In his latest volume, Dr. Guthrie makes a fierce and persuasive argument for a paradigm shift in how researchers and policy makers consider educational reform in developing countries. He challenges us to recognize the failings of the progressive education agenda and to move instead toward a formalistic framework that is responsive to and respectful of the educational practices in many emerging economies. Far from wanting to maintain the status quo, however, Dr. Guthrie urges a paradigm shift so that future efforts toward educational improvement might be more impactful and lead directly to positive results for students. His book is a must read for anyone who is committed to strengthening teaching and learning and building educational equity and excellence in developing countries.

Heather Lattimer, EdD, *Professor of Education, University of San Diego*

This book presents a compelling argument for why 'formalism' should be the primary conceptual underpinning informing curriculum work in schools in developing country contexts. A core strength of the book is a careful illustration, based on strong evidence, that a progressivist centred curriculum approach favoured by many countries over the last 40 years has not replaced teacher-centred formalistic classroom practice. In this light, the author presents a convincing argument for reconsidering the role of such curricular approaches in developing contexts. This is a well-argued and convincing text which should be compulsory reading for students, academics, and education policy and planners in developing and other country contexts.

Aslam Fataar, *Distinguished Professor, Department of Education Policy Studies, Stellenbosch University*

Classroom Change in Developing Countries

Progressive education, derived mainly from Anglo-American culture, has been the primary frame of reference for student-centred classroom change in developing countries for over 50 years. Yet in many developing countries, strong evidence shows that progressivism has not replaced teacher-centred formalistic classroom practice. *Classroom Change in Developing Countries: From Progressive Cage to Formalistic Frame* presents a robust case for why formalism should be the primary frame of reference for upgrading classroom teaching in developing countries. Theoretically rich yet grounded in practice, the book draws on case studies from Africa, China and Papua New Guinea to show how culturally intuitive formalistic teaching styles can induce positive classroom change.

Synthesising research and evaluation literature on classroom change in developing countries, Guthrie examines some of the methodological flaws in the literature. The book considers the progressive cage, and looks at Confucian influences on teaching in China, progressive reform failures in both Sub-Saharan Africa and Papua New Guinea, and offers a critical take on some failings in comparative education. It examines the formalistic frame, addresses methodological issues in culturally grounded research and offers a model of teaching styles for basic classroom research. The book concludes by returning the focus back to teachers and considers the so-called teacher resistance to change.

The book will be an essential purchase for academics and research students engaged in the fields of classroom teaching, teacher education and curriculum, and will also be of interest to academics, aid officials and decision makers in developing countries.

Dr Gerard Guthrie is an educationalist with 45 years of experience who has specialised in teaching styles in developing countries.

Routledge Research in International and Comparative Education

This is a series that offers a global platform to engage scholars in continuous academic debate on key challenges and the latest thinking on issues in the fast-growing field of International and Comparative Education.

Books in the series include:

Globalization and Japanese "Exceptionalism" in Education
Insider's Views into a Changing System
Edited by Ryoko Tsuneyoshi

Canadian Teacher Education
A Curriculum History
Edited by Theodore Michael Christou

The Shifting Global World of Youth and Education
Edited by Mabel Ann Brown

The Making of Indigeneity, Curriculum History, and the Limits of Diversity
Ligia L. López López

Civil Society Organizations in Latin American Education
Case Studies and Perspectives on Advocacy
Regina Cortina and Constanza Lafuente

Navigating the Common Good in Teacher Education Policy
Critical and International Perspectives
Edited by Nikola Hobbel and Barbara L. Bales

Classroom Change in Developing Countries
From Progressive Cage to Formalistic Frame
Gerard Guthrie

For more information about the series, please visit www.routledge.com.

Classroom Change in Developing Countries
From Progressive Cage to Formalistic Frame

Gerard Guthrie

LONDON AND NEW YORK

First published 2018
by Routledge
2 Park Square, Milton Park, Abingdon, Oxon OX14 4RN

and by Routledge
711 Third Avenue, New York, NY 10017

Routledge is an imprint of the Taylor & Francis Group, an informa business

© 2018 Gerard Guthrie

The right of Gerard Guthrie to be identified as author of this work has been asserted by him in accordance with sections 77 and 78 of the Copyright, Designs and Patents Act 1988.

All rights reserved. No part of this book may be reprinted or reproduced or utilised in any form or by any electronic, mechanical, or other means, now known or hereafter invented, including photocopying and recording, or in any information storage or retrieval system, without permission in writing from the publishers.

Trademark notice: Product or corporate names may be trademarks or registered trademarks, and are used only for identification and explanation without intent to infringe.

British Library Cataloguing-in-Publication Data
A catalogue record for this book is available from the British Library

Library of Congress Cataloging-in-Publication Data
A catalog record for this book has been requested

ISBN: 978-0-8153-5519-9 (hbk)
ISBN: 978-1-351-13047-9 (ebk)

Typeset in Bembo
by Apex CoVantage, LLC

For Xiaoli

Contents

List of figures   xiii
List of tables   xiv
Preface   xv

PART I
Overview   1

1 Soft power and the culture wars   3
    1.1 From progressive cage to formalistic frame 6
    1.2 The Progressive Education Fallacy 8
    1.3 Progressivism as cultural imperialism 9
    1.4 Global English and cultural clusters 13
    1.5 Cultural relativity 16
    1.6 Intergenerational and organisational culture 17
    1.7 Teaching styles, paradigms and epistemology 18
    1.8 The progressive cage 20
    1.9 The formalistic frame 21
    1.10 Conclusion 22
    References 23

PART II
The progressive cage   31

2 Typology of progressive reform findings   33
    2.1 The typology 34
    2.2 Sound positive findings 36
    2.3 Vested consultancy findings 37
    2.4 Further technical inputs 38
    2.5 Interim formalism 39

    2.6   *Structural change 40*
    2.7   *Rejection of universal progressivism 41*
    2.8   *Global distribution of findings 42*
    2.9   *Progressivism as an axiom 46*
    2.10 *Conclusion 50*
    References 51

3 Theoretical and methodological limitations   58
    3.1   *Theoretical shaping 59*
    3.2   *Theoretical limitations 60*
    3.3   *Methodological limitations 64*
    3.4   *An example of review bias 68*
    3.5   *An example of evaluation failure 69*
    3.6   *Independent evidence 73*
    3.7   *Cultural imperialism in action 75*
    3.8   *Conclusion 77*
    References 78

4 Formalistic tradition in China   82
    4.1   *History of Confucianism 83*
    4.2   *Chinese epistemology 85*
    4.3   *Confucianism as an educational paradigm 86*
    4.4   *Confucian pedagogy 87*
    4.5   *Modern educational developments 89*
    4.6   *Recent perspectives on schooling in China 91*
    4.7   *Curriculum reforms since 2001 92*
    4.8   *Communities of professional learning 95*
    4.9   *Conclusion 97*
    References 98

5 The formalistic paradigm in Africa   102
    5.1   *African pedagogical commonalities 102*
    5.2   *A case study of classroom formalism 104*
    5.3   *Progressive reform across Sub-Saharan Africa 107*
    5.4   *Theoretical and methodological issues 113*
    5.5   *Findings about formalism 116*
    5.6   *Conclusion 117*
    References 118

6 Culture and schooling in Papua New Guinea   123
    6.1   *Traditional education 123*
    6.2   *Continuities in colonial formalism 126*

    6.3 Effects of tradition in modern times 127
    6.4 Failure of progressive reforms 130
    6.5 Prevalence of formalism 135
    6.6 Conclusion 137
    References 138

7   **The failure of progressive paradigm reversal**   143
    7.1 Progressive paradigm shift in the classroom? 143
    7.2 Gestalt-switch and paradigm reversal in the literature? 146
    7.3 Cultural issues and cognitive dissonance 149
    7.4 A cosmology of cumulative progressive hallucination 152
    7.5 Progressive delusions 154
    7.6 Conclusion 156
    References 157

PART III
The formalistic frame   159

8   **Theory of formalism**   161
    8.1 Lessons learned from progressive failure 162
    8.2 Universal versus local 164
    8.3 Revelatory epistemology and the formalistic paradigm 166
    8.4 Lessons about formalism 168
    8.5 Formalistic borrowings? 174
    8.6 Cognition 176
    8.7 Conclusion 178
    References 180

9   **Culturally grounded methodology**   184
    9.1 Research strategy 185
    9.2 Design for field experiments on teaching styles 186
    9.3 Relevant research methods 189
    9.4 Classroom observation 192
    9.5 Examples of variables in field research 194
    9.6 Decision-making about classroom reforms 199
    9.7 Conclusion 203
    References 203

10 **Teaching Styles Model**   206
    10.1 The model 207
    10.2 Changing styles 213

10.3 Systemic barriers to change 214
10.4 Financial implications 219
10.5 Conclusion 221
References 222

11 Teacher constructs and classroom change 224
11.1 Teachers' constructs 225
11.2 Perceptions of change 227
11.3 Adopters of innovation 228
11.4 Students' constructs 230
11.5 Improving formalistic teaching 231
11.6 Conclusion 237
References 239

Index 243

Figures

2.1	Typology of findings about progressive educational reforms in developing country schools	35
3.1	Theoretical influences on types of research finding	59
9.1	Invalid curriculum experiment	187
9.2	Valid teaching styles experiment	188
9.3	Bloom's Revised Taxonomy of Educational Objectives	191
9.4	Evaluation of curriculum impact on classroom teaching	196
9.5	Evaluation of impact of certification on student achievement	197
9.6	Simplified flow chart for decisions on teaching styles	201
9.7	Relationships between amount and likelihood of change	202

Tables

2.1	Global distribution of negative findings about progressivism in developing countries	44
3.1	Limitations in school effectiveness and classroom improvement research	61
8.1	Contrasts between formalistic and progressive teachers in Nepal and the United States	169
10.1	Teaching Styles Model	208
11.1	Adopters of innovation	229

Preface

Classroom Change in Developing Countries: From Progressive Cage to Formalistic Frame is intended to be a cutting-edge synthesis of the literature on classroom change in 'developing' countries. The evidence is that progressive reforms have struck severe difficulties in a statistically representative range of such countries. The research and evaluation literature that nonetheless sustains the progressive paradigm has widespread methodological limitations. The book's critique leads to a rejection of the progressive paradigm. Rather, a foundation for formalist pedagogy lies in revelatory epistemologies, leading to a theoretical analysis that takes formalism seriously as a legitimate cultural paradigm and a foundation for change rather than an obstacle. Paradigm shift is needed in the academic and policy literature to reflect the prevalence of formalism. This conclusion is controversial, but the priority is to analyse, not proselytise.

One of the methodological themes that runs through the book is that interpretation of research should be grounded in the data and not be a bad science case of theory seeking supporting evidence. My view of the interpretations herein is that they are grounded soundly in meta-analyses of the literature on classroom reforms in developing countries. This data exists at three levels. One is the research evidence about classroom reforms as such, which leads to the conclusion that progressivism has not succeeded outside its Anglo-American cultural hearth. The second level is about the politics of progressive reforms. The indication is that comparative education has elements of cultural imperialism that take the progressive side in an ideological struggle with formalism in developing countries that is embedded in the international culture wars.

The third set of evidence goes beyond the cognitive to the affective domain, even more fundamentally to the conscious and unconscious worldviews of adherents to the progressive paradigm. Progressivism typically is a worldview posing as a theory. As an axiomatic theoretical starting point and a desirable but unquestioned professional end point, it is a value position to be implemented rather than a theory subject to logical analysis and field testing. The research evidence about its failures should lead to Gestalt-shift and paradigm reversal among progressive adherents; instead, superficial assumptions about the benefits of progressivism for classroom improvement hold fast. The literature demonstrates cognitive dissonance and blindness to failure, such that progressivism has become a cage rather than a frame. Indeed, one chapter goes beneath the polite third person fiction in academia that theories are independent of their creators to analyse the progressive paradigm as a delusional intellectual straightjacket. The effect is that progressives can be caged in a cosmology of cumulative hallucination where errors compound, leading to a vicious circle of misinformation for continuing the irrational pursuit of the unattainable.

It is possible such interpretations will not win me friends. Progressive change agents serious about classroom reform can retain a stubborn and long-lasting faith in the paradigm as a panacea, demonstrate intellectual confusion over findings about its failures, and may not like to be confronted with their personal responsibility in this. Cultural imperialists with a conscious ideological mission masked by progressive educational language are even less likely to be persuaded. However, those targeted for change in developing countries can know that the comprehensive evidence reported here does not support progressive reforms. They should be wary of cultural imperialism underlying dubious claims for progressive education. The paradigm has lost credibility as the primary frame of reference for reform of developing country classrooms.

These analyses are an evolutionary development of my 2011 book on the topic, *The Progressive Education Fallacy in Developing Countries: In Favour of Formalism* (*PEF*), which addressed the axiomatic assumption that the progressive teaching process will produce the enquiry learning product. Some saw *PEF* as 'persuasive'; if so, my view is that the evidence was persuasive not the writing that drew attention to it. Some also saw the conclusions that this led to as 'polemical', but that just seems to be a pejorative used by those with a different perspective. My later use of the metaphor of child soldiers in the culture wars has also been accused of trying to start a war, when actually it is trying to stop one. Contributing to such interpretations is a stylistic issue, a consequence of writing both for academic audiences (where conclusions are reached only at the end of a piece) and for time-pressed administrative decision makers (where conclusions are summarised first). *PEF* melded both styles, possibly to the dissatisfaction of both audiences. This book also targets both academics and educational policy-makers and therefore maintains these traits, no doubt still to the collective dissatisfaction.

None of this is intended as an attack on progressivism in its own domain. Indeed, as I also stated in the preface to *PEF*, I actually do share many progressive educational values within my own cultural context. What I do not share is the position that progressive values should be transferred to other cultures and that developing countries should attempt to follow Western, predominantly Anglo-American, educational paths regardless of the evidence that progressive educational reforms are widely prone to failure in the developing world. In short, do not do unto others as you would have them do unto you: they may have different preferences.

PEF was structured around Popperian conjectures and refutations, while this book is structured around Kuhnian paradigm change. With permissions from the publishers, parts of four chapters derive from *PEF* (albeit with many

Preface xvii

omissions, such as a deconstruction of C. E. Beeby's 'stages' of educational development, details about education in Papua New Guinea and some historical discussion of school effectiveness research, where I have little new to add). Parts of other chapters derive from nine articles published since 2012, mainly for regional audiences in journals that receive limited international exposure. Other material explores the empirical data, methodological issues, the implications of paradigm reversal, and cognitive dissonance.

> Part I, consisting of Chapter 1, is an overview that locates the issues, defines some key terms, and summarises the material that follows.
> Part II focusses on the progressive cage, starting in Chapter 2 with a synthesis of the research and evaluation literature on classroom change in developing countries.
> Chapter 3 examines some of the methodological flaws in the literature, illustrated with examples of dubious review and evaluation.
> Chapter 4 updates material on Confucian history and its influence on teaching styles and recent classroom reforms in China.
> Chapter 5 expands considerably material on progressive reform failures widespread in Sub-Saharan Africa.
> Chapter 6 analyses reasons for the longitudinal failure of several major progressive reforms in Papua New Guinea over 50 years.
> Chapter 7 is a highly critical take on the failures of comparative educationists to adjust to formalistic reality.
> Part III turns to the formalistic frame. Chapter 8 syntheses the theoretical basis for treating formalism as the primary frame of reference for classroom change in developing countries.
> Chapter 9 addresses methodological issues in culturally grounded research.
> Chapter 10 presents a model of teaching styles for basic classroom research.
> Chapter 11 concludes the book by focussing back on the teachers who are at the heart of classroom change, with analysis of so-called teacher resistance to change.

In all cases, any source material (identified in the endnotes to each chapter) has been paraphrased, edited for content and style, updated and expanded where new evidence has become available, and cut to reduce internal repetition across the book. However, some repetition does remain, partly because of the complexity of interweaving elements of the analysis and partly because of a publishing exigency to sell chapters online and therefore for them to be self-contained. Although there are extensive recent references, I have kept older publications that still have relevant theoretical perspectives and as a counter to ahistorical research that misinterprets anomalies in progressive implementation as new challenges rather than evidence of chronic failure.

Classroom Change in Developing Countries has eclectic multidimensional perspectives that reject progressivism as widely irrelevant to the developing world. Not only does the book make use of the concept of dialectics (usually but not necessarily associated with materialism) in addressing the conflict between incommensurable formalistic and progressive paradigms, but it also has elements of an equally unfashionable cultural relativism with roots in idealist philosophy. Of course, books that synthesise a wide range of material run the risk that they will not please specialists in each area who are able to operate within narrower conventions, and all this presents at least something for the unpersuaded or unidimensional to seize upon. While some may think that I am losing my marbles in my old age, these perspectives actually reflect my private thoughts for the last 50 years (and open the possibility the unkind may claim my marbles actually went missing back then). Sinner that I am, a few of my publications along the way have had a radical element in the political sense, although I prefer to think of them as being radical in the sense of going to the fundamental issues: in this book, cultural imperialism, paradigm change, cognitive dissonance and academic responsibility. The moral obligation is to the children in Third World classrooms, and I no longer have the patience for putting such issues aside in case I offend people.

Gerard Guthrie

www.researchgate.net/profile/Gerard_Guthrie/

Part I
Overview

1 Soft power and the culture wars

Political analysts interested in international realpolitik draw a distinction between 'hard power' – coercive diplomatic, economic and military sanctions by countries exercisable in international conflicts – and 'soft power', which is persuasive effort to gain international influence, especially through cultural and institutional means (Nye 2009). Alliance Française, the British Council, the Goethe Institutes and the Confucian Institutes, for example, are government sponsored agencies that project their countries' images positively. Bilateral foreign aid programmes, whether or not overtly tied to national interest as part of foreign policy, also project soft power, including through educational scholarships in donor 'developed' countries and aid activities implemented in recipient 'developing' countries. As well, national governments actively promote their international interests through membership of multilateral agencies such as the World Bank and forums such as the Development Assistance Committee of the Organisation for Economic Co-operation and Development (OECD). Underlying the projection of soft power by Western countries, in particular, is what Huntington (1996a) described as a clash of civilisations, although analysts have tended subsequently to emphasise a clash of cultures (e.g. Malitza 2000; Hauk and Mueller 2015). The continuing effect is such that Huntington's (1996b) observation remains highly pertinent: 'Westerners have assured themselves and irritated others by expounding the notion that the culture of the West is and ought to be the culture of the world.... [A view] to varying degrees misguided, arrogant, false, and dangerous' (28).

Whether or not they are conscious of such influences, comparative educationalists and other well-meaning academics who provide international educational services are often funded from governmental programmes that export cultural tradition. Governmental funding for aid projects, university scholarships, or consultancies is intended to project national values in a positive light. As well as the political interests of governments and foundations, economic interests are involved in education as a major and expanding export industry (Verger, Lubienski, and Steiner-Khamsi 2016). Countries derive foreign exchange earnings, universities increase their financial strength, and academics find employment. The collective effect, as this book will show, is that a considerable part of soft power projection by English-speaking countries has involved promotion of progressive educational values where, in effect, many educationalists act as secular missionaries. As Schweisfurth (2015a, 645–646) put it,

> Comparative Education as a community of scholars, and educational policy makers and practitioners all need to be on guard against cultural imperialism in its many forms. Whether such inappropriate transfers of practice reflect a conscious imposition of norms of practice, or whether they are based on well-meaning but misjudged value-laden readings of effectiveness, they disrespect indigenous knowledge and ways of knowing. This is not only morally problematic. When it comes to pedagogy, on a practical level, learning is more effective when it is not in dissonance with local values.

Central to cultural imperialism in education are attempts to replace formalistic teaching with progressive styles in developing country classrooms. Progressive education, derived mainly from Anglo-American culture, has been for some 50 years the primary frame of reference in curriculum and teaching reforms targeting classroom change, as well as for school-focussed investment in the school effectiveness field (Barrett *et al.* 2006; Guthrie 2017). Since the 1960s, the progressive paradigm has also been a central tenet of 'travelling policies' among bilateral and multilateral aid agencies, and of many locally supported educational reforms in developing countries. The most tangible benefit of foreign aid has been to contribute to increased school enrolments, especially at the primary level (Riddell and Nino-Zarazua 2016). However, attempts to replace formalistic teaching with progressive styles have had two major issues: they are usually culturally inappropriate, and they usually fail. The history of progressive failure is, in fact, a long and often overlooked one, although discussion in comparative education has regained momentum in recent years, in part framed by interest in the influence of context on teaching styles (Guthrie 1980, 1990, 2011; Crossley 1984, 2000; Tabulawa 1997, 2013; Alexander 2000; Barrett 2007; Schweisfurth 2013a, 2015b). Problematic consequences of international policy transfers have also been again a focus of attention (Steiner-Khamsi and Waldow 2012; Auld and Morris 2014; Crossley 2014; Tan 2015, 2016; Portnoi 2016). As one of the leaders in these fields has framed the discussion, 'context matters, and comparative and international research in education is especially well placed to demonstrate this' (Crossley 2000, 323).

The literature on education in developing countries has a wide range of theoretical influences, so that its two main fields have considerable differences despite their primary focusses on the school. One field is econometric school effectiveness research by educational economists and statisticians driven by aid agency interests in cost-effective investment and seeking international policy generalisations about school improvement. The other field – with which this book is consistent – is classroom improvement research. It usually comprises educational sociologists concerned with classroom interaction and the influence of context, and subject specialists who evaluate the impacts of curriculum and teacher education. In a comprehensive review of educational effectiveness by Reynolds et al. (2014), a lack of integration between the fields was apparent, with little reference to the classroom improvement field or developing country findings. Nonetheless, researchers refer to findings from both fields, and Auld and Morris (2014, 132), coming from the classroom improvement field, considered they are distinctive, albeit related, comparative genres rather than separate research paradigms because of common interests in the identification of educational best practices to substantiate policy transfer.

Policy roles lead to a crucial distinction between the two fields. Classroom improvement research has more credibility within the educational sociology often found in academic comparative education. However, as Auld and Morris (2014, 129) put it in their critique of international policy transfer,

> The task of comparing foreign systems of education is no longer the reserve of specialised academics, if it ever was. The practice has spread and metamorphosed over the last 30 years, and is now dominated by transnational agencies, consultancies, policy entrepreneurs, policy makers and the media.

The school effectiveness field is by far the greater influence on the policy discourses of official agencies, in part because of its foundation in economics, as well as its role in analysing the student achievement surveys that generate international statistical indicators. Auld and Morris labelled this policy approach as the 'New Paradigm', a quantitative approach to neo-liberal managerialist reform that downplays context in the search for policy direction from measurable outputs. Auld and Morris (2014, 149) found the evidentiary foundations to be weak, however:

> Despite its self-portrayal as non-ideological and scientific, the [policy] ambition has not been pursued following the conventions of scholarly analysis. Its rationale and assumptions embody and reinforce an ideology that sees education as an economic investment designed to cultivate human capital so as to maximise a nation's competitiveness in the global economy . . . its methodology . . . is reductionist; downplays context and non-educational factors; tends to confirmation bias; uses correlations to infer causality.

In effect, labelling progressivism a travelling policy uses a benign term for cultural imperialism that directly or indirectly is a soft power policy plank in the culture wars. The progressive education paradigm predates the New Paradigm, but has been subsumed into it as a vehicle for 'democratisation', particularly through aid conditionality. This educational role is heavily entwined with Western cultural, political and economic interests and permeates the World Bank (2011) *Learning for All* Strategy for 2020, which is a key example of international policy about developing countries (Verger and Altinyelken 2013; Heyneman and Lee 2016). Auld and Morris (2014) were scathing about the New Paradigm as 'a form of ideological transfer', an 'intellectual swindle', and 'simplistic school effectiveness snake oil' (152).

1.1 From progressive cage to formalistic frame

Cultural imperialism, the role within it of comparative education, and the extensive failures of progressive classroom reforms in developing countries are all contentious matters that generate issues for the primary focus of this book inside the classroom. Part I, comprising this introductory chapter, locates the issues, defines some key terms, and summarises what follows. Part II explores some of the traps through which culture-bound value judgements, whether conscious or unconscious, cage comparative education studies of classroom reform. Chapter 2 brings together overwhelming evidence that progressivism has not replaced formalistic classroom practice in the many developing country cultural contexts despite the extensive international aid support. The chapter identifies studies from 32 statistically representative developing countries which have shown that progressive reforms were inappropriate and/or had major implementation difficulties, which appears to be the first statistical demonstration that progressive reform difficulties are widespread and systematic, not just aberrant or interim cases. Detailed evidence leading to these conclusions is in Chapters 2–3, while further examples occur in the systematic area studies in Chapters 4–6. The first area study, on the influence of Confucianism, provides a detailed case of an ancient formalistic paradigm and its current impact in China; the second is a geographically wide review of the lack of success of progressive classroom reforms across Sub-Saharan Africa; while the third is a historical review of multiple progressive failures over 50 years in Papua New Guinea (PNG).

Centred within the book is a challenge to progressivism as the 'normal science' paradigm and to adherents exhibiting classic symptoms of values-based resistance to change. Despite the absence of paradigm shift from formalism to progressivism in developing country classrooms, the academic literature and international travelling policies remain imbued with the maintenance of universalistic claims for the progressive worldview. Progressivism typically is an axiomatic theoretical starting point and a desirable but unquestioned professional end point, rather than a theory subject to logical analysis and field testing in developing countries. A large research and evaluation literature sustains the paradigm, but that literature is subject to widespread validity, reliability, relevance and generalisability issues. Little evidence of reversal of the progressivism paradigm is found, while denial of evidence that contradicts progressive values amounts to cognitive dissonance, in Leon Festinger's (1957) widely recognised concept, as manifest in surface redefinitions of teaching styles. All this points to a failure of comprehension about the cultural depths and epistemological substance underlying the formalist paradigm. The grip of progressivism on educational theory and official policy despite the evidence is such that it has become a cage rather than a frame, to use Anthony Ryle's (1975) terms. Indeed, Chapter 7 analyses the foundering of the progressive paradigm in a cosmology of cumulative hallucination that generates compounding errors of judgement.

The sensible conclusion from the failure of progressivism is that paradigm shift should occur in the academic and policy literature to match classroom reality. Evidence and logic point to formalism becoming the primary frame of reference for classroom change in developing countries rather than being perceived as an obstacle to change. Part III therefore starts in Chapter 8 with a theoretical foundation for taking the formalistic paradigm seriously as a theory of teaching for transmission of modern as well as traditional knowledge. In sum, incommensurable epistemological assumptions and educational values underlie the international clash of educational cultures. In revelatory cultures, epistemology holds that important knowledge comes from truths revealed by gods and previous generations, which provides the philosophical foundations for formalistic educational paradigms centrally concerned with the inter-generational transmission of knowledge. In revelatory cultural systems, formalism is a body of teacher-centred pedagogy valued highly for its congruence with traditional beliefs and its effectiveness in transmitting them. In modern times, the pedagogy is usually adopted in primary and secondary classrooms to transmit modern knowledge, including scientific knowledge. However, the nature of progressive or formalistic theory as such is not the primary issue; in many ways, the primary issue is methodology for identifying culturally appropriate teaching styles. Chapter 9 therefore considers basic grounded methodology for eliciting the nature of the contexts into which teaching styles must fit. A Teaching Styles Model in Chapter 10 provides a framework for classifying research data arising from application of grounded methodological principles. As well, it explores some of the decision-making consequences for upgrading formalistic teaching. Finally, the book explores the widespread misunderstanding by reformers that problems of implementation lie with teachers rather than misjudged reforms. Failure of teachers to innovate may be rational, reasoned responses to complex progressive reforms that offer no relative advantage in the classroom, are not compatible with existing methods and offer no observable outcomes for students and parents concerned with examination results. Rather than treating formalistic teachers as obstructive, Chapter 11 concludes the book by considering teachers' perceptual constructs, different types of innovators, and some evidence-based paths that fit with formalistic constructs. The influence of context-specific cultural paradigms on teachers' and students' formalistic constructs may well outweigh – quite rationally from their perspective – the alleged benefits of any progressive reform.

Nonetheless, worldviews that promote cultural imperialism can encompass more than progressivism. For example, the imposition of formalistic pedagogy in the South can involve cultural epistemology with roots in continental European disciplinary tradition (Section 8.5). Superficially, South-South borrowings may seem another resolution, but they have two issues. One, as Lam (2014) stated, is that 'the literature related to South-South transfer can be perceived as another form of "north-south south" borrowing' (3). The second issue is that cultural contexts vary so widely in the South that southern borrowings may be as inappropriate as northern ones. Possibly such borrowings will be more relevant than direct North-South transfer from developed countries, but borrowings will always need adaptation to local circumstances. The nuances also include South to North borrowings (Forestier and Crossley 2015). However, the predominant issue is progressive educational norms and their relevance in the South, which is the focus of this book.

1.2 The Progressive Education Fallacy

All these issues come to bear on the central concern with teaching inside primary and secondary classrooms in developing countries. Various teaching styles are defined more fully in Chapter 10 for ongoing research and policy purposes. Sufficient for discussion in the meantime is the understanding that *progressivism* encapsulates a variety of student-centred classroom practices (variously labelled 'child-centred', 'learner-centred', 'learning-centred', 'active learning', 'enquiry', 'problem-solving', 'heuristic', 'discovery', 'participative', 'constructivist', 'competence mode', 'meaning', 'liberal' or 'democratic'), while *formalism* is shorthand for teacher-centred practices (including 'traditional', 'didactic', 'whole-class', 'expository', 'direct instruction', 'performance mode' and 'instructivist' labels) (Guthrie 2011, 3–5). Some claims have existed that the distinctions between formalism and progressivism are insufficiently nuanced (e.g. Alexander 2000; Barrett 2007), with subtleties generated through redefinition, such as 'learning-centred' for 'learner-centred' (O'Sullivan 2004), or reconstruction of teacher-dominated lessons in China as a form of 'student-centredness' (Mok 2006). A deeper view is that formalistic and progressive teaching styles are embedded in constructs founded on intellectually antagonistic epistemologies (Tabulawa 1997, 2013; Guthrie 2011, 2015a). The seemingly irreconcilable differences between revelatory and scientific epistemologies, of which teacher- and student-centred styles are but a surface manifestation, seem ultimately to explain international focus on the two generic styles.

Progressive Anglo-American theories have been by far and away the main impetus for classroom change in developing countries, but this thrust has been based on a false premise that I have labelled the Progressive Education Fallacy (Guthrie 2011). The Fallacy is that enquiry teaching methods are necessary to develop enquiry skills in primary and secondary schools in developing countries. The confusion is between the teaching process and the learning product, which misunderstanding generates continuing efforts to change teachers away from formalistic classroom methods on an assumption little researched cross-culturally that progressive methods actually help students learn enquiry skills. Yet, in the widespread absence of controlled field experiments on the effectiveness of teaching styles,

- There is no necessary indication that enquiry intellectual skills must be introduced in primary and secondary schools in revelatory cultures where knowledge is there to be revealed rather than created; or
- That changing teaching styles is a necessary precondition.

The fallacy helps explain why the evidence strongly suggests that progressive education reforms generally fail in cultures with revelatory epistemologies. These failures are a reality check to ethical arguments for progressive education. The high likelihood of failure may seem the only necessary reason to reject progressive curriculum reforms. However, in rationalising the failures, reformers often misdirect attention to teachers, teacher training and educational bureaucracy, rather than to the lack of cultural fit of progressivism and their own lack of understanding about this.

1.3 Progressivism as cultural imperialism

Progressive tenets hold progress to be a unilinear and inevitable process of 'modernisation', with Western values influencing strongly the assumed directions for worldwide economic, political and educational change. After World War II, a belief that education was the most important factor in 'development' became central to the thinking of many in the field of education and national development, coming to dominate among academics, scholars, policymakers, multilateral agencies and practitioners (Hawkins 2007, 147). Education was not just one of many factors in socio-cultural development, it was often seen – naively – as the most crucial factor, such that by the 1980s progressivism was the dominant paradigm for reform of curriculum, teacher education and classroom schooling in developing countries.

Progressive educational forms have been entwined with Western cultural, political and economic interests in developing countries (Heyneman and Lee 2016). Phillips (2009) described three types of *policy transfer*: (1) transfers imposed under totalitarian and/or authoritarian rule (e.g. colonies required to adopt the colonial powers' approaches to education), (2) transfers required under constraint (e.g. in defeated or occupied countries), and (3) transfers negotiated under constraint (e.g. World Bank loans with New Paradigm conditionality). Progressivism is recognised widely as a pervasive travelling policy among international and multilateral organisations (Barrett et al. 2006; Schweisfurth 2013b, 2015b), including the OECD (Alexander 2000; Hawkins 2007) and the United Nations (Jones and Coleman 2005). Within the UN system, progressive educational policies are found in the World Bank (Klees, Samoff, and Stromquist 2012), UNESCO (Beeby 1992; Hawkins 2007; Cerqua, Gautheir, and Dembele 2014) and UNICEF (Jones 2006). Policy in these organisations has been influenced strongly by UNESCO's Education for All (EFA) resolutions from the 1990 Jomtien and 2000 Dakar conferences, which brought human rights and active learning into the international educational agenda. Another area of progressive influence has been on the educational projects of bilateral aid agencies in countries such as the United States (e.g. Ginsburg 2010) and Australia (Guthrie 2012). As well, progressivism has also been perceived by national governments and local innovators as an attractive path for overcoming political and cultural legacies, including with outcomes-based education in South Africa (Jansen and Taylor 2003; Fataar 2006; Hoadley 2017). Thus, Phillips

(2009) also included two types of *policy borrowing* in his categories: (4) purposeful borrowing by developing countries (e.g. South Africa), and (5) borrowing introduced through the general influence of educational ideas (such as those of John Dewey, C. E. Beeby, Jerome Bruner and Hilda Taba).

A notable influence on international policies that equate teacher quality with progressive teaching practices was Beeby's (1966) classic book, which embedded quality of education in 'stages' of educational development (Guthrie 1980; Barrett *et al.* 2006). Beeby was one of UNESCO's founding figures after World War II (Beeby 1992). His approach was rapidly taken up in the international education literature (Barrington 1980), and he was a major influence on education policy in PNG in the 1960s and 1970s (Chapter 6), influenced education in neighbouring Indonesia (Beeby 1979), and directly influenced World Bank staff in the 1980s to add teaching quality to more purely economic investment issues (Heyneman and White 1986; Alcorn 1999, 354–355; Barrett *et al.* 2006, 4–8). Beeby's book, which was valuable for its experiential insights, described a transition through five stages from the 'Dame School', through 'Formalism' to progressive teaching for 'Meaning'. In the World Bank, adoption of progressive teaching became a surrogate for quality of schooling in building on the work of human capital theorists, rates of return and school effectiveness research to argue for cost-effective investment in primary school education. A key example was an influential 1990 World Bank Primary Education Policy Paper, based on an extensive literature review by Lockheed and Verspoor (1991), which identified three key issues for teacher effectiveness. These issues (knowledge of subject matter, pedagogical skills and teacher motivation) contained the progressive assumption that students need to participate actively in classrooms. Following on, Lockheed and Levin (1993) argued that effective schools in developing countries require, among other things, teaching that promotes student active learning and pedagogical flexibility, while Heneveld's (1994) influential conceptual framework for school effectiveness had 16 factors organised into four groups, including variety in teaching strategies as a component of the teaching/learning process. During this period in the Bank, Verspoor and Leno (1986, 11–14) and Verspoor and Wu (1990) also loosely adapted Beeby's stages model, in turn influencing some writers particularly concerned with the implications for teacher in-service, especially in southern Africa (De Feiter, Vonk, and van den Akker 1995; De Feiter and Ncube 1999; Harvey 1999; Rogan and Grayson 2003). While these writers cautioned about the speed of progressive reform, qualifications were about the speed of attainment of the higher 'stages' and teaching for 'meaning', rather than questions about the progressive destination.

A continuing influence, Barrett *et al.* (2006, 4–6) found, is that there is little to distinguish Beeby's approach from later writings on educational quality, which have evolved to embrace contemporary preoccupations with democracy, human rights and environmental sustainability, so that (cast in terms such as learner-centred, active learning, participative and democratic) progressivism is an enduring tradition within academic education. As well, the tradition has become a soft power policy plank. The neo-liberal New Paradigm promotes, and an active literature discusses, democratisation. Recent examples include encouragement of critical thinking as a counter to authoritarianism in Kazakhstan (Burkhalter and Shegebayev 2012); student-centred learning intended to promote democratisation in the classroom in Turkey (Altinyelken 2013); learner-centred philosophy in teacher education in Namibia that has functioned more than anything as a rhetorical device for nation-building (Arreman, Erixon, and Rehn 2016); and a discussion from South Africa of curriculum issues that arise when retraining teachers, socialised previously in authoritarian regimes, to be autonomous professionals (Slonimsky 2016).

The intertwining of progressive educational with Western cultural, political and economic interests has not been without contention over the decades. My own critiques deconstructed serious methodological flaws in Beeby's so-called stages, which were dead ends that apparently gave form and structure but which had so many loose elements that they generated few hypotheses of lasting value for serious research. In particular, his approach had unexamined, culture-bound assumptions about Western teaching styles as a liberal objective for reform of classroom quality in developing countries (Guthrie 1980, 1990, 2011, 21–60). Other criticisms of the progressive values and their implicit cultural bias came from studies about Korea (Lee, Adams, and Cornbleth 1988), the South Pacific (Thaman 1991) and PNG (Crossley 1992; O'Donoghue 1994). All criticised the dependency model implicit in the stages mentality, which assumed that the solution to educational problems in these areas involved the application of Western progressive models.

As the story moved forward, others extended the cultural argument to concerns that progressive values represent Western political and economic interests. Sweeting (1996) argued that globalisation of learning is a doubtful concept. Tikly (1999) argued that consideration of post-colonial issues was necessary for developing a less Eurocentric understanding of the relationship between globalisation and education. Later he wrote about education as a key policy plank for multilateral development agencies instrumental in developing a new regime of international governance that serves Western interests, and labelled the global system of governance that promotes such views as the 'new imperialism' (Tikly 2004). Critics in Africa, in particular, have also commented on underlying political assumptions in progressive reforms. Tabulawa (2003, 17–44) analysed learner-centred pedagogy as an inherently ideological political artefact with questionable justification on educational grounds. His case was that the pedagogy is embedded in economic and political rationales for stimulating economic growth and of Western desire to globalise a liberal democratic ethos that is a political and ideological element of competitive capitalism. Post-colonial analysis of Sub-Saharan Africa found that aid agencies sought to encourage liberal democracy. The ascendancy of neo-liberalism as a development paradigm in the 1980s and 1990s elevated political democratisation as a prerequisite for economic development, with learner-centred methods intended to develop democratic social relations in the schools of aid-receiving countries. The methods, Tabulawa found, brought an ideological outlook, a worldview intended to develop a preferred kind of society and people, and represented a process of westernisation disguised as quality and effective teaching. Similarly, Quist (2003) criticised the implicit dependency that assumed that the solution to educational problems in Ghana involved the application of Western progressive models and underestimated contextual factors. From analyses like these, it is difficult to escape the conclusion that educational progressivism is embedded in individualistic values which, at best, are culture-bound and, at worst, have long been regarded by many as embedded in notions of Northern political and cultural superiority.

In particular, World Bank educational policies remain a perennial subject of controversy (e.g. Klees 2002; Heyneman 2003; Barrett *et al.* 2006; Auld and Morris 2014; Tikly 2014). Stein (2008) reactivated important critiques from the 1960s by Gunnar Myrdal and Simon Kuznets of W. W. Rostow's economic 'stages' theory in arguing that the Bank's development strategies still downplay social and political contexts because they are based on a teleological view of development internationally as following a singular route to progress (115), while Klees, Samoff, and Stromquist (2012) roundly criticised the Bank's global approach to educational policy over more than three decades as being ideologically driven, insensitive to local contexts, and treating education as independent of international dynamics and of national and local economies and cultures. It should be noted that some Bank documents have reflected a need to adapt policy to local contexts, for example a sector study of schooling in Madagascar that emphasised local economic, cultural and political realities and did not foreground student-centred reforms (Heneveld 1995). However, the dominant impression is that Bank educational policy remains an ongoing vehicle for globalising Western economic interests. This is not only through curriculum and teaching styles but also through the New Paradigm, which the current World Bank (2011) EFA Strategy for 2020 promotes through the adoption in education systems of private sector managerial culture that is insensitive to context (Verger and Altinyelken 2013). Heyneman and Lee (2016) reported positively and Zapp (2017) enthusiastically on the Bank's influence. More soberly, Verger, Edwards, and Altinyelken (2014) found that even participation by the Netherlands, German and UK government aid agencies in development of the Strategy resulted in little contestation of the Bank's policy ideas; indeed, the agencies contributed inadvertently to reproducing the Bank's predominance in the education for development field.

The existence of international organisation travelling policies promulgated by staff can generate tensions with the national rights of developing country member nations, as a recent analysis of the pedagogical discourse of UNESCO demonstrates (Cerqua, Gautheir, and Dembele 2014). The authors asked how UNESCO uses research-based evidence to establish a bridge between research and policy, in particular on the issue of teaching practices. Their study analysed 45 UNESCO publications on teachers from the previous 15 years and conducted interviews with representatives of five strategic country members. UNESCO, they found, seemed caught in a contradiction between the content of its publications and the representatives' perspectives. The interviewees argued strongly that pedagogical orientations are a matter of national sovereignty and that UNESCO should not cross this line, while the publications timidly but recurrently promoted learner-centred constructivist approaches even though these were not supported by strong evidence. The authors suggested dryly that the organisation should at least base advice to member states on research evidence.

Similarly critical of UNESCO's research quality, an analysis by Alexander (2015) of the EFA Global Monitoring Report (UNESCO 2014) identified that the report highlighted quality of teachers and teaching, but its monitoring methodology had only a limited range of variables that failed to capture pedagogy's pivotal role in generating educational quality. Culture was treated 'not as an all pervasive feature to be handled with care, sensitivity and humility but as just another variable to be confidently factored and crunched' (256). Likewise, Sayed and Ahmed (2015, 330) found that in discussion on EFA's future,

> quality is still being defined as literacy and numeracy and still being constrained by what can be measured. While teachers are identified as crucial to the quality agenda, there is still a failure to engage more broadly with teaching and learning as well as the diverse contexts of teaching and learning.

Such critiques place this book in good company, but criticisms of cultural imperialism in international education policies usually come from the geographic and academic wildernesses and usually remain there. The critiques have been an influence on debate over schooling and educational transfer, and many problematic consequences of internationally influenced efforts at educational modernisation are recognised. However, Section 2.9 will find the progressive paradigm has remained axiomatic in the academic and evaluation literature associated with reforms in developing country schools.

1.4 Global English and cultural clusters

An example that brings the themes about cultural imperialism together from a developing country perspective is a study in Myanmar. Lall (2011) reported that rote learning there is the norm, but a network (comprising international and national aid and education organisations, commercial teacher training providers and consultants) was pushing a child-centred approach in Buddhist monastic schools. Lall's fieldwork involved classroom observations in 11 non-state-sector schools, interviews with 66 teachers and 19 teacher trainers, and focus groups with 58 parents or grandparents across four schools. While many said that child-centred was a 'better' approach to teaching and learning, the principal issue identified by teachers, head monks and parents was that this Western approach undermined traditional hierarchical structures of respect for teachers and elders, leading to a culture clash at home and in the classroom.

In contrast to Buddhist traditions, judgement in the comparative education literature that progressive change is desirable remains based on the norms of an individualistic, liberal Western academic subculture with a hidden agenda of moral and philosophical values about desirable psycho-sociological traits for individuals and for society (Guthrie 1990, 222). Progressivism has been influenced by predominantly European traffic in educational philosophy, but Alexander (2000) identified that the individualistic cultural values encoded in the progressive worldview are essentially Anglo-American. In continental Europe, Alexander showed, older formalistic traditions still involve highly structured lessons, whole-class teaching, the breaking down of learning tasks into small graduated steps, and the maintenance of economy in organisation, action and the use of time and space. The effect is a major cultural divide between English and non-English speaking countries that have communal and collective value sets that differently shape and explain pedagogy.

The modesty with which claims for the universal predominance of progressive Anglo-American educational values should be exercised is demonstrated by figures on English usage globally. Estimates of the numbers of second language users vary widely, from around half a billion to over one billion, depending on how language competence is defined, but international use of English as an academic, commercial and diplomatic language does not reflect a spread of its embedded cultural values (Guthrie 2011, 244–246). English has considerably less global currency as a mother tongue and therefore the initial vehicle for transmission of sociolinguistic cultural identity. A recent Summer Institute of Linguistics estimate had Chinese with more first speakers than any of 7,097 recognised languages (Lewis 2016). Chinese was spoken by some 1.302 billion people in 35 countries, 20% of the cited world population of 6.506 billion. Next at 6.6% was Spanish, growing rapidly with 427 million first speakers in 31 countries. English was third at 339 million, but in 106 countries. Only 5.2% of the world's population used English as a first language and therefore were likely to have it as the mother tongue vehicle for transmission of intergenerational culture. The clue to the global influence of English is that it has the highest number of countries with first language speakers and it is the most common language for international communication (Pennycook 2013). However, the use of English as a second language indicates its practical global utility, not the distribution of deep Anglo-American educational values.

The notion that the educational values of the 5% of first language English speakers will become those of the remaining 95% of the world's population seems improbable mathematically, to say the least. Indeed, Schweisfurth (2015a) questioned progressivism's success in making the transition from policy to practice even in its own cultural hearth. Other indications exist in Alexander's identification of the divide between Anglo-American educational paradigms and non-Anglophone ones, while beyond Europe, Regan (2005) described seven major indigenous traditions in Africa, South America, North America and Asia (with its Confucian, Hindu, Buddhist and Islamic cultures). Among these traditions, the area studies that illustrate this book demonstrate lack of progressive success in fundamentally changing teaching styles in Confucian countries, Sub-Saharan Anglophone Africa and PNG, which together encompass 30% of the world's population. Children do indeed appear to be valued in all cultures, but the ways in which they are valued and the expectations of appropriate intellectual and emotional development, and of appropriate behaviours, vary greatly around the world (Lancy 2014).

An important perspective is found in the recent borrowing by Zhang, Khan, and Tahirsylag (2015) of the concept of *cultural clusters* or 'world cultures' from management theory to show patterns in schooling indicators within and across country groups. Cultural clusters are distinct entities 'wherein countries share similarities in patterns of collective behavior and attitudes along specific dimensions of group characteristics . . . [studies of which] identify cultural nuances that give rise to the diversity of cultures across societies and countries' (44). The researchers used a classification of countries into ten clusters. The Anglo Cluster comprised Australia, Canada, Ireland, New Zealand, the United Kingdom and the United States, which together accounted for just 6.2% of the world's population in 2015 (this and all subsequent population data are from World Bank 2016). The nine other clusters were Arab, Confucian, Eastern Europe, Germanic Europe, Latin America, Latin Europe, Nordic Europe, South Asia and Sub-Saharan African Cultures. This classification came from GLOBE (Global Leadership and Organisational Behavior Effectiveness), a mega-project on cultural clustering that developed a comprehensive framework to explain the effects of cultural variables on leadership and organisations across countries and cultures (House *et al.* 2004). GLOBE factor analysis of survey data from 62 countries identified the ten clusters using quantitative measures of nine cultural dimensions (performance orientation, uncertainty avoidance, humane orientation, institutional collectivism, in-group collectivism, assertiveness, gender egalitarianism, future orientation and power distance). Regression analysis of 2009 PISA (Programme for International Student Assessment) data by Zhang and colleagues revealed striking similarities in educational performance among countries within many cultural clusters, including numerous developing countries (except the Sub-Saharan cluster, which had no PISA data). Collectively, the cluster variables had very high explanatory power indeed, explaining 65.9% of total variance in average student performance and 50.1% of school performance in 65 PISA countries. This is very strong quantitative evidence of the importance of culture in school systems.

The outcome is that the progressive educational paradigm derives from first-language English cultures – the Anglo Cluster – where scientific epistemology predominates. In contrast, in non-Anglo cultural clusters progressivism is usually subordinate to the formalistic paradigm, especially in cultures where revelatory epistemologies prevail. While educational reforms in developing countries face many practical barriers to classroom change (Sections 10.3–10.4), individualistic values in the cultures from which progressivism derives have often led educational reformers to underestimate countervailing communal and collective value sets associated with the dominant formalism.

1.5 Cultural relativity

The effect of cultural context on pedagogy has become an increasing concern in mainstream comparative education in recent decades, including among critical theorists who question the effects of globalisation in demarginalising local intellectual traditions. The much fraught area of cultural relativism, in which these transcultural issues often lie, has complex and contested meanings in fields ranging from philosophy, human rights, politics and law to anthropology, sociology and psychology. The field closest to this book's educational concerns with cultural context is anthropology, from which cultural understandings of epistemologies and pedagogies often derive. While noting over 20 kinds of cultural relativism across various fields, Brown (2008, 367–370) distinguished three main usages in anthropology: methodological, epistemological and ethical relativism.

Methodological relativism is the practice of suspending judgement until a belief or practice can be understood within its total context, which usage is only rarely objected to in anthropology or philosophy. In this book, methodological relativism is involved in recommending research to establish (preferably through grounded field experiments) which teaching style is most effective in generating student learning against the educational standards set within particular countries (Chapter 9). An important element is treatment as a hypothesis of the usually uncontested universalistic assumption that Anglo-American progressive educational values should be the primary frame of reference for classroom reform in developing countries. A second, more contested usage is *epistemological relativism*, which holds that members of different societies live in different and incommensurable knowledge worlds. Encompassed by this general principle are two interrelated sub-themes. One sub-theme claims that societies may exhibit ways of thinking that are radically different from our own: in this book, in Kuhnian analyses of incommensurable revelatory and scientific epistemologies and of the competition between pedagogical paradigms that frequently involves proponents of established paradigms in values-based resistance to change (below, also Chapter 7). The other epistemological sub-theme challenges the assumption that positivist scientific methods have transcultural validity, which is involved in the book's challenges to universal laws that may give theoretically elegant predictions about the educational future (as found in the school effectiveness field). The third and most contested usage is *ethical* or *moral relativism*, which goes further in insisting that each people's values are unique and self-validating, requiring outsiders to assess them by that group's own standards rather than universal ones.

Methodological and epistemological relativism are reflected in multicultural perspectives that provide respect for 'other' cultures, which this book shares, although it stops short of moral relativism. Rather, it fits within Epstein's (2008, 380) characterisation of a mainstream epistemology in comparative education that he labelled historical functionalism. This conceptual position synthesises positivist and relativist ones to probe the historical and social contexts of education to understand their interactions. Historical functionalism also uses cross-national generalisation to show the universality of theories about education. Thus, none of the usages herein is a rejection of scientific methods, positivism or progressivism as such, and I am not averse in principle to such quests. The approach is evidence-based, leading to reflection on the lack of evidence about progressivism increasing student achievement outside its own cultural domain and a rejection of ill-considered assumptions about learning theories and practices from education in developed countries that are often embedded in searches for universalities. Part III encourages eclectic mixed method research using objectivist and subjectivist methodologies to seek local solutions to local problems (Guthrie 2015b). The concern is establishing which teaching styles are effective in various developing country classrooms and which are not.

1.6 Intergenerational and organisational culture

Central to all this is the influence of context on schooling. Such a role is now virtually unchallenged in comparative education (e.g. Barrett 2007; Alexander 2008; Vavrus 2009; Schweisfurth 2013a), and researchers now commonly find that international policy borrowing does not absorb contextual lessons (e.g. Cerqua, Gautheir, and Dembele 2014, on UNESCO; Lattimer 2015, on Kenya; Shah and Quinn 2016, on Timor-Leste; and Courtney 2017, on Cambodia). However, usages vary in part because some writers focus on the cultural aspects of context and others on structural elements in society. As Section 7.4 will discuss in more detail, one current conceptualisation focusses on behaviour change inside the classroom (Guthrie 2011, 217–228, 2017). This approach follows Hall (1983) and Sternberg (2007) in considering *intergenerational culture* for understanding attitudes, values and beliefs that influence classroom behaviours; a background variable that is observable but not readily altered. Another current conceptualisation focusses on *organisational culture* as an intervening variable, a problematic implementation barrier between progressive theories and their intended effects (Schweisfurth 2011, 2013a, 2013b). This approach frequently follows Alexander's (2000) definition of pedagogy as both the act of teaching and the discourse in which it is embedded, which usage has expanded attention to school communities and organisations, especially if influenced by structural elements in Basil Bernstein's (2000) theories (e.g. Barrett 2007; Sriprakash 2012; Hoadley 2017).

Key propositions in this book agree fully with Alexander that pedagogy is contextually based, but collapsing the meaning of cultural context and teaching style into the one term removes a useful analytical distinction that I will retain, so that *pedagogy* as used here refers to teaching styles. Two other issues arise. One is the value of keeping a clear distinction between *cultural* and *structural* elements of context. The difficulty in not maintaining these distinctions is illustrated by Schweisfurth's (2015a, 2015b) interpretation of school environments as 'a situated and resilient "pedagogical nexus" . . . in which culture, structures, and materials resonate across mutually-reinforcing dimensions of life in and out of school, including assessment, relationships, cohort formation, and parental and pupil aspiration' (2015b, 646). Such abstractions may have theoretical merit, but from a pragmatic perspective the interweaving of so many elements is merely confusing in its failure to prioritise potential classroom interventions. A second issue for classroom reform is that even were systemic structural barriers resolved outside the classroom, intergenerational culture is much less prone to interventions and would remain intuitive for teachers and students inside the classroom.

1.7 Teaching styles, paradigms and epistemology

Insightful analysis of cultural effects occurs in many of the publications cited in this book as providing varying degrees of support for progressivism, but even these publications tend to skate on the cultural surface. While a focus on formalistic versus progressive teaching styles has been rejected by some, recognition is needed of formalism and progressivism as pedagogical paradigms (Kuhn 1962; Tabulawa 1997, 1998, 2011, 2013; Guthrie 2011; as discussed in Chapter 7). As Patton (2008) put it, paradigms provide a 'worldview built on implicit assumptions, accepted definitions, comfortable habits, values defended as truths, and beliefs projected as reality' (267). Thus, the deeper view of teaching styles is that the two paradigms are social constructs which constitute ways of viewing reality that are ultimately to be explained by seemingly irreconcilable differences between the underlying revelatory and scientific epistemologies. International debate over teacher- and student-centred styles is a surface manifestation of the implicit culture war.

Deep-rooted *revelatory epistemologies* provide the philosophical foundations for *formalistic educational paradigms* centrally concerned with the inter-generational transmission of cultural knowledge, especially through formal rather than informal or non-formal education. The principle underpinning such epistemologies is that knowledge is based on revealed truths from gods and previous generations so that important knowledge comes from deities and the ancestors rather than human inquiry. Such beliefs can be secular or non-secular: they are commonly but not only found in fundamentalist branches of all the major religions. In Confucianism, as a major example, revealed truths (derived from a moral order originating in an idealised golden age) have been embedded in Chinese philosophy for at least 3,000 years (Chapter 4). Likewise, studies in Islamic culture suggest that Islamic traditions have formalistic classrooms underpinned by concern for the development of student understanding founded in deep textual knowledge (e.g. Dhofier 1999; Minnis 1999; Boyle 2006; Moosa 2015). In Botswana, Richard Tabulawa (1997) found formalistic and progressive paradigms with opposed assumptions about the social world, the nature of reality and the learner (Chapter 5). The same is true of tribal PNG, where study of traditional religion found a unified epistemology going back to the ancestors such that myths were the sole and unquestionable source of all important truth (Lawrence 1964; Chapter 6). Commonalities in cultures with revelatory epistemology like these include a formalistic preference for teacher-centred methods to transmit given knowledge.

Traditional revelatory epistemologies are consistent with the underlying assumption in modern formalism that teachers know and transmit, and students do not know and receive. In China, classrooms embedded in ancient Confucian culture are functional for strong international achievement outcomes. The philosophy of knowledge embedded in traditional Tswana cosmology, in a society that emphasised subordination of children to their elders, underpins Botswana's prevalent teacher-centred method of school teaching. Similarly in Melanesia, for students 'the problem is to find the right source or text, rather than engaging with the source or text in a creative fashion', with the consequence that 'learning is, above all, a social construction based on relationships with teachers that are immediate, dialogical, and hierarchical' (Guy, Haihuie, and Pena 1997, 36). Formalistic paradigms provide long-term patterns for teachers' and students' behaviour, notably a didactic approach to revelation of knowledge to learners. Both traditional and modern formalism require students to play passive roles in receiving old and new knowledge through memorisation of a curriculum of basic facts and principles.

In contrast, central concerns in Western philosophy are with the metaphysical, rational thought as a distinguishing characteristic of humans, and the scientific study of nature based on *scientific epistemology* (Needham 1956). Karl Popper (1979, 60–61), for example, in developing his philosophy of science, strongly opposed the 'bucket theory' of knowledge – the assumption that an empty mind is to be filled with existing knowledge. In apposition, the *progressive paradigm* in Anglo-American education systems values questioning, creativity and problem-solving to construct new knowledge. In some contexts where scientific epistemologies prevail, the progressive view of pedagogy is that the student is the centre of the classroom rather than the teacher, and knowledge is to be discovered rather than transmitted. The lack of emphasis on enquiry, reflectivity and creativity in revelatory epistemology, as found in many religions for example, is fundamentally incompatible with progressive reforms that encourage all these types of thought. The deep epistemological substance that underlies the surface classroom forms of Southern formalistic paradigms, this book posits, is the fundamental explanation for the failures to generate shift to the progressive paradigm outside its own Anglo-American cultural context.

Revelatory epistemologies are highly compatible with formalistic pedagogy, but not with progressive pedagogy (at least at primary and secondary school levels). In contrast, scientific epistemology can be taught both with formalistic and progressive pedagogies. Indeed, formalistic methods were the norm for transmission of scientific knowledge in the Anglo Cultural Cluster until half a century ago, and still are in much of non-Anglophone Europe. Thus, formalistic pedagogy is often a vehicle for transmission of modern knowledge. The relationship between curriculum content and teaching styles, to reduce these concepts to their practical effect in the classroom, is complex and has many local nuances. The central focus of the book is teaching styles, within which the analysis prioritises culturally relevant local pedagogical paradigms over any assumption that Eurocentric classroom methods should prevail, although the approach is agnostic about curriculum content, which is a separate issue for national authorities (Section 9.3).

1.8 The progressive cage

Over some 50 years, the progressive paradigm has rarely demonstrated fundamental changes to its constructs to consider its failure in developing countries. An extensive literature continues to sustain the progressive paradigm despite the widespread evidence in Chapters 2–7 that witnesses the foundering of progressivism on cultural traditions. Chapter 2 derives from syntheses of 611 meta-analyses, research studies, evaluations and policy studies on education from the last half century. This literature, classified into a continuum with six types of findings from positive to negative, contains little if any sound evidence to support sustained progressive success in developing country classrooms. Numerous researchers have reported that progressive reforms were inappropriate and/or had major implementation difficulties in at least 32 statistically representative developing countries, including Azerbaijan, Botswana, Cambodia, China, Egypt, Ethiopia, Ghana, India, Indonesia, Jamaica, Kenya, Kyrgyzstan, Lesotho, Libya, Malawi, Mexico, Morocco, Mozambique, Myanmar, Namibia, Nigeria, Pakistan, PNG, Peru, Senegal, South Africa, Tanzania, Timor-Leste, Turkey, Uganda, Vietnam and Zambia. A similar list previously identified 12 such countries (Guthrie 2011, 7–8), which indicates that the lack of sustained success of progressivism and the prevalence of formalism in developing country classrooms are becoming increasingly acknowledged in the literature. However, reasons and responses remain in dispute, and the mainstream literature continues to hold progressivism as axiomatic despite being fraught with validity, reliability, relevance and generalisability issues (Section 3.3). At one level, these are technical matters, but they interact with and compound the conflicted intellectual cage that progressivism has become.

A lack of systematic attention to and rectification of methodological issues is indicative of proponents treating progressivism as a value position to be implemented rather than a theory to be judged on the evidence. Partly the faith in progressivism is a form of cultural imperialism founded in individualistic Western values; too, it has a foundation in issues to do with *paradigm shift*. Thomas Kuhn's (1962) seminal work saw science as conservative, with competition between incommensurable paradigms frequently involving proponents of established paradigms in values-based resistance to change (Bird 2013). In revelatory cultural systems formalistic pedagogy is the 'normal science' paradigm, a body of teacher-centred methods valued highly by adherents for its congruence with traditional beliefs and its effectiveness in transmitting them. Kuhn's pro-change position implies intellectually revolutionary change would be required in formalists' constructs (a *Gestalt-switch*) to resolve the tension between progressivism and formalism and to generate paradigm shift to progressivism. The anomaly that now exists is between progressive theory and sustained formalistic classroom practice. The failure for paradigm shift to occur when progressivism is exposed to competition outside its own cultural domain implies that progressive *paradigm reversal* is required, i.e. revolutionary reversal of the progressive worldview (Guthrie 2017; Section 7.2). However, paradigm reversal has not occurred and, ironically, the progressive paradigm is now the normal science position under attack and exhibiting resistance to intellectual change. Comparative education – which in so many ways is a cross-culturally enlightened field of study – nonetheless has this failure of imagination, which indicates a fundamental need for reflection. Commentary in Sections 7.3–7.5 will further ask, why the stubborn and long-lasting faith in progressivism as an axiomatic panacea and the cognitive dissonance generated by findings about its failures? Limited recognition of the authenticity of formalistic pedagogy and few reversals of universal claims for the progressive worldview indicate cognitive dissonance embedded in a cumulative progressive hallucination in which errors of judgement compound.

1.9 The formalistic frame

The most fundamental issue in this book is not actually teacher versus student, as embedded in the dialectic between formalistic and progressive paradigms, highly important though it is. Rather, the most important issue is contextual relevance, not only of progressivism but also of different forms of teacher-centredness. Pedagogies, be they student- or teacher-centred, from one cultural environment may be highly inappropriate in another, and there are no blanket formalistic solutions any more than there may be progressive ones because these countries and their cultures vary so widely. This contextual approach has similarities with Scheerens' (2015) model of educational effectiveness, which he conceptualised as an integration of top-down system-level, school-level, classroom-level and student factors. One theoretical explanation, Scheerens noted, is contingency theory, which has as its central thesis that the effectiveness of organisations depends on certain more basic and contextual conditions. It holds that there is no universal best way to organise and success depends on a good fit among internal organisational characteristics and between them and contextual antecedents and conditions (Section 8.2). In Scheerens' systems analysis, policy influence runs hierarchically from higher levels to lower levels, with higher level processes contextualising and controlling lower levels; however, the lower levels have considerable autonomy. The effect for teaching styles is that progressive national policies are generally ineffective where they run counter to cultural antecedents and where teachers have a large measure of independence in classroom practice. The evidence is clear that in developing countries formalism prevails.

The theoretical foundation in Chapter 8 shows that formalism is appropriate in the many educational and cultural contexts where it has value in itself and that it is more realistic than progressivism as the primary frame of reference for classroom change. However, in many ways, the methodology for identifying culture-specific teaching styles is more important than the theory because the grounded approach implies that it is not the nature of formalism (or of formalistic theory as such) that is the primary issue, but the methodology for eliciting the nature of the cultural contexts into which teaching styles need to fit. The way forward in applied policy and action research is methodology that investigates teaching and its improvement as culturally embedded acts to provide a constructive path for the development of culturally effective teaching styles (Chapters 9 and 10). From the extensive evidence about the long history of progressive failure, it can be predicted that in most non-Anglo cultural clusters in developing countries field experiments will find that formalistic teaching styles are equally or more effective than progressive ones in most types of primary and secondary classroom.

Whole-class formalistic processing of fixed syllabuses and textbooks, with the emphasis on memorising basic facts and principles, can be effective at promoting learning, particularly at the lower cognitive levels required in primary and secondary schools, thus providing building blocks for later intellectual endeavour. Formalistic teaching is consistent with the formalistic teacher training, inspections and examinations that provide coherence in many educational systems, providing a base on which to build in the many situations where teachers and students feel comfortable with it. The functionality of formalism in schools and classrooms with poor facilities is a considerable advantage, although formalism is not merely a response to lack of resources. Even were financing of education and working conditions in schools and classrooms improved, formalism would still prevail, such that the most effective use of funding is actually to improve formalistic conditions (Sections 10.3–10.4). As well, the affective consequences of formalistic teaching can be rather more positive than is commonly assumed. While a considerable barrier to the international acceptance of formalism is its connotation of a domineering authoritarianism, authoritative formalistic teaching can be benevolent. Thus, formalism is compatible with societies that value respect for knowledge and for authority.

1.10 Conclusion

A scarcity of deep reflection on findings is such that the progressive paradigm has often not been deconstructed. Despite the paradigm's failure to compete beyond its own cultural domain, it remains a soft power plank and the primary frame of reference for classroom change in developing country contexts. The effect is that the progressive paradigm remains axiomatic as a travelling policy. Widespread failure to generate paradigm shift in classroom practice has not led to paradigm reversal so that the academic and policy literature might align with classroom reality. Instead, the progressive paradigm has become an intellectually caged, distorted and history-free educational ideology that can manifest as a worldview posing as a theory and exhibiting resistance to deep-rooted alterations to its basic assumptions. The paradigm now amounts to a set of constructs that, in claiming to produce more reliable and dependable knowledge than non-scientific paradigms, has become the opposite: an intellectual cage distorted by culture-bound value judgements and frequently blind to the cultural imperialism in which it is embedded.

For educators, improving teaching is a legitimate act. Formalism, this book concludes, should not be regarded as a classroom problem readily subject to educational remediation – it is remarkably difficult to change – but as a deep-rooted cultural paradigm capable of adaptation and of performing important educational functions now and in the foreseeable future. Classroom formalism is frequently portrayed as an obstruction to modernisation and, at best, an intermediary stage on the path to progressive educational development. Rather, the teaching style is likely to remain embedded in many school systems because it is symptomatic of pervasive cultural continuities compatible with traditional and ongoing practices in formal education. The issue is not how to change the quality of teaching by promoting alternatives to formalism, but how to improve the quality of formalism. There is no point in using progressive styles just because they appear to represent modern thinking in developed countries. Different teaching styles are not 'better' or 'worse' than each other, only more or less appropriate, so that progress can well be a case of improving within a style (Guthrie 1981, 166, 1990, 228, 2011, 208–210). The thrust of the evidence is that incremental change within the formalistic teaching style may well succeed, but attempts to change to progressivism have not. Progressivism has not provided a virtuous circle of increasingly informed decisions on improvement of classroom teaching. If it continues as the primary frame of reference, the risk is continuation of a vicious circle of misinformation perpetuating the irrational pursuit of the unattainable.

References

Alcorn, N. 1999. *'To the Fullest Extent of His Powers': C.E. Beeby's Life in Education*. Wellington: Victoria University Press.

Alexander, R. 2000. *Culture and Pedagogy: International Comparisons in Primary Education*. Oxford: Blackwell.

Alexander, R. 2008. *Education for All, the Quality Imperative and the Problem of Pedagogy*. Create Pathways to Access Monograph No.20. London: Institute of Education, University of London.

Alexander, R. 2015. "Teaching and Learning for All? The Quality Imperative Revisited." *International Journal of Educational Development* 40: 250–256.

Altinyelken, H. 2013. "Teachers' Principled Resistance to Curriculum Change: A Compelling Case from Turkey." In *Global Managerial Education Reforms and Teachers: Emerging Policies, Controversies and Issues in Developing Contexts*, edited by A. Verger, H. Altinyelken, and M. de Koning, 109–126. Brussels: Education International.

Arreman, I., Erixon, P-O., and Rehn, K-G. 2016. "Postcolonial Teacher Education Reform in Namibia: Travelling of Policies and Ideas." *European Educational Research Journal* 15 (2): 236–259.

Auld, E., and Morris, P. 2014. "Comparative Education, the 'New Paradigm' and Policy Borrowing: Constructing Knowledge for Educational Reform." *Comparative Education* 50 (2): 129–155.

Barrett, A. 2007. "Beyond the Polarization of Pedagogy: Models of Classroom Practice in Tanzanian Primary Schools." *Comparative Education* 43 (2): 273–294.

Barrett, A., Chawla-Duggan, R., Lowe, J., Nikel, J., and Ukpo, E. 2006. *The Concept of Quality in Education: Review of the 'International' Literature on the Concept of Quality in Education*. EdQual Working Paper No.2. Bristol: University of Bristol.

Barrington, J. 1980. "The Teacher and the Stages of Educational Development." *British Journal of Teacher Education* 6 (2): 100–114.

Beeby, C.E. 1966. *The Quality of Education in Developing Countries*. Cambridge: Harvard University Press.

Beeby, C.E. 1979. *Assessment of Indonesian Education: A Guide in Planning*. Wellington: New Zealand Council for Educational Research.

Beeby, C.E. 1992. *The Biography of an Idea: Beeby on Education*. Wellington: New Zealand Council for Educational Research.

Bernstein, B. 2000. *Pedagogy, Symbolic Control and Identity: Theory, Research, Critique*. Lanham: Rowman & Littlefield.

Bird, A. 2013. "Thomas Kuhn." In *The Stanford Encyclopedia of Philosophy*, edited by E. Zalta. Stanford: Stanford University. plato.stanford.edu/entries/thomas-kuhn/

Boyle, H. 2006. "Memorization and Learning in Islamic Schools." *Comparative Education Review* 50 (3): 478–495.

Brown, M. 2008. "Cultural Relativism 2.0." *Current Anthropology* 49 (3): 363–383.

Burkhalter, N., and Shegebayev, M. 2012. "Critical Thinking as Culture: Teaching Post-Soviet Teachers in Kazakhstan." *International Review of Education* 58 (1): 55–72.

Cerqua, A., Gautheir, C., and Dembele, M. 2014. "Education Policy, Teacher Education, and Pedagogy: A Case Study of UNESCO." In *Annual Review of Comparative and International Education 2014*, edited by A. Wiseman and E. Anderson, 235–364. Bingley: Emerald.

Courtney, J. 2017. "An Exploration of the Interaction Between Global Education Policy Orthodoxies and National Education Practices in Cambodia, Illuminated Through the Voices of Local Teacher Educators." *Compare*. doi.org/10.1080/03057925.2017.1338937

Crossley, M. 1984. "Strategies for Curriculum Change and the Question of International Transfer." *Journal of Curriculum Studies* 16 (1): 75–88.

Crossley, M. 1992. "Teacher Education in Papua New Guinea: A Comment on Comparative and International Observations." *Journal of Education for Teaching* 23 (1): 23–28.

Crossley, M. 2000. "Bridging Cultures and Traditions in the Reconceptualisation of Comparative and International Education." *Comparative Education* 36 (3): 319–332.

Crossley, M. 2014. "Global League Tables, Big Data and the International Transfer of Educational Research Modalities." *Comparative Education* 50 (1): 15–26.

De Feiter, L., and Ncube, K. 1999. "Towards a Comprehensive Strategy for Science Curriculum Reform and Teacher Development in Southern Africa." In *Science and Environment Education: Views from Developing Countries*, edited by S. Ware, 177–198. Secondary Education Series 19659. Washington, DC: World Bank.

De Feiter, L., Vonk, H., and van den Akker, J. 1995. *Towards More Effective Teacher Development in Southern Africa*. Amsterdam: Vrije University Press.

Dhofier, Z. 1999. *The Pesantren Tradition: The Role of the Kyai in the Maintenance of Traditional Islam in Java*. Tempe: Monograph Series, Program for Southeast Asian Studies, Arizona State University.

Epstein, E. 2008. "Setting the Normative Boundaries: Crucial Epistemological Benchmarks in Comparative Education." *Comparative Education* 44 (4): 373–386.
Fataar, A. 2006. "Policy Networks in Recalibrated Political Terrain: The Case of School Curriculum Policy and Politics in South Africa." *Journal of Education Policy* 21 (6): 641–659.
Festinger, L. 1957. *A Theory of Cognitive Dissonance*. Evanston: Row and Peterson.
Forestier, K., and Crossley, M. 2015. "International Education Policy Transfer – Borrowing Both Ways: The Hong Kong and England Experience." *Compare* 45 (5): 664–685.
Ginsburg, M. 2010. "Improving Educational Quality through Active-Learning Pedagogies: A Comparison of Five Case Studies." *Educational Research* 1 (3): 62–74.
Guthrie, G. 1980. "Stages of Educational Development? Beeby Revisited." *International Review of Education* 26 (4): 411–438.
Guthrie, G. 1981. "Teaching Styles." In *Teachers and Teaching: Proceedings of the 1980 Extraordinary Meeting of the Faculty of Education*, edited by P. Smith and S. Weeks, 154–168. Port Moresby: UPNG.
Guthrie, G. 1990. "To the Defense of Traditional Teaching in Lesser Developed Countries." In *Teachers and Teaching in the Developing World*, edited by V. Rust and P. Dalin, 219–232. New York: Garland.
Guthrie, G. 2011. *The Progressive Education Fallacy in Developing Countries: In Favour of Formalism*. New York: Springer.
Guthrie, G. 2012. "The Failure of Progressive Classroom Reform: Lessons from the Curriculum Reform Implementation Project in Papua New Guinea." *Australian Journal of Education* 56 (3): 241–256.
Guthrie, G. 2015a. "Child Soldiers in the Culture Wars." *Compare* 45 (4): 635–642.
Guthrie, G. 2015b. "Culturally-grounded Pedagogy and Research Methodology." *Compare* 45 (1): 163–168.
Guthrie, G. 2017. "The Failure of Progressive Paradigm Reversal." *Compare* 47 (1): 62–76.
Guy, R., Haihuie, S., and Pena, P. 1997. "Research, Knowledge and the Management of Learning in Distance Education in Papua New Guinea." *Papua New Guinea Journal of Education* 33 (1): 33–41.
Hall, E. 1983. *The Dance of Life*. New York: Doubleday.
Harvey, S. 1999. "Phasing Science InSET in Developing Countries: Reflections on the Experience of the Primary Science Program in South Africa." *International Journal of Science Education* 21 (6): 595–609.
Hauk, E., and Mueller, H. 2015. "Cultural Leaders and the Clash of Civilizations." *Journal of Conflict Resolution* 59 (3): 367–400.
Hawkins, J. 2007. "The Intractable Dominant Educational Paradigm." In *Changing Education: Leadership, Innovation and Development in a Globalizing Asia-Pacific*, edited by P. Hershock, M. Mason, and J. Hawkins, 137–162. Hong Kong: Comparative Education Research Centre, University of Hong Kong.
Heneveld, W. 1994. *Planning and Monitoring the Quality of Primary Education in Sub-Saharan Africa*. Technical Note No.14. Washington: World Bank Human Resources and Poverty Division.
Heneveld, W. 1995. *Madagascar: Towards a School-based Strategy for Improving Primary and Secondary Education*. Washington, DC: World Bank Population and Human Resources Division, Central Africa and Indian Ocean Department.
Heyneman, S. 2003. "The History and Problems in the Making of Education Policy at the World Bank 1960–2000." *International Journal of Educational Development* 23 (3): 315–337.
Heyneman, S., and Lee, B. 2016. "International Organizations and the Future of Educational Assistance." *International Journal of Educational Development* 48: 9–22.

Heyneman, S., and White, D. (Eds.). 1986. *The Quality of Education and Economic Development: A World Bank Symposium*. Washington, DC: World Bank.

Hoadley, U. 2017. *Pedagogy in Poverty: Lessons from Twenty Years of Curriculum Reform in South Africa*. London: Routledge.

House, R., Hanges, P., Javidan, M., Dorfman, P., and Gupta, V. 2004. *Culture, Leadership, and Organizations: The GLOBE Study of 62 Cultures*. Thousand Oaks: Sage.

Huntington, S. 1996a. *The Clash of Civilizations and the Remaking of World Order*. New York: Simon and Schuster.

Huntington, S. 1996b. "The West: Unique, Not Universal." *Foreign Affairs* 75 (6): 28–46.

Jansen, J., and Taylor, N. 2003. "Educational Change in South Africa 1994–2003: Case Studies in Large-scale Education Reform." *Country Studies in Education Reform and Management* 2 (1). Washington, DC: World Bank.

Jones, P. 2006. "Elusive Mandate: UNICEF and Educational Development." *International Journal of Educational Development* 26 (6): 591–604.

Jones, P., and Coleman, D. 2005. *The United Nations and Education: Multilateralism, Development and Globalisation*. London: Routledge Farmer.

Klees, S. 2002. "World Bank Education Policy: New Rhetoric, Old Ideology." *International Journal of Educational Development* 22 (5): 451–474.

Klees, S., Samoff, J., and Stromquist, N. (Eds.). 2012. *The World Bank and Education: Critiques and Alternatives*. New York: Springer.

Kuhn, T. 1962. *The Structure of Scientific Revolutions*. Chicago: University of Chicago Press.

Lall, M. 2011. "Pushing the Child Centred Approach in Myanmar: The Role of Cross National Policy Networks and the Effects in the Classroom." *Critical Studies in Education* 52 (3): 219–233.

Lam, E. 2014. "'South-South' Borrowing: Lessons from the Caribbean and Implications for Post 2015 Agenda." *Canadian and International Education* 43 (2): Article 5. http://ir.lib.uwo.ca/cie-eci/vol43/iss2/5

Lancy, D. 2014. *The Anthropology of Childhood: Cherubs, Chattel, Changelings*. Cambridge: Cambridge University Press.

Lattimer, H. 2015. "Translating Theory into Practice: Making Meaning of Learner Centered Education Frameworks for Classroom-based Practitioners." *International Journal of Educational Development* 45 (1): 65–76.

Lawrence, P. 1964. *Road Belong Cargo*. Melbourne: Oxford University Press.

Lee, J., Adams, D., and Cornbleth, C. 1988. "Transnational Transfer of Curriculum Knowledge: A Korean Case Study." *Journal of Curriculum Studies* 20: 233–246.

Lewis, M. (Ed.). 2016. *Ethnologue: Languages of the World* (19th ed.). Dallas: SIL International.

Lockheed, M., and Levin, H. 1993. "Creating Effective Schools." In *Effective Schools in Developing Countries*, edited by H. Levin, and M. Lockheed, 1–19. London: Falmer.

Lockheed, M., and Verspoor, A. 1991. *Improving Primary Education in Developing Countries*. Oxford: Oxford University Press.

Malitza, M. 2000. "Ten Thousand Cultures: A Single Civilization." *International Political Science Review* 21 (1): 75–89.

Minnis, P. 1999. "Is Reflective Practice Compatible With Malay-Islamic Values? Some Thoughts on Teacher Education in Brunei Darussalam." *Australian Journal of Education* 43 (2): 172–185.

Mok, I. 2006. "Shedding Light on the East Asian Learner Paradox: Reconstructing Student-centredness in a Shanghai Classroom." *Asia-Pacific Journal of Teacher Education* 26 (2): 131–142.

Moosa, E. 2015. *What Is a Madrasa?* Chapel Hill: University of North Carolina Press.

Needham, J. 1956. *Science and Civilization in China, Volume 2: History of Thought*. Cambridge: Cambridge University Press.

Nye, J. 2009. *Understanding International Conflicts* (7th ed.). New York: Pearson.

O'Donoghue, T. 1994. "The Need for Educational Reform and the Role of Teacher Training: An Alternative Perspective." *International Journal of Educational Development* 14 (2): 207–210.

O'Sullivan, M. 2004. "The Reconceptualisation of Learner-Centred Approaches: A Namibia Case Study." *International Journal of Educational Development* 24 (6): 585–602.

Patton, M. 2008. *Utilization-Focused Evaluation*. Thousand Oaks: Sage.

Pennycook, A. 2013. *The Cultural Politics of English as an International Language*. London: Routledge.

Phillips, D. 2009. "Aspects of Educational Transfer." In *International Handbook of Comparative Education*, edited by R. Cowen and A. Kazamias, 1061–1078. Dordrecht: Springer.

Popper, K. 1979. *Objective Knowledge: An Evolutionary Approach* (2nd ed.). Oxford: Oxford University Press.

Portnoi, L. 2016. *Policy Borrowing and Reform in Education: Globalized Processes and Local Contexts*. New York: Palgrave Macmillan.

Quist, H. 2003. "Transferred and Adapted Models of Secondary Education in Ghana: What Implications for National Development?" *International Review of Education* 49 (5): 411–431.

Regan, T. 2005. *Non-Western Educational Traditions: Indigenous Approaches to Educational Thought and Practice*. Mahwah: Erlbaum.

Reynolds, D., Sammons, P., De Fraine, B., Van Damme, J., Townsend, T., Teddlie, C., and Stringfield, S. 2014. "Educational Effectiveness Research (EER): A State-of-the-Art Review." *School Effectiveness and School Improvement* 25 (2): 197–230.

Riddell, A., and Nino-Zarazua, M. 2016. "The Effectiveness of Foreign Aid to Education: What Can Be Learned?" *International Journal of Educational Development* 40: 23–36.

Rogan, J., and Grayson, D. 2003. "Towards a Theory of Curriculum Implementation With Particular Reference to Science Education in Developing Countries." *International Journal of Science Education* 25 (10): 1171–1204.

Ryle, A. 1975. *Frames and Cages: The Repertory Grid Approach to Human Understanding*. London: Chatto & Windus.

Sayed, Y., and Ahmed, R. 2015. "Education Quality, and Teaching and Learning in the Post-2015 Education Agenda." *International Journal of Educational Development* 40: 330–338.

Scheerens, J. 2015. "Theories on Educational Effectiveness and Ineffectiveness." *School Effectiveness and School Improvement* 26 (1): 10–31.

Schweisfurth, M. 2011. "Learner-Centred Education in Developing Country Contexts: From Solution to Problem?" *International Journal of Educational Development* 31 (5): 425–432.

Schweisfurth, M. 2013a. *Learner-Centred Education in International Perspective: Whose Pedagogy for Whose Development?* London: Routledge.

Schweisfurth, M. 2013b. "Learner-Centred Education in International Perspective." *Journal of International and Comparative Education* 2 (1): 1–8.

Schweisfurth, M. 2015a. "Make Learning, Not War." *Compare* 45 (4): 644–647.

Schweisfurth, M. 2015b. "Learner-Centred Pedagogy: Towards a Post-2015 Agenda for Teaching and Learning." *International Journal of Educational Development* 40: 259–266.

Shah, R., and Quinn, M. 2016. "Mind the Gap: Global Quality Norms, National Policy Interpretations and Local Praxis in Timor-Leste." *Compare* 46 (3): 394–413.

Slonimsky, L. 2016. "Teacher Change in a Changing Moral Order: Learning from Durkheim." *Education as Change* 20 (1): 1–17.

Sriprakash, A. 2012. *Pedagogies for Development: The Politics and Practice of Child-Centred Education in India*. New York: Springer.

Stein, H. 2008. *Beyond the World Bank Agenda: An Institutional Approach to Development*. Chicago: University of Chicago Press.

Steiner-Khamsi, G., and Waldow, F. (Eds.). 2012. *World Yearbook of Education 2012: Policy Borrowing and Lending in Education*. London: Routledge.

Sternberg, R. 2007. "Culture, Instruction, and Assessment." *Comparative Education* 43 (1): 5–22.

Sweeting, A. 1996. "The Globalization of Learning: Paradigm or Paradox?" *International Journal of Educational Development* 16 (4): 379–391.

Tabulawa, R. 1997. "Pedagogical Classroom Practice and the Social Context: The Case of Botswana." *International Journal of Educational Development* 17 (2): 189–194.

Tabulawa, R. 1998. "Teachers' Perspectives on Classroom Practice in Botswana: Implications for Pedagogical Change." *International Journal of Qualitative Studies in Education* 20: 249–268.

Tabulawa, R. 2003. "International Aid Agencies, Learner-centred Pedagogy and Political Democratisation: A Critique." *Comparative Education* 39 (1): 7–26.

Tabulawa, R. 2011. "The Rise and Attenuation of the Basic Education Programme (BEP) in Botswana: A Global-Local Dialectic Approach." *International Journal of Educational Development* 31 (5): 443–442.

Tabulawa, R. 2013. *Teaching and Learning in Context: Why Pedagogical Reforms Fail in Sub-Saharan Africa*. Dakar: Codesria.

Tan, C. 2015. "Education Policy Borrowing and Cultural Scripts for Teaching in China." *Comparative Education* 51 (2): 196–211.

Tan, C. 2016. "Tensions and Challenges in China's Education Policy Borrowing." *Educational Research* 58 (2): 195–206.

Thaman, K. 1991. "Towards a Culture-Sensitive Model of Curriculum Development for the Pacific Countries." *Directions* 13: 1–13.

Tikly, L. 1999. "Postcolonialism and Comparative Education." *International Review of Education* 45 (5–6): 603–621.

Tikly, L. 2004. "Education and the New Imperialism." *Comparative Education* 40 (2): 173–198.

Tikly, L. 2014. "The World Bank and Education." *Comparative Education Review* 58 (2): 344–355.

UNESCO. 2014. *Teaching and Learning: Achieving Quality for All, EFA Global Monitoring Report*. Paris: UNESCO.

Vavrus, F. 2009. "The Cultural Politics of Constructivist Pedagogies: Teacher Education Reform in the United Republic of Tanzania." *International Journal of Educational Development* 29 (3): 303–311.

Verger, A., and Altinyelken, H. 2013. "Global Education Reform and the New Management of Teachers: A Critical Introduction." In *Global Managerial Education Reforms and Teachers: Emerging Policies, Controversies and Issues in Developing Contexts*, edited by A. Verger, H. Altinyelken, and M. de Koning, 1–18. Brussels: Education International.

Verger, A., Edwards, D., and Altinyelken, H. 2014. "Learning from All? The World Bank, Aid Agencies and the Construction of Hegemony in Education for Development." *Comparative Education* 50 (4): 381–399.

Verger, A., Lubienski, C., and Steiner-Khamsi, G. 2016. "The Emergence and Structuring of the Global Education Industry: Towards an Analytical Framework." In *World Yearbook of Education 2016: The Global Education Industry*, edited by A. Verger, C. Lubienski, and G. Steiner-Khamsi, 3–24. New York: Routledge.

Verspoor, A., and Leno, J. 1986. *Improving Teaching: A Key to Successful Educational Change*. Report EDT50. Washington, DC: World Bank Educational and Training Department.

Verspoor, A., and Wu, K. 1990. *Textbooks and Educational Development*. PHREE Background Paper PHREE/90/31. Washington, DC: World Bank.

World Bank. 2011. *Learning for All: Investing in People's Knowledge and Skills to Promote Development, Education Sector 2020 Strategy Report*. Washington, DC: World Bank.

World Bank. 2016. *World Development Indicators Database*, 16 December 2016. Washington, DC: World Bank. http://data.worldbank.org/data-catalog/world-development-indicators

Zapp, M. 2017. "The World Bank and Education: Governing (through) Knowledge." *International Journal of Educational Development* 53: 2–22.

Zhang, L., Khan, G., and Tahirsylag, A. 2015. "Student Performance, School Differentiation, and World Cultures: Evidence from PISA 2009." *International Journal of Educational Development* 42: 43–53.

Part II
The progressive cage

2 Typology of progressive reform findings

Over the last 50 years, progressivism has been entrenched as an axiom – an assumed starting point – and as an unexamined end point in much of the academic literature. It became a travelling policy among international and multilateral aid organisations, and was taken up by many decision makers in 'developing' countries who were influenced by international trends. Initially, classroom effects of the policy transfers and borrowings described by Phillips (2009) were analysed in three overlapping phases (Crossley 1984a, 1984b; Guthrie 1986, 2011, 62–65). The first phase was to blame teachers for an inability to change away from formalism to more progressive teaching styles, more pre-service and in-service teacher education being the perceived remedies. The second phase blamed lack of change on teacher training and curriculum, and attempted to alter either or both. Lack of cultural understanding contributed to the widespread failure of both these phases. A third phase involved more systematic project-based management of the change process. More recently, a fourth phase is the growing concern for context, for identifying culturally appropriate teaching styles.

An extensive research and evaluation literature sustains the progressive paradigm as the primary frame of reference for educational theory and policy in developing countries. Does evidence support sustained progressive success inside classrooms? If not, has progressive theory aligned with classroom reality or does progressivism usually remain axiomatic? This chapter systematises research, evaluations and policy studies. As well, independent meta-analyses by other researchers illustrate a typology in the chapter and analysis in the next chapter of theoretical and methodological limitations in this literature. The review derives primarily from long, deep and wide literature searches (including but not limited to comparative education journals and Google Scholar and ResearchGate searches of key terms and authors). A previous search synthesised 412 publications relevant to teaching styles in developing countries (Guthrie 2011). Of these, 150 older ones have been omitted from the present book (mainly about 'stages' of educational development, Papua New Guinea, and early school effectiveness research, where I have nothing new to add), while 239 new publications update the literature to provide 501 references in this book. Of the total of 651 references in both works, 613 are directly on education in developing countries, while the other 38 are mainly on research methodology and neuropsychology. So culturally irrelevant are findings on 'developed' country education that almost none have been used.

Of the 501 references herein, 211 are of literature current in the ten years from 2008 to 2017. This chapter draws heavily on recent literature, but included and on occasion added to is older material, especially on methodological discussions and the areas studied in Chapters 4–6. This material is relevant where it provides seminal concepts, the analyses remain valid, they provide research evidence that remains useful (either by having established major empirical findings or where subsequent research has not updated or refuted it) and/or they demonstrate historical perspectives. In part, such material is intended as a corrective to ahistorical writing in the progressive literature because the book considers continuities in progressive educational thought since the middle of the last century and other educational traditions that date back centuries.

2.1 The typology

The baseline is that formalistic classroom practices dominate in primary and secondary schools in developing countries. A recent broad-based literature analysis by Nag *et al.* (2014) that reconfirmed this widely agreed generalisation included 260 research reports on foundation learning published from 1990 to 2013. The reports contained primary data from experimental or observational studies using statistical, ethnographic or other qualitative descriptive methods, and from interventions using randomised controls or quasi-experimental designs. A wide range of developing countries in Africa, South and Central America, South, Southeast and North Asia, and the South Pacific was included. In particular, 14 ethnographic studies in literacy and numeracy classes in Ethiopia, Eritrea, Ghana, India, Kenya, Mexico, Pakistan and Peru consistently showed deeply entrenched formalistic practices. Rote and surface learning dominated, with chorus, copy writing and drill the most visible aspects of instruction, albeit with some variety in these practices (13–15). Progressive reforms seek to alter formalistic practices like these in developing country classrooms. Consideration suggests that the literature on such reforms can be classified into six types along the continuum from positive findings to negative ones in Figure 2.1.

As research and evaluations are categorised from left to right in the figure, they have increasingly negative findings. From a measurement perspective, the typology is in the form of a continuum with six analytically distinct but empirically arbitrary divisions that represent differences of degree rather than of kind. The typology represents for explanatory purposes a continuous variable as an ordinal scale. Such typologies are commonly used in social science, but it is worth reiterating some of the measurement properties of ordinal scales to clarify what the figure is and is not intended to represent. Ordinal scales are based on a continuous variable, with each category incorporating transitivity (i.e. if $a > b$,

Typology of progressive reform findings 35

Sound positive findings	Vested consultancy findings	Further technical inputs	Interim formalism	Structural change	Rejection of universal progressivism
Methodologically sound findings about progressive innovations in developing countries that are successful in the long-term rather than just during pilot programmes.	Supportive findings from commercially contracted evaluations with vested interests in reporting positive outcomes from progressive pilot projects.	Findings that progressive reforms have not had the desired effect but future success perceived as lying in further technical inputs.	Evaluations question the effectiveness of progressive reforms on pragmatic grounds and look to interim improvement in formalistic teaching methods.	Recognition that technical inputs or time are insufficient. More sophisticated recommendations for structural reforms to promote progressive change.	Rejection of universal claims for progressivism. The only evaluation group for which progressivism is non-axiomatic.

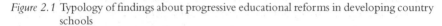

Increasingly negative findings about progressivism

Figure 2.1 Typology of findings about progressive educational reforms in developing country schools
Source: Author.

and $b > c$, then $a > c$), but without specifying the size of the interval. There may be less difference, for example, between recommendations for technical inputs and structural change than between recommendations for structural change and rejection of progressivism. Labels are assigned to the categories for convenience, but other labels could be used or other categories added. Boundaries between the categories are drawn in the figure as broken lines, the implication being that they are arbitrary to a degree and capable of being redefined. Such redefinition, however, would have to be consistently transitive in relation to the underlying variable of negativity of findings. The most positive findings at the left-hand end have methodologically sound data about innovations with sustained success. In the negative findings at the right-hand end of the continuum, progressivism is not an axiomatic basis for reform.

This chapter does not attempt to classify all the publications, but illustrates the typology with pertinent examples and, it should be noted, many studies have elements that fit more than one category, e.g. vested consultancy findings with recommendations for further technical inputs. Further and more detailed examples are in the methodological issues discussed in Chapter 3 and the three area studies that follow.

2.2 Sound positive findings

The first type of evaluation is methodologically sound findings about progressive innovations in developing countries that have remained successful in the long-term rather than just during pilot programmes.[1]

The 2011 literature search did not actually find methodologically sound evidence that demonstrated long-term survival of progressive classroom reforms, nor have three updates (expanded and further updated in Chapters 4–6). One, of classroom studies in China since curriculum policy changes in 2001, found that the effect had been to upgrade the level of formalism rather than to adopt progressive teaching (Guthrie 2012a). Another review of Sub-Saharan Anglophone Africa consolidated studies spanning 30 years in nine countries (Guthrie 2013). Field studies with strong methodology found equal or superior performance from formalistic teaching. Reviews on the literature on Papua New Guinea (PNG), covering 100 studies spanning 50 years, found that eight major efforts to change the formalistic teaching paradigm through curriculum reform in primary and secondary classrooms all failed despite large-scale professional, administrative and financial support (Guthrie 2014, 2015a). Independently, Schweisfurth (2011) surveyed 72 studies from the *International Journal of Educational Development* spanning 20 years and 39 countries, finding the literature 'riddled with stories of failures grand and small' (425). The only review uncovered that claimed systematic evidence favouring progressive practices was undertaken for the UK Department for International Development (Westbrook *et al.* 2013), but its Executive Summary overgeneralised from studies that the body of the report showed had weak methodological foundations (as discussed in Section 3.4).

Nearly all the literature found in these reviews was based on case studies and surveys. More widely, a search by Glewwe *et al.* (2011) of over 9,000 worldwide school effectiveness studies from 1990 to 2010 found only 13 randomised trials among 43 high-quality econometric studies on developing countries. The studies focussed on quantifiable school and teacher characteristics rather than classroom behaviour. The only variables with significant effects on student learning were availability of desks, teacher subject knowledge and teacher absence, which threw little light on teaching styles (although some of the implications of their negative as well as positive findings return in the final chapter). The authors' conclusion was that 'despite a large and increasingly sophisticated literature, remarkably little is known about the impact of education policies on student outcomes in developing countries' (46). Another school effectiveness review of 90 African studies by Yu (2007) concluded that developed country findings do not provide a blueprint for the creation of more effective schools and should not be applied without reference to the particular contexts, nor should it be assumed that developing countries are a single entity.

Field experiments directly on the effect of classroom teaching styles on student achievement remain rare. One in Zambia researched the effectiveness of traditional and discovery approaches for teaching scientific facts, understandings and attitudes (Mulopo and Fowler 1987). Sixty randomly selected concrete operational and 60 formal operational grade 11 male chemistry students in two schools were randomly assigned to traditional and discovery approaches for 10 weeks and pre- and post-tested with the same standard tests. Two-way analysis of covariance found the traditional group outperformed the discovery group on achievement. Teaching style did not make a difference among concrete reasoners for understanding of science but the formal reasoner discovery group scored significantly higher. Students in the traditional group had significantly lower scientific attitude scores than those taught by discovery. The authors concluded that the traditional, formalistic approach was efficient for teaching scientific facts and principles, especially for concrete operational students, while the progressive discovery approach was more effective among formal reasoners in promoting scientific attitudes and understandings. This Zambian finding supports a long-standing but rarely tested hypothesis derived from earlier literature reviews that formalistic styles are more effective with the lower cognitive levels found in primary and secondary schools (Guthrie 1982, 2011, 77–101). Conversely, some mixed support exists for the hypothesis that progressive teaching styles are more effective with higher cognitive levels and some affective aspects of learning. However, where these findings might apply and the meanings ascribed to them by the actors are highly dependent on cultural context, as illustrated by a recent study that even found difficulty transferring learner-centred skills from Scotland to tertiary teachers at a university in Iraq (Jordan *et al.* 2014).

The net effect of the various literature searches, especially seen in historical perspective, is that there is no reliable evidence showing that progressivism has made the transition from theory to classroom practice when exposed outside its own Anglo-American cultural domain to competition with formalism in developing countries.

2.3 Vested consultancy findings

A second type of evaluation contains supportive findings about progressivism that are derived from commercially contracted evaluations that can have vested interests in reporting positive outcomes from pilot projects. Commonly such studies have terms of reference from multilateral and bilateral aid agencies.

The United Nations Children's Fund report on UNICEF's child-friendly schools (CFS) programme was a mixed method study contracted from American Institutes for Research (UNCF 2009). While an appendix detailed data collection instruments, statistical methods and sophisticated data analysis techniques, broader methodological issues lacked rigour and were glossed over in the Executive Summary (viii–xvii). A first issue was that a report entitled 'global' was based on only six countries. School samples were claimed in the Executive Summary to include 'the range of CFS schools in terms of location, duration of implementation and demography' (viii), however the methodology appendix showed they were judgement samples chosen non-randomly and in part for convenience by UNICEF representatives (139). There was no clarification whether these were pilot schools, and possibly well-resourced, and an absence of quasi-experimental controls with 'non-child friendly' schools. Any randomisation in the sampling applied only to selection of interviewees within schools. The Child-Centred Pedagogy observation schedule contained 16 items. Inspection suggests that several could be as valid in teacher-centred classrooms as child-centred ones (e.g. the teacher presents lessons in a well-prepared and organised manner, moves around the classroom, communicates in a positive and friendly manner, and students pay attention and are respectful) (151). The study purported to find that 'CFSs in varying contexts successfully apply the three key principles of CFS models – inclusiveness, child-centredness and democratic participation' (ix), but the apparently contradictory classroom result was that 'Observations and student and teacher reports suggest that many teachers in CFSs are using child-centred pedagogical approaches. However, teachers are not necessarily following the pedagogical approaches one would expect in a CFSs' (xi), whatever that means. In sum, the report failed several methodological tests: sampling was non-random, the classroom data collection instrument was unfocussed, and findings were generalised far beyond the six-country study. Confusing claims were also made about classroom findings. Weak evaluation practices were also followed by the contractor managing a large bilateral Australian curriculum reform project in PNG from 2000–2006 (Guthrie 2012b), which will be presented at length in Sections 3.5–3.7.

While commercialised evaluations are often unpublished, they can be influential in the contracting agencies. When such material is published, routine acknowledgement of funding sources does not obviate the underlying influences, so a cool eye is needed. As Cannon (2012) put it,

> where is the evidence for 'what works' in education interventions? The evidence commonly comes from the 'grey literature'; from education project reports and special studies commissioned by donors as part of a development activity. This literature has important advantages of recency and specificity. However, unlike peer reviewed, published research undertaken by universities and research organizations, many of these studies are done at very short notice, by teams of professionals unknown to one another and drawn from different countries, implemented within tight completion deadlines and subject to donor review before release. Such circumstances raise reasonable questions about the quality and independence of these studies.

2.4 Further technical inputs

A third group of evaluations – perhaps the most common – finds progressive reforms have not had the desired effect but perceives future success lying in further technical inputs.

Often, ideological commitment and lack of understanding of the depths of culturally derived constructs and the paradigms of which they are a part have led to teacher conservatism being blamed for failure to innovate, with the consequent supposition that their resistance can be overcome by funding more facilities, training and curricular resources. For example, Ginsburg (2010), in another contracted evaluation by American Institutes for Research, synthesised case studies of teacher in-service projects supported by the US Agency for International Development (USAID) in Cambodia, Egypt, Jordan, Kyrgyzstan and Malawi that focussed on active-learning pedagogies. None of the five pilot projects apparently used student learning as the dependent variable. Evaluations assessed teachers' classroom behaviour using indirect reportage primarily from focus groups, supplemented in some countries by interviews, finding that teachers could articulate active-learning policies. While interviews and focus groups are subject to validity issues in many cultures, especially with professional and group pressures for conformity to researchers' expectations (Section 3.3), changes in actual classroom behaviour were nonetheless inferred. However, in Egypt, the only study that added systematic classroom observation, any changes towards active learning were modest. Despite the limited findings in the five case studies, the conclusion went beyond the data to claim that real classroom change did occur, which conclusion justified further funding (71–72).

Tabulawa's (2013) extensive analysis found that emphasis on financial and technical inputs was typical of internationally influenced efforts at educational modernisation in Sub-Saharan Africa, which in essence had failed because technicist approaches considerably underestimated context. An example from Africa consistent with this finding was a questionnaire and observation study in Ethiopia, which found little application in the classroom of government policy promoting active learning in basic education and recommended a variety of further inputs such as teacher training, curricular materials and classroom resources (Serbessa 2006). In contrast, Rogers's (2003) approach to attributes of innovations provides understanding that deeply held, culturally based constructs can provide a rational basis for rejecting complex progressive innovations where they offer little comparative advantage over formalistic styles for teachers targeted for change in schools (Sections 7.2 and 11.2–11.3). The effect is to subvert the intentions of administrators and change agents who assume falsely that teachers will passively and similarly implement change directives or that money and resources will overcome any 'resistance'. However, almost invariably, the published research and evaluation studies that recommend such inputs do not discuss or estimate their financial costs, or where the funding might come from.

2.5 Interim formalism

A not uncommon fourth type of evaluation questions the effectiveness of progressive reforms on pragmatic grounds and looks to interim improvement in formalistic teaching methods.

40 *The progressive cage*

Essentially, this was a position held by Beeby (1966) in his classic book on educational 'stages', which were a considerable influence on curriculum reform in PNG (Chapter 6). It also strongly influenced several writers associated with the World Bank who focussed on educational reform in southern Africa (Section 5.1). All accepted variations on Beeby's progressive stages approach, but cautioned against pursuing it too rapidly. They predominantly argued that the higher progressive stages were too advanced for formalistic teachers and recommended a slower, pragmatic approach to teacher education and curriculum development. These were qualifications about the speed of attainment of the higher stages, rather than about the progressive destination, which remained axiomatic (Guthrie 2013). Although the stages model has long been debunked (Guthrie 1980, 1990, 2011), Beeby's book has remained an influence on the axiomatic equation of 'quality' with student-centred classrooms (Barrett *et al.* 2006; Section 1.3), and the 'stages' still occasionally surface as justification for progressive reform (e.g. Ginsburg 2010).

An allied but methodologically unsound variation on the temporal theme is that progressive reforms should be allowed more time to succeed. Renwick (1998) took this position in positing that a Popperian refutation of the universality of Beeby's 'stages' could be based on a demonstration that a stage could be skipped. However, this attempt at refutation addressed only the proposition that stages are sequential and could not test Beeby's teleological conjecture of an inevitable progressive end point. A skipped stage could disprove the proposition that the stages are sequential, but a failure to change from one stage to the next 'higher' one would merely be lack of time (i.e. an interim false negative), such that testing of the stages could slide irrefutably and pseudo-scientifically into the future (Guthrie 2011, 49–51).

2.6 Structural change

A small fifth group of analyses recognises that technical inputs or time are insufficient and makes more sophisticated recommendations for structural reforms to promote progressive change.

Sriprakash (2012), for example, drew on Bernstein's sociology of British pedagogy for her ethnographic case study of the introduction in South India of child-centred education in two projects. Her research was conducted in 16 rural primary school communities. In particular, in-depth interviews with 22 teachers who were key participants in the research found teachers' voices were largely absent from policymaking processes and often they were unconvinced child-centred approaches would help students learn syllabus content. Even so, the recommendation was that greater material and systemic focus was needed in the school arena to promote child-centred education by generating structural change, defined moderately as addressing teachers' professional status, investment in teacher education, and increased teacher participation in policymaking processes.

More radical structural change was part of the philosophy behind 'The Education Reform' in PNG, which had a long-term effect (Section 6.4). While notionally emphasising 'participation', essentially a major school reorganisation recommended by a key report in 1986 was based in the Marxist-influenced view that structural upheaval is necessary in society to remove tradition as an obstacle to modernisation. Avalos (1992a, 1992b), an active leader in the process, placed the reforms in the South American context of Ivan Illich and Paulo Freire and in the socialist tradition of Antonio Gramsci, Agnes Heller and Jürgen Habermas. The relevance of Latin American radicalism to an entirely different context on the far side of the Pacific was never established, nonetheless recommendations for a far-reaching series of structural changes to the school system were implemented by 2001, including widespread creation of elementary schooling and shifting grades between primary, lower secondary and upper secondary schools, with major implications for teacher training and curriculum. Follow-through with attempts at progressive curriculum change had dubious success (Guthrie 2014). The structural changes remain in place, but quite unclear in the upheaval to the school system were the merits of high levels of administrative reorganisation, professional dislocation and financial cost. The restructuring gave the appearance of educational change, but the intended curricular substance did not actually require restructuring the school system.

2.7 Rejection of universal progressivism

A sixth and uncommon type of publication rejects universal claims about progressivism, which means this is the only group for which progressivism is not axiomatic.

Universalistic claims may variously be found in a quest for elegant predictions about the educational future (as underlying much school effectiveness research), in psychological assumptions about human learning, and in generalisation of educational theories and practices from developed countries to developing ones (on which, see Sections 3.1 and 8.2). Such claims are based in the positivist scientific tradition, explicitly so in Beeby's (1980, 468–473) and Renwick's (1998) failed Popperian defences of the 'stages'. The single refutation necessary to demonstrate that universal applicability of the stages does not exist was provided by the continual failure of successive curriculum reforms in PNG (Guthrie 2011, 107–172; summarised in Section 6.4). Otherwise, Bowers (2005, 2013) located progressivism alongside global neo-liberal reforms and the impact on ecological crisis of their undermining of cultures; Dasen and Akkari (2008) focussed on the ethnocentrism of Western models of schooling; while Tabulawa (2013) focussed on underestimation of social and cultural contexts in Africa. Other writers, also outside the comparative education mainstream, have long rejected international influences on developing country educational systems if they are embedded in economic and political imperialism (Carnoy 1974; Tikly 2004; Nguyen et al. 2009), including in aid programmes that have unstated economic and political rationales as part of globalising a liberal democratic ethos (Tabulawa 2003; Section 1.3). An accompanying recognition is of formalism and progressivism as a dialectic based in antithetical worldviews (Tabulawa 2011; Guthrie 2015b). However, even writers who avoid politically radical language can comment that there is 'a donor monopoly over client interests' (Heyneman 2010, 518), comparative educationists 'need to be on guard against cultural imperialism' (Schweisfurth 2015a, 645) and 'there is a need to give voice to scholars from developing countries' in educational policy formation (Brown 2015, 1).

Elsewhere, the continually growing body of evidence about contextual appropriateness tends to come from an eclectic mix of grounded multidisciplinary classroom culture studies, cross-cultural psychology and anthropology. One of the best researched examples of successful formalistic teaching is the Confucian tradition, which provides a paradigm encompassing large elements of China, Hong Kong, Japan, Korea, Macau, Mongolia, Taiwan, Singapore and Vietnam – together having 23.6% of the world's population. A research foundation was laid by the psychologist John Biggs (1996), who identified the Paradox of the Chinese Learner, with mathematics, science and language scores in international achievement studies that were (and still are) nearly always higher than American students despite formalistic teaching methods. Progressive curriculum changes in China since 2001 appear to have upgraded formalism rather than leading to adoption of progressive teaching (Sections 4.7–4.8), reinforcing Biggs's (1996, 49) comment that

> We thus have some explaining to do, otherwise some well-supported propositions about the nature of teaching and learning are at risk. And what of the political implications (not to mention the face lost by researchers), if large classes, outdated teaching methods, poor equipment, inadequate public expenditure per student, and relentless low-level examining can produce students who see themselves as engaging in high-level processing, and who outperform Western students in many subject areas!

Critical theorists, such as Santos (2009), use the label ecologies of knowledge to consider the epistemology of ways of knowing embedded in different societies. From a different perspective, Lancy's (2014) anthropology demonstrated a wide range of assumptions about childhood and learning in different cultures worldwide. The effect, as Sternberg (2007, 17) concluded from cross-cultural psychology literature, is that when cultural context is taken into account, individuals are better recognised for and are better able to make use of their talents, schools teach and assess children better, and society uses rather than wastes the talents of its members:

> We need to teach to who the students are, not some idealisation of who we might want them to be. In that way, we make instruction culturally relevant rather than culturally blind, deaf, and dumb.

2.8 Global distribution of findings

Amid the research and evaluation categorised in the typology, researchers in at least 32 developing countries have found from individual projects and/or

Typology of progressive reform findings 43

literature reviews that progressive reforms failed in the sense that they were inappropriate and/or had major implementation difficulties. Wide variations occurred in interpretation of this ineffectiveness and in recommended actions. Most studies did not reject progressivism as such, but none implied that sustained paradigm shift occurred in classroom practice, including in:

- Azerbaijan (Chapman *et al.* 2005)
- Botswana (Tabulawa 1997, 2013)
- Cambodia (Ogisu 2014; Song 2015)
- China (Halstead and Zhu 2010; Guthrie 2012a)
- Egypt (Mansour 2010)
- Ethiopia (Serbessa 2006; Frost and Little 2014; Mitchell 2014)
- Ghana (Quist 2003; Zimmerman 2011; Akyeampong *et al.* 2013)
- India (Clarke 2003; Sriprakash 2012; Miglani, Subramanian, and Agnihotri 2017)
- Indonesia (Chang *et al.* 2014; Sopantini 2014)
- Jamaica (Jennings-Wray 1984; Jennings 2001)
- Kenya (Daley *et al.* 2005)
- Kyrgyzstan (Chapman *et al.* 2005; de la Sablonniere, Taylor, and Sadykova 2009)
- Lesotho (Dembele and Lefoka 2007)
- Libya (Orafi and Borg 2009)
- Malawi (Mtika and Gates 2010)
- Mexico (Brooke 1982)
- Morocco (Chafi, Elkhouzai, and Ouchouid 2016; Chafi and Elkhouzai 2017)
- Mozambique (Alderuccio 2016)
- Myanmar (Lall 2011; Clifford and Khaing Phyu Htut 2015)
- Namibia (O'Sullivan 2002, 2004; Arreman, Erixon, and Rehn 2016)
- Nigeria (Lockheed and Komenan 1989)
- Pakistan (Shamim 1996)
- Papua New Guinea (Guthrie 2014, 2015a)
- Peru (Balarin and Benavides 2010)
- Senegal (Miyazaki 2016)
- South Africa (Jansen and Taylor 2003; Nykiel-Herbert 2004; Hoadley 2017)
- Tanzania (Barrett 2007; Vavrus 2009; Mtahabwa and Rao 2010; Tarmo 2016)
- Timor-Leste (Shah and Quinn 2016)
- Turkey (Altinyelken 2011, 2013; Aksit, Niemi, and Nevgi 2016)
- Uganda (Altinyelken 2010a, 2010b)
- Vietnam (Saito and Tsukui 2008)
- Zambia (Mulopo and Fowler 1987).

Are these findings about the ineffectiveness of progressive reforms confined to only some types of developing country (e.g. the poorer ones, as is often

44 *The progressive cage*

assumed) or are they representative of all such countries? Much research in the school effectiveness field derives from international educational achievement surveys but, in the absence of useful work on teaching styles in this field, the available research is otherwise an accumulation of ad hoc case studies and surveys. The original choices about research sites were usually haphazard or purposive rather than random and the English-language comparative education journals publish predominantly on Africa and Asia. Accurate mapping of formalism's geographic distribution is not possible so far, and this book is as much bounded by that as any other in the field despite the extensive educational publications on which it is based.

Even so, the 32 countries with negative findings are statistically representative of the three main developing country lists used internationally. The three lists are the World Bank categorisation by per capita national income, the Organisation for Economic Co-operation and Development's (OECD) list of countries eligible to receive foreign aid (which is also primarily based on income levels), and the United Nations Development Programme's (UNDP) broader Human Development Index (HDI), which includes two indicators of length of schooling. Table 2.1 allocates the 32 countries to the categories in each list.

Table 2.1 Global distribution of negative findings about progressivism in developing countries

Developing Country Types	Total Countries	Negative Findings	Statistical Significance
World Bank Income			
Upper Middle	56	10	
Lower Middle	52	16	
Low	31	6	
Total	139	32	$X^2 = 2.19, df = 2, p = .34$
DAC ODA Recipients			
Upper Middle Income	58	10	
Lower Middle Income	36	10	
Least Developed & Other Low Income	52	12	
Total	146	32	$X^2 = 1.17, df = 2, p = .56$
UNDP Human Development Index			
Very High & High	56	8	
Medium	36	12	
Low	45	12	
Total	137	32	$X^2 = 3.72, df = 2, p = .16$
Geographic Distribution			
Africa	54	17	
Asia and Pacific	52	12	
Central and South America	30	3	
Total	136	32	$X^2 = 3.79, df = 2, p = .15$

Source: Author. Where indicated by ampersands, source categories were collapsed if the combinations were meaningful to ensure that expected frequencies were sufficiently large for the purpose of the chi square one-sample test.

A first test allocated the 32 according to the World Bank (2016) categorisation of 139 developing countries into Upper Middle, Lower Middle, and Low Income groups by gross national income per capita in 2015. As the table shows, a statistically significant difference was not found between the observed number of countries with negative findings and the expected number in each income group, i.e. the countries with negative findings were proportionately from the three national income groups.

The 32 countries were also grouped into three categories used in the OECD Development Assistance Committee (DAC 2014) list of 146 countries and territories for which foreign aid was eligible to be counted as Official Development Assistance from 2014–2016. The differences were not significant either.

The DAC list identified 137 developing countries for which data was available in the 2014 Human Development Index (UNDP 2015, which did not identify the countries covered by its use of the term 'developing countries'). The tendency among the 32 countries with ineffective progressive reforms was for under-representation in the Very High & High HDI group, however the overall differences were not statistically significant.

The 32 countries were also grouped broadly by geography into Asian (including Southwest, Central, North, South and Southeast Asia, and the Pacific), African (North and Sub-Saharan), and Central and South American (including the Caribbean), excluding High Income and European developing countries. The tendency was for South America to be under-represented, but the overall differences were not statistically significant either.

The outcome of this testing was that the list of 32 developing countries identified as having difficulties with progressive reforms was not biased significantly by national per capita income, eligibility for foreign aid, levels of human development, or geographic distribution. Although the list had non-random origins and the groupings used for statistical testing were necessarily coarse, the outcome appears to be the most systematic evidence to date on the distribution of findings about the failure of progressive reforms to achieve paradigm shift in developing country classrooms.

An area of research that provides potential for international generalisations about teaching styles and their cultural underpinnings is the country coverage of the ten GLOBE cultural clusters. Zhang, Khan, and Tahirsylag (2015), using 2009 Programme for International Student Assessment (PISA) data, found very high levels of variance in student achievement explained by the clusters, although the analysis was limited by the absence from the source GLOBE and PISA studies of data on most developing countries (Section 1.4). Strong quantitative support could exist for the cultural connections in education if further research increases the GLOBE survey coverage. As a work in progress, the value currently lies in providing an indication of the potential for quantitative analysis of global cultural clusters to inform interpretation of educational patterns. In the meantime, other cultural patterns are consistent with such data. Of the 32 studies above, 21 occurred in countries with revelatory religious traditions encompassing at least 80% of the population: Buddhism in Cambodia and

Myanmar; Christianity in Botswana, Kenya, Lesotho, Malawi, Mexico, Namibia, PNG, Peru, Timor-Leste and Zambia; Hinduism in India; and Islam in Azerbaijan, Egypt, Indonesia, Libya, Morocco, Pakistan, Senegal and Turkey (CIA 2017). Also, the area studies in Chapters 4–6 illustrate three of the six clusters that contain developing countries (i.e. the African, Confucian and Southeast Asian Clusters). These studies demonstrate the lack of progressive success in fundamentally changing teaching styles in countries encompassing some 30% of the world's population.

2.9 Progressivism as an axiom

Despite the now demonstrable global distribution of findings about the difficulties and failures with attempted progressive reforms, progressive theory usually does not appear to have aligned with classroom reality. The middle four categories in the typology of research findings particularly sustain the progressive paradigm with identification of input deficiencies and structural issues. Yet, the studies in them typically have two major limitations. The first, to be explored in the next chapter, is widespread methodological problems in research purporting to find sufficient evidence of progressive success to recommend continuing attempts at reform. The second issue is the axiomatic acceptance of progressive theory despite the lack of methodologically sound evidence of success, such that faith in progressivism is rarely subjected to fundamental questioning. Beeby himself was quite explicit about this in writing, 'The ultimate aims in education are not given by reason but by a feeling in the pit of one's stomach. Sooner or later in life, one must say, for no very obvious reason, "I believe in X," and never challenge it again' (quoted by Alcorn 1999, 371). The problem, as Tan (2016, 90) put it, is that paradigms can be part of a 'taken-for-granted world-picture', and,

> far from being objective and universal . . . [they] are the cultural products of socialization, enculturation and scholarship . . . laden with the researchers' beliefs, values, assumptions and expectations, which in turn shape their observations, perceptions and interpretation of data.

The irony is that in representing an educational philosophy founded in scientific epistemology that questions the type of revelatory epistemology in which the formalist paradigm is embedded, proponents do not usually question progressivism itself. Progressivism is both an assumed theoretical starting point and a desirable but unquestioned professional end point in much of the academic literature. When proponents promote their views in developing countries, they can echo imperialism in becoming secular missionaries.

Unquestioned axioms open up a key epistemological issue, which is the fatal logical flaw of teleology. *Teleology* is a long-standing if difficult philosophical concept that attacks circular logic, particularly usage of ultimate causes to rationalise prior actions. 'By a teleological approach is meant one in which a purpose, which is not explicitly intended by anyone, is fulfilled while the process of fulfilment is presented as an inevitable sequence of events' (Myrdal 1968, 1851). Teleology is inherent in much of the literature simply because progressivism is the criterion of advancement – the ultimate cause – but usually it is assumed and not subject to explicit analysis or independent assessment in particular cultures. This is the issue at the heart of the Progressive Education Fallacy, with its identification of the confusion between enquiry learning as a process and the enquiring mind as a product. Thus, axiomatic assumptions abound about the merits of progressive reforms and their continuation, and are maintained despite the evidence that they do not generate substantive change in teaching styles.

The assumptions are often found in the opening paragraphs of publications and reverted to in the closing paragraphs despite contrary evidence in between. A case in point is the American Institutes for Research synthesis of case studies of USAID teacher in-service projects in Cambodia, Egypt, Jordan, Kyrgyzstan and Malawi that focussed on 'active-learning pedagogies' (Ginsburg 2010). These projects were found squarely within the Progressive Education Fallacy, focussing on reforms advanced within international organisations during the previous 25 years and influenced by Beeby's 'stages'. An introductory statement (Ginsburg 2010, 64) appeared to provide balance in stating,

> there is some, albeit contradictory research evidence on the impact of active-learning versus rote memory-oriented pedagogies. . . . Nevertheless, it seems that many of the arguments for active-learning, student-centered pedagogy are grounded more in philosophy and educational theory than they are warranted by empirical evidence.

Despite this, as noted earlier in this chapter, a key conclusion went way beyond the evaluation evidence to claim that classroom change did occur: 'While it would be an overstatement to say that teachers involved in projects radically transformed their instructional practices, it seems appropriate to conclude that real changes occurred as a result of sustained training and supervisory support' (72). The inference is that the consultants did not consider empirical evidence was important enough to challenge USAID's philosophical attachment to active learning, which interpretation is consistent with Tabulawa's (2003) critique of aid programmes with economic and political rationales as part of globalising a liberal democratic ethos.

Even authors who are understanding of cultural context – and this is becoming more common – often retain a progressive baseline for reform. Schweisfurth's (2011) review found that the literature is riddled with stories of 'failures grand and small' (425) and 'there is not a great deal of proof that LCE [learner-centred education] can achieve the grand aims that its proponents claim' (430). Nonetheless, she stated that the evidence only occasionally made her query the foundations of LCE; rather it raised questions about where and how it is best implemented (426), and she dismissed pejoratively as 'recidivism' teachers' reversion to formalism despite progressive training (428). Later, she argued for an emancipatory role for progressivism on the grounds that human rights arguments rise above research evidence, so that the effort to implement LCE 'must go on' (Schweisfurth 2013, 5), especially as an enabling goal on which other goals and targets depend (Schweisfurth 2015b).

Barrett (2007), in a well-recognised study in Tanzania, noted the equation of formalism with poor quality, authoritarian, inequitable and teacher-dominated classrooms and, while acknowledging the difficulties in changing from formalism, argued for pedagogical flexibility in the classroom: 'It is possible to recognise and build on learners' prior knowledge; to recognise and cater for different learning styles; to value individuals' contributions and celebrate individuals' achievements within whole-class "teacher-centred" practice' (290). The essence of her case was that formalism and progressivism should not be polarised, but they could be combined in the classroom in a flexible middle ground. As Tabulawa (2013, 49) has pointed out, this does not grapple with the deeper epistemological issues:

> It is difficult to see how the polarized view can disappear before the epistemological differences are resolved ... such resolution is nowhere in sight, meaning that the pedagogical paradigms are enduring and that perhaps there is something about the differences that demands closer attention ... [unless and until then] it will not be possible to utilize the 'substance' of learner-centred pedagogy. Only its 'form' (use of techniques) would be possible. Unfortunately, it is the evidence of the teachers' utilization of the 'form' of the pedagogy that Barrett (2007) and others have mistaken for (and conflated with) its 'substance'.

A Tanzanian ethnography by Vavrus (2009) foregrounded cultural issues confronting the progressive paradigm in formalistic contexts, and argued sensibly that social, cultural and economic contexts of teachers' practice needed to be considered in efforts to reform education systems. What is required, she suggested, is 'contingent constructivism' that weaves together methods of engaging students in learning adapted to local cultural and material contexts. Vavrus and Bartlett (2012) analysed this approach further in examining how epistemological differences regarding knowledge production and material differences in teaching conditions influence understandings of learner-centred pedagogy. A principal issue involved scepticism about progressivism 'as conceptualized in specific contexts in the global North serving as a global gold standard by which teachers and teacher educators worldwide should be evaluated' (654). Nonetheless, it was adapting progressivism to local conditions that was a given in the term 'contingent constructivism', not situating formalism, which the authors previously made explicit in a set of policy guidelines for encouraging learner-centred techniques in Sub-Saharan Africa (Vavrus, Thomas, and Bartlett 2011, 85–94).

Other examples of progressivism as an axiom include Sriprakash's (2012) study of the introduction in South India of child-centred education, which found that teachers' voices were largely absent from policymaking processes and they were unpersuaded that child-centred approaches would help students learn syllabus content. Even so, the conclusion that structural change was needed to promote child-centred education contradicted a call for greater consultation with teachers. Overriding their views was an axiomatic acceptance of 'the enduring promise in development discourses that child-centred pedagogies can achieve "quality" education for the poor' (188). Similarly, Mtika and Gates (2010) found constraints in Malawi on the application of practices from learner-centred teacher education, which were either not appropriated fully by the trainee teachers or, when they were appropriated, were resisted or completely negated by the school system and the national curricular orientation. The progressive notions promoted in teacher education resulted in only minor attempts at change in classroom practice. Nonetheless, the apparent solution retained progressivism as axiomatic: 'Teacher educators and policy makers need to ... examine relevant ways and possibly adaptations that can be reasonably made to ensure that secondary teaching appropriately benefits from the strength of learner-centred pedagogy' (396). Other material with similar issues includes Akyeampong et al. (2013) on teacher education in Ghana, Kenya, Mali, Senegal, Tanzania and Uganda; Harber (2017, 138–141), who quoted the research by Altinyelkin, Barrett and Vavrus as demonstrating hybridisation of teaching styles and a step forward in Sub-Saharan Africa; and Westbrook et al. (2013) in a geographically wide review of pedagogy, curriculum and teacher education (Section 3.4). In effect, where such studies consider culture it is usually as an organisational barrier to change, an intervening variable rather than an intergenerational background variable that is a precondition for teaching styles.

It can be noted also that in recent years some awareness of the nature of formalism is being demonstrated in the literature (e.g. Nag et al. 2014; Lattimer 2015; Tan 2015). However, it is too early to say whether this represents a groundswell in theoretical reorientation. As Tan (2015, 306) put it,

> various authors have highlighted the problem of learner-centredness as a floating signifier, and draw our attention to variations in learner-centred philosophies and practices that reflect a wider cultural base. . . . But such writings, although important, are relatively small in number compared to the extant published works that promote a Western-centric version of learner-centred education. The fact remains that the dominant conception of learner-centred education is one that is primarily traced to European philosophies, focuses on active learning, learner choice, and a shift of power from the teacher to the learner . . . and is propagated by the spread of innovations especially in the U.S. and U.K.

Challenges to the affective, child-centred value position embedded in the progressive paradigm can be sensitive, as illustrated by a range of reactions to my use of a metaphor about child soldiers in a forum in the journal *Compare* (Guthrie 2015b). The metaphor was of classroom students in developing countries positioned by progressive reforms as child soldiers in the battle zones of the international culture wars. Like teaching, local occurrences of child warfare are embedded in place, in systematic and complex processes of recruitment and induction within particular social structures and cultures (Honwana 2006). In such contexts, the roles of children can range from active combatants, to auxiliaries, to passive players. However, child soldiering does not occur as isolated aberrations, but interweaves with complex economic, political, religious and ideological conflicts in hard power warfare (Wessells 2006; Drumbl 2012). The educational analogy is with the role of pupils in developing country classrooms who are cast in the frontline of the soft power culture wars implicit in progressive educational reforms that project a worldview that often runs counter to local educational cultures. Unsurprisingly, the metaphor generated varied responses in the forum. Sarangapani (2015) saw fit to ignore it; Tabulawa (2015) commented that the metaphor underestimated the role of children as active agents; Hugo and Wedekind (2015) alleged (wrongly) that I must hate progressivism to use such language; while Schweisfurth (2015a) indignantly found the language inflammatory, creating new frictions, and diminishing of real child soldiers. All I can add is that recognising the culture war is not trying to start a war, but is trying to stop one.

2.10 Conclusion

Little if any evidence supports sustained progressive success in generating paradigm shift in developing country classrooms. On the contrary, findings about the lack of sustained success of progressive reforms have a global spread. The cumulative evidence is not biased significantly by national per capita income in developing countries, their eligibility levels for foreign aid, levels of human development or geographic distribution. Despite such evidence, the middle four categories of research and evaluation outlined in the typology particularly treat the progressive paradigm as axiomatic and, despite the implementation problems, sustain it with recommendations for further inputs and promotion of the progressive destination.

Thus, progressive theory usually has not aligned with classroom reality. Progressive resistance to construct change manifests in many ways. One is retention of an axiomatic faith in progressivism as a universal panacea even though its culturally biased and problematic assumptions about teaching styles in other cultures often are not contested. Even research that is understanding of cultural context – and this is becoming more common – often retains a progressive baseline for reform. Another manifestation is theoretically superficial and ahistorical studies with weak findings, notably in vested commercialised evaluations subject to financial conflicts of interest. Where implementation difficulties are found, the commonplace response has been to recommend more resource inputs or time.

The poor quality of the research and evaluation is not merely a consequence of methodological and technical issues, but (as Sections 7.3–7.5 will explore) cognitive dissonance in consideration of the evidence is also demonstrated when anomalies incorrectly are ignored, downplayed or mistreated as acceptable error. In effect, random false positives are treated as indications of future possibilities and dissonant elements are ignored as false negatives, so that negative feedback ('the reform is less than successful') is mistreated as positive ('now we know what further inputs are required to generate success'). Research that ignores the history of progressive failure, an absence of evaluation findings showing sustained progressive adoption, ritual recommendations for yet more technical inputs or, more radically, calls for structural change collectively embody the misinterpretation of difficulties in progressive implementation as new challenges and a state of denial about the evidence of chronic failure to generate paradigm shift in the classroom. The children allegedly at the heart of progressivism are not so much in need of rescue from the forces of formalism; rather, attempts to impose progressive thought through educational reform position them in the battle zones of the international culture wars.

Note

1 Sections 2.2–2.7 derive from an article published in *Compare* (Guthrie 2017), available online: www.tandfonline.com/doi/full/10.1080/03057925.2016.1138396.

References

Aksit, F., Niemi, H., and Nevgi, A. 2016. "Why Is Active Learning So Difficult to Implement: The Turkish Case?" *Australian Journal of Teacher Education* 41 (4): 94–109.

Akyeampong, K., Lussier, K., Pryor, J., and Westbrook, J. 2013. "Improving Teaching and Learning of Basic Maths and Reading in Africa: Does Teacher Preparation Count?" *International Journal of Educational Development* 33: 272–282.

Alcorn, N. 1999. *'To the Fullest Extent of His Powers': C. E. Beeby's Life in Education.* Wellington: Victoria University Press.

Alderuccio, M. 2016. *Curriculum Innovations and the 'Politics of Legitimacy' in Teachers' Discourse and Practice in a Mozambican Primary School.* Unpublished Doctor of Education thesis, University of Sussex.

Altinyelken, H. 2010a. "Curriculum Change in Uganda: Teacher Perspectives on the New Thematic Curriculum." *International Journal of Educational Development* 30 (2): 145–150.

Altinyelken, H. 2010b. "Pedagogical Renewal in Sub-Saharan Africa: The Case of Uganda. *Comparative Education* 46 (2): 151–171.

Altinyelken, H. 2011. "Student-Centred Pedagogy in Turkey: Conceptualisations, Interpretations and Practices." *Journal of Education Policy* 26 (2): 137–160.

Altinyelken, H. 2013. "Teachers' Principled Resistance to Curriculum Change: A Compelling Case from Turkey." In *Global Managerial Education Reforms and Teachers: Emerging Policies, Controversies and Issues in Developing Contexts*, edited by A. Verger, H. Altinyelken, and M. de Koning, 109–126. Brussels: Education International.

Arreman, I., Erixon, P-O., and Rehn, K-G. 2016. "Postcolonial Teacher Education Reform in Namibia: Travelling of Policies and Ideas." *European Educational Research Journal* 15 (2): 236–259.

Avalos, B. 1992a. "Education for the Poor: Quality or Relevance?" *British Journal of Sociology of Education* 13 (4): 419–436.

Avalos, B. 1992b. "The Need for Educational Reform and the Role of Teacher Training: The Case of Papua New Guinea." *International Journal of Educational Development* 12 (4): 309–318.

Balarin, M., and Benavides, M. 2010. "Curriculum Reform and the Displacement of Knowledge in Peruvian Rural Secondary Schools: Exploring the Unintended Local Consequences of Global Education Policies." *Compare* 40 (3): 311–325.

Barrett, A. 2007. "Beyond the Polarization of Pedagogy: Models of Classroom Practice in Tanzanian Primary Schools." *Comparative Education* 43 (2): 273–294.

Barrett, A., Chawla-Duggan, R., Lowe, J., Nikel, J., and Ukpo, E. 2006. *The Concept of Quality in Education: Review of the 'International' Literature on the Concept of Quality in Education*. EdQual Working Paper No.2. Bristol: University of Bristol.

Beeby, C.E. 1966. *The Quality of Education in Developing Countries*. Cambridge: Harvard University Press.

Beeby, C.E. 1980. "The Thesis of Stages Fourteen Years Later." *International Review of Education* 26 (4): 451–474.

Biggs, J. 1996. "Western Misperceptions of the Confucian-Heritage Learning Culture." In *The Chinese Learner: Cultural, Psychological and Contextual Influences*, edited by D. Watkins and J. Biggs, 45–67. Hong Kong: Comparative Education Research Centre, University of Hong Kong.

Bowers, C. 2005. *The False Promises of Constructivist Theories of Learning: A Global and Ecological Critique*. New York: Peter Lang.

Bowers, C. 2013. *In the Grip of the Past: Educational Reforms That Should Address What Needs to Be Changed and What Needs to Be Conserved*. Eugene: Eco-Justice Press.

Brooke, N. 1982. "Relevance in Pedagogy and the Problem of Educational Quality in Latin America." *International Journal of Educational Development* 2 (1): 73–79.

Brown, C. (Ed.). 2015. *Globalization, International Educational Policy and Local Policy Formation: Voices from the Developing World*. New York: Springer.

Cannon, R. 2012. *The Progressive Education Fallacy in Developing Countries, by Gerard Guthrie: A Review*. Development Policy Blog, Canberra: Australian National University: http://devpolicy.org/the-progressive-education-fallacy-in-developing-countries-by-gerard-guthrie-a-review-20120924/. Accessed 8 August 2017.

Carnoy, M. 1974. *Education as Cultural Imperialism*. New York: John Wiley.

Chafi, M., and Elkhouzai, E. 2017. "Reculturing Pedagogical Practice: Probing Teachers' Cultural Models of Pedagogy." *International Journal of Education and Literacy Studies* 5 (1): 78–85.

Chafi, M., Elkhouzai, E., and Ouchouid, J. 2016. "Teacher Excessive Pedagogical Authority in Moroccan Primary Classroom." *American Journal of Educational Research* 4 (1): 134–146.

Chang, M., Shaeffer, S., Al-Samarrai, S., Ragatz, A., de Ree, J., and Stevenson, R. 2014. *Teacher Reform in Indonesia The Role of Politics and Evidence in Policy Making*. Washington, DC: World Bank.

Chapman, D., Weidman, W., Cohen, J., and Mercer, M. 2005. "The Search for Quality: A Five Country Study of National Strategies to Improve Educational Quality in Central Asia." *International Journal of Educational Development* 25 (5): 514–530.

CIA. 2017. *The World Factbook*. Washington, DC: CIA. www.cia.gov/library/publications/the-world-factbook/geos/us.html

Clarke, P. 2003. "Culture and Classroom Reform: The Case of the District Primary Education Project, India." *Comparative Education* 39 (1): 27–44.

Clifford, I., and Htut, K.P. 2015. *A Transformative Pedagogy for Myanmar? Paper presented to Learning for Sustainable Futures Conference*. Oxford: University of Oxford, 15–17 September. https://englishagenda.britishcouncil.org/sites/ec/files/efect_academic_paper.pdf

Crossley, M. 1984a. "Relevance Education, Strategies for Curriculum Change and Pilot Projects: A Cautionary Note." *International Journal of Educational Development* 4 (3): 245–250.

Crossley, M. 1984b. "Strategies for Curriculum Change and the Question of International Transfer." *Journal of Curriculum Studies* 16 (1): 75–88.

DAC (Development Assistance Committee). 2014. *DAC List of ODA Recipients Effective for Reporting on 2014, 2015 and 2016 Flows*. Paris: OECD. www.oecd.org/dac/stats/documentupload/DAC%20List%20of%20ODA%20Recipients%202014%20final.pdf

Daley, T., Whaley, S., Sigman, M., Guthrie, D., Neumann, C., and Bwibo, N. 2005. "Background and Classroom Correlates of Child Achievement, Cognitive, and Behavioural Outcomes in Rural Kenyan Schoolchildren." *International Journal of Behavioral Development* 29 (5): 399–408.

Dasen, P., and Akkari, A. (Eds.). 2008. *Educational Theories and Practices from the Majority World*. New Delhi: Sage.

de la Sablonniere, R., Taylor, D., and Sadykova, N. 2009. "Challenges of Applying a Student-centered Approach to Learning in the Context of Education in Kyrgyzstan." *International Journal of Educational Development* 29 (6): 628–634.

Dembele, M., and Lefoka, P. 2007. "Pedagogical Renewal for Quality Universal Primary Education: Overview of Trends in Sub-Saharan Africa." *International Review of Education* 53 (5–6): 531–553.

Drumbl, M. 2012. *Reimagining Child Soldiers in International Law and Policy*. Oxford: Oxford University Press.

Frost, M., and Little, A. 2014. "Children's Learning Practices in Ethiopia: Observations from Primary School Classes." *Oxford Review of Education* 40 (1): 91–111.

Ginsburg, M. 2010. "Improving Educational Quality through Active-Learning Pedagogies: A Comparison of Five Case Studies." *Educational Research* 1 (3): 62–74.

Glewwe, P., Hanushek, E., Humpage, S., and Ravin, R. 2011. *School Resources and Educational Outcomes in Developing Countries: A Review of the Literature from 1990 to 2010*. Working Paper 17554. Cambridge: National Bureau of Economic Research.

Guthrie, G. 1980. "Stages of Educational Development? Beeby Revisited." *International Review of Education* 26 (4): 411–438.

Guthrie, G. 1982. "Reviews of Teacher Training and Teacher Performance in Developing Countries: Beeby Revisited (2)." *International Review of Education* 28 (3): 291–306.

Guthrie, G. 1986. "Current Research in Developing Countries: The Impact of Curriculum Reform on Teaching." *Teaching and Teacher Education* 2 (1): 81–89.

Guthrie, G. 1990. "To the Defense of Traditional Teaching in Lesser Developed Countries." In *Teachers and Teaching in the Developing World*, edited by V. Rust and P. Dalin, 219–232. New York: Garland.

Guthrie, G. 2011. *The Progressive Education Fallacy in Developing Countries: In Favour of Formalism*. New York: Springer.

Guthrie, G. 2012a. "Progressive School Teaching in China?" *International Journal of Comparative Education and Development* 14: 98–111.

Guthrie, G. 2012b. "The Failure of Progressive Classroom Reform: Lessons from the Curriculum Reform Implementation Project in Papua New Guinea." *Australian Journal of Education* 56 (3): 241–256.

Guthrie, G. 2013. "Prevalence of the Formalistic Paradigm in African Schools." *Southern African Review of Education* 19 (1): 121–138.

Guthrie, G. 2014. "The Failure of Progressive Paradigm Shift in Papua New Guinea." *Papua New Guinea Journal of Education* 41 (1): 1–28.

Guthrie, G. 2015a. "The Formalistic Educational Paradigm in Papua New Guinea." *Contemporary PNG Studies* 22: 33–47.

Guthrie, G. 2015b. "Child Soldiers in the Culture Wars." *Compare* 45 (4): 635–642.

Guthrie, G. 2017. "The Failure of Progressive Paradigm Reversal." *Compare* 47 (1): 62–76.

Halstead, J., and Zhu, C. 2010. "Autonomy as an Element in Chinese Educational Reform: English Lessons in a Senior High School in Beijing." *Asia-Pacific Journal of Education* 29 (4): 443–446.

Harber, C. 2017. *Schooling in Sub-Saharan Africa: Policy, Practice and Patterns*. London: Palgrave Macmillan.

Heyneman, S. 2010. "Education and Development: A Return to Basic Principles." *Development* 53 (4): 518–521.

Hoadley, U. 2017. *Pedagogy in Poverty: Lessons from Twenty Years of Curriculum Reform in South Africa*. London: Routledge.

Honwana, A. 2006. *Child Soldiers in Africa*. Philadelphia: University of Pennsylvania Press.

Hugo, W., and Wedekind, V. 2015. "Climbing Out of the Trenches: A Response to Guthrie." *Compare* 45 (4): 650–654.

Jansen, J., and Taylor, N. 2003. "Educational Change in South Africa 1994–2003: Case Studies in Large-scale Education Reform." *Country Studies in Education Reform and Management* 2 (1). Washington, DC: World Bank.

Jennings, Z. 2001. "Teacher Education in Selected Countries in the Commonwealth Caribbean: The Ideal of Policy Versus the Reality of Practice." *Comparative Education* 37 (1): 107–134.

Jennings-Wray, Z. 1984. "Implementing the 'Integrated Approach to Learning': Implications for Integration in the Curricula of Primary Schools in the Caribbean." *International Journal of Educational Development* 4: 265–278.

Jordan, L., Bovill, C., Othman, S., Saleh, A., Shabila, N., and Watters, N. 2014. "Is Student-Centred Learning a Western Concept? Lessons from an Academic Development Programme to Support Student-Centred Learning in Iraq." *Teaching in Higher Education* 19 (1): 13–25.

Lall, M. 2011. "Pushing the Child Centred Approach in Myanmar: The Role of Cross National Policy Networks and the Effects in the Classroom." *Critical Studies in Education* 52 (3): 219–233.

Lancy, D. 2014. *The Anthropology of Childhood: Cherubs, Chattel, Changelings*. Cambridge: Cambridge University Press.

Lattimer, H. 2015. "Translating Theory into Practice: Making Meaning of Learner Centered Education Frameworks for Classroom-based Practitioners." *International Journal of Educational Development* 45 (1): 65–76.

Lockheed, M., and Komenan, A. 1989. "Teaching Quality and Student Achievement in Africa: The Case of Nigeria and Swaziland." *Teaching and Teacher Education* 5 (2): 93–113.

Mansour, N. 2010. "The Impact of the Knowledge and Beliefs of Egyptian Science Teachers in Integrating an STS Based Curriculum." *Journal of Science Teacher Education* 21 (5): 513–534.

Miglani, N., Subramanian, J., and Agnihotri, V. 2017. "Unpacking Participation: The Case of Child-Centered Pedagogy in India." In *Participatory Action Research and Educational Development: South Asian Perspectives*, edited by H. Kidwai, R. Iyengar, M.A. Witenstein, E.J. Byker, and R. Setty, 129–159. New York: Springer.

Mitchell, R. 2017. "Democracy or Control? The Participation of Management, Teachers, Students and Parents in School Leadership in Tigray, Ethiopia." *International Journal of Educational Development* 55: 49–55.

Miyazaki, T. 2016. "Is Changing Teaching Practice the Mission Impossible? A Case Study of Continuing Professional Development for Primary School Teachers in Senegal." *Compare* 46 (5): 701–722.

Mtahabwa, L., and Rao, N. 2010. "Pre-Primary Education in Tanzania: Observations from Urban and Rural Classrooms." *International Journal of Educational Development* 30 (3): 227–235.

Mtika, P., and Gates, P. 2010. "Developing Learner-Centred Education among Secondary Trainee Teachers in Malawi: The Dilemmas of Appropriation and Application." *International Journal of Educational Development* 30 (4): 396–404.

Mulopo, M., and Fowler, H. 1987. "Effects of Traditional and Discovery Instructional Approaches on Learning Outcomes for Learners of Different Intellectual Developments: A Study of Chemistry Students in Zambia." *Journal of Research in Science Teaching* 24 (3): 217–227.

Myrdal, G. 1968. *Asian Drama: An Enquiry into the Poverty of Nations* (3 Vols). New York: Twentieth Century Fund.

Nag, S., Chiat, S., Torgerson, C., and Snowling, M. 2014. *Literacy, Foundation Learning and Assessment in Developing Countries: Final Report*. Education Rigorous Literature Review. London: Department for International Development.

Nguyen, P-M., Elliott, J., Terlouw, C., and Pilot, A. 2009. "Neocolonialism in Education: Cooperative Learning in an Asian Context." *Comparative Education* 45 (1): 109–130.

Nykiel-Herbert, B. 2004. "Mis-Constructing Knowledge: The Case of Learner-Centred Pedagogy in South Africa." *Prospects* 34 (3): 249–265.

Ogisu, T. 2014. *How Cambodian Pedagogical Reform Has Been Constructed: A Multi-level Case Study*. Unpublished PhD dissertation, Michigan State University.

Orafi, S., and Borg, S. 2009. "Intentions and Realities in Implementing Communicative Curriculum Reform." *System* 37 (2): 243–253.

O'Sullivan, M. 2002. "Reform Implementation and the Realities within which Teachers Work: A Namibian Case Study." *Compare* 32 (2): 219–237.

O'Sullivan, M. 2004. "The Reconceptualisation of Learner-Centred Approaches: A Namibia Case Study." *International Journal of Educational Development* 24 (6): 585–602.

Phillips, D. 2009. "Aspects of Educational Transfer." In *International Handbook of Comparative Education*, edited by R. Cowen and A. Kazamias, 1061–1078. Dordrecht: Springer.

Quist, H. 2003. "Transferred and Adapted Models of Secondary Education in Ghana: What Implications for National Development?" *International Review of Education* 49 (5): 411–431.

Renwick, W. 1998. "Clarence Edward Beeby (1902-98)." *Prospects* 28 (2): 335–348.

Rogers, E. 2003. *Diffusion of Innovation* (5th ed.). New York: Free Press.

Saito, E., and Tsukui, A. 2008. "Challenging Common Sense: Cases of School Reform for Learning Community under an International Cooperation Project in Bac Giang Province, Vietnam." *International Journal of Educational Development* 28 (5): 571–584.

Santos, B. 2009. "A Non-Occidentalist West? Learned Ignorance and an Ecology of Knowledge." *Theory, Culture and Society* 26 (6): 103–125.

Sarangapani, P. 2015. "Viewing CCE Through an 'Indigenous' Lens." *Compare* 45 (4): 647–650.

Schweisfurth, M. 2011. "Learner-Centred Education in Developing Country Contexts: From Solution to Problem?" *International Journal of Educational Development* 31 (5): 425–432.

Schweisfurth, M. 2013. "Learner-Centred Education in International Perspective." *Journal of International and Comparative Education* 2 (1): 1–8.

Schweisfurth, M. 2015a. "Make Learning, Not War." *Compare* 45 (4): 644–647.

Schweisfurth, M. 2015b. "Learner-Centred Pedagogy: Towards a Post-2015 Agenda for Teaching and Learning." *International Journal of Educational Development* 40: 259–266.

Serbessa, D. 2006. "Tension Between Traditional and Modern Teaching-Learning Approaches in Ethiopian Primary Schools." *Journal of International Cooperation in Education* 9 (1): 123–140.

Shah, R., and Quinn, M. 2016. "Mind the Gap: Global Quality Norms, National Policy Interpretations and Local Praxis in Timor-Leste." *Compare* 46 (3): 394–413.

Shamim, F. 1996. "Learner Resistance to Innovation in Classroom Methodology." In *Society and the Language Classroom*, edited by H. Coleman, 105–121. Cambridge: Cambridge University Press.

Song, S. 2015. "Cambodian Teachers' Responses to Child-Centred Instructional Policies: A Mismatch between Beliefs and Practices." *Teaching and Teacher Education* 50: 24–35.

Sopantini. 2014. *Reforming Teaching Practice in Indonesia: A Case Study of the Implementation of Active Learning in Primary Schools in North Maluku*. Unpublished Doctor of Education thesis, University of Tasmania.

Sriprakash, A. 2012. *Pedagogies for Development: The Politics and Practice of Child-Centred Education in India*. New York: Springer.

Sternberg, R. 2007. "Culture, Instruction, and Assessment." *Comparative Education* 43 (1): 5–22.

Tabulawa, R. 1997. "Pedagogical Classroom Practice and the Social Context: The Case of Botswana." *International Journal of Educational Development* 17 (2): 189–194.

Tabulawa, R. 2003. "International Aid Agencies, Learner-Centred Pedagogy and Political Democratisation: A Critique." *Comparative Education* 39 (1): 7–26.

Tabulawa, R. 2011. "The Rise and Attenuation of the Basic Education Programme (BEP) in Botswana: A Global-Local Dialectic Approach." *International Journal of Educational Development* 31 (5): 443–442.

Tabulawa, R. 2013. *Teaching and Learning in Context: Why Pedagogical Reforms Fail in Sub-Saharan Africa*. Dakar: Codesria.

Tabulawa, R. 2015. "Response to Guthrie's 'Child Soldiers in the Culture Wars'." *Compare* 45 (4): 642–644.

Tan, C. 2015. "Teacher-Directed and Learner-Engaged: Exploring a Confucian Conception of Education." *Ethics and Education* 10 (3): 302–312.

Tan, C. 2016. "Investigator Bias and Theory-Ladenness in Cross-Cultural Research: Insights from Wittgenstein." *Current Issues in Comparative Education* 18 (1): 84–95.

Tarmo, A. 2016. "Pre-service Science Teachers' Epistemological Beliefs and Teaching Reforms in Tanzania." *Cogent Education* 3 (1). https://doi.org/10.1080/2331186X.2016.1178457

Tikly, L. 2004. "Education and the New Imperialism." *Comparative Education* 40 (2): 173–198.

UNCF. 2009. *Child Friendly Schools Programming: Global Evaluation Report*. New York: UNCF Evaluation Office.

UNDP. 2015. *Human Development Report 2015: Work for Human Development*. New York: UNDP.

Vavrus, F. 2009. "The Cultural Politics of Constructivist Pedagogies: Teacher Education Reform in the United Republic of Tanzania." *International Journal of Educational Development* 29 (3): 303–311.

Vavrus, F., and Bartlett, L. 2012. "Comparative Pedagogies and Epistemological Diversity: Social and Materials Contexts of Teaching in Tanzania." *Comparative Education Review* 56 (4): 634–658.

Vavrus, F., Thomas, M., and Bartlett, L. 2011. *Ensuring Quality by Attending to Inquiry: Learner-centered Pedagogy in Sub-Saharan Africa*. Addis Ababa: UNESCO.

Wessells, M. 2006. *Child Soldiers: From Violence to Protection*. Cambridge: Harvard University Press.

Westbrook, J., Durrani, N., Brown, R., Orr, D., Pryor, J., Boddy, J., and Salvi, F. 2013. *Pedagogy, Curriculum, Teaching Practices and Teacher Education in Developing Countries, Education Rigorous Literature Review*. London: Department for International Development.

World Bank. 2016. *World Development Indicators Database*, 16 December 2016. Washington, DC: World Bank. http://data.worldbank.org/data-catalog/world-development-indicators

Yu, G. 2007. *Research Evidence of School Effectiveness in Sub-Saharan Africa*. EdQual Working Paper No.12. Bristol: University of Bristol.

Zhang, L., Khan, G., and Tahirsylag, A. 2015. "Student Performance, School Differentiation, and World Cultures: Evidence from PISA 2009." *International Journal of Educational Development* 42: 43–53.

Zimmerman, J. 2011. "'Money, Materials, and Manpower': Ghanaian In-Service Teacher Education and the Political Economy of Failure, 1961–1971." *History of Education Quarterly* 51 (1): 1–27.

3 Theoretical and methodological limitations

The literature on education in 'developing' countries has a wide range of theoretical influences. The two main fields are classroom improvement research, which is framed by educational theory, and school effectiveness research, which is framed by economic theory. A comprehensive review of educational effectiveness by Reynolds *et al.* (2014) demonstrated a lack of theoretical or methodological integration between the fields, with little reference to the classroom improvement field or developing country findings. Nonetheless, researchers refer to findings from both fields, and Auld and Morris (2014, 132), coming from the classroom improvement field, considered they are distinctive, albeit related, comparative genres rather than separate research paradigms because of common interests in policy transfer. However, as noted in Chapter 1, the school effectiveness field is far more influential in international agency policy discourse.

The classroom improvement field is especially the domain of teaching subject specialists who evaluate the impacts of curriculum and teacher education on teaching, and educational sociologists concerned with classroom interaction and the influence of context. The field is overtly imbued with theory, but frequently in the form of axiomatic and only superficially examined assumptions about the benefits of progressive theory for classroom improvement, as seen at some length in Chapter 2. The school effectiveness field is also imbued with a progressive worldview, but in contrast to the educational focus on classroom process, the focus is on student achievement as product. Theoretical concerns are assumed in econometric regression models that quantify structural variables and technical inputs to educational systems that might improve the cost-efficiency of investments in school effectiveness (Guthrie 2011, 77–101). Typically, student achievement is measured through the various international testing regimes, especially in mathematics and science. The underlying economic theory and progressive influences are discussed rarely; instead, publications usually focus on the statistical models and measurement issues.

Contrasting theoretical and methodological strengths and weaknesses bound the two fields. Their limitations contribute to the technical issues seen in the research and evaluation literature in Chapter 2 and to issues arising in interpretation of that research. This chapter outlines the theoretical influences on recommendations for educational reform before turning to limitations in the two fields. Limitations in classroom improvement evaluations are illustrated by two examples: one of bias in progressive review, the other of evaluation failure in a large aid project in Papua New Guinea, which also happens to be a very clear case of cultural imperialism. This discussion also informs interpretation of research in the area studies that follow in the next three chapters.

3.1 Theoretical shaping

Both the classroom improvement and school effectiveness fields generate findings with implied or stated remedies for lack of progressive success. Attributed causes for progressive shortfalls range from surface understandings embodied in recommendations for improving resources conditions, through societal conditions, to deeper cultural conditions (as seen across the typology in Chapter 2). Multiple and often overlapping theoretical influences inform these layers, as indicated in Figure 3.1.

The first, most common and most surface influence frequently comes from policy-oriented school effectiveness research, which is shaped by econometric

Attributed Causes	Theoretical Influences
Resource Conditions	
Classroom and school facilities, e.g. staff:student ratios, desks.	Economics.
Professional inputs, e.g. teacher education, curriculum, textbooks.	Education, Subject specialisations.
Societal Conditions	
Education system, e.g. professional status, working conditions.	Management Theory.
Social structure, e.g. class reproduction.	Dependency Theory, Political Economy.
Cultural Conditions	
Organisational culture, e.g. bureaucracy as barrier to change.	Sociology of Society.
Intergenerational culture, e.g. paradigms, epistemology.	Anthropology, Cross-cultural Psychology, Cultural Sociology.

Increasingly more fundamental responses ↓

Figure 3.1 Theoretical influences on types of research finding
Source: Author.

models that seek to quantify the extent to which inputs might improve student achievement as assessed in international testing. The most basic set of recommendations relates to improving physical conditions in schools, where overcrowded classrooms, lack of furniture, shortages of books and other learning materials, and so on, are readily identifiable as practical barriers to classroom change. A less basic approach to resource conditions, as indicated by the arrow, is recommendations for further professional inputs such as improved pre-service teacher education, more in-service teacher education (INSET), reformed curricula and textbooks. Similar recommendations in the classroom improvement field often derive differently from professional concerns shaped by progressive theories applied to curriculum, teacher education and teaching subjects. Recommendations for more such inputs assume, often naively, that they can overcome professional barriers and generate progressive success.

The next two layers of theoretical influence are more academic in orientation. The second layer often derives from neo-liberal management theory (as found in the 'New Paradigm') where the focus is on education systems, the working conditions they provide (such as inadequate pay and housing), and their reflection in teachers' low professional status. Much more radically, post-colonial analyses shaped by political economy, dependency theory and critical theory turn attention to social, political and economic systems as obstacles to change. At this deeper level, the education system is seen as shaping formalistic knowledge in the interest of reproducing social class structures.

The third layer, more fundamental but much less radical in the political sense, sees the underpinning cultural elements, either organisational culture as a barrier to change or culture as an intergenerational grammar and a foundation for culturally embedded educational practice. Recent theoretical debate has focussed recently on this layer, with influences coming from fields such as cultural anthropology and cross-cultural psychology. Attention has turned to paradigms and epistemology to provide deep explanations for the lack of paradigm shift from formalism to progressivism in developing country classrooms.

Clearly, this book is in the last group, and it will take up again the more fundamental cultural issues in Chapter 8. However, an important qualification is that the focus on cultural conditions is not a denial of the importance of technical inputs and structural change. The thrust of the evidence and analysis is that investment in the production and delivery of classroom equipment, textbooks, teaching materials and professional training would be more efficiently and effectively applied to upgrading formalism than to promoting progressive classroom change (Sections 10.3–10.4).

3.2 Theoretical limitations

The school effectiveness and classroom improvement fields are caged by contrasting theoretical and methodological limitations that provide trade-offs among validity, reliability, relevance and generalisability. The often corresponding strengths and weakness of the two fields are summarised in Table 3.1, while

Section 9.5 has two studies from Indonesia that provide examples of the respective limitations.

Classroom improvement studies typically are contextualised within individual national education systems, as seen in Chapter 2, albeit prone to make recommendations that extend far beyond their sampling bases. In contrast, the school effectiveness field is broader in scale. It is strongly founded academically in a positivist quest for elegant predictions about the educational future and for universal generalisations, as reflected in *School Effectiveness and School*

Table 3.1 Limitations in school effectiveness and classroom improvement research

	School Effectiveness Field	Classroom Improvement Field
Theoretical Limitations	• Cross-fertilisation with classroom improvement field uncommon. • Universal basis in econometric models. • Anthropology, education and sociology theory usually absent.	• Cross-fertilisation with school effectiveness field uncommon. • Universal theoretical basis dominated by usually unexamined axioms about progressive benefits. • Economic theory usually absent.
Methodological Limitations *Validity*	• Student achievement as dependent variable gives valid output measure. • Statistical trawling typically measures large numbers of structural and school variables, but rarely includes cultural context or classroom processes. • Misuse of questionnaire surveys as proxy for classroom behaviours.	• Common misuse of teaching style rather than student achievement as dependent variable. • Mixed methods studies of classroom processes can have insights to cultural context. • Often correct use of observation to assess classroom behaviours.
Reliability	• Lack of statistical discrimination for formalistic teaching styles. • Disaggregated classroom process variables overlook the bigger teaching styles picture.	• Qualitative classroom studies can lack replicability.
Relevance	• False assumption that developed country findings relevant to developing countries.	• False assumption that progressive theory relevant to formalistic systems.
Generalisability	• Surveys may not be relevant to other populations.	• Case studies rarely selected randomly, usually involve small numbers and lack controls. • Hawthorne effects in pilot projects.

Source: Author.

Improvement, where articles and reference lists rarely contain titles that state the countries in which studies take place, seemingly because interest in universal generalisations makes location seem unimportant. A newer, allied field on teacher effectiveness has received less attention (Muijs *et al.* 2014; Reynolds *et al.* 2014). It has primarily concentrated on 'developed' countries, as reflected in an influential synthesis by Hattie (2009), which derived from studies in English-speaking, 'highly developed' countries and unusually, but correctly, excluded non-English-speaking and developing countries from its generalisations (13). The overall effect in both the school effectiveness and classroom improvement fields is that progressivism is often based in universal claims to knowledge that rarely are treated as hypotheses to be tested experimentally in developing countries.

The sheer volume of econometric research is overwhelming. Hattie (2009) found over 800 meta-analyses of teacher effectiveness; Glewwe *et al.* (2011) identified over 9,000 worldwide school effectiveness studies from 1990 to 2010; while Auld and Morris (2014) reviewed four compendiums published from 1996 to 2010. A consequence is that individual school effectiveness studies are absorbed into policy discourse through meta-analyses and are recycled without much cognizance of their theoretical and methodological limitations. The underlying economic theory appears to have been remarkably stable, especially compared to the less bounded classroom improvement field. Econometric modelling is the unquestioned 'normal science' paradigm and for decades discussion has focussed on reliability issues such as measurement error and statistical test effects (Guthrie 1982; Boissiere 2004; Glewwe and Kremer 2006; Reynolds *et al.* 2014).

A long-term absence has been classroom process studies, which has been reflected historically in little openness to educational theory that might lead in this direction. Scheerens (2001), working within the field, reported 'instructional and pedagogical theory appeared to be practically missing as a source of inspiration for educational effectiveness studies in developing countries' (365). This was still the case 12 years later, when a further review of 109 school effectiveness studies found only six were driven by any theory at all (Scheerens 2013). One consequence of the lack of educational theory is an absence of much qualitative data and of many mixed methods studies to explain statistical relationships, which has made the school effectiveness field and its findings difficult to access (Reynolds *et al.* 2014, 201). When teaching quality is considered in the school effectiveness field, the conventionally implied assumption is that quality equates to more progressive teaching methods, as explored in Section 1.3 with the influence of Beeby's 'stages' in the World Bank. Generally, however, classroom processes have been treated historically as constants or background noise, which a Bank review exemplified. Boissiere (2004, 18) observed with no apparent regret that

> Curriculum design also includes decisions about teaching methods and teacher preparation – for example on best ways to teach reading. . . . It is difficult to do good production function studies on details such as this,

since data on teaching methods for a particular subject are not easily available or difficult to generate, even in the most advanced countries.

Apparently, teaching of reading was merely a classroom detail rather than one of the most important functions of schooling.

In contrast, classroom studies have been common in the classroom improvement field, but its theory-laden research has often used qualitative data to argue for what should happen rather than to analyse what does happen. The field is overtly imbued with theory, but frequently in the form of axiomatic and only superficially examined assumptions about the benefits of progressive theory for classroom improvement, as already discussed in Chapter 2. A practical constraint that also influences the field's limitations is that many classroom improvement publications derive from the authors' doctoral studies, which are restricted by the requirement for the research to be solely that of the candidate, thus limiting the scope of solo researchers with limited resources and able only to make marginal use of research assistants. In contrast, as the examples of Indonesian research in Section 9.5 illustrate, classroom effectiveness studies, especially those with extensive aid agency funding, can engage large teams to collect and/or analyse data. While the result is usually large samples and careful statistical cross-analysis, the absence of educational and cultural theory is a major contrast with classroom improvement research.

School effectiveness studies often acknowledge cultural context but are prone to consider it as organisational culture and to ignore the influence of intergenerational culture. Recognition of sociological elements usually has been confined to more easily measured structural-functional variables, with the operational focus mainly on student and teacher socio-economic status (Tatto 2008, 500–502 contains illustrations). As part of an analysis of some 90 school effectiveness studies in Sub-Saharan Africa by Yu (2007), none of nine systematic reviews had any apparent findings about cultural context (5–14), only two of 11 research studies apparently raised cultural issues (14–26) and only four of seven models of educational effectiveness referred to culture (32–47). The effect is that cultural context (like classroom process) was treated as background noise, as part of the unexplained residuals. Combined with the absence of theory about teaching, anthropological and sociological theory that might guide cultural analysis usually has also remained absent (Scheerens 2001, 2013). Thus, the field has often been a form of empiricism involving statistical trawling among loosely connected socio-economic variables that generate little understanding of cultural context, teaching styles or intergenerational culture in the classroom (Guthrie 2011, 86–98). A still surprising example comes from Glewwe *et al.* (1995), who conducted two analyses in Jamaica, each containing 56 variables, finding only 10%–13% of results were positive, i.e. significant findings were so infrequent that nearly half may have been false positives, an explanation not considered by the authors. In contrast, classroom culture studies have been more open to exploring cultural context or ecological validity through grounded mixed method designs (below).

64 *The progressive cage*

There are exceptions to all generalisations, including consideration of criticisms like these from inside and outside the school effectiveness field (Reynolds *et al.* 1994; Reynolds and Teddlie 2001); research in Kenya by Daley *et al.* (2005) that did include the influence of cultural context (Section 5.4); Hattie's (2009) exclusion of developing countries from his generalisations; inclusion by Chang *et al.* (2014) of classroom observation in a large Indonesian study; and Scheerens' (2015) recent inductive process of theory formation. However, even this approach to theory conceptualised educational effectiveness as an integration of system-level, school-level, classroom-level, and student factors, and omitted cultural context as a factor. Progress could be made in this direction if Scheerens' framework were expanded to include cultural factors, integrated with the empirical work on cultural clusters by Zhang, Khan, and Tahirsylag (2015), and if classroom-level factors included observational data on teaching styles.

3.3 Methodological limitations

The theoretical limitations in both fields are often reflected in a number of methodological issues involving validity, reliability, relevance and generalisability, as summarised in Table 3.1.[1]

Validity

In contrast to its theoretical weaknesses, a major strength of the school effectiveness field is use of student achievement as dependent variable to give a highly valid output measure when test objectives match the taught curriculum. The field's emphasis on empirical data has contributed to its influence on evidence-based decision-making. Often, classroom improvement evaluations of curriculum and teacher education reforms have not matched these particular strengths because they assume rather than demonstrate that changes in teaching style and classroom interaction will improve student performance. For example, Hardman, Abd-Kadir, and Smith (2008) in Nigeria and Hardman *et al.* (2009) in Kenya found that primary school-based teacher development programmes impacted on teaching styles in progressive directions, but offered no evidence about any effects on student achievement, thus in both cases embodying the Progressive Education Fallacy in not testing the axiomatic assumption that the teaching process would produce the learning product.

The theoretical narrowness of school effectiveness research has commonly been reflected in technical problems measuring classroom factors and cultural context. A particular validity issue arises from the lack of classroom observation studies in this field. Rather than direct observation, data such as use of class time usually has come indirectly from questionnaire surveys with teachers and administrators (e.g. African examples in Yu's 2007 extensive review). A similar problem can also arise in curriculum and teacher education evaluations that focus on classroom improvement using questionnaires, interviews and focus groups, which are not direct means of establishing classroom behaviours.

Indirect data on the classroom from these sources is not valid when interpreted as representing observable behaviours that actually occur inside the classroom (for example, by Ginsburg 2010). Questionnaires and interviews are prone to elicit the views that respondents consider researchers seek, while focus groups can add to such pressures because there is no confidentiality about participants' views, especially when the groups contain members who hold positions of authority. In particular, the tendency of teachers to present pictures of their classrooms that are more consistent with reform ideologies than their actual classroom behaviours can be an issue in evaluating official reforms (Guthrie 2011, 90–92). The evidence for this has long been found in widespread mixed methods classroom improvement studies, which commonly show that questionnaires find teacher acceptance of reforms but classroom observation finds the same teachers do not implement them. Morris (1983, 1985) in Hong Kong, O'Sullivan (2004) in Namibia, Barrett (2007) and Tarmo (2016) in Tanzania, Halstead and Zhu (2010) in China, Song (2015) in Cambodia, and Shah and Quinn (2016) in Timor-Leste all reported teachers professing progressive change but actually teaching formalistically. As Altinyelken (2010), who found the same issue in Uganda, put it, 'teacher self-report is a weak proxy in analysing the progress of reform policies in practice' (162). A more rigorous application of questionnaires, interviews and focus groups is to investigate students' and teachers' perceptions of and attitudes to the classroom and its processes, and their cultural explanations of classroom behaviour.

It should be noted that adherence here to the core meaning of validity as the correctness of the data collected is no longer conventional practice in the field of testing and measurement. This raises two issues. One is that definition is a chronic issue in social science research. A plethora of definitions of validity exist – for example, construct, content and criterion validity in measurement; internal and external validity in experimental design; ecological validity in cultural sociology; and validity as logic in philosophy, among many others – and these sometimes move far from the core meaning of validity (see continuing discussion in a Special Edition on Validity in *Assessment in Education: Principles, Policy & Practice* 23 (2), 2016). The best one can do is make one's own usages clear (Guthrie 2010, 1, 10–11). The other issue is that concerns in psychology about assessing validity often rest in a positivist construct of scientific research as a hypothetico-deductive search for universalities that is itself bounded in the culture of science. This can create limitations when trying to find out what classroom behaviours do occur in other cultures and – a separate issue – what the meanings and perceptions of the behaviours are in those cultures.

Reliability

A statistical clue to a lack of operational recognition of both teaching styles and cultural context in school effectiveness research lies in Scheerens' (2001, 361, 368) observation that the range of variation in teaching practices in some developing countries may be quite limited, thus providing a lack of statistical discrimination. Categorisation of teaching styles as present or absent may provide too little information to analyse through measures of variance, such as regression analysis, which assume interval and ratio data that allows for differences in degree rather than kind. Advanced parametric techniques are usually robust with nominal and ordinal measurement, but when cultural commonalities are widespread and basically occur in whole rather than in part they effectively provide lower-level binary data. The inadequacy of multivariate regression techniques in accounting for the presence or absence of pervasive cultural phenomena is not just a reliability matter, but is a statistical artefact raising validity issues.

In recent years, analysis of teaching process variables through classroom video has appeared in response to critiques that econometric production function estimates usually do not include classroom processes. For example, Carnoy, Ngware, and Oketch (2015) included teacher pedagogical skills in their model of grade 6 mathematics teaching in Botswana, Kenya and South Africa. A 12-item teaching protocol was used to rate teacher quality as low/better/best. Four items rated cognitive demand based on memorisation, procedures without connections, procedures with connections, and doing mathematics. However, these were measures of the quality of the mathematics rather than teaching styles, which received no consideration as such. Chang *et al.* (2014) in their study of grade 8 mathematics in Indonesia, made what they considered to be 'a pioneering in-depth analysis of secondary school mathematics teaching that directly links student outcomes with teacher knowledge and behaviors' (45). In analysing the 'classroom black box', their discussion of classroom process focussed on the amount of time spent on exposition, discussion, problem-solving, practical work, and investigation, and they also divided whole class time into teacher-only, teacher-student, and student-student interaction (132–136). Nonetheless, there was only passing reference to the overall pattern of formalistic teaching, which the categories suggest would have been a fertile area for in-depth discussion (see also Section 9.5). It appears that statisticians disaggregating classroom teaching variables to quantify mathematics lessons have a mindset that is prone to overlook the bigger teaching styles picture.

Relevance

Considerable effort has been expended in both fields trying to plant findings from developed to developing countries on an apparent methodological assumption that they have universal validity. Auld and Morris (2014, 130) have described the syllogistic reasoning involved:

> Crudely stated, this takes the form: countries X and Y perform well in cross-national comparative assessment surveys and exhibit educational system feature A. Country Z underperforms in cross-national comparative assessment surveys and does not exhibit educational system feature A. Therefore, if country Z were to adopt educational system feature A (or

a contextualised variant of educational system feature A), its educational outcomes would be improved.

However, with an absence of cross-cultural validation, school effectiveness studies have provided only weak and inconclusive evidence on the effects in developing countries of instructional factors that have received empirical support in developed ones (Scheerens 2001; Yu 2007). Yu's review of African school effectiveness studies concluded that developed country findings do not provide a blueprint for the creation of more effective schools and should not be applied mechanically without reference to the particular contexts of a school or country, nor should it be assumed that developing countries are a single entity. Rather, meta-analyses over more than 40 years have demonstrated that teacher education and teaching style effects are so highly dependent on context that claims promoting international educational transfer are highly dubious (Guthrie 1982, 2011, 77–86). The complexity of the findings actually demonstrates that they have been highly oriented to context, not only to socio-economic conditions but also to the cultural milieu.

Generalisability

Operational constraints usually mean that the most common research methods in developing country school systems involve surveys (especially in curriculum and school effectiveness research) and case studies of pilot projects (especially for classroom studies). However, basic sampling principles provide limitations that should restrict prediction, generalisation or the maintenance of axiomatic claims from such methods (Guthrie 2010, 53–98), but often do not. Surveys can provide reliable generalisations to the populations from which they are drawn, but not to other populations. Case studies are rarely selected randomly, usually involve small numbers, and lack controls. They are suited to formative evaluation and action research within study sites but should not be used to generalise beyond the case (although, as Vulliamy 1990, 230, observed, cumulative case studies within a particular developing country can be used for refutation of claims to universal applicability). However, many reports fall breathlessly into the trap of announcing from small-scale studies that teachers support progressive reforms and implementation is successful. As an example, Burner et al.'s (2017) case study of an apparently successful introduction of student-centred learning (SCL) in Iraqi Kurdistan involved close support for just three teachers. On this slim basis, the authors' optimism was sufficient to recommend for the whole of Kurdistan that SCL topics should be a part of teacher education and in-service practicum, and that textbooks and classroom furniture should be adapted to SCL to smooth a transition phase from traditional teacher-centred teaching.

Short-term progressive pilot projects may generate temporary change in parts of formalistic systems, but they are unlikely to change the whole system. In particular, the Hawthorne effect makes prediction risky from any apparent early success to sustainability (Guthrie 2011, 218–222). Under trial conditions, considerable Hawthorne effects can occur with commitments of time from those singled out for attention through, for example, INSET. However, project extension phases requiring the same high levels of commitment, often without relief from normal duties and usually with less in-service support, are usually unsustainable. As Gauthier and Dembele (2004) properly cautioned, 'it should be borne in mind that beyond the novelty syndrome of the pilot project, and beyond the whims of fashion trends, it is important to measure the stability of student learning gains' (35). The longer-term perspective on pilot projects is that traditional paradigm behaviour usually overwhelms progressive behaviours, despite technicist inputs, so that initial appearances of paradigm shift do not sustain.

3.4 An example of review bias

Many of these limitations are illustrated by a meta-analysis by Westbrook *et al.* (2013) for the UK Department for International Development (DfID) that held progressivism as axiomatic. The review was placed in the context of UNESCO's Education for All strategy and donor pressure for progressive curriculum and progressive reform. A thorough search found 489 studies from low or middle income countries since 2000, of which 45 were analysed in depth as having 'methodological trustworthiness and quality of contextualisation' (1). The main claim in the Executive Summary (Westbrook *et al.* 2013, 1–2) was that

> teachers' use of communicative strategies encourages pedagogic practices that are interactive in nature, and is more likely to impact on student learning outcomes and hence be effective. This claim . . . has emerged from an interpretation of the overall body of evidence.

The overall strength of the evidence was said to be 'moderate' and mostly derived from observational-descriptive studies, but was 'strongest in the consistency of findings on the extent to which teachers are able to implement the pedagogical strategies and practices envisaged by reforms and training' (2). The pedagogical key was reported to be classroom interaction, with six effective teaching practices identified: flexible use of whole-class, group and pair work with student discussion; frequent and relevant use of learning materials beyond the textbook; open and closed questioning, expanding responses, and encouraging student questioning; demonstration and explanation drawing on sound content knowledge; use of local languages; and planning and varying lesson sequences. The Summary (Westbrook *et al.* 2013, 2) claimed:

> While all teachers may use the above practices, the key difference is that the most effective teachers use them communicatively, paying attention to their students and placing them centrally in their construction of the teaching-learning process. These effective teachers recognise the need to

provoke a positive response in students and do so in more interactive, communicative ways, so that students engage, understand, participate and learn.

However, like the UNCF (2009) report on UNICEF's child-friendly schools discussed in Section 2.3, the Executive Summary was not consistent with numerous qualifications noted in the body of the report about gaps in research design, so that the methodological base for the progressive interpretation was shaky. From the initial group of studies, the 203 with positive findings did not far outnumber the 179 with negative findings about pedagogic practices. The body of the review, in reporting on the in-depth analysis of the higher quality studies, noted that findings frequently came from self-evaluations (and which thus had limitations involving lack of independence), and acknowledged possible publication bias towards positive findings (Westbrook *et al.* 2013, 23–24, 36). A small number of apparently effective interventions based on structured pedagogy were not thoroughly evaluated, while a number of studies pointed only to superficial uptake of progressive forms. Teachers could often enunciate progressive principles pedagogy and direct instruction; however, observation of lessons showing the principles did not translate into practice. Circular bias was inherent in reporting of teacher attitude, strategies and practices as positive by definition if they were progressive and as negative if they were formalistic (36–39). As well, none of the studies used control schools; evidence on how communicative practices impacted on learning outcomes was not robust because very few observational-descriptive studies used pre-tests as well as post-tests, or school or national student achievement data; many studies claimed greater student engagement and confidence without rigorous evidence; the small number of effectiveness studies that did correlate specific practices with student achievement missed details of pedagogic practices; while qualitative studies that looked at reforms or existing conditions and classroom practices did not systematically assess student learning (44, 65).

The effect of all these qualifications is that the search strategy collecting the studies may have been rigorous, but all the methodological limitations detailed in the body of the report beg the question of why these studies were considered in the Executive Summary to be trustworthy and why its progressive interpretation was valid. The discussion of vested consultancy findings in Section 2.3 seems pertinent, as does further discussion in Section 7.2 of bias originating from caged progressive, theory-laden observation. At least the DfID review and this book agree that the way forward is controlled field experiments with classroom innovations to provide the greatest potential for generalisations within their particular cultural context (Section 9.2).

3.5 An example of evaluation failure

Evaluation failure in an Australian aid project in Papua New Guinea (PNG) provides a further and more detailed example of numerous pitfalls that project designers and evaluators should avoid. The project illustrates how far astray progressive curriculum evaluation can go, to the extent that most of the weaknesses of classroom improvement studies in Table 3.1 were manifest and few if any of the trade-offs between validity, reliability, relevance and generalisability were realised.[2]

As part of a series of education system reforms in PNG (Section 6.4), the Australian Agency for International Development (AusAID) contracted out management of the large Curriculum Reform and Implementation Project (CRIP) to an Australian company, SAGRIC. From 2000–2006, at a cost of some AUD 42 million, CRIP introduced curriculum reforms, including outcomes-based education (OBE), generalist teaching in primary schools, and progressive subject syllabuses for elementary, primary and secondary schools (AusAID 2002; CRIP 2002, 2004, 13–14). Major evaluation issues stemmed from a design flaw by AusAID, which required the managing contractor to conduct both formative and summative evaluations of its own project work. This generated a lack of reliability such that independent evaluators contradicted CRIP's claims about OBE's success in schools.

Central to CRIP's implementation programme was its decision to implement the OBE curriculum. OBE has been associated with a number of progressive themes, such as variety in teaching methodologies matched against learner needs, flexible timing to meet individual needs, and the teacher as a facilitator (Norman 2006a). The approach is centrally based on measuring student cognitive outcomes, understood as what students can actually do to be effective citizens, and then designing the curriculum, instruction and assessment backwards from the outcomes to ensure they are met. 'Traditional' OBE aims to produce academically competent students, with a focus on student mastery of subject-related academic outcomes (which can fit within a formalistic system); 'transitional' OBE is characterised more progressively by a wide range of teaching practices; and 'transformational' OBE aims to produce competent future citizens and has long-term cross-curricular outcomes that are intended to relate directly to students' future life. The transformational role was adopted in PNG because it fitted with community education goals: 'One of the reasons for the current curriculum reform was that the previous curriculum was not enabling the young to lead useful, happy and healthy lives in the community' (51).

An important aspect of AusAID's project design was a requirement for SAGRIC to undertake an overriding evaluation of the impact of curriculum reform on student learning outcomes and teacher practice (CRIP 2004, 89–92). In conformity, in a paper delivered the year before CRIP ended (Dawson 2006, 220), the Project Director stated that,

> it is critical that the fundamental policy decisions about the nature and extent of the reform process, and ongoing decisions about the progress and impact of educational reform, are based on reliable evidence rather than assumption. . . . [including] reviewing and analysing relevant research to guide the development of the program of reform, collecting baseline

data about ... student performance, [and] collecting and analysing ongoing performance data.

In practice, CRIP's self-evaluations had fallen well short of this.

The design requirement was to provide an output measure of the impact of the reform on student achievement. A baseline study was to commence in Impact Study 1 with a five-year longitudinal evaluation in pre-reform and reform schools using quantitative and qualitative data to, where possible, identify causal relationships between key variables. In principle, this would subject progressive assumptions to field experiment. A 2001 pilot study found two major problem areas in implementing the impact evaluation (CRIP 2004, 13–14). The first problem arose from an absence of suitable instruments to meet an AusAID requirement to use test data collected by the PNG Department of Education and instead CRIP developed literacy and numeracy tests. Alongside Impact Study 1 in 2003–2004, the Australian Council for Educational Research also developed new national literacy and numeracy tests for primary grades (Freeman, Anderson, and Morgan 2005), which provided baseline but not longitudinal data. Student achievement was tested using the CRIP instruments in three grade cohorts from a representative sample of 12 schools in eight provinces. However, CRIP did not provide evidence about the validity of its replacement instruments, and the design now focussed attention on the effectiveness of vernacular elementary schooling at increasing student achievement in English-language primary schools, rather than testing the effect on student achievement of the teaching style embedded in the new primary curriculum and teacher in-service.

Thus, the second problem area was that the original AusAID requirement to undertake an overriding evaluation of the impact of curriculum reform on student learning outcomes and teacher practice now focussed on curriculum implementation issues. A true experimental design would have involved a control group of teachers and students using the previous teaching methods (which would have been possible given the phased introduction of the reform curriculum). However, teaching styles were not controlled in the testing programme, which focussed on curriculum effects. The untested CRIP assumption in this research was that the curriculum changes would drive changes in teaching style and, in turn, a change from formalism would improve student outcomes, i.e. it is another example of the Progressive Education Fallacy.

Results were reported from 'Reform Status 1' students who had not attended vernacular elementary schools, 'Reform Status 2' students who started in elementary schools before previous curricula introduced in the 1990s were replaced by the CRIP-developed curriculum in 2002 and 2003, and 'Reform Status 3' students who started in elementary schools with the reform curriculum. Baseline data came from 881 students in 2002. Initial longitudinal data came in 2003 from 518 of the 2002 sample. A third round of testing in 2004 was to be reported in 2005 (CRIP 2004, 12), but the results do not appear to be publicly available and were not referred to by an AusAID education sector evaluation (Packer, Emmott, and Hinchcliffe 2009).

The first two rounds of testing gave rise to a number of highly variable and confusing results that generated data interpretation issues.

- Both male and female students in the lowest cohort, elementary grade 1 in 2002, performed less well in mathematics and language in 2003, although not significantly so in three out of four t-tests (CRIP 2004, 27–31). This unexpected finding gave rise to three possible interpretations: the extra year had not added to literacy and numeracy, the assessment instruments were invalid, or test administration changed from 2002 to 2003. The third explanation was considered most likely, in effect treating the result as a false negative.
- Primary grade 3 and 5 cohorts did have statistically significant improvements from 2002 to 2003 in all eight statistical comparisons categorised by reform status. These results were accepted at face value, albeit with caution, because a grade 3 group without elementary schooling had greater improvements than a group with elementary schooling, while the reverse was true for the grade 5 cohort. Thus, cognitive dissonance was apparent when the report considered that lack of reliability in administration gave false negatives with the grade 1 cohort, but ignored the possibility that the same issue in grades 3 and 5 could have created false positives.
- PNG has over 800 languages (Lewis 2016). A recognised problem with vernacular pre-schooling was training primary teachers to cope with the transition into English of pupils arriving from vernacular elementary schools into grade 3 in primary schools (Siegel 1997; Guy *et al.* 2006; Kale 2006). Many primary teachers simply did not know the vernacular of the locations in which they were posted and had difficulties with language transition if they could not use the vernacular in which pupils had been schooled. The CRIP research did not explore the possibility that the variable student results could have been affected by the vernacular knowledge of the teachers.
- Impact Study 1 attributed wastage of 39% of the students between the pretest and the follow-up to student movement and non-payment of school fees. Test data also suggested that less able students had dropped out or repeated in each cohort (CRIP 2004, 25–26), thus the longitudinal data was biased towards students who were more able.
- Additionally, consideration of the value added by statistically significant learning gains in the grades 3 and 5 cohorts was based only on percentage change in magnitude rather than on variance. Hattie (2009, 7–22) considered that an effect size of 0.4 of a standard deviation should be the benchmark to judge whether effects on schooling are below or above average. Consideration of the CRIP data suggests that three-quarters of the significant positive results may have been below this benchmark. Only two of the eight improvements among the two cohorts had an effect size greater than 0.4 (mathematics and language for the grade 5 group with

elementary education, at .86 and .65, compared to a range from .04 to .38 for the other groups). However, proper assessment requires pooled standard deviations from pre- and post-tests, which the report did not provide, and this estimate is based on the means of each pair of standard deviations.

Some findings relevant to teaching style issues appeared in 3 of 31 papers in the proceedings of a curriculum reform conference in 2005. The three studies used teacher reports rather than direct classroom observation, indicating support expressed in principle for the reform curriculum but concerns about its application due to lack of materials, school support and language issues (Guy et al. 2006; Kaleva et al. 2006; Murphy 2006). Another project study gave some consideration to the impact of the syllabuses on teacher practice, with passing but unspecified reference to classroom observation by project researchers (CRIP 2006, 90–97). On this sketchy basis, it was claimed that teachers were using the new teaching strategies with varying competence, marked change in classroom management, and integration across the curriculum.

In sum, CRIP had manifest weaknesses from aid project design, management and evaluation perspectives. Design documentation did require field experiments to evaluate whether proposed teaching style innovations would improve student achievement, but left this to a conflict of interests by the contractor. The evidence available from CRIP's incompetent self-evaluation was skimpy and incomplete. In the absence of a true experimental design, no effort was made to identify the impact of teaching styles, as originally required. CRIP management articulated a need for evidence-based decision-making rather than acting on assumption, however its weak evaluation processes did not subject its progressive assumptions to systematic classroom scrutiny. Insofar as CRIP did provide passing comment on actual classroom behaviour, it was apparently based on casual rather than systematic observation. Impact study data on classroom implementation of the curriculum relied heavily on questionnaires and did not delve into the tendency of teachers to present pictures of their classrooms that are more consistent with reform ideologies than their actual classroom behaviours. Other reliability issues were more technical. Baseline data was collected but instruments were not validated; any learning gains were uneven; incomplete longitudinal data was biased towards students who were more able; teacher vernacular competency was not considered; and there were inconsistencies in interpretation of test results. Test data on primary student learning gains from 2002 to 2003 scarcely presented a compelling picture. Nor did CRIP present any valid evidence that substantive changes occurred to teaching styles.

3.6 Independent evidence

In contrast to CRIP's generally positive claims about school and classroom change, two independent studies found an absence of them. One study, by

Agigo (2010), was a summative evaluation of CRIP impacts in four primary and two secondary schools in one province from each of the four regions in PNG, including questionnaires and interviews with 159 participants. Agigo found a major project impact at the national level with professional training for curriculum officers, however at provincial, district and school levels, a targeted cluster approach to INSET did not adhere to national guidelines for systematic curriculum development and implementation. Rushed training prior to completion of the syllabuses also had a negative impact on the development, implementation and sustainability of the curriculum reform at school level. Many teachers did not receive training and materials at the same time, which possibly contributed to 74% of 112 teachers responding that they were not using their training to teach curriculum reform subjects effectively. Despite a 1991 Department of Education Sector Review support for objectives, CRIP had not provided reasons why outcomes were appropriate, and the evaluation found that classroom learning was ineffective under the student-centred outcomes model (3–5, 29–35). Seventy-eight percent of teachers did not agree that the curriculum was easy to program and teach, while 65% did not agree that students were learning well with it. Only 26% said the curriculum reform had changed their way of teaching. Although there was support in PNG for OBE (e.g. Norman 2006a, 2006b), the outcomes approach meant considerable confusion in the teaching profession (Guthrie 2005), and Agigo (2010) concluded that it was 'unsustainable and not appropriate for the country' (47).

Agigo's independent summative evaluation was much more negative than the CRIP-contracted formative evaluations, but did not incorporate classroom observation to triangulate against the professional perceptions reported from questionnaires and interviews. A second independent study by Le Fanu (2011) did include lesson observation along with interviews with teachers and stakeholders. This qualitative case study of three rural primary schools in Eastern Highlands Province in 2008–2009 gave situational detail about progressive reform implementation in the schools. The new curriculum identified various inclusive precepts that teachers should follow, with the research assessing the precepts' impacts on teaching and learning practices. One precept required subject integration. The teachers admitted that they found it conceptually difficult to synthesise the different learning areas of the curriculum, and that their teaching was more focussed and intelligible when they taught subjects separately. A second precept required teachers to provide students with opportunities to take charge of their own learning. Teachers found difficulty providing opportunities given the lack of learning resources in schools, particularly print materials, consequently they tended to give students identical tasks and to control the learning process tightly. A third precept recommended peer tutoring through explanation and demonstration of problem-solving processes. Although the teachers encouraged their students to help one another, lesson observation indicated that peer tutoring generally meant answer sharing, and students were highly reliant on the remedial support provided by teachers patrolling the classroom. A fourth precept, derived from the intent in OBE to measure student outcomes, expected teachers to deploy expertly 13 assessment instruments. Unsurprisingly, teachers said they lacked the time, energy and expertise to use many of them, and they tended to rely on previous methods.

The formalistic teachers were not necessarily averse to change as such. Although they ignored many of the precepts, some had developed their own contextually appropriate approaches for promoting student learning. Often these reflected cultural tradition in assuming that teachers should centrally control teaching and learning, and so were contrary to the spirit as well as the letter of the new curriculum (Le Fanu 2010). Teachers expertly used a variety of strategies to transmit skills and knowledge, including showing respect towards their students – an essential approach in a shame-based society. Strategies also included speaking in short simple sentences, providing examples relevant to students' own experiences, providing concise definitions, using visual aids and scrutinising facial expressions for understanding. Like Agigo, Le Fanu found that non-implementation could be partly attributed to the gap between the technical demands of the progressive curriculum and the capacity of the teachers to meet those demands. Importantly, Le Fanu added, non-implementation could also be attributed to culturally embedded teacher resistance to the facilitative roles expected in the classroom and to teachers' scepticism about constructivist learning theories. In essence, this independent research showed that the progressive ideas inherent in the new curriculum were little used, with improvements in teaching being predominantly within a formalistic rather than a progressive approach. The implication was 'policymakers should work with rather than against educational realities' (1).

3.7 Cultural imperialism in action

CRIP also happens to be a particularly clear example of cultural imperialism. The historical political and economic connection as such came from the fact that PNG was effectively an Australian colony for much of its modern history. The southern part, Papua, was a British colony from 1888 to 1906, then an Australian territory until 1975. New Guinea, to the north, was a German colony from 1884 to 1914, became a League of Nations Mandated Territory under Australia from 1921 to 1946, then an Australian trusteeship under the United Nations. The two parts were administered jointly by Australia and in later years came under the purview of the United Nations Committee on Colonialism (Weeks and Guthrie 1984). Since independence in 1975, Australia has been PNG's predominant international partner and there is a large bilateral aid programme (estimated at AUD 477 million in 2016–2017) (DFAT 2016, 11). CRIP was managed from 2000–2006 by an Australian company, SAGRIC, which was contracted by AusAID, the Australian government aid agency. CRIP's curriculum work imposed progressive OBE theories derived from the United States that were then fashionable in Australia.

Somewhat late in the life of the project, CRIP's project director stated that 'one of the interesting counter-effects of globalisation which is driving the development of culturally relevant curricula is an appreciation of the threat to traditional cultural values . . . by an "internationalised culture"' (Dawson 2006, 215). Despite this articulation of a need for appreciation of cultural influences, there is no indication in any of the available project documentation that CRIP management considered the relevance of progressive reforms to PNG or that the project actually addressed the historical and cultural context in which classroom behaviour is situated. Instead, SAGRIC's project staff undertook a very proactive role in OBE curriculum development, which compounded the lack of independence of CRIP's self-evaluation. So active was CRIP's role that it was 'criticised on the basis that its technical advisers drive policy decisions and the development of the national curriculum for PNG through project activities' (Guy 2009, 136). Although the Department of Education officially denied this claim, a quasi-independent AusAID-funded evaluation noted that the decision to pursue an outcomes-based curriculum was not in the original design. It found that 'given the lack of specification of curriculum in the design, ultimately the decision rested with key individuals in the National Department of Education and the managing contractor' (Packer, Emmott, and Hinchcliffe 2009, 32). Other evidence also supports the claims about CRIP's role. Ryan (2008), a participant observer who worked within the Department's Curriculum Unit, angrily wrote of the unit's ruthless exclusion from the syllabus development process by CRIP. Agigo's (2010, 47) independent evaluation found that the Department

> lacked the leadership capacity to deal with the CRIP Project consultants and to be involved in the design and development of the curriculum . . . [it] relied on the model proposed by the CRIP consultants . . . [who] took the lead in designing the . . . curriculum model.

Le Fanu (2011, 178–214) found that much evidence suggested that the curriculum formation process was driven by exogenous rather than endogenous influences, 'possibly because expatriate CRIP staff – consciously or unconsciously – exploited their superior cultural capital . . . to dominate proceedings' (213).

The 'outcome' was that Australian progressive cultural values were imposed on the primary and secondary school curriculum in part because of weak counterpart management systems, and regardless of contrary evidence that PNG values are different or of ample literature on the failure of several previous progressive attempts to change teaching styles in PNG (Section 6.4). CRIP management articulated a need for appreciation of cultural influences, yet there is no suggestion in its evaluations that CRIP actually addressed the historical and cultural context in which classroom behaviour in PNG is situated, it examined the cultural validity of OBE, or it even attempted to research the large literature on Melanesian pedagogy that is readily available in PNG. The biases in and mediocrity of CRIP's evaluation work, coupled with the cultural imperialism inherent in its curriculum development processes, makes clear that AusAID would have done better to contract independent project evaluators rather than leave evaluation subject to a conflict of interest for a rampant contractor.

3.8 Conclusion

A variety of theoretical influences has been layered through the literature on educational reform in developing countries. Three types can be observed in the research findings on progressive educational reforms that were seen in Chapter 2. The first, most common and most surface layer is often found in the school effectiveness field and in mainstream educational analyses centred on classroom improvement. Perceptions that the lack of success of progressive reforms is due to poor resources led to recommendations for further physical and professional inputs. A second layer of findings shaped variously by organisational sociology and post-colonial analyses turns attention to educational, social, political and economic systems as obstacles to change. The third, more fundamental layer sees underpinning cultural elements either as organisational culture to be overcome as a barrier to change or to accept culture as an intergenerational grammar and a foundation for culturally embedded educational practice. The fundamental professional issue underlying curriculum development and teacher training in many developing countries since the 1960s has been the cultural conflict between progressive and formalistic approaches in the classroom.

The first layer has been the most common. Widespread studies in the school effectiveness and classroom improvement fields have particularly focussed on school and classroom issues rather than contextual ones. As the area studies in the next three chapters will continue to show, these fields are bounded by research paradigms with reciprocal theoretical and methodological limitations involving trade-offs among validity, reliability, relevance and generalisability. Econometric school effectiveness studies typically use quantitative data to measure large numbers of school variables that reveal little about teaching styles. In contrast, the classroom improvement field is imbued with axiomatic theory and superficial literature surveys about the benefits of progressive theory. The effect in both fields is that progressivism is often based on universal claims to knowledge that rarely are treated as hypotheses to be tested experimentally in developing countries.

Limitations like these pervade the progressive research and evaluation literature, as illustrated by the contracted DfID review and CRIP's self-evaluation. Lack of independence has added to the Hawthorne effect in formative evaluations of pilot projects. In the absence of true experimental designs, lack of identification of causal relationships between key variables highlights a need for evidence-based decision-making that subjects progressive assumptions to careful classroom scrutiny. Like much of the research in Chapter 2, the two examples of review and evaluation bias in this chapter manifested an axiomatic faith in progressivism as a universal panacea, such that culturally biased and problematic assumptions about teaching styles were not contested. Many of the research studies in the area chapters have similar issues. However, the theoretical, methodological and technical limitations are only part of a picture that Chapter 7 will explore at greater length. Underlying them is cognitive dissonance in consideration of the evidence, which is demonstrated when anomalies incorrectly are ignored, downplayed or mistreated as acceptable error. The outcome is that theoretically superficial, methodologically flawed, and ahistorical research often sustains misjudged attempts at progressive reform.

Notes

1 Section 3.3 derives in part from an article published in *Compare* (Guthrie 2017), available online: www.tandfonline.com/doi/full/10.1080/03057925.2016.1138396.
2 The PNG case study in Sections 3.5–3.7 derives from parts of an article published in the *Australian Journal of Education* (Guthrie 2012, Copyright © Australian Council for Educational Research 2012) by permission of SAGE Publications, available online: http://journals.sagepub.com/doi/pdf/10.1177/000494411205600304.

References

Agigo, J. 2010. *Curriculum and Learning in Papua New Guinea Schools: A Study on the Curriculum Reform Implementation Project 2000 to 2006*. Special Publication No.57. Port Moresby: National Research Institute.

Altinyelken, H. 2010. "Pedagogical Renewal in Sub-Saharan Africa: The Case of Uganda." *Comparative Education* 46 (2): 151–171.

Auld, E., and Morris, P. 2014. "Comparative Education, the 'New Paradigm' and Policy Borrowing: Constructing Knowledge for Educational Reform." *Comparative Education* 50 (2): 129–155.

AusAID (Australian Agency for International Development). 2002. *Papua New Guinea: Program Profiles 2001–02*. Canberra: AusAID.

Barrett, A. 2007. "Beyond the Polarization of Pedagogy: Models of Classroom Practice in Tanzanian Primary Schools." *Comparative Education* 43 (2): 273–294.

Boissiere, M. 2004. *Determinants of Primary Education Outcomes in Developing Countries: Background Paper for the Evaluation of the World Bank's Support to Primary Education*. Washington, DC: World Bank Operations Evaluation Department.

Burner, T., Madsen, J. Zako, N., and Ismail, A. 2017. "Three Secondary School Teachers Implementing Student-centred Learning in Iraqi Kurdistan." *Educational Action Research*: 25 (3): 402–419.

Carnoy, M., Ngware, M., and Oketch, M. 2015. "The Role of Classroom Resources and National Educational Context in Student Learning Gains: Comparing Botswana, Kenya, and South Africa." *Comparative Education Review* 59 (2): 199–232.

Chang, M., Shaeffer, S., Al-Samarrai, S., Ragatz, A., de Ree, J., and Stevenson, R. 2014. *Teacher Reform in Indonesia: The Role of Politics and Evidence in Policy Making*. Washington, DC: World Bank.

CRIP (Curriculum Implementation Reform Project). 2002. *Second Annual Plan July 2002–June 2003*. Adelaide: SAGRIC.

CRIP. 2004. *Impact Study 1: Mid-Term Review Report* (Vol. 1). Adelaide: SAGRIC.

CRIP. 2006. *Impact Study 6: Final Report*. Adelaide: SAGRIC.

Daley, T., Whaley, S., Sigman, M., Guthrie, D., Neumann, C., and Bwibo, N. 2005. "Background and Classroom Correlates of Child Achievement, Cognitive, and Behavioural

Outcomes in Rural Kenyan Schoolchildren." *International Journal of Behavioral Development* 29 (5): 399–408.

Dawson, G. 2006. "Supporting Curriculum Reform in the Pacific: Lessons Learned from the Curriculum Reform Implementation Project (CRIP)." In *Sustainable Curriculum Development: The PNG Curriculum Reform Experience*, edited by P. Pena, 214–222. Port Moresby: Department of Education.

DFAT (Department of Foreign Affairs and Trade). 2016. *Australian Aid Budget Summary 2016-17*. Canberra: DFAT.

Freeman, C., Anderson, P., and Morgan, G. 2005. *Implementation Project Report on the Pilot Curriculum Standards Monitoring Test*. Canberra: AusAID.

Gauthier, C., and Dembele, M. 2004. Quality of Teaching and Quality of Education: A Review of the Research Findings. Paper commissioned for the UNESCO Education for All Global Monitoring Report 2005, The Quality Imperative. http://unesdoc.unesco.org/images/0014/001466/146641e.pdf

Ginsburg, M. 2010. "Improving Educational Quality through Active-Learning Pedagogies: A Comparison of Five Case Studies." *Educational Research* 1 (3): 62–74.

Glewwe, P., Grosh, M., Jacoby, H., and Lockheed, M. 1995. "An Eclectic Approach to Estimating the Determinants of Achievement in Jamaican Primary Education." *World Bank Economic Review* 9 (2): 231–258.

Glewwe, P., Hanushek, E., Humpage, S., and Ravin, R. 2011. *School Resources and Educational Outcomes in Developing Countries: A Review of the Literature from 1990 to 2010*. Working Paper 17554. Cambridge: National Bureau of Economic Research.

Glewwe, P., and Kremer, M. 2006. "Schools, Teachers, and Education Outcomes in Developing Countries." In *Handbook of the Economics of Education*, Vol. 2, edited by E. Hanushek and F. Welsh, Ch.16. Amsterdam: North-Holland.

Guthrie, G. 1982. "Reviews of Teacher Training and Teacher Performance in Developing Countries: Beeby Revisited (2)." *International Review of Education* 28 (3): 291–306.

Guthrie, G. 2005. *PNG Primary and Secondary Teacher Education Project: Independent Completion Report*. Canberra: Educo.

Guthrie, G. 2010. *Basic Research Methods: An Entry to Social Science Research*. New Delhi: Sage.

Guthrie, G. 2011. *The Progressive Education Fallacy in Developing Countries: In Favour of Formalism*. New York: Springer.

Guthrie, G. 2012. "The Failure of Progressive Classroom Reform: Lessons from the Curriculum Reform Implementation Project in Papua New Guinea." *Australian Journal of Education* 56 (3): 241–256.

Guthrie, G. 2017. "The Failure of Progressive Paradigm Reversal." *Compare* 47 (1): 62–76.

Guy, R. 2009. "Formulating and Implementing Education Policy." In *Policy Making and Implementation: Studies from Papua New Guinea*, edited by R. May, 131–154. Studies in State and Governance in the Pacific No.5. Canberra: State, Society and Governance in Melanesia Program, Australian National University.

Guy, R., Paraide, P., Kippel, L., and Reta, M. 2006. "Review of the Catch-Up Bridging to English Workshops – CRIP Impact Study 2." In *Sustainable Curriculum Development: The PNG Curriculum Reform Experience*, edited by P. Pena, 112–122. Port Moresby: Department of Education.

Halstead, J., and Zhu, C. 2010. "Autonomy as an Element in Chinese Educational Reform: English Lessons in a Senior High School in Beijing." *Asia-Pacific Journal of Education* 29 (4): 443–446.

Hardman, F., Abd-Kadir, J., Agg, C., Migwi, J., Ndambuku, J., and Smith, F. 2009. "Changing Pedagogical Practice in Kenyan Primary Schools: The Impact of School-Based Training." *Comparative Education* 45 (1): 65–86.

Hardman, F., Abd-Kadir, J., and Smith, F. 2008. "Pedagogical Renewal: Improving the Quality of Classroom Interaction in Nigerian Primary Schools." *International Journal of Educational Development* 28 (1): 55–69.

Hattie, J. 2009. *Visible Learning: A Synthesis of Over 800 Meta-Analyses Relating to Achievement*. London: Routledge.

Kale, J. 2006. "Bilingual Schooling in Papua New Guinea: A Sharp Tool Easily Blunted." In *Sustainable Curriculum Development: The PNG Curriculum Reform Experience*, edited by P. Pena, 201–213. Port Moresby: Department of Education.

Kaleva, W., Maha, A., Maha, N., and Badenoch, R. 2006. "The Development and Perceptions of the Reformed Upper Primary Curriculum, CRIP Impact Study 4." In *Sustainable Curriculum Development: The PNG Curriculum Reform Experience*, edited by P. Pena, 141–150. Port Moresby: Department of Education.

Le Fanu, G. 2010. *Promoting Inclusive Education in Papua New Guinea*. EdQual Quality Brief No.7. Bristol: University of Bristol.

Le Fanu, G. 2011. *The Transposition of Inclusion: An Analysis of the Relationship between Curriculum Prescription and Practice in Papua New Guinea*. Unpublished Doctoral dissertation, University of Bristol.

Lewis, M. (Ed.). 2016. *Ethnologue: Languages of the World* (19th ed.). Dallas: SIL International.

Morris, P. 1983. "Teachers' Perceptions of their Pupils: A Hong Kong Case Study." *Research in Education* 29: 81–86.

Morris, P. 1985. "Teachers' Perceptions of the Barriers to the Implementation of a Pedagogic Innovation: A South East Asian Case Study." *International Review of Education* 31 (1): 3–18.

Muijs, D., Kyriakides, L., van der Werf, G., Creemers, B., Timperley, H., and Earl, L. 2014. "State of the Art – Teacher Effectiveness and Professional Learning." *School Effectiveness and School Improvement* 25 (2): 231–256.

Murphy, P. 2006. "What Do Teachers Think of the Reform Curriculum?" In *Sustainable Curriculum Development: The PNG Curriculum Reform Experience*, edited by P. Pena, 23–33. Port Moresby: Department of Education.

Norman, P. 2006a. "Outcomes-Based Education: A PNG Perspective." *Contemporary PNG Studies* 5: 45–57.

Norman, P. 2006b. "Impact of Curriculum Reforms on Some Teacher Education Programs." In *Sustainable Curriculum Development: The PNG Curriculum Reform Experience*, edited by P. Pena, 65–74. Port Moresby: Department of Education.

O'Sullivan, M. 2004. "The Reconceptualisation of Learner-Centred Approaches: A Namibia Case Study." *International Journal of Educational Development* 24 (6): 585–602.

Packer, S., Emmott, S., and Hinchcliffe, K. 2009. *Improving the Provision of Basic Education Services to the Poor in Papua New Guinea: A Case Study*. Canberra: AusAID.

Reynolds, D., Creemers, B., Nesselrodt, P., Shaffer, E., Stringfield, S., and Teddlie, C. (Eds.). 1994. *Advances in School Effectiveness Research and Practice*. Oxford: Pergamon.

Reynolds, D., Sammons, P., De Fraine, B., Van Damme, J., Townsend, T., Teddlie, C., and Stringfield, S. 2014. "Educational Effectiveness Research (EER): A State-of-the-Art Review." *School Effectiveness and School Improvement* 25 (2): 197–230.

Reynolds, D., and Teddlie, C. 2001. "Countering the Critics: Responses to Recent Criticisms of School Effectiveness Research." *School Effectiveness and School Improvement* 12 (1): 41–82.

Ryan, A. 2008. "Indigenous Knowledge in the Science Curriculum: Avoiding Neo-Colonialism." *Cultural Studies of Science Education* 3 (3): 663–683.

Scheerens, J. 2001. "Monitoring School Effectiveness in Developing Countries." *School Effectiveness and School Improvement* 12 (4): 359–384.

Scheerens, J. 2013. "The Use of Theory in School Effectiveness Research Revisited." *School Effectiveness and School Improvement* 24 (1): 1–38.

Scheerens, J. 2015. "Theories on Educational Effectiveness and Ineffectiveness." *School Effectiveness and School Improvement* 26 (1): 10–31.

Shah, R., and Quinn, M. 2016. "Mind the Gap: Global Quality Norms, National Policy Interpretations and Local Praxis in Timor-Leste." *Compare* 46 (3): 394–413.

Siegel, J. 1997. "Formal vs. Non-Formal Vernacular Education: The Education Reform in Papua New Guinea." *Journal of Multilingual and Multicultural Development* 18 (3): 206–222.

Song, S. 2015. "Cambodian Teachers' Responses to Child-Centred Instructional Policies: A Mismatch between Beliefs and Practices." *Teaching and Teacher Education* 50: 24–35.

Tarmo, A. 2016. "Pre-service Science Teachers' Epistemological Beliefs and Teaching Reforms in Tanzania." *Cogent Education* 3 (1). https://doi.org/10.1080/2331186X.2016.1178457

Tatto, M. 2008. "Teacher Policy: A Framework for Comparative Analysis." *Prospects* 38: 487–508.

UNCF. 2009. *Child Friendly Schools Programming: Global Evaluation Report.* New York: UNCF Evaluation Office.

Vulliamy, G. 1990. "Research Outcomes: Postscript." In *Doing Educational Research in Developing Countries: Qualitative Strategies*, edited by G. Vulliamy, K. Lewin, and D. Stephens, 228–233. London: Falmer.

Weeks, S., and Guthrie, G. 1984. "Papua New Guinea." In *Schooling in the Pacific Islands: Colonies in Transition*, edited by R. Thomas and T. Postlethwaite, 29–64. Oxford: Pergamon.

Westbrook, J., Durrani, N., Brown, R., Orr, D., Pryor, J., Boddy, J., and Salvi, F. 2013. *Pedagogy, Curriculum, Teaching Practices and Teacher Education in Developing Countries, Education Rigorous Literature Review.* London: Department for International Development.

Yu, G. 2007. *Research Evidence of School Effectiveness in Sub-Saharan Africa.* EdQual Working Paper No.12. Bristol: University of Bristol.

Zhang, L., Khan, G., and Tahirsylag, A. 2015. "Student Performance, School Differentiation, and World Cultures: Evidence from PISA 2009." *International Journal of Educational Development* 42: 43–53.

4 Formalistic tradition in China

The Confucian education tradition is one of the best-researched examples of the success of formalistic teaching. In GLOBE terminology, the Confucian Cultural Cluster comprises China, Hong Kong, Japan, both Koreas, Macau, Mongolia, Taiwan, Singapore and Vietnam – together having 23.6% of the world's population. What Biggs (1996) labelled the Paradox of the Chinese Learner highlighted that the sort of classrooms commonly considered in Anglo-American progressive thought to be required for good learning were rarely observable in Confucian-heritage schools. Learners from Confucian-heritage countries consistently scored towards the top in International Association for the Evaluation of Educational Achievement (IEA) studies (and continue to do so – see Sellar and Lingard 2013; Kember 2016; Tan 2017), even though classrooms generally had over 40 students, appeared highly authoritarian to Western observers, had formalistic teaching methods aimed at stressful low-level examinations, and were funded poorly. Nonetheless, a 2001 curriculum policy introduced some progressive elements in China (Zhu 2007). Indeed, Chan and Rao (2009, 12–22, 326–330) claimed optimistically that decentralisation, school-based development, redefinition of educational goals, and emphasis on lifelong learning in China and Hong Kong represented a paradigm shift from knowledge transmission to knowledge construction. Chan (2009) called this 'transforming pedagogy' by drawing on constructivist and problem-based learning. However, borrowings from Japan as well as the West influenced the policies, so that Tan (2015a, 199) observed,

> we should not conclude that the Chinese leaders and educators have thereby adopted foreign (especially 'Western') policies and practices wholesale. On the contrary ... what is clear is the awareness of the Chinese government to endeavour to strike a balance between borrowing Western ideas and preserving the local traditions.

Chinese history has long been well documented, notably in dynastic histories that provide rich detail about the intertwining of its philosophy, religion and education. This chapter synthesises material derived from and critiquing these sources to outline at some length the ancient Confucian educational paradigm that still pervades modern classrooms in China. China thus provides an in-depth example of a revelatory epistemology very different from that prevalent in the Anglo-American philosophical world. The shaping of pedagogy by Confucian philosophy helps explain the continuing prevalence of formalistic teaching in China today, to be seen later in the chapter in findings from 16 field studies about teaching after reform efforts began in 2001. The evidence is that classrooms continue to demonstrate a stable and widespread pattern of formalistic teaching and in-service teacher education (INSET) in primary and secondary schools. Policy is apparently not fundamentally changing classroom behaviour, which is unsurprising given the ancient history of formalistic, teacher-centred pedagogy makes unlikely the wholesale adoption in China of current Anglo-American models for progressive, student-centred classrooms.

4.1 History of Confucianism

Traditional interpretations based on China's official dynastic histories portray a continuous empire led by northern China.[1] Recent archaeological evidence suggests that other areas within modern China's boundaries were just as advanced, competing kingdoms existed, and there were long periods with lack of central control in many times since the 3rd millennium BCE. Regardless of the continuities and discontinuities among the political entities, Confucianism provided philosophical continuity linking dynasties and it remains a direct influence on Chinese education (Guo 2006, 7–8; Keay 2008, 3–7, 25–49, *passim*).

Schools and a rudimentary examination system have existed in China for over three millennia. From the 11th to the 8th century BCE, education became more sophisticated and intellectual ferment was precipitated by rival schools of thought (Cleverley 1991; Guo 2006, 128–153). Confucius (*Kong Qiu*) lived in the 6th and 5th centuries BCE. The tradition he established dominated existing philosophical schools and, eventually, subsequent ones (Needham 1956, 3–215; abridged in Ronan 1978, 78–126). Historically, Confucius the philosopher was somewhat equivalent to Socrates, but how much he contributed to the writings imputed to him is problematic: some writings derive from his students, but succeeding layers of scholarship modified and added to them over the centuries (Keay 2008, 66–71, *passim*). Confucian moral philosophy laid the basis, first, for a state religion; later it became pervasive as the religion of the ruling classes in particular; and eventually it became the cultural equivalent of the Judeo-Christian tradition in European civilisation.

China's governance early came to synthesise ethical Confucian and authoritarian Legalist principles which dated from the 4th century BCE (Needham 1956, 204–215; Ronan 1978, 187–189, 273–275; Keay 2008, 75–77, *passim*). Confucian political views were paternalistic. They concerned the orderly administration of affairs based on historical precedent. In contrast, Legalists codified laws and regulations. Confucianism won the intellectual debate, but the authoritarian Legalist approach to administrative regulation became practice in governance in the Qin state in the 3rd and 2nd centuries BCE. However, after being ignored officially for several centuries, a revitalisation of Confucian thought in the 3rd century BCE by the second great Confucian philosopher, Mencius (*Mengzi*), contributed to Confucianism becoming slowly entrenched as the ritualistic state religion during the Han dynasty from the 2nd century BCE to the 3rd century CE. As the state religion, it provided a prototype for a system of bureaucratic governance. In turn it acquired institutional substance and a veneer of orthodoxy through state endorsement. The influence on government came in considerable part from the principle of the Mandate of Heaven, which legitimised rule passing from an unjust dynasty to a new one when rebellion meant power could no longer be maintained. The Mandate reinforced the role of officials in conducting Confucian rituals to legitimise emperors, writing the dynastic histories, applying precepts that could legitimise (often retrospectively) changes of government from one dynasty to another, and giving the appearance of continuity to maintain stable governance (Dawson 1972, 20–29, *passim*; Keay 2008, 129, 216–218, *passim*).

Chinese civilisation remained largely self-contained and stable until the 19th century, but change did happen. Three main religions – Confucianism, Taoism and Buddhism – were mutually influential at a philosophical level, usually coexisted comfortably during times of peace, and were often intermixed in daily religious practice. Keay (2008, 196–209) very helpfully typified the role of Confucianism as the state religion and guiding philosophy of the ruling elites, but paying little attention to the ordinary people and despising trade. Taoism provided an alternative for the commercial and agricultural classes, and for dynastic challengers from within China. Its influence was greater in some periods (part of the 8th century CE, for example, when candidates for civil service examinations could choose to be tested on Taoist rather than Confucian texts), and reached a popular peak in the 12th century. Buddhism more typically was the religion of outside challengers. Its influence began in the 4th century CE and was particularly strong from the 7th to 9th centuries, and again in the 13th century when the Mongol invader Kublai Khan established the Yuan dynasty.

Like Taoism and Buddhism, Confucianism waxed, waned and changed. During the 12th and 13th centuries CE, a renaissance by the school known as Neo-Confucianism attempted to invigorate the moral authority of Confucian thought, although it too came to be regarded as tyrannical. A reform of the civil service examination system was short-lived, but a longer lasting national school system was established with the intention that students would have to attend before further classical education in senior institutions prepared candidates for civil service selection. From the end of the Buddhist-influenced Yuan dynasty in the 14th century, Neo-Confucianism was the dominant ideology through the Han Ming and Manchu Qing dynasties until the end of the Imperial period at the beginning of the 20th century (Keay 2008, 346–350).

4.2 Chinese epistemology

Early revelatory concerns central to Confucian epistemology focussed on the customary transmission of ancient wisdoms about social relations and the moral authority of good leaders. Confucianism taught that there was moral order to the universe in the sense that there was an ideal way to order human society, and thus has a teleological basis as a belief in design in nature. Modern interpretations impute various materialist and idealist standpoints to different Confucians over the millennia (e.g. Guo 2006, 98–99, *passim*), but Confucius himself treated nature as a given and emphasised a social sense of justice as part of the moral order revealed in the writings, rites, poetry and song of an idealised golden age about five centuries previously (Needham 1956, 3–32; Guo 2006, 38–46). Chinese philosophy's dominant concerns with social and ethical principles contrast with central concerns in Western philosophy with the metaphysical, rational thought as a distinguishing characteristic of humans, and the scientific study of nature.

Confucian contributions to science were almost entirely negative even though it was headed by scholars and officials rather than priests, according to Joseph Needham (1956, 1), the major source of Western knowledge about the history of Chinese science (Winchester 2008). Instead, proto-scientific thinking developed from four other schools of philosophy with naturalistic worldviews, although none of these came to dominate the intertwined systems of governance and elite education in the same way as Confucianism (Needham 1956, 33–203; Wilkinson 1997; Guo 2006, 132–141). Chief among the other schools in the long term was Taoism, which laid the basis for pragmatic Chinese invention. Its beginnings were ascribed traditionally to a slightly older contemporary of Confucius, Lao Tzu (*Lao Zi*), but modern scholarship considers that Taoist philosophy (like Confucianism) was probably an anthology of thought from later centuries. Taoism incorporated magic and science, which were then indistinguishable, developing into a popular religion by the time that Confucianism become the state religion in the 2nd century CE. Additionally, the Mohist School in the 4th century BCE had a particular interest in mechanics and physics for defensive military purposes. This interest reached a threshold for scientific reasoning, with an understanding of conceptual models, induction and deduction, but did not develop into a theory of science. A third school, the Naturalists, gave rise to the earliest Chinese scientific theories in the 4th and 3rd centuries BCE. Naturalists developed schemes for classifying the basic properties of material things into five elements (water, fire, wood, metal and earth) and two fundamental forces (*Yin* and *Yang*), which were codified symbolically through the *Book of Changes* (*I Ching*) (Needham 1956, 216–345; Cleary 2005, 3–35). These schemas represented a view of nature as an organic, patterned and harmonious whole. The Logicians, a fourth school differentiated in the 1st century CE, had similarities with Mohists. They were also concerned with logic, particularly the use of paradoxes to analyse change in nature. Both schools were lost over time, but some of their proto-scientific thought became incorporated into Taoism.

Taoism came to include three relevant differences from Confucianism (Needham 1956, 55–56; Ronan 1978, 93). First, it sought both inorganic and biological knowledge about order in nature through observation and naturalistic practical experimentation in an empirical and atheoretical fashion. Second was a denial of the teleological acceptance of design in nature held in Confucianism. Third, Taoism admitted a pragmatic interest in change. It never developed a systematic natural philosophy, but Taoists were very adept at developing practical technology. Later influential philosophies, such as Buddhism, also admitted elements of scientific thinking, but none led to scientific epistemology in the Western sense of developing theories from which to deduce hypotheses to be tested under controlled conditions. For indeterminate reasons, the type of formal scientific epistemology that eventually developed in Europe in the 17th century did not develop in China (Winchester 2008, 259–261). Both Confucian and Taoist epistemology have remained revelatory in that they rely predominantly on textual authority that traces back to Confucius and Lao Tzu.

4.3 Confucianism as an educational paradigm

Confucianism did not lead to scientific epistemology, but its moral philosophy did give rise to a pedagogical paradigm based on formalistic teaching of truths revealed in classical texts. Confucius held in principle that the capacity to govern had no necessary connection to birth, wealth or position. This capacity, he taught, depended solely on character and knowledge, which depended on education. In principle, every man (schooling was not relevant to women) was capable of being educated. Needham (1956, 6) viewed Confucius as greatest as an educator,

> the first who pointed out that in teaching there should be no class-distinctions. No qualifications of birth were necessary in acceptance for the ... training that Confucius gave. In this we see one of the germs of the bureaucratic system, according to which whoever was teachable and ambitious for letters could become a scholar and serve his prince.

After Confucianism became the state religion in the Han period, memorisation of its classical texts was regarded as providing the ideal educational curriculum. The key *Book of Rites* was compiled during the 2nd and 1st centuries BCE from the writings of Confucian scholars (Tan 2015a, 2015b). It laid down a system with first-level village and district schooling and second-level education for nine years in universities in the capitals. The texts became the basis for an examination system, which, though not designed to select scientists or even to encourage an interest in science, nevertheless selected educated people for positions of power; something that was not even contemplated under feudalism in Europe (Needham 2004, 227). Selection of career officials by examination was revolutionary as a vehicle for opening up government appointments based on ability, however, in practice examination access became limited to ruling class families with the leisure and resources for a classical education for their sons. 'The examination system thus came to perpetuate the interests of the ruling classes. The great respect for learning . . . together with the idea of choosing officials steeped in Confucian literature, survived as fundamental characteristics of Chinese civilization' (Dawson 1972, 22). In the 7th century CE, Confucianism was also embedded in local government with Confucian teaching temples established in all provinces and counties. In the temples, stone tablets (steles) displayed imperial decrees for study and for dissemination through stone rubbings. Together with a script that has been standardised for some 3,000 years and the development of printing before the end of the first millennium CE, steles made Confucian precepts accessible over the centuries.

During the 12th and 13th centuries CE, Confucian writings were pared down to the *Four Books* by *Zhu Xi*, the key figure in the development of Neo-Confucianism. Memorisation of the books became required for the examination system and the mark of an educated man. In the second half of the 14th century, the first Ming emperor further extended the coverage of Confucian schools to every county, sub-prefecture and prefecture to augment temples and private schools. The associated examination system had a systematic comprehensiveness unknown in Europe until the mass education systems early in the 19th century. The ritualistic and highly competitive system was the only path to official employment. It imbued the ruling elite with Confucian doctrine and success could result in progressively higher trappings of office and wealth. In addition, a network of small private Taoist-influenced popular schools taught literacy to traders and artisans (Dawson 1972, 142–146, 204–205; Cleverley 1991; Bol 1997; Keay 2008, 346–350, 395–396). These schools were subject to less state control and were much under-resourced compared with the elite's Confucian schools. Taoist education was more practical than Confucian, although teaching methods were similar. The values of filial propriety were taught along with some 2,000 characters a year and calligraphy, but arithmetic and practical skills were usually taught outside school. The outcome was two distinct types of formalistic schooling. One taught Confucian-based high culture to the sons of the governing elite. The other provided schooling for artisans and traders that was closer to Taoist concerns with nature and the practical.

4.4 Confucian pedagogy

Three key elements underpinned the long dominance of Confucian philosophy as a revelatory educational paradigm. One was respect for traditional moral authority, another was the emphasis on memorising the revealed truths in the ancient lore documented by Confucius, and a third was its pivotal role in social advancement through the examination system. Confucianism has always taught that a moral code linked individual and state as part of a harmonious whole. An educated man investigated the complex relationships that ordered social life rather than investigated empirically or was curious about other areas of knowledge. Content about human relations also reinforced respect for the teacher as the fount of traditional wisdom.

Confucian teaching methods evolved over time (Gu 2001, 34–38, 48–75, 189–194). Confucius's own school used active non-formal educational methods in which the teacher set the example in developing moral and intellectual qualities among gentlemen scholars. Some confusion in the educational literature exists about the age groups to which Confucius applied this method, but the dominant impression is that it applied to older students in higher education and not at the lower levels of schooling: in today's terms, to university level and adult learning in the higher cognitive and affective domains rather than to primary and secondary school study.

The development of Confucian thought on teaching by Mencius during the 3rd century BCE stressed the teacher's role as identifying the most talented individuals to teach and nourish them. The teacher's formalistic job was to present ethical precepts rather than to advocate critical thinking, but question and answer methods encouraged students to persist, in part through reflection on the texts (Guo 2006, 94–109). Within a few centuries, formalistic schooling became the Confucian norm. Following the *Book of Rites* in the 1st century BCE, schooling was closely structured, with formalistic observance of rituals, lectures and memorisation of texts for examinations. One volume, *Record of Learning*, systematically elucidated elements of teaching and learning, especially for higher education of government officials. It guided teachers to use open-ended questions to elicit students' thinking, elaborate teachers' answers, drill students, and use analogies. Teachers were required to undergo strict training and were given absolute authority to generate respect for doctrines (Guo 2006, 153–168). However, Tan (2015b, 304) emphasised, this classroom approach to questioning does not fit the description of learner-centred education as commonly understood in the Western literature. Rather, the *Record of Learning* (*Xueji*)

> advocated a 'teacher-directed and learner-engaged' approach by giving the teacher control over the curriculum and authority over the learners. At the same time, the learners are encouraged to participate actively in the learning process so as to obtain deep understanding and moral self-cultivation. In proposing a conception that is not exactly learner-centred, the *Xueji* challenges the assumption that 'good' education must necessarily be learner-centred.

Compared to Anglo-American notions of learner-centred education, students had a low level of choice over the content of learning and little power, but were intended to be thoughtfully engaged with lessons to obtain deep understanding and moral self-cultivation.

Confucian obligations were initially taught informally within the family, for which the Neo-Confucian, Zhu Xi, later produced a handbook on family rituals (Keay 2008, 349–350). Its precepts set the basis for upbringing in the ruling classes, starting with rules for pregnant women on how to nurture the unborn. Young children were to be taught hygiene, courtesy and correct ways of reading and writing through imitation and persistence until learned behaviours became habit. A detailed textbook for children prescribed nine years of formalistic primary schooling until the age of 15. Social relationships revolved around the patriarchal family, where an expectation that extended families related by descent and marriage would share wealth and good fortune was conducive to nepotism. Beyond the family, society's aim was for harmony and unity through educational prescription, ruled over by emperors who were expected to maintain ethical principles and good management. The five key human relationships were those of ruler and minister, father and son, husband and wife, older and younger brother, and friend to friend. The relationships were notionally reciprocal, but depended in practice on the junior partner's deference and devotion. Within families, the old had more rights that the young, males more than females, and the head of the household more than other members. Children were bound by filial piety requiring absolute obedience and complete devotion to parents and, by extension, to teachers, whom students were taught to revere (Cleverley 1991, 1–14).

Once in school, the examination system was intended to direct boys to learn rational principles from the works of the sages. The system produced more graduates than the civil service required, but conferred considerable prestige even on lower-level degree holders who were unplaced in the civil service and for whom teaching became an option (Cleverley 1991, 15–19, 25; Guo 2006, 287–309). Teachers were required to have well-planned formalistic programmes following set standards using uniform syllabuses set by bodies of literary superintendents and chancellors, and controlled by an inspection system. The teachers' first task was to teach characters through imitation and repetition. At 8, a boy began tutoring to rote learn the *Four Books* and the *Five Classics* and by 15 was apparently expected to have memorised over 400,000 characters of text (at 2–3 English words per character, perhaps equivalent to some 10 books the size of this one). Once the texts were learned, students were taught the longer commentaries on them and began work on specimen examination answers: they should read articles until they were memorised, respect the explanations of the ancient masters, practise the message in their own life, read with concentration, and persist. They were forbidden to ask questions lest they transgressed their rank, and a sharp slap from the teacher's ruler was possible for inattention. Many similarities continue in the modern period.

4.5 Modern educational developments

China's 'modern' history from the opening up forced by the first Opium War in the early 1840s has three distinct educational periods. The first spanned about 120 years including the end of the Qing dynasty in 1911, through the Republic that followed, to the early Communist years in the 1950s and 1960s. Both Confucian and Taoist ideas coexisted and there was little apparent change to formalistic teaching (Guo 2006, 384–577). A major event was the abolition of the Imperial examinations in 1905, which contributed to the main outcome from this period, the widening of educational opportunity. Content also widened, while Chinese intellectuals adopted some elements of progressive Western educational philosophy. They criticised rigid teaching of the classics and grappled with bringing together broader Western academic and technical knowledge with Taoist-influenced practical learning. Mission education of girls was a distinct change, and the opening up of education to girls became a major accomplishment in the post-Liberation period after 1949 as part of a push towards universal education under Communism (Keay 2008, 481, 519). The early years of the Communist dynasty prior to the Cultural Revolution also saw modelling of the education system on the Soviet Russian approach, which had strong formalistic traditions influenced by German thought (Gu 2001, 184–186; Hayhoe 2001).

The second period was the Cultural Revolution, seemingly the most thoroughgoing educational revolution of all. Mao Zedong's early educational writings were progressive, emphasising that student learning should focus actively on moral, intellectual and physical development and that students should not be overburdened with rote learning and examinations. In 1929, he laid out ten teaching methods, which should be heuristic, use lively language, and encourage students to learn in a lively and active way, and he was increasingly against examinations (Gu 2001, 94–95). By the start of the Cultural Revolution in 1964, Mao's views were radical rather than progressive. He emphasised class struggle, integration of education and manual labour and of theory and practice. Carried to a 'destructive extreme' (Hayhoe 2001, 11), the Cultural Revolution left a generation undereducated. From 1966 to 1976, very restricted school programmes mainly required political education. Millions of young people were sent to the countryside for non-formal education aimed at breaking feudal tradition and political opposition. Universities were closed until 1977, when worker, peasant and soldier students were admitted. While initially studied internationally and often naively for its educational philosophy, the Cultural Revolution is now seen primarily as a disastrous political strategy within which educational philosophy was used by Mao as a weapon against his political enemies (Chang and Halliday 2005, 534–569; Keay 2008, 519–522). The significance of the Cultural Revolution for this book is that it included a comprehensive, highly radical and very unsuccessful revolutionary attempt to overthrow an educational philosophy that embodied classroom formalism. The failure saw reversion to traditional formal teaching.

With the death of Mao, the third period since 1978 has seen modernisation of the Chinese economy, the development of trade, and China's growth as an international 'partial power', including with soft power projection through its Confucius Institutes (Shambaugh 2013; Lo and Pan 2016). Considerable expansion and structural reform of education occurred (Hayhoe 2001; Rao, Chi, and Cheng 2009; Tan and Chua 2015). A major expansion of the very large and increasingly well-funded formal education system has been notable for providing nine years of compulsory schooling, as well as nationwide curriculum reforms in 2001. Even so, from the late 1980s Confucian influence was central to concern for moral and ethical education in a 'back to tradition' movement. The movement began at the grass roots implicitly teaching traditional Confucian-based virtues, spread to 3,000 schools and one million students within four years, gained governmental support in 1994 in the name of 'Chinese traditional virtues', and was still strong over ten years later (Yu 2008). The moral aspects emphasised following truth and respecting ethics, the cultivation of sound personal character, benevolence towards others and trustworthiness (Guo 2006, 578–590). These traditional virtues were a reaction against commercialisation and modernisation that could lead to 'insatiable' and 'avaricious' ways. Interest like this in Confucian education is consistent with official attempts to help develop greater respect for laws and to combat corruption through the traditional Confucian emphasis on moral qualities as well as intellectual ones. Today, China is largely a secular country. Confucian philosophy is studied, but practitioners of Confucianism as a religion are uncommon. However, like Judeo-Christian values in Western culture, Confucian-heritage values permeate the constructs even of non-believers.

4.6 Recent perspectives on schooling in China

One of the major influences on study of Chinese schooling during the most recent of the three periods has been the educational psychologist, John Biggs, who used systems theory as a conceptual framework. The systems theory perspective meant that classroom teaching should be understood in terms of its own system, not an exotic one (thus with a similar regard for the importance of context as comparative educationalists influenced by anthropology and sociology). Biggs (1996) put his Paradox of the Chinese Learner in the Dunkin and Biddle (1974) framework of student presage, teaching presage, process and product factors operating in interaction in a system tending towards equilibrium. He observed that Western progressive confusion over Confucian formalistic pedagogy came from too narrow a focus on the components of classroom learning and not understanding that high-quality outcomes could emerge from poor conditions. Several researchers have investigated Confucian-heritage learning from this perspective, notably in papers in two volumes edited by Watkins and Biggs (1996, 2001) and revisited in Chan and Rao (2009, overviewed at 3–32).

Ginsberg, Nackerud, and Larrison (2004, 99) reported that the Confucian influence emphasises benevolence and doing what is right, so that the intelligent person spends much effort in learning, enjoys learning and persists in lifelong learning with enthusiasm, while the Taoist tradition emphasises the importance of humility, freedom from conventional standards of judgement, and full knowledge of oneself and external conditions. The underlying conceptions of intelligence include nonverbal reasoning ability, verbal reasoning ability and (notably, given the derogatory view of it often held in progressivism) rote memorisation. Memorisation, however, means more than mere rote learning without thought to meaning. It is not as an end in itself, but is a basic repetitive building block to ensure accurate recall as a basis for ongoing, deeper understanding (Lee 1996; Biggs 1996, 54; Kember 2016; Kwok, Kato, and Hung 2016 and other papers in Issue 48 (1) of *Educational Philosophy and Theory*). As noted, Tan (2015b) has explored Confucian influences in generating a 'teacher-directed and learner-engaged' approach by giving the teacher control over curriculum and authority over learners, who are encouraged to think actively to obtain deep understanding and moral self-cultivation.

The way in which the Confucian influence has permeated everyday life is seen in the concept of 'vernacular Confucianism', the common beliefs about the nature of teaching and learning that are held by Chinese teachers, parents and students (Chang 2000). Vernacular Confucianism as a form of intergenerational culture includes beliefs that praise spoils children, scolding builds character, failure results from laziness rather than lack of ability, and learning requires painful effort. Chang asked for ethnographic research into these beliefs: the available research since coming mainly from Hong Kong, where the examination system reflects both historical tradition and the highly competitive life chances for children. Salili (2001) found traditional Confucian traits that teachers valued in their students included honesty, self-discipline, respectfulness to parents, responsibility, diligence, humbleness and obedience. Teachers' classroom behaviour reflected traditional child-rearing beliefs about praise and punishment. They should appear stern, especially with new classes; they seldom praised and provided only limited feedback. 'Cultural values are also reflected in educational policies such as the length of the schooling, the type of role models the textbooks promote, as well as the manner in which students and teachers interact' (79). Additionally, respect and obedience to superiors, including teachers, was expected, such that questioning a teacher could be considered disrespectful. Ability was perceived as achievable and dependent on effort through memorisation and repetition. Many of these vernacular Confucian beliefs would not be recognised by Confucius or endorsed by him as Confucian (Watkins and Biggs 2001, 4–5 ff.). Nor is the formalistic teaching style incorporating vernacular beliefs apparently consistent with Confucius's own approach to higher education; rather it is more consistent with Mencian and Neo-Confucian approaches to lower-level schooling.

4.7 Curriculum reforms since 2001

In mainland China, the state promulgates syllabuses, textbooks and teacher training requirements, so that the school system has much in common across the whole country. Top-down nationwide curriculum reforms introduced in 2001 included a more student-focussed policy for teaching and learning (Zhu 2007). Given centralised control and very effective institutionalised procedures for teacher development, the policies were disseminated quickly. Twenty-two new primary and 16 senior middle school subject syllabuses focussed on student competencies with practical applications and attempted to move away from domination by examinations. Policy moved away from single national subject textbooks, and emphasised discovery and cooperative learning to lay a foundation for lifelong learning. What have classroom studies shown about the impact of the reforms?[2]

The curriculum approach encouraged more active student involvement in lessons, however studies have predominantly shown that this aspect of the policy has not been implemented in classroom practice much beyond apparently increased attention to closed questioning to check student engagement in lessons. Here, a critical distinction between formalistic and progressive teaching styles comes from types of classroom questions: 'The formalist will use closed questions to check student recall, whereas the progressive teacher will tend to ask open questions designed to promote student understanding' (Guthrie 2011, 206–207). For example, Ma, Zhao, and Tuo (2004) compared mathematics teaching in two urban and two rural primary schools in Jilin Province for over one month in each. Observation and interviews showed that teachers structured their formalistic lessons consistently. In 40-minute lessons, teachers on average spent about 15 minutes questioning students from the front of the class, but commonly used closed question/answer format for checking understanding. Students seldom initiated questions.

A further ethnographic report by Ma, Lam, and Wong (2006) found similarly that mathematics teachers in two primary schools in Jilin closely followed the new primary mathematics syllabus, but they had not taken effective steps to adapt it to students' individual differences, particularly because of the examination culture. Another study of mathematics teaching by Rao, Chi, and Cheng (2009) was of grades 3 and 5 in six urban, semi-rural and rural schools in Zhejiang Province. Despite average class sizes of 48, videotape showed well-disciplined children who were very engaged in the learning process. Teachers did not have to manage disruptive behaviour, children were seldom criticised and the classroom atmosphere was very pleasant. Formalistic lesson structures were very similar across all schools and both grades, with whole-class teaching used for the majority of lesson time. Teachers typically introduced a new topic, then generally questioned students about it, assigned class work, and finally summarised the lesson. Consistent with the new curriculum, questioning was used to ensure student attention, but the teachers generally used short closed questions and students never asked questions. Lower student achievement occurred in rural schools, but teaching styles were similar. Fan et al. (2004) contains several other studies of formalistic mathematics classrooms.

Martin (2006) examined the development and implementation of the new geography curriculum in secondary schools in Shanghai. Analysis of the processes and mechanisms which underlie curricular change in China revealed embedded bureaucratic, social and cultural norms that profoundly influenced the degree to which the geography curriculum reforms achieved the desired results. Interviews with teachers, extensive classroom observations, and a review of the new curriculum and geography textbooks revealed deep differences between the stated goals of curricular reform, the processes of curriculum development and implementation, and an examination system that compelled teachers to maintain traditional teaching methods using lecturing and rote learning. Wang (2011) found similar outcomes from his ethnographic study of a rural elementary school in southwest China. Teachers' pedagogical choices were heavily constrained by both the centralised curriculum and schedule and the social context of rural-urban disparities. Together these constraints created a dilemma of time allocation that significantly limited the room for teachers to experiment with student-centred methods.

Halstead and Zhu (2010) usefully distinguished between the 'personal autonomy' of the individual as a self-actualised decision maker as a central goal of Western progressive education and the emphasis in China's educational reforms on a more limited 'learner autonomy', with individuals taking more responsibility for their own learning (balanced by a recognition of interdependence and collectivism). The research included observation of 12 lessons in a senior high school English class in Beijing and semi-structured interviews with the teacher and 10 randomly selected students. Even limited learner autonomy was hardly a reality in the classroom. The teacher and students reflected curriculum policy in expressing a desire for student autonomy and management of class activities for which the students had responsibility, however implementation was very limited. The teacher's hands were tied by her own tendency to dominate the learning process (in accordance with traditional expectations) and by examination requirements.

In a recent study, Tan (2016a) found similar themes. Her study was based on 119 questionnaires and 47 interviews with primary and secondary teachers, principals and vice principals between 2013 and 2015, all of whom had at least seven years working with the New Curriculum Reform (NCR). Tan found that examination demands conflicted with school-based curriculum development, de-emphasis on teacher-centred pedagogy had led to a perceived lowering of standards, and stakeholders still preferred quantitative assessments to qualitative ones. The effect, Tan (2016a, 203) stated, was that the

> tensions and challenges . . . reflect the interaction between, and a clash of, ideologies: a quality-oriented educational worldview propagated by the NCR (with an emphasis on all-rounded development, student-centred pedagogy and formative assessment) versus an examination-oriented educational worldview subscribed to by the Chinese educational stakeholders (with an emphasis on academic development, teacher-centred pedagogy and summative assessment).

Similarly, Peng et al. (2014) found from interview and focus group data in three senior high schools that pressures from changing societal patterns and the demands of the far-reaching curriculum reforms highlighted tensions between a traditional reliance on examination results and a newer demand for all round development and lifelong learning.

Apparently more positive evidence in support of the curriculum reforms came from a 2004 Gansu study reported by Sargent (2009). Questionnaires from 961 children in 137 rural schools showed perceptions that reform teachers lectured less, praised more, and placed greater emphasis on the development of students' self-expression and thinking abilities than teachers using traditional methods. Additionally, a mixed method survey in 15 rural primary schools used qualitative classroom observation in 10 mathematics and 20 Chinese lessons, and interviews with the teachers. In schools that had not begun implementation, teachers stated that they did not know much about the reforms. Where implementation had begun with new materials and INSET, interview data suggested that the reforms figured heavily in lesson planning and pedagogy, with a greater stated emphasis on student self-expression, greater valuing of student contributions and opportunity for students to contribute. Classroom observation found that the environment in classrooms following the new curriculum was more relaxed, with more praise and encouragement by the teachers. The evidence was claimed to suggest that the reforms were generating methods that were more progressive. However, the claim that more open-ended questions were in use was not supported by quantitative data and some important qualifications are needed about the methodology, especially the use of questionnaires and interviews as proxies for classroom behaviour (Section 3.3). Classroom observation in each school did take place, but on one day only and based on high inference judgements by the researcher rather than structured observation schedules or long-term ethnography. Additionally, study classes were chosen non-randomly by head teachers who, being subject to conformist Chinese political culture, seem unlikely to have selected classes unsuccessfully implementing the reforms.

4.8 Communities of professional learning

Classroom findings in China are framed by an institutionalised group culture in which formalistic teaching is usually a highly developed professional form. Cortazzi and Jin (2001) reported that the school system provided incentives for teachers to learn from each other, act as mentors and model practices within a school-teacher culture of collective support, an approach consistent with international use of the label 'communities of learning'. A case study by Tsui and Wong (2009) reported that use of schools as the prime site for teacher development derived from the Soviet model adopted in the 1950s. Formal qualifications in teacher education from normal universities were a start; after graduation much INSET happened daily within schools. Standard approaches included 'lesson research' (including collective lesson preparation, lesson observation and post-observation conferencing), demonstration lessons and one-on-one mentoring. The case study used interviews with participants in a Shanghai INSET programme that was recognised as an outstanding success and modelled elsewhere in China. In a number of schools, teacher professional development was organised systematically, including subject groups working on collective lesson preparation. The approach used an apprenticeship model that initially gave light loads to inexperienced teachers. They were assigned mentors whom they observed and who provided feedback from classroom observation of subject knowledge and instructional strategies. Collective lesson preparation was used to develop 'virtuoso lessons' (Paine 1990) that were carefully planned, critiqued, refined into a standard piece, rehearsed and repeated perhaps for decades with standard material. Teaching demonstrations (also held at district, province and national levels) were open to critique from large audiences. The programme leader was guided by Confucian thinking on the integration of teaching, learning and doing, which provided a framework within which any Western influences were applied (Tsui and Wong 2009, 290–304).

Mok (2006) conduced a case study of 15 videotaped lessons from a Shanghai mathematics classroom influenced by this INSET programme. The teacher was formalistic. Sixty-seven percent of lesson time was whole-class instruction, 22% was individual work, and 11% was small group or pair work. Whole-class instruction included frequent questions to the students, although very few student-initiated questions, but there was some variation within lessons. The students were consistently attentive, valued memorisation, and actively reflected on the lessons. Based on this, Mok argued the somewhat convoluted notion that a teacher-dominated lesson may actually be interpreted as an alternative form of student-centredness. Perhaps it is more straightforward to suggest that one implication of this type of INSET is that formalistic teachers' objective behaviour may not be very student-centred in the classroom, but their subjective thought may nonetheless consider student learning needs during lesson planning. While not all reports on teacher morale are positive (e.g. Wang, D. 2013), others have also found effective professional learning communities in schools in different parts of China (Wong 2010; Sargent 2015; Wang, T. 2015).

Otherwise, many areas remain for further classroom research. The studies reported in the international English-language literature are quite limited in volume and scope. Much scope exists for review of Chinese-language classroom research and to broaden the subject and geographical range of research, although many papers published in China advocate safely for the curriculum reforms but do not present research on classroom impacts (see www.en.cnki.com.cn). The findings about classroom questioning are consistent thus far, but they reflect limited samples and non-random access to classrooms. Findings predominantly come from mathematics classes and from urban and coastal areas, and further observational research may indicate wider variation in practice than is apparent so far. Too, 'what remains relatively under-explored is the epistemological basis for cultural views on teaching that mediate policy transfer' (Tan 2015a, 196; see also Tan 2016b).

A further caution is that much research into Confucian-heritage education derives from studies in Hong Kong and Singapore, not mainland China. Within Hong Kong classrooms, progressive influences have often come from Western-educated teachers and educators (Salili 2001, 78). Perhaps this explains some cognitive dissonance from the contradiction between the Confucian heritage emphasising the importance of learning revealed truths and Western scientific epistemologies emphasising the importance of individual discovery. The Chinese educationalist Gu Mingyuan (2001, 105–110; see also Wu 2009) argued sensibly that China, as a country with strong educational traditions, must aim both to preserve cultural identity and to modernise. For Gu, modernisation did not mean westernisation as such. Rather, indigenous cultural traditions must change and develop, and the assimilation of foreign cultural elements should be based on considered choices, which, indeed, is what Tan (2016a) found to be occurring in practice. The effect is that working to improve traditional formalistic teaching is a more constructive path than working against it by attempting (and apparently failing) to introduce progressive teaching practices derived in part from an Anglo-American culture that differs so much from the Confucian heritage.

4.9 Conclusion

Confucian culture generated an educational paradigm that persists in modern times and differs markedly from progressive Anglo-American constructs. Teaching styles 2,000 years later still resonate with the formalism of the Mencian *Book of Rites* and, especially, with the later Neo-Confucian approach to first-level schooling. An apparently stable and widespread approach to classroom teaching and teacher development exists in mainland China. Since 2001, policy has been for teachers to pay more attention to student learning. Given centralised control, the policies were disseminated quickly; however, the overall effect of classroom research is to find that the heritage of formalistic Confucian pedagogy continues to dominate. The observation studies summarised here found predominantly that teachers directed more closed rather than open questions to students during the conventional whole-class lessons. Such questions appear to be a device to check student attention and recall with a view to them thinking actively about the lessons (and in the long term to provide a foundation for greater understanding of the given knowledge) rather than to encourage their own constructions of knowledge. Thus, classroom practice does not demonstrate large-scale adoption of constructivist techniques. The evidence is that the effect of progressive policy elements has actually been to upgrade the level of formalism rather than to adopt a progressive teaching style. As Tan (2016b, 90) has similarly concluded, Chinese formalism is symptomatic of age-old cultural preferences:

> A salient feature of the current education reform in China is the promotion of student-centered learning. . . . Such a move reflects an international trend that links student-centered learning to twenty-first century competencies in an era of globalization. . . . Despite concerted efforts by the Chinese authority to change the dominant pedagogy from teacher-centeredness to student-centeredness, research shows that the former, far

from being jettisoned, continues to be valued by Chinese educators and featured prominently in Chinese classrooms. . . . A researcher whose prior cultural worldview and theoretical presuppositions are critical of didacticism (e.g. equates it with rote-memorization and indoctrination) may view the dominant teacher-centred approach in China as outdated and inferior. Such a judgment echoes the ideologically biased assumptions held by some Western historians about why a phenomenon (in this case, pedagogical reform in China) does or does not go as it should.

In such a context, formalism is not an intermediary step on the path to progressive classroom teaching, but is likely to remain central to the school system because it is compatible with traditional and ongoing cultural practices. In China, it leads to high academic outcomes and need not be a problematic obstruction to modernisation. Formalistic teaching there does not have to be regarded as a classroom problem, but is a deep-rooted cultural behaviour capable of improvement and of continuing to play an important role long into China's future. Fifteen years of mild policy change do not seem to carry the potential or demonstrate a need to alter dramatically well over 2,000 years of formalistic Confucian tradition.

Notes

1 Sections 4.1–4.5 derive from Guthrie (2011, 174–183, https://doi.org/10.1007/978-94-007-1851-7_9, © Springer Science+Business Media B.V. 2011) with permission of Springer Nature.
2 Material in Sections 4.7–4.8 on recent classroom reforms in China derives in part from Guthrie (2012), an article in *Comparative Education Bulletin*, now *International Journal of Comparative Education and Development* published by Emerald UK, available online: www.fe.hku.hk/cerc/ceshk/doc/CEB2011_13.pdf.

References

Biggs, J. 1996. "Western Misperceptions of the Confucian-heritage Learning Culture." In *The Chinese Learner: Cultural, Psychological and Contextual Influences*, edited by D. Watkins and J. Biggs, 45–67. Hong Kong: Comparative Education Research Centre, University of Hong Kong.
Bol, K. 1997. "Examinations and Orthodoxies: 1070 and 1313 Compared." In *Culture and State in Chinese History: Conventions, Accommodations, and Critiques*, edited by T. Huters, B. Wong, and P. Yu, 29–57. Stanford: Stanford University Press.
Chan, C. 2009. "Classroom Innovation for the Chinese Learner: Transcending Dichotomies and Transforming Pedagogy." In *Revisiting the Chinese Learner: Changing Contexts, Changing Education*, edited by C. Chan and N. Rao, 169–210. Hong Kong: Comparative Education Research Centre, University of Hong Kong.
Chan, C., and Rao, N. (Eds.). 2009. *Revisiting the Chinese Learner: Changing Contexts, Changing Education*. Hong Kong: Comparative Education Research Centre, University of Hong Kong.
Chang, J., and Halliday, J. 2005. *Mao: The Unknown Story*. London: Cape.

Chang, W. 2000. "In Search of the Chinese in All the Wrong Places!" *Journal of Psychology in Chinese Societies* 1 (1): 125–142.
Cleary, T. (Trans.). 2005. *The Taoist I Ching*. Boston: Shambhala.
Cleverley, J. 1991. *The Schooling of China: Tradition and Modernity in Chinese Education* (2nd ed.). Sydney: Allen & Unwin.
Cortazzi, M., and Jin, L. 2001. "Large Classes in China: 'Good' Teachers and Interaction." In *Teaching the Chinese Learner: Psychological and Pedagogical Perspectives*, edited by D. Watkins and J. Biggs, 115–134. Hong Kong: Comparative Education Research Centre, University of Hong Kong.
Dawson, R. 1972. *Imperial China*. London: Hutchinson.
Dunkin, M., and Biddle, B. 1974. *The Study of Teaching*. New York: Holt Rinehart & Winston.
Fan, L., Wong, J., Cai, J., and Li, S. (Eds.). 2004. *How Chinese Learn Mathematics: Perspectives from Insiders*. Singapore: World Scientific.
Ginsberg, L., Nackerud, L., and Larrison, C. 2004. *Human Biology for Social Workers: Development, Ecology, Genetics, and Health*. Boston: Pearson.
Gu, M. 2001. *Education in China and Abroad: Perspectives from a Lifetime in Comparative Education*. Hong Kong: Comparative Education Research Centre, University of Hong Kong.
Guo, Q. 2006. *A History of Chinese Educational Thought*. Beijing: Foreign Languages Press.
Guthrie, G. 2011. *The Progressive Education Fallacy in Developing Countries: In Favour of Formalism*. New York: Springer.
Guthrie, G. 2012. "Progressive School Teaching in China?" *International Journal of Comparative Education and Development* 14: 98–111.
Halstead, J., and Zhu, C. 2010. "Autonomy as an Element in Chinese Educational Reform: English Lessons in a Senior High School in Beijing." *Asia-Pacific Journal of Education* 29 (4): 443–446.
Hayhoe, R. 2001. "Introduction." In *Education in China and Abroad: Perspectives from a Lifetime in Comparative Education*, edited by M. Gu, 5–23. Hong Kong: Comparative Education Research Centre, University of Hong Kong.
Keay, J. 2008. *China: A History*. London: Harper.
Kember, D. 2016. "Why Do Chinese Students Out-perform Those from the West? Do Approaches to Learning Contribute to the Explanation?" *Cogent Education* 3. https://doi.org/10.1080/2331186X.2016.1248187
Kwok, D-J., Kato, M., and Hung, R. 2016. "The Confucian Concept of Learning Revisited for East Asian Humanistic Pedagogies." *Educational Philosophy and Theory* 48 (1): 1–6.
Lee, W. 1996. "The Cultural Context for Chinese Learners: Conceptions of Learning in the Confucian Tradition." In *The Chinese Learner: Cultural, Psychological and Contextual Influences*, edited by D. Watkins and J. Biggs, 25–41. Hong Kong: Comparative Education Research Centre, University of Hong Kong.
Lo, J., and Pan, S. 2016. "Confucius Institutes and China's Soft Power: Practices and Paradoxes." *Compare* 46 (94): 512–532.
Ma, Y., Lam, C., and Wong, N. 2006. "Chinese Primary School Mathematics Teachers Working in a Centralised Curriculum System: A Case Study of Two Primary Schools in North-east China." *Compare* 36 (2): 197–212.
Ma, Y., Zhao, D., and Tuo, Z. 2004. "Differences Within Communities: How Is Mathematics Taught in Rural and Urban Regions in Mainland China?" In *How Chinese Learn Mathematics: Perspectives from Insiders*, edited by L. Fan, J. Wong, J. Cai, and S. Li, 413–441. Singapore: World Scientific.

Martin, A. 2006. "The Cultural Politics of Curricular Reform in China: A Case Study of Geographical Education in Shanghai." *Journal of Contemporary China* 15 (47): 233–254.

Mok, I. 2006. "Shedding Light on the East Asian Learner Paradox: Reconstructing Student-Centredness in a Shanghai Classroom." *Asia-Pacific Journal of Teacher Education* 26 (2): 131–142.

Needham, J. 1956. *Science and Civilization in China, Volume 2: History of Thought*. Cambridge: Cambridge University Press.

Needham, J. 2004. *Science and Civilization in China, Volume 7 Part II: General Conclusions and Reflections*. Cambridge: Cambridge University Press.

Paine, L. 1990. "The Teacher as Virtuoso: A Chinese Model of Teaching." *Teachers College Record* 92: 49–81.

Peng, W., McNess, E., Thomas, S., Wu, X., Zhang, C., Li, J., and Tian, H. 2014. "Emerging Perceptions of Teacher Quality and Teacher Development in China." *International Journal of Educational Development* 34: 77–89.

Rao, N., Chi, J., and Cheng, K. 2009. "Teaching Mathematics: Observations from Urban and Rural Schools in China." In *Revisiting the Chinese Learner: Changing Contexts, Changing Education*, edited by C. Chan and N. Rao, 211–231. Hong Kong: Comparative Education Research Centre, University of Hong Kong.

Ronan, C. 1978. *The Shorter Science and Civilization in China: An Abridgement of Joseph Needham's Original Text, Volume 1*. Cambridge: Cambridge University Press.

Salili, F. 2001. "Teacher-student Interaction: Attributional Implications and Effectiveness of Teachers' Evaluative Feedback." In *Teaching the Chinese Learner: Psychological and Pedagogical Perspectives*, edited by D. Watkins and J. Biggs, 77–98. Hong Kong: Comparative Education Research Centre, University of Hong Kong.

Sargent, T. 2009. *Revolutionizing Ritual Interaction in the Classroom: Constructing the Chinese Renaissance of the 21st Century*. Gansu Survey of Children and Family Papers. Pittsburgh: University of Pennsylvania.

Sargent, T. 2015. "Professional Learning Communities and the Diffusion of Pedagogical Innovation in the Chinese Education System." *Comparative Education Review* 59 (1): 102–132.

Sellar, S., and Lingard, B. 2013. "Looking East: Shanghai, PISA 2009 and the Reconstitution of Reference Societies in the Global Education Policy Field." *Comparative Education* 49 (4): 464–485.

Shambaugh, D. 2013. *China Goes Global: The Partial Power*. Oxford: Oxford University Press.

Tan, C. 2015a. "Education Policy Borrowing and Cultural Scripts for Teaching in China." *Comparative Education* 51 (2): 196–211.

Tan, C. 2015b. "Teacher-Directed and Learner-Engaged: Exploring a Confucian Conception of Education." *Ethics and Education* 10 (3): 302–312.

Tan, C. 2016a. "Tensions and Challenges in China's Education Policy Borrowing." *Educational Research* 58 (2): 195–206.

Tan, C. 2016b. "Investigator Bias and Theory-Ladenness in Cross-cultural Research: Insights from Wittgenstein." *Current Issues in Comparative Education* 18 (1): 84–95.

Tan, C. 2017. "PISA and Education Reform in Shanghai." *Critical Studies in Education*. https://doi.org/10.1080/17508487.2017.1285336

Tan, C., and Chua, C. 2015. "Education Policy Borrowing in China: Has the West Wind Overpowered the East Wind?" *Compare* 45 (5): 686–704.

Tsui, A., and Wong, J. 2009. "In Search of the Third Space: Teacher Development in Mainland China." In *Revisiting the Chinese Learner: Changing Contexts, Changing Education*, edited by C. Chan and N. Rao, 281–311. Hong Kong: Comparative Education Research Centre, University of Hong Kong.

Wang, D. 2011. "The Dilemma of Time: Student-centered Teaching in the Rural Classroom in China." *Teaching and Teacher Education* 27 (1): 157–164.

Wang, D. 2013. *The Demoralization of Teachers: Crisis in a Rural School in China*. Lanham: Lexington.

Wang, T. 2015. "Contrived Collegiality Versus Genuine Collegiality: Demystifying Professional Learning Communities in Chinese Schools." *Compare* 45 (6): 908–930.

Watkins, D., and Biggs, J. (Eds.). 1996. *The Chinese Learner: Cultural, Psychological and Contextual Influences*. Hong Kong: Comparative Education Research Centre, University of Hong Kong.

Watkins, D., and Biggs, J. 2001. "The Paradox of the Chinese Learner and Beyond." In *Teaching the Chinese Learner: Psychological and Pedagogical Perspectives*, edited by D. Watkins and J. Biggs, 3–23. Hong Kong: Comparative Education Research Centre, University of Hong Kong.

Wilkinson, R. 1997. "Introduction." In *Lao Tzu, Tao Te Ching*, translated by A. Waley, vii–xix. Ware: Wadsworth.

Winchester, W. 2008. *The Man Who Loved China*. New York: Harper.

Wong, J. 2010. "Searching for Good Practice in Teaching: A Comparison of Two Subject-Based Professional Learning Communities in a Secondary School in Shanghai." *Compare* 40 (5): 623–639.

Wu, D. 2009. "Reflection on Prosperity: Localization of Pedagogy in China." *Frontiers of Education in China* 4 (3): 453–465.

Yu, T. 2008. "The Revival of Confucianism in Chinese Schools: A Historical-Political Review." *Asia-Pacific Journal of Education* 28 (2): 113–129.

Zhu, M. 2007. "Recent Chinese Experiences in Curriculum Reform." *Prospects* 37 (2): 223–235.

5 The formalistic paradigm in Africa

Unprecedented interest in reforming pedagogical practices in Sub-Saharan Africa since the 1990s has usually been characterised by efforts to change from teacher-centred to child-centred pedagogy using variously labelled progressive and constructivist teaching practices (Dembele and Lefoka 2007; Altinyelken 2010a, 2010b; Vavrus, Thomas, and Bartlett 2011). One of the contextual matters commonly underestimated in the progressive reforms has been the impact of widely differing social values on education. Alexander (2000) identified three basic value sets that are highly pervasive internationally. Individualism occurs especially in Anglo-American cultures. In contrast, collectivism particularly occurs in Confucian cultures, while communal values are widespread across Africa. The individualistic values embodied in the progressive paradigm have been a major influence on schools of thought about educational quality in Africa, but an important issue is whether progressive curriculum reforms based in individualistic values actually are appropriate in African communal contexts.

The previous chapter on the Confucian tradition detailed an effective formalistic paradigm with a cohesive underpinning of Chinese philosophy in countries encompassing 23.6% of the world's population in 2015. This chapter consolidates widespread evidence from 57 studies in 12 Sub-Saharan Anglophone countries, all members of the African Cultural Cluster. Botswana, Ghana, Kenya, Lesotho, Malawi, Namibia, Nigeria, South Africa, Tanzania, Uganda, Zambia and Zimbabwe together total another 6.2% of the world's population.[1] Compared to philosophy written down over millennia in China, traditional African education is less well documented, but research into recent progressive reforms is far more detailed. Conceivably, Anglophone countries could absorb progressive influences more readily than China, either from their time in the British Empire and Commonwealth or from post-independence study by their educational professionals in English-language universities; however, extensive research findings do not demonstrate sustained classroom change from formalistic to progressive paradigms.

5.1 African pedagogical commonalities

Africa contains many similar and deeply embedded educational traditions based around formalistic, teacher-centred methods from which students learn revealed knowledge (Regan 2005; Omolewa 2007; Tabulawa 2013). The primary purpose of African educational traditions is the intergenerational transmission of cultural heritage, as shown in an extensive handbook with 44 contributions about 16 countries (Nsamenang and Tchombe 2011). In particular, Gwanfogbe (2011) identified three significant educational heritages (derived from indigenous African, Islamic-Arabic, and Western-Christian civilisations) that now coexist in Africa. A considerable variety of theological interpretations of revelation exists among these traditions (Thomas 2015). Their common element is that they are held to reveal the various truths held by the traditions and their branches. In particular, the maintenance of indigenous traditions is 'accomplished by passing down cultural traditions through rituals, ceremonies, and writings' (Ukpokodu 2012, 23). Formal religious classes are for an exclusive few such as priests and custodians of shrines (40), while informal and non-formal education are a process of lifelong education from parents, family members and the community. Omolewa (2007), in a review of traditional education across Africa, reported that traditional informal and non-formal education in villages is often activity-based and collaborative in transmitting local culture, religion and history from generation to generation through language, music, dance and oral tradition. Practical skills and utilitarian knowledge are also imparted during childhood and adolescence in a combination of cultural, empirical and hierarchical training methods. In apprenticeship systems, for example, specialised crafts taught to children come with taboos and sanctions to enforce conformity and respect for the master and an appreciation of lifelong learning. Rites, such as initiations, mark the passage of learners through different levels of knowledge and into quasi-religious cults. Indigenous traditions long pre-dated European colonialism and, despite disruption by European missions from the 15th century, traditional education has continued to inculcate moral and ethical values, notably through proverbs and myths.

The colonial period layered unevenly over traditional education a different institutional approach (Vavrus, Thomas, and Bartlett 2011, 29–33). Education in schools was new, but formalistic colonial teaching was different from pre-colonial formalism in degree not kind (Tabulawa 2013, 138). European colonial administrations usually left in Christian hands most of the little schooling that was provided, but Koranic schools existed too. Both institutionalised formal education in classrooms, where teachers' and students' intuitive, culturally derived assumptions about the nature of knowledge, the ways it ought to be transmitted, and their perceptions of the goals of schooling continue to influence their behaviours. Tabulawa's (1998) analysis showed, for example, that Botswana's prevalent didactic, teacher-centred method of teaching was underpinned by a philosophy of knowledge embedded in traditional Tswana cosmology in a society that emphasised domination and subordination of children to their elders. In Zimbabwe, Madzima's (2010) case study of high school students in Harare found they interpreted their situation in terms of Shona *hunhu* practices and related their school experiences to traditional cultural explanations rather than to Northern ones, thus understanding their modern school setting according to traditional ontology. In South Africa, Kubow (2017) identified communal cultural assumptions in *ubuntu* (a moral ethic about humanness, where the individual is viewed as not separate from, but rather embedded in, the birth community) that affect convergences and divergences between Western and indigenous knowledge in democratic citizenship education. As cultural relativism tells us and these studies illustrate, peripheral Southern intellectual and linguistic capital can exist in indigenous cultures, even if it is not readily apparent in Eurocentric terms.

Omolewa (2007) and Nsamenang and Tchombe (2011) promoted the progressive view that traditional activity-based and collaborative methods from informal and non-formal education should be adapted to the requirements of student-centred formal schooling. Omolewa (2007, 609) specifically supported outcomes-based schooling so that

> The teacher's role might have to change from being a transmitter of knowledge to a mediator and facilitator of learning. The expectation for the student would need to change from a passive receiver of knowledge to an autonomous learner, reflective thinker and problem solver, who is actively involved in his/her own learning and construction of knowledge.

However, traditional informal and non-formal methods are often ill-adapted to formal education in modern classrooms (Guthrie 2011, 154–157). The risks include teachers who may not be familiar with local language and culture if they teach outside their own area, and thus may lack local knowledge on which to build curricula. Attempts to have teachers be flexible and self-reliant, use improvised materials, and integrate syllabuses with community activities can also founder on teachers' and parents' expectations that the school's role is a formal one aimed at examinations that might provide the children with a rare and hopefully corruption-free opportunity to escape from poverty. A more direct source of inspiration for modern classrooms is traditional formal education.

5.2 A case study of classroom formalism

Formalistic educational traditions have been treated widely as problematic obstructions to modernisation in Africa, but reforms have had limited success in generating paradigm reversal in the classroom. A particularly clear example of the countervailing effect of a traditional formalistic paradigm underpinned by traditional epistemology comes from Tabulawa's (1997, 1998, 2004) brilliant research into the meanings attached to pedagogical practices by both teachers and students in Botswana. His grounded case study of geography teachers in a rural secondary school in 1993 mainly used qualitative methods, especially unstructured classroom observation of the school's three geography teachers over a two-month period, semi-structured interviews with them and four other departmental teachers, and interviews with 10 students. The research took place in a school system where internationally influenced official policy was to change student-teacher relationships in a progressive, democratic, learner-centred direction.

The research found a textbook example of formalism (Tabulawa 1998). Classes moved as a whole from one activity to another, with little variation in routine classroom practices. Teacher-student relationships were paternalistic and formal, with teachers expecting traditional respect and deference and maintaining a social distance. Teachers emphasised attentiveness, formality and orderliness in their lessons: essentially, they treated the students as a single mass, had little individual contact, and paid little attention in the classroom to individual student needs. Usually, teachers started lessons with recapitulation of the previous lesson, followed by lecturing and brief notes written on the board. Few questions came from the students, who generally sat quietly, and student-student interaction was conspicuously absent except in occasional small-group discussions. The lessons usually ended with recapitulation by the teachers or quizzing of the students. The limited verbal contact was initiated by the teachers in highly formalised question and answer sessions where considerable emphasis was put on students demonstrating the 'right answers' to closed questions, part of a central concern about maintaining teacher control. Corporal punishment, which was common in the school, was an option, but mastery of subject matter, which depended on good lesson preparation and presentation, was an important aspect of control that made corporal punishment unnecessary.

Tabulawa found that progressive policies were ineffective because teachers and students shared common expectations about the value of formalistic classroom teaching. Knowledge was a utilitarian commodity: the teachers' job was to impart it, the students' job to acquire it. All the teachers saw schooling as a vocational route to employment and, possibly, higher education, mediated by the examination system. Teachers perceived that 'imparting' and 'delivery' of curriculum knowledge and keeping order in class were their main responsibilities so that students could gain the knowledge to pass the public exams. The students' role was 'receiving' the teachers' knowledge. Students should read, listen to the teacher in class, and be ready to receive instruction. They were doing meaningful work when they answered questions, wrote assignments and took notes, and therefore learned school knowledge from teachers and textbooks. Thus, Tabulawa (1998, 264) wrote,

> if the role of the teacher is that of purveying knowledge, then his/her role is to 'teach'. If the role of the student is perceived as that of a receptacle of knowledge, then his/her role is to 'learn' by way of assimilating the teacher's knowledge.

The distinction between teaching and learning defined and simplified the actors' classroom roles. A stable and orderly classroom atmosphere came from adherence to the roles and the actors were conscious of deviations from them. 'In fact, the study shows how teachers employed overt and more subtle strategies to maintain their dominant role in class and how students, likewise, employed strategies to keep the teachers in an information-giving position' (264).

Importantly, students had a very similar perspective to teachers. Students viewed knowledge as external, a commodity possessed by the school and teachers, and found in textbooks. If they wanted to pass the exams, they had to get it from these sources. 'Thus, attempts to have them construct knowledge in the classroom would be a waste of time, and group discussions are, therefore, resisted' (Tabulawa 1998, 263). Exploration of power relations in the classroom further showed that students did not necessarily perceive teacher dominance as just a product of teachers' inherent desire for social control (Tabulawa 2004). In many instances teachers were 'forced' into a dominant position by the students themselves. Teacher dominance was thus a mutually constructed, negotiated product resulting from students and teachers exercising power on each other within the constraints set by their social and cultural context. Students contributed to teacher-centredness through their expectations of teacher behaviour and they had considerable informal power over teachers' reputations. In turn, teachers were conscious of their reputations and actively avoided teaching behaviours that might get them labelled as incompetent by students. The students especially defined teachers' competence as deriving from their subject knowledge and their ability to teach it efficiently. Rather than student silence in class being a sign of laziness, deviance or powerlessness, silence rationally communicated the expectation that teachers would fill it with the required knowledge. Silence, Tabulawa identified, was actually a form of countervailing power. The teachers' apparent dominance was not so much imposed as a co-constructed, negotiated authority that was a product of teachers' and students' mutual expectations of schooling derived from their shared cultural context. In Weberian terms, teachers did not so much wield power as legitimate authority.

Tabulawa's research can be seen against an earlier study in the same country by Fuller and Snyder (1991), which found similar formalistic patterns. Structured classroom observation of three lessons each by 154 junior secondary and 127 primary teachers found that the teachers were vocal and dominant in most classrooms. Teachers were predominantly formalistic but, in a larger sample with both primary and secondary schools, and with more teachers and subjects, there was more variety than in Tabulawa's study. Teachers did not always use chalk-and-talk, and substantial variation occurred in the use of textbooks, written exercises and materials, in part depending on the subject and the size of the class. Pupils were not always passive and silent. A good deal of time was spent on question, answer and recitation (mainly involving closed-ended questions), but with considerable variation and many teachers attempting to generate pupil action. The inference was that there were overriding cultural commonalities in teachers' formalistic approach, but practices could be flexible to some extent. More recently, Tawana (2009, 306–341) found from observation and semi-structured interviews with 11 teachers of chemistry in four Botswanan secondary schools that only modest levels of implementation of the student-centred approach of the curriculum (which the researcher took as axiomatic) occurred because the teachers preferred lecturing.

One conclusion from the three studies by Fuller and Snyder, Tabulawa, and Tawana is that formalism in Botswana remained consistently resistant to change across more than two decades. A major reason, as Tabulawa's (1998) analysis showed, was that Botswana's prevalent didactic, teacher-centred method of teaching was underpinned by a philosophy of knowledge embedded in the wider culture. The culture provided a value system for both teachers and students that contributed to the failure of attempts to change didactic practices. Formalism was deeply anchored in traditional Tswana cosmology in a society that emphasised domination and subordination of children to their elders. Children were exposed to this from earliest childhood: it was part of the culture they brought into the classroom so that teachers and students shared the same educational philosophy. The resulting deductive, product-oriented classrooms, Tabulawa found, were antithetical to official policy of generating a more inductive, learner-centred approach where teachers would facilitate student learning processes because learning-centred teaching was not congruent with teachers' and students' deep-seated and shared assumption that the goal of schooling was to impart knowledge as a vocational commodity. The failure of the progressive reforms did not come from a lack of resources, but from ignoring the cultural contexts within which schools operated. Teachers' classroom practices were influenced by many non-technical factors, including their assumptions about the nature of knowledge and the ways it should be transmitted, and their perceptions of students and the goal of schooling. Thus, issues arising from the cultural context were at the bottom of the failure of the misplaced technicist focus on classroom change that aimed to deliver innovation through resource inputs.

5.3 Progressive reform across Sub-Saharan Africa

International policy borrowings aimed at changing formalistic teaching occurred in many parts of Africa, especially when countries took progressive reforms as an opportunity to break with the colonial past and overcome cultural and societal obstacles to change. In Ghana, for example, progressivism was embraced with special zeal as a path to modernisation in the early years after Independence in 1957, so that education policy resolved to prepare a largely untrained teaching force in progressive methods (Zimmerman 2011). Across the 1960s and across subject areas, in-service teacher education (INSET) promoted group projects, inquiry learning and the other aspects of progressive pedagogy: 'Education should be child-centered, progressives said, not teacher-centered; active, not passive; grounded in experience, not simply in books; and focussed on the community, not just the school' (Zimmerman 2011, 3). However, the reforms rarely took hold in classrooms. Resource problems identified by Zimmerman were a sheer lack of money and personnel; too, the political tyranny that developed in Ghana was incompatible with progressive pedagogy. A connection to current reforms is support for progressive forms of teaching as desirable for promoting democratisation or opposing authoritarianism (e.g. Arreman, Erixon, and Rehn 2016, on Namibia; Slonimsky 2016, on South Africa; and Harber 2017, across Sub-Saharan Africa).

Foreign interests have often aligned with local change agents. The World Bank's 'stages' mentality (Section 1.3) influenced some writers concerned in particular with the implications for teacher in-service, especially in southern Africa. Harvey (1999, 604–608), for example, argued that Beeby's (1966) work helped define the type of INSET appropriate for teachers at different 'stages'. De Feiter and Ncube (1999) similarly held the view that 'more student centred methodologies can be introduced at higher levels of school development' (184). School development and curriculum innovation were also seen as a movement towards more sophisticated higher levels by Rogan and Grayson (2003, 1174). In their defence, these writers did realistically caution about the speed of progressive reform: Verspoor (1989, 134) pointed to problems that lay in underestimation of implementation difficulties in large curriculum projects; De Feiter and Ncube (1999, 184) qualified their approach with the view that educational support must be realistic about the effects of working conditions on reform; while Rogan and Grayson (2003, 1174) usefully noted that the stages approach implied a linear view of complex and idiosyncratic curriculum change processes, and that higher levels should be seen as inclusive of the lower ones rather than replacements. Even so, these were qualifications about the speed of attainment of the 'higher stages', rather than questions about the progressive destination.

Subsequently, a review by Chisholm and Leyendecker (2008) of curriculum reforms in Sub-Saharan Africa, which used evidence particularly from Namibia and South Africa, reported that learner-centredness, outcomes- and competency-based education, and national qualifications frameworks all found favour. Critical writers such as Tabulawa (2003), Quist (2003) and Fataar (2006) identified not just technical and cultural difficulties with such reforms, but commented on their underlying political assumptions and the role of aid agencies in internationally-funded teacher education and curriculum projects (Section 1.3). Nonetheless, progressive theories were recognised and ambiguous enough to be borrowed locally as vehicles for achieving economic, social and political goals, but they did not result in widespread change in classroom practice.

South Africa

In recent decades, perhaps the most widely studied progressive curriculum reforms was the home-grown in South Africa. The driver of reform in the 1990s was an entirely praiseworthy political drive to counter apartheid (Botha 2002; Fiske and Ladd 2004; Fataar 2006; Hoadley 2017). A main focus quickly became replacement of formalism with outcomes-based education (OBE) under the Curriculum 2005 programme. Like in Papua New Guinea (as seen in Sections 3.5–3.7 and 6.4), the approach to OBE was 'transformational' (Norman 2006). The programme was implemented from 1998 and was initially subject to little critical analysis (Jansen 1998). Jansen's prediction of a negative impact upon schools was subsequently supported by research that found the curriculum changes did not improve achievement levels (Mouton, Louw, and Strydom 2012). For example, an IEA study of mathematics standards tested 8,147 students in 194 secondary schools, finding the lowest levels among 38 participating countries and no increase from 1995 to 1999 (Howie 2002, 103–118). Nakabugo and Sieborger's (2001) case study of seven 4th grade teachers of English found that they had not made changes in assessment from old formalistic practices to the new ones necessary for the paradigm shift required for OBE. The official approach, they concluded, was very dubious and in need of much closer attention to what actually happened in classrooms and to ways of facilitating meaningful change.

As has been pointed out extensively, in effect the official assumption that overthrowing the racism of apartheid required a rapid paradigm shift to progressive, outcomes-based schooling was political symbolism. The transformational role was based on fallacious grounds educationally and was unrelated to professional realities, especially in schools not inhabited by the middle class (Jansen 1998, 2002; Harley *et al.* 2000; Cross, Mungadi, and Rouhani 2002; Allais 2003; Chisholm 2003; Jansen and Taylor 2003, 38–41; Hoadley 2017). The many complexities that reformers dealt with included the negative legacy of apartheid educational systems, such as Bantu education, that explicitly used authoritarianism to create passive workers. However, formalistic classrooms are not necessarily authoritarian (Section 8.4), so the reform equation of classroom formalism with political and social authoritarianism means that the progressive curriculum was fundamentally flawed in terms of the concern of this book with processes inside the classroom. Nykiel-Herbert (2004) was particularly scathing about the curriculum reformers, 'who chose on ideological rather than pragmatic grounds a radical progressive/constructivist pedagogy model, with the expectation that it would help to redress . . . inequalities of the country's inglorious racist past' (250). The actual outcome was that 'a severe shortage of the necessary expertise . . . turned the intended recipe for educational success into a new variety of educational malpractice, producing yet another generation of illiterate, innumerate South Africans' (250).

Curriculum 2005 was revised in 2002 with a hybrid National Curriculum Statement and again in 2005, but still was unsuccessful (Chisholm and Wildeman 2013; Maher 2015; Hoadley 2017). A further review in 2009 finally dispensed with OBE and a new Curriculum and Assessment Policy marked a decisive shift towards a knowledge-based curriculum. This change, Hoadley (169) commented, was a surprising shift from the scriptural status that OBE had achieved for its transformational intent, with the new policy understanding social justice in education as being grounded in access to formal knowledge. Hoadley traced the classroom impacts of the three curriculum reforms through detailed ethnographic classroom studies in early primary school classrooms in the same poor communities near Cape Town, which were conducted just after the implementation of each reform. While the policies changed substantially, classroom formalism endured through all three (211).

Namibia

In Namibia, educational reform in the 1990s also reacted to the formalistic teaching found under the previous apartheid system. The focus typically was on curriculum (as in South Africa), with a strong emphasis on introducing progressive elements and extensive teacher development programmes (Dembele and Lefoka 2007). O'Sullivan (2002, 2004) found that implementation of constructivist approaches was unsuccessful. Her mixed methods action research on an in-service programme included 450 hours of lesson observation among 145 unqualified teachers in 31 predominantly rural primary schools from 1995–1997. She found that teachers were familiar with reform policy and claimed to use the learner-centred methods, but rote teaching dominated in classroom practice. Two school-based reasons for the lack of use of the new teaching skills were limited resources (including inability to provide small classes) and teacher professional capacity to understand the language of the policy documents. Other reasons were contextual. Learners had expectations derived from traditional formalistic approaches, where children were expected to be respectful of authority, and a background as semi-nomadic rural herders, which meant the interests of the individual tended to be subsumed into the group.

Some basic elements of epistemology that the progressive reforms overlooked led to a major underestimation of requirements (O'Sullivan 2004, 594–595). Constructivist education required highly qualified and experienced staff, specific assumptions and great skill, which the teachers in the case study schools did not have. A central requirement to recognise learners as cognate individuals could only be applied successfully if the contribution of learners to knowledge development was acknowledged and teachers accommodated learners as social beings reliant on interaction with others to generate meaning, which they did not. Teachers had to be aware of the types of ideas brought to school subjects by learners and to be knowledgeable about strategies to restructure and extend these conceptions in a constructivist manner, which they were not. Even degree-level workshop participants had major difficulties attempting to adopt a constructivist view. Instead, teachers tended to view knowledge as fixed, objective and detached from the learner, and believed their function was to transmit this knowledge to the children, usually through rote learning. Effectively, constructivist requirements were in direct contrast to the local cultural context and teachers' expectations. Teachers would not just need new teaching skills; they would have to change their cultural framework about teaching and learning completely (as also found in Tabulawa's Botswanan study). O'Sullivan did find some teachers in Namibia could reconsider such a view and, in the short term at least, change their teaching. Whether or not change would be sustained (and no evidence was presented either way) would likely depend on the extent to which teachers perceived that helping students would violate cultural standards about self-reliance.

Tanzania

The relationship between progressive educational policy and actual practice has been of considerable interest in Tanzania. One study, by Mtahabwa and Rao (2010), videoed 15 lessons by five teachers in two urban and two rural pre-primary schools. Classroom practice was formalistically characterised by adult dominance rather than student interaction. The authors' explanation particularly focussed on school facilities, which had considerable urban-rural differences. The rural classes had considerably less space, larger groups, less favourable teacher/pupil ratios, fewer instructional resources and less qualified teachers. Although it is unclear from the report whether this resulted in more formalistic classroom behaviour in the rural settings, teacher professional qualifications were thought to influence the quality of classroom interaction more than the physical setting and resources.

A more insightful study by Barrett (2007) is well recognised. In 2002–2003, she interviewed 32 teachers in 18 primary schools and observed 28 lessons to compare what teachers said was good practice with their classroom behaviour. A belief by some teachers in the importance of understanding pupils' conceptualisation of subject matter meant that they had some values consistent with Bernstein's (2000) learner-centred 'competence mode', but they operated predominantly within his teacher-centred 'performance mode'. Thus, teachers' professed beliefs reflected official progressive reform policy, but they actually taught much more formalistically. However, the stereotype that teaching in Sub-Saharan Africa is rigid was challenged by variation among teachers. Even in classes averaging around 45 students and in fairly standardised lessons, there was some variety that seemed influenced by school culture, exposure to INSET, plus teacher confidence, subject knowledge and pedagogical skill. A second stereotype that Barrett challenged was that formalistic teaching cannot be upgraded. She considered there was scope to avoid the tendency to promote uncritically educational ideas from English-speaking countries. Improvement of teacher practice could occur within the existing pedagogical palette and be combined in a flexible middle ground, albeit a position criticised by Tabulawa (2013, 43) for not recognising the underlying epistemological substance of formalism (Section 2.9).

Unlike much other research, cultural issues confronting the progressive paradigm were in the foreground of a year-long ethnography of a teacher training college by Vavrus (2009) in 2006–2007. The college was founded on the principles of social constructivism and aimed to challenge the formalistic, teacher-centred pedagogy of the typical Tanzanian secondary school. The approach was consistent with government policy that encouraged teachers to view themselves as facilitators in the classroom who elicit students' knowledge and enable peer learning. This policy was coupled with a move from content-based curricula towards a competency-based approach that necessitated student-centred teaching and learning. The case study found adoption of the policy by students was problematic, and that the cultural, economic and political dimensions of teachers' practice needed to be considered alongside efforts to reform the education system. Vavrus and Bartlett (2012) further examined how epistemological differences regarding knowledge production and material differences in the conditions of teaching influenced teachers' and teacher educators' understandings of learner-centred pedagogy. This research focussed on six Tanzanian secondary schools whose teachers participated in a workshop on learner-centred pedagogy and pedagogical content knowledge. The research found that teachers' views of knowledge production were profoundly shaped by the cultural, economic and social contexts in which they taught. Teachers had a mixture of professional and practical difficulties implementing policy, including with social and intellectual authority, noise, size of classes and time for preparation, all of which might shape pedagogical practices. Material diversity in working conditions was an important contextual factor, the researchers found, but epistemological diversity also needed to be conceptualised more fully in theories of knowledge production and global/local reforms of teacher education.

Elsewhere

Progressive reforms in other parts of Sub-Saharan Anglophone Africa have also had major implementation difficulties. In Lesotho, Dembele and Lefoka (2007) reviewed three studies that highlighted a gap between progressive theory in teacher education and formalistic classroom practice, while a small case study by Moloi, Morobe, and Urwick (2008) found the formalistic teachers rejected individual learning methods. Likewise, in Malawi, Mtika and Gates (2010) found constraints on the application of practices from learner-centred teacher education. Their qualitative mixed methods study used data from four secondary pre-service student teachers drawn from a more detailed sample of 22 trainees. Theoretical learner concepts advocated in initial teacher education were either not appropriated fully by the trainee teachers or, where they were, applied only a surface feature of the learner-centred approach, such as group work, where pupils still worked individually. Even these attempts met resistance or complete negation in classrooms. Appropriation and application of learner-centred education was comprehensively constrained by the teacher education system, the student teacher's personal disposition, school culture, and the national curriculum.

In Uganda, progressive pedagogical principles had also been adopted as policy, in particular with a thematic curriculum promoting classroom interaction in primary schools. Altinyelken's (2010a, 2010b) fieldwork in Kampala in 2007 used interviews and observation to explore teachers' views on the reforms, their classroom practices, and the perceived challenges in implementation. The majority of teachers were enthusiastic about the new curriculum, but were not implementing it as fully as they claimed. In general, teachers used a hybrid of traditional and progressive practices. Some surface aspects of the reforms (such as arrangement of desks and use of teaching aids) were more easily adopted, but deeper ones (such as student participation or open questions) were less apparent. Systemic inhibitions ranged from heavy workload and lack of teaching and learning materials to large classes and inadequate teacher training. The discrepancy between policy and practice raised questions also about the cultural appropriateness of progressivism. The pedagogy required children to question and challenge teachers directly, which contradicted the relationship norm for adults and children as one of respect and authority.

An underlying element in much of the research outlined here was highlighted in a comparative study of teacher education in Ghana, Lesotho, Malawi, South Africa, and Trinidad and Tobago. Lewin and Stuart (2003) demonstrated that different approaches to teacher education were related intimately to theories of learning, ontology and epistemology. They found that epistemological diversity had important implications for the study of pedagogy and teacher education. Formalism, with ties to behaviourism and positivism, predominated among teacher educators in the institutions they examined. Improving teacher education would require training that developed professional reasoning ability and recognised the value of trainees' personal, experiential and craft knowledge. Epistemological diversity also signalled the importance of historical, political and social situating of all types of knowledge, making it essential to locate teachers' understood and enacted theories of teaching and learning in social and material contexts and to provide contextually grounded training materials.

5.4 Theoretical and methodological issues

Most of the African studies seen so far fall within the classroom improvement rather than the school effectiveness field, partly because countries have opted out of international testing. With the preeminent exception of Tabulawa's work, two types of response to progressive difficulties are found. The technicist approach focusses on increasing material and professional inputs. Less frequently, and usually only partially, has research seen beneath resource matters to more fundamental contextual issues, particularly the underlying cultural ones, further illustrating the theoretical and methodological issues in the progressive literature that were identified in Chapters 2 and 3.

Technicist evaluations in Africa, as elsewhere, commonly interpret insufficient physical and professional resource inputs as the predominant barriers to progressive change. Approaches like these are often bound by the Progressive Education Fallacy, which has been a long-standing problem in studies caged by the progressive axiom that classroom quality requires students to participate actively, and which prejudge teacher-dominated formalistic classrooms as obstacles to reform. An early study of Nigerian primary schools by Urwick and Junaidu (1991) judged teaching processes largely on the extent to which teacher methods were pupil-centred and on the variety of methods of communication used in lessons, as well as the variety of activities organised during lessons. More recently, the Fallacy was typified by a group of researchers working across Kenya, Nigeria, Tanzania and Uganda (Hardman, Abd-Kadir, and Smith

2008; Hardman *et al.* 2009, Hardman *et al.* 2011). Their findings appeared to stem from the view that formalistic classrooms are necessarily dull and repetitive, teachers bored and uninterested, and pupils quiet and passive (Ackers and Hardman 2001, 256). Classroom observation in the four countries found a prevalence of teacher explanation, recitation, and rote in primary classroom discourse, with little attention to pupil understanding, but did find school-based INSET could impact on teaching styles in a progressive direction. The Nigerian study, for example, investigated classroom practices in primary schools using interaction and discourse analysis of video recordings of 42 lessons and 59 teacher questionnaires from ten states, mainly from the north (Hardman, Abd-Kadir, and Smith 2008). The axiomatic assumption was of a need to transform classroom talk from the familiar teacher talk to include a wider repertoire of dialogue and discussion in whole-class, group-based and one-to-one interactions. Likewise, the Kenyan study reported on the impact of a national INSET programme on learning and teaching in primary schools (Hardman *et al.* 2009). Mixed methods research collected 144 video-recorded lessons on English, mathematics and science in Standards 3 and 6, which were analysed to investigate whole-class teaching and group-based learning. Interviews on the impact of the training programme on learning and teaching were also held with school management committees, head teachers, teachers and pupils. The study found that compared to an earlier baseline study, teachers were more interactive with the pupils in their whole-class teaching and greater use was made of group work. Lesson plans, teaching resources and flexible classroom layouts were also evident. Like the other studies, the circular progressive assumption was apparent in the standard recommendations for more progressive-oriented teacher training inputs. However, the studies offered no evidence about effects on student achievement, whether practices were sustained, or much in-depth analysis of cultural context, thereby having three major limitations. As Tabulawa (2013) identified, a common failing in this technicist approach in Africa is underestimation of context.

The second type of response to progressive difficulties does go past findings about lack of resources to recognise fundamental contextual issues that make implementation problematic. As discussed in Sections 2.6 and 3.1, the primary focus is usually on structural issues in the societal context, but even studies that recognise cultural issues generally treat them as organisational barriers to change and still hold progressive values as axiomatic. This is true even of studies widely and properly recognised in the literature for their cultural insights. For example, O'Sullivan's (2002, 2004) Namibian action research recognised that teachers would have to change their cultural framework about constructivist teaching and learning completely, which they did not, although limited classroom skills did introduce some variety and improved student reading skills. Keen to avoid labelling the outcome as still formalistic, O'Sullivan reconceptualised the official progressive policy approach as 'learning'-centred teaching rather than 'learner'-centred: albeit, on reflection, she admitted the teachers' skills were close to Rosenshine's (1979) formalistic direct instruction.

Barrett (2007) argued that aspects of formalism and progressivism in Tanzania could be combined in a flexible middle ground, which did not grapple with the deeper epistemological issues. Vavrus's (2009) study in Tanzania offered 'contingent constructivism' as an alternative to the international consensus on a single model of excellent teaching. This construct recognised epistemological diversity, but the axiomatic assumption was of the value of adapting progressivism, not of situating formalism.

Still, a growing number of classroom improvement studies in Africa are grappling with cultural complexities, unlike the school effectiveness field, where analysis of cultural context remains rare. The field's quantitative techniques have a plethora of variables caged by serious technical problems in measuring both cultural context and classroom processes and a neglect of structured and unstructured observation within the classroom where the tested learning is designed to occur (Sections 3.1–3.3). A recent school effectiveness study that partly addressed such limitations was undertaken by Carnoy, Ngware, and Oketch (2015) in 6th grade mathematics in Botswana, Kenya and South Africa using large random surveys. The focus was on national educational contexts and classroom resources, including the use of classroom observation to assess the contribution of the quality of the teaching process to student performance. Mixed methods were used to measure teacher characteristics and some teaching process variables, to estimate learning gains associated with students' exposure to these, and to consider national institutional factors influencing student achievement. A model of classroom learning consisted of five main components: teacher mathematical and pedagogical knowledge, teacher pedagogical skills, student opportunity to learn through the curriculum, student socioeconomic background, and student learning gains. Teachers' pedagogical skills were categorised from videos of lessons by two expert maths educators into low/better/best using a 12-item protocol developed from the maths teaching literature. In South African, Botswanan and low-scoring Kenyan school samples, better classroom teaching, as evaluated from the videos, had a positive impact on student achievement. However, two critical variables were not included in the complex mathematical models used to analyse the data. Pedagogical skill sets went to the level of conceptual demand, reasoning, problem-solving and maths application required of students rather than to teaching style as discussed in this book; nor did the models include cultural context variables. These omissions perhaps help explain the authors' finding that 'a large "residual effect"... cannot be explained by differences in the socioeconomic background of the students or the variables we use to measure teacher quality or classroom conditions' (228).

More successfully, Daley *et al.* (2005) incorporated national and local beliefs, values, and norms about education and achievement in a Kenyan study involving 531 grade 1 students in 15 classes in 12 primary schools, with an average attendance of 37 students in each lesson observed. A conventional range of school effectiveness measures was used, with depth added from classroom observation to include variables such as child behaviour and classroom quality ratings reflecting local beliefs. Culturally grounded ratings came from classroom observation of teacher tone and behaviour, classroom organisation, and interest in student learning. Also used were multiple outcome variables: student off-task behaviour (from observation of behaviour such as talking to other students about non-school topics and playing with an object) and teacher end-of-term ratings of students (including attention, task persistence, participation and learning difficulties). The authors recognised limitations in their techniques, but linear regression analysis did show some interesting results. Addition of classroom variables to student background variables provided a significant increase in the variance explained. A major finding was the rejection of a research hypothesis that more open, encouraging, patient and interested behaviour by teachers would correlate positively with more on-task behaviour by students. The research actually found the opposite: less strict teaching was associated with less student attention. Further, greater teacher interest in student learning was a negative predictor of examination scores. Clear discipline provided greater control and more student attention, the likelihood of more rote learning, and higher examination scores. The authors, grappling with some of their more progressive assumptions, found this counter-intuitive but recognised that 'these findings reflect ... [the] assertion that "Western" styles of teaching may not be appropriate markers of quality in developing countries' (407).

5.5 Findings about formalism

In most of the studies discussed so far, progressivism axiomatically shaped theory-laden research that assumed formalism should be replaced. Research that treated its merits more objectively has been uncommon.

An old but still rare matched field experiment was the Zambian field study of teaching styles and learning gains reported by Mulopo and Fowler (1987). A key feature was a focus on student achievement as dependent variable, thus avoiding the dubious assumption that teaching style should be the objective (Section 3.3). The groups were also categorised by Piaget's cognitive levels as an intervening variable: lower cognitive level concrete reasoners and higher cognitive level formal reasoners. For science achievement, the formalistic control group outperformed the experimental discovery group. For science understanding, the mode of teaching did not make a difference among concrete reasoners, but among formal reasoners the discovery group scored significantly higher. With scientific attitudes, students in the formalistic group had significantly lower scores than the discovery group. Thus, the traditional, formalistic approach was efficient for teaching scientific facts and principles, while the progressive discovery approach tended to be more effective among formal reasoners in promoting scientific understanding and attitudes. The achievement finding was consistent with several other studies. Fuller and Clarke (1994, 139) noted that when developing country teachers displayed more participatory forms of pedagogy, achievement gains were not always observed, citing Lockheed and Komenan (1989, 110), who found in Nigeria and Swaziland that time spent by pupils listening to lecturing and at deskwork, respectively, were positively associated with achievement. Indeed, in grade 8 and 9 mathematics in Botswana, more open-ended questions by teachers actually suppressed achievement (Fuller, Hua, and Snyder 1994). Likewise, the Kenyan school effectiveness study by Daley *et al.* (2005) found clear discipline provided greater control and more student attention, the likelihood of more rote learning, and higher examination scores.

A recent study in Kenya by Lattimer (2015) involved basic research to identify teaching styles used in secondary mathematics lessons in two similar schools in Nairobi (Section 10.1). Observation found a majority of teachers used similar formalistic methods but variations in instructional practice did occur. A number of teachers engaged students with elements of learner-centred practices, and variations in teacher questioning, student participation and assessment practices contributed to different learning environments. Testing against student achievement was not undertaken but, rather than assuming the desirability of progressive elements, Lattimer cautioned that the analysis was not an endorsement for a flexible teaching style compared to a more formalistic one. Rather, in-depth analysis of classroom practices could inform decisions about methods for implementing instructional goals (74). Thus, the research was not bounded by the axiomatic cage provided by the progressive paradigm, as seen in so much of the other research in Sub-Saharan Africa, but provided groundwork for identifying classroom practices that could be educationally effective.

5.6 Conclusion

Numerous research studies in primary and secondary schools across 12 Anglophone countries in Sub-Saharan Africa invariably have found lack of success with implementation of progressive reforms. Extensive field evidence from Botswana, Ghana, Kenya, Lesotho, Malawi, Namibia, Nigeria, South Africa, Tanzania, Uganda, Zambia and Zimbabwe continues to demonstrate that Anglophone influences have been strong at policy level but have not translated to paradigm shift away from formalism in the classroom. Many of the studies illustrate the theoretical and methodological limitations identified in Chapters 2 and 3, as well as the remarkable difficulty of replacing the formalistic paradigm with progressivism. The research findings help explain why African schools abound with the remains of unproductive progressive reforms.

The failures have generally been attributed to structural conditions, but the more insightful studies point to cultural incompatibility. A small number of studies that have focussed on formalism as such have also found that it was equally or more effective with the type of student achievement typically measured in high-stakes public examinations. The field evidence is consistent with the view that (a) formalism is effective in primary and secondary schools in many examination-oriented contexts in Sub-Saharan Africa, and (b) progressive education reforms usually fail in cultures where epistemology is revelatory rather than scientific. Common reasons for failures given by progressive researchers are poor classroom conditions, insufficient resource inputs and problems in project delivery, but these limited findings leave open the false inference that progressive classroom change merely requires more resources in future. Given the perennial progressive failures, the indication is that any such inputs would be more effectively applied to upgrading conditions within a formalistic framework.

In Africa, as elsewhere, the profound reason for formalism's continuing prevalence is that classroom behaviours are intuitively influenced by teachers', students' and parents' intergenerational beliefs about the nature of knowledge, how it should be transmitted, and their perceptions of the goals of schooling. The cultural roots of revelatory epistemology about the nature of truth and how it should be revealed are the basis for formalistic educational paradigms that provide long-lasting patterns for teachers' and students' behaviour, notably a didactic approach to revelation of knowledge to learners. Even where teachers are not particularly conscious of the underlying epistemology, formalism provides a model with assumptions that students can and do share with them. Rather than an intermediary 'stage' on the path to educational development, formalism is likely to remain in African classrooms because it is a symbiotic part of traditional and current culture.

Note

1 Chapter 5 expands considerably an article published in the *Southern African Review of Education* (Guthrie 2013) with permission of the journal.

References

Ackers, J., and Hardman, F. 2001. "Classroom Interaction in Kenyan Primary Schools." *Compare* 31 (2): 245–261.

Alexander, R. 2000. *Culture and Pedagogy: International Comparisons in Primary Education*. Oxford: Blackwell.

Allais, S. 2003. "The National Qualifications Framework in South Africa: A Democratic Project Trapped in a Neo-Liberal Paradigm?" *Journal of Education and Work* 16 (3): 305–323.

Altinyelken, H. 2010a. "Curriculum Change in Uganda: Teacher Perspectives on the New Thematic Curriculum." *International Journal of Educational Development* 30 (2): 145–150.

Altinyelken, H. 2010b. "Pedagogical Renewal in Sub-Saharan Africa: The Case of Uganda. *Comparative Education* 46 (2): 151–171.

Arreman, I., Erixon, P-O., and Rehn, K-G. 2016. "Postcolonial Teacher Education Reform in Namibia: Travelling of Policies and Ideas." *European Educational Research Journal* 15 (2): 236–259.

Barrett, A. 2007. "Beyond the Polarization of Pedagogy: Models of Classroom Practice in Tanzanian Primary Schools." *Comparative Education* 43 (2): 273–294.

Beeby, C.E. 1966. *The Quality of Education in Developing Countries*. Cambridge: Harvard University Press.

Bernstein, B. 2000. *Pedagogy, Symbolic Control and Identity: Theory, Research, Critique*. Lanham: Rowman & Littlefield.

Botha, R. 2002. "Outcomes-Based Education and Educational Reform in South Africa." *International Journal of Leadership in Education* 5 (4): 361–371.

Carnoy, M., Ngware, M., and Oketch, M. 2015. "The Role of Classroom Resources and National Educational Context in Student Learning Gains: Comparing Botswana, Kenya, and South Africa." *Comparative Education Review* 59 (2): 199–232.

Chisholm, L. 2003. "The State of Curriculum Reform in South Africa: The Issue of Curriculum 2005." In *State of the Nation: South Africa 2003–2004*, edited by J. Daniel, A. Habib, and R. Southall, 268–289. Cape Town: HSRC Press.

Chisholm, L., and Leyendecker, R. 2008. "Curriculum Reform in Post-1990s Sub-Saharan Africa." *International Journal of Educational Development* 28: 195–205.

Chisholm, L., and Wildeman, R. 2013. "The Politics of Testing in South Africa." *Journal of Curriculum Studies* 45 (1): 89–100.

Cross, M., Mungadi, R., and Rouhani, S. 2002. "From Policy to Practice: Curriculum Reform in South Africa." *Comparative Education* 38 (2): 171–187.

Daley, T., Whaley, S., Sigman, M., Guthrie, D., Neumann, C., and Bwibo, N. 2005. "Background and Classroom Correlates of Child Achievement, Cognitive, and Behavioural Outcomes in Rural Kenyan Schoolchildren." *International Journal of Behavioral Development* 29 (5): 399–408.

De Feiter, L., and Ncube, K. 1999. "Towards a Comprehensive Strategy for Science Curriculum Reform and Teacher Development in Southern Africa." In *Science and Environment Education: Views from Developing Countries*, edited by S. Ware, 177–198. Secondary Education Series 19659. Washington, DC: World Bank.

Dembele, M., and Lefoka, P. 2007. "Pedagogical Renewal for Quality Universal Primary Education: Overview of Trends in Sub-Saharan Africa." *International Review of Education* 53 (5–6): 531–553.

Fataar, A. 2006. "Policy Networks in Recalibrated Political Terrain: The Case of School Curriculum Policy and Politics in South Africa." *Journal of Education Policy* 21 (6): 641–659.

Fiske, E., and Ladd, H. 2004. *Elusive Equity: Education Reform in Post-Apartheid South Africa*. Washington, DC: Brookings.

Fuller, B., and Clarke, P. 1994. "Raising School Effects While Ignoring Culture – Local Conditions and the Influence of Classroom Tools, Rules, and Pedagogy." *Review of Educational Research* 64 (1): 119–157.

Fuller, B., Hua, H., and Snyder, C. 1994. "When Girls Learn More Than Boys: Do Teaching Practices Influence Achievement in Botswana?" *Comparative Education Review* 38 (2): 347–376.

Fuller, B., and Snyder, C. 1991. "Vocal Teachers, Silent Pupils? Life in Botswana Classrooms." *Comparative Education Review* 35 (2): 274–294.

Guthrie, G. 2011. *The Progressive Education Fallacy in Developing Countries: In Favour of Formalism*. New York: Springer.

Guthrie, G. 2013. "Prevalence of the Formalistic Paradigm in African Schools." *Southern African Review of Education* 19 (1): 121–138.

Gwanfogbe, M. 2011. "Africa's Triple Education Heritage: A Historical Comparison." In *Handbook of African Educational Theories and Practices: A Generative Teacher Education Curriculum*, edited by A. Nsamenang and T. Tchombe, 39–54. Bamenda: Human Development Resource Centre.

Harber, C. 2017. *Schooling in Sub-Saharan Africa: Policy, Practice and Patterns*. London: Palgrave Macmillan.

Hardman, F., Abd-Kadir, J., Agg, C., Migwi, J., Ndambuku, J., and Smith, F. 2009. "Changing Pedagogical Practice in Kenyan Primary Schools: The Impact of School-based Training." *Comparative Education* 45 (1): 65–86.

Hardman, F., Abd-Kadir, J., and Smith, F. 2008. "Pedagogical Renewal: Improving the Quality of Classroom Interaction in Nigerian Primary Schools." *International Journal of Educational Development* 28 (1): 55–69.

Hardman, F., Ackers, J., Abrishamian, N., and O'Sullivan, M. 2011. "Developing a Systemic Approach to Teacher Education in Sub-Saharan Africa: Emerging Lessons from Kenya, Tanzania and Uganda." *Compare* 41 (5): 669–683.

Harley, K., Barasa, F., Bertram, C., Mattson, E., and Pillay, S. 2000. "'The Real and the Ideal': Teacher Roles and Competences in South African Policy and Practice." *International Journal of Educational Development* 20 (4): 287–304.

Harvey, S. 1999. "Phasing Science InSET in Developing Countries: Reflections on the Experience of the Primary Science Program in South Africa." *International Journal of Science Education* 21 (6): 595–609.

Hoadley, U. 2017. *Pedagogy in Poverty: Lessons from Twenty Years of Curriculum Reform in South Africa*. London: Routledge.

Howie, S. 2002. *English Language Proficiency and Contextual Factors Influencing Mathematics Achievement of Secondary School Pupils in South Africa*. Unpublished Doctoral thesis, University of Twente.

Jansen, J. 1998. "Curriculum Reform in South Africa: A Critical Analysis of Outcomes-Based Education." *Cambridge Journal of Education* 28 (3): 321–331.

Jansen, J. 2002. "Political Symbolism as Policy Craft: Explaining Non-Reform in South African Education after Apartheid." *Journal of Education Policy* 17 (2): 199–215.

Jansen, J., and Taylor, N. 2003. "Educational Change in South Africa 1994–2003: Case Studies in Large-scale Education Reform." *Country Studies in Education Reform and Management* 2 (1). Washington, DC: World Bank.

Kubow, P. 2017. "Exploring Western and Non-Western Epistemological Differences in South Africa: Theorising a Critical Democratic Citizenship Education." *Compare*. https://doi.org/10.1080/03057925.2017.1305881

Lattimer, H. 2015. "Translating Theory into Practice: Making Meaning of Learner Centered Education Frameworks for Classroom-based Practitioners." *International Journal of Educational Development* 45 (1): 65–76.

Lewin, K., and Stuart, J. 2003. "Insights into the Policy and Practice of Teacher Education in Low Income Countries: Multi-Site Teacher Education Research (MUSTER) Project." *British Educational Research Journal* 29 (5): 691–707.

Lockheed, M., and Komenan, A. 1989. "Teaching Quality and Student Achievement in Africa: The Case of Nigeria and Swaziland." *Teaching and Teacher Education* 5 (2): 93–113.

Madzima, L. 2010. *Low Socio-Economic Status and Identity Formation: A Case of Selected Successful Learners in a Secondary School in Harare*. Unpublished Doctoral dissertation, University of Cape Town.

Maher, M. 2015. "Lighting Up Learning: Mathematics Becoming Less of a 'Killer Subject' in KwaZulu-Natal, South Africa." *International Journal for Mathematics Teaching and Learning*. www.cimt.org.uk/journal/maher.pdf.

Moloi, F., Morobe, N., and Urwick, J. 2008. "Free but Inaccessible Primary Education: A Critique of the Pedagogy of English and Mathematics in Lesotho." *International Journal of Educational Development* 28 (5): 612–621.

Mouton, N., Louw, G., and Strydom, G. 2012. "A Historical Analysis of the Post Apartheid Dispensation Education in South Africa (1994–2011)." *International Business & Economics Research Journal* 11 (11): 1211–1222.

Mtahabwa, L., and Rao, N. 2010. "Pre-primary Education in Tanzania: Observations from Urban and Rural Classrooms." *International Journal of Educational Development* 30 (3): 227–235.

Mtika, P., and Gates, P. 2010. "Developing Learner-Centred Education Among Secondary Trainee Teachers in Malawi: The Dilemmas of Appropriation and Application." *International Journal of Educational Development* 30 (4): 396–404.

Mulopo, M., and Fowler, H. 1987. "Effects of Traditional and Discovery Instructional Approaches on Learning Outcomes for Learners of Different Intellectual Developments: A Study of Chemistry Students in Zambia." *Journal of Research in Science Teaching* 24 (3): 217–227.

Nakabugo, M., and Sieborger, R. 2001. "Curriculum Reform and Teaching in South Africa: Making a 'Paradigm Shift'?" *International Journal of Educational Development* 21 (1): 53–60.

Norman, P. 2006. "Outcomes-Based Education: A PNG Perspective." *Contemporary PNG Studies* 5: 45–57.

Nsamenang, A., and Tchombe, T. (Eds.). 2011. *Handbook of African Educational Theories and Practices: A Generative Teacher Education Curriculum*. Bamenda: Human Development Resource Centre.

Nykiel-Herbert, B. 2004. "Mis-Constructing Knowledge: The Case of Learner-Centred Pedagogy in South Africa." *Prospects* 34 (3): 249–265.

Omolewa, M. 2007. "Traditional African Modes of Education: Their Relevance in the Modern World." *International Review of Education* 53 (5–6): 593–612.

O'Sullivan, M. 2002. "Reform Implementation and the Realities Within Which Teachers Work: A Namibian Case Study." *Compare* 32 (2): 219–237.

O'Sullivan, M. 2004. "The Reconceptualisation of Learner-Centred Approaches: A Namibia Case Study." *International Journal of Educational Development* 24 (6): 585–602.

Quist, H. 2003. "Transferred and Adapted Models of Secondary Education in Ghana: What Implications for National Development?" *International Review of Education* 49 (5): 411–431.

Regan, T. 2005. *Non-Western Educational Traditions: Indigenous Approaches to Educational Thought and Practice*. Mahwah: Erlbaum.

Rogan, J., and Grayson, D. 2003. "Towards a Theory of Curriculum Implementation with Particular Reference to Science Education in Developing Countries." *International Journal of Science Education* 25 (10): 1171–1204.

Rosenshine, B. 1979. "Content, Time and Direct Instruction." In *Research on Teaching: Concepts, Findings and Implication*, edited by P. Peterson and H. Walberg, 28–56. Berkeley: McCutchan.

Slonimsky, L. 2016. "Teacher Change in a Changing Moral Order: Learning from Durkheim." *Education as Change* 20 (1): 1–17.

Tabulawa, R. 1997. "Pedagogical Classroom Practice and the Social Context: The Case of Botswana." *International Journal of Educational Development* 17 (2): 189–194.

Tabulawa, R. 1998. "Teachers' Perspectives on Classroom Practice in Botswana: Implications for Pedagogical Change." *International Journal of Qualitative Studies in Education* 20: 249–268.

Tabulawa, R. 2003. "International Aid Agencies, Learner-Centred Pedagogy and Political Democratisation: A Critique." *Comparative Education* 39 (1): 7–26.

Tabulawa, R. 2004. "Geography Students as Constructors of Classroom Knowledge and Practice: A Case Study from Botswana." *Journal of Curriculum Studies* 36 (1): 53–73.

Tabulawa, R. 2013. *Teaching and Learning in Context: Why Pedagogical Reforms Fail in Sub-Saharan Africa*. Dakar: Codesria.

Tawana, L. 2009. *Identifying Relevant Factors in Implementing a Chemistry Curriculum in Botswana*. Unpublished Doctoral thesis, University of the Witwatersrand.

Thomas, D. 2015. *African Traditional Religion in the Modern World*. Jefferson: McFarland.

Ukpokodu, P. 2012. "African Indigenous Education: Formal and Informal." In *Contemporary Voices from the Margin: African Educators on African and American Education*, edited by N. Ukpokodu and P. Ukpokodu, 3–28. Charlotte: Information Age.

Urwick, J., and Junaidu, S. 1991. "The Effects of School Physical Facilities on the Processes of Education: A Qualitative Study of Nigerian Primary Schools." *International Journal of Educational Development* 11: 19–29.

Vavrus, F. 2009. "The Cultural Politics of Constructivist Pedagogies: Teacher Education Reform in the United Republic of Tanzania." *International Journal of Educational Development* 29 (3): 303–311.

Vavrus, F., and Bartlett, L. 2012. "Comparative Pedagogies and Epistemological Diversity: Social and Materials Contexts of Teaching in Tanzania." *Comparative Education Review* 56 (4): 634–658.

Vavrus, F., Thomas, M., and Bartlett, L. 2011. *Ensuring Quality by Attending to Inquiry: Learner-centered Pedagogy in Sub-Saharan Africa*. Addis Ababa: UNESCO.

Verspoor, A. 1989. *Pathways to Change: Improving the Quality of Education in Developing Countries*. Washington, DC: World Bank.

Zimmerman, J. 2011. "'Money, Materials, and Manpower': Ghanaian In-Service Teacher Education and the Political Economy of Failure, 1961–1971." *History of Education Quarterly* 51 (1): 1–27.

6 Culture and schooling in Papua New Guinea

Lack of understanding of the depths of culturally derived constructs and the paradigms of which they are a part has played out at length in Papua New Guinea (PNG) since attempts to introduce 'modern' curriculum began to target so-called teacher conservatism in the 1960s. Over 50 years of reform efforts provide a longitudinal country study of the failure of successive progressive reforms, and a further example of the inter-relationship between cultural epistemology and formalistic paradigms, which is a fundamental part of the explanation for the progressive failures. Such perspectives can be overlooked in ahistorical research that treats current failures as aberrant cases rather than chronic patterns. Although PNG's population is only 7.6 million, the progressive failures in PNG also provide a Popperian refutation of any universal claims for progressive 'stages' of educational development, as undertaken at length in *The Progressive Education Fallacy* (Guthrie 2011, 103–172). This is germane because of the influence of the stages mentality on much academic and official literature on educational reform in non-Western cultures that was seen in Chapter 1.

Notionally, given the present level of research, PNG is a member of the Southeast Asian Cultural Cluster. PNG contains over 800 recognised languages (Lewis 2016) and a variety of cultures; albeit the cultures share a commonality in the depths of traditional formalism. In contrast to China's dynastic histories, but as with many other former colonies, indigenous historical perspectives must rely on contact histories, anthropological studies and oral history. An extensive research and evaluation literature, much of it from the 1970s to the 1990s and readily available only in PNG, demonstrates the depth that can be added from in-country publications with insights not available internationally. The analysis in this chapter derives from 160 publications on education in PNG, 70% of which were published locally. Some of their insights also were illustrated by the detailed example in Chapter 3 of methodological traps in the evaluation processes of the Curriculum Reform Implementation Project.

6.1 Traditional education

PNG demonstrates several long-recognised types of education.[1] One is *informal education*, which includes childhood socialisation. Socialisation into intergenerational culture (in the sense defined in Section 1.6 as unspoken, implicit rules of behaviour and thought) occurs from children's earliest years. The process gives young children their identity through the learning of constructs from their elders and siblings that define who they are and what it means to be a member of their particular group. Ochs and Schieffelin's (1984) well-recognised ethnography showed how Kaluli mothers in the Southern Highlands Province defined their babies' development through physical, emotional and verbal interaction. Kaluli described young babies as helpless and with no understanding. Babies were always accompanied, but rarely were spoken to directly or were the focus of attention. Mothers tended to hold their babies outwards to be part of the social group. Others might address the baby, but the mother responded on its behalf. She used well-formed language that was assertive, controlled and competent, which defined her expectations for the child's own language. Exchanges were not based on anything initiated by the baby, partly because in Kaluli culture discussion of others' feelings was inappropriate. As a baby aged, it was addressed directly and if necessary corrected by shaming, but responses were not expected. Babbling was not recognised as communicative or related to speech when it emerged. A baby was only regarded as beginning to speak when it used the words for 'mother' and 'breast'. Then the mother provided assertive adult phrases to be copied and promoted the child into situations requiring their use. The child's own utterances were corrected to take adult form as part of a hardening process so that it could converse eventually as an assertive adult in a face-to-face egalitarian society, which ability defined its cultural identity.

A second type of education is *non-formal education*, where knowledge is passed on the job from experts in a particular field to others who are learning these skills, for example in fishing, gardening or tribal warfare. Technical skills were available generally (depending on age and gender) and satisfying in their practicality and relevance to village life (McLaughlin 1994). Among the Abelam in East Sepik Province, for example, every villager participated in teaching and learning of non-sacred activities, such as gardening, hunting and fishing, building food houses, domesticating animals and rearing children (Wallangas 2003). Among the Bundi on the border of Madang and Simbu Provinces, children, once weaned about the age of 4 or 5, received informal instruction in the skills and beliefs necessary for the physical and social environment (Fitz-Patrick and Kimbuna 1983, 44–47). Boys moved from the women's house to the men's house and received an arrow to mark the first ceremonial period of their life. They learned by watching and imitating arrow and spear making, house building and pig raising. Much time was also spent playing games with a range of hunting and fighting skills required for inter-tribal warfare. Throughout childhood, emotional punishment (such as shaming) and, less frequently, corporal punishment were used to ensure behaviour complied with traditional expectations.

Third, and less well recognised as existing in oral societies, is *formal education* (Elkin 1945). The anthropological literature describes a PNG paradigm, probably going back millennia, that provided a basis for formalistic instruction through which particular forms of highly valued knowledge were – and still are – passed from one generation to another in systematically structured, elaborate and varied ways (Lawrence 1964; Carrier 1980, 1984; Lancy 1983). The teaching process often required lengthy separations from the rest of the community and extraordinary amounts of time and effort could go into elaborate ceremonies and rituals. Institutionalised teachers did not exist, but knowledgeable people acted as mentors, providing guidance through leading, instructing and demonstrating. These leaders were acknowledged and they personally taught initiates, whether individually or in groups. They often gave didactic verbal instruction based on esoteric, sacred knowledge. Learners had to master this curriculum; it could not be newly generated, but could only be passed to initiates by those who already possessed it.

Among the Bundi, boys' passage to manhood required a period of authoritarian formal instruction starting with a flute ceremony when they were some 10–14 years old (Fitz-Patrick and Kimbuna 1983, 48–52). Learning involved much practice of skills and recitation of instructions, with beatings for bad behaviour and brutal punishment by fire. However, correct behaviour could generate respect and earn praise and other rewards. Completion of this period of the boys' learning was marked by another initiation ceremony involving exchange of pig meat, after which they were men capable of taking part in tribal warfare. Increasingly, esoteric knowledge about sacred rites and sorcery, which were an important aspect of life, was available later in adulthood to initiated males selected by recognised leaders such as the clan wizard. Among the Abelam too, sacred activities were only taught and performed by initiated elders and village leaders, and only selected adult men could learn construction of spirit houses, cultivation of sacred yams, special dances, magic rituals, sorcery and witchcraft (Wallangas 2003). Training involved fasting, special dieting, ritual reciting, study of herbs and their processing, and the application of skills to improve food production, heal sicknesses and kill people. Each stage of initiation had its own entry requirements, a prerequisite being passing of all tests at the preceding level.

Despite the variety of cultures in PNG, a unified epistemology going back to the ancestors and the deities underlies traditional formal education. An important anthropological work noted that traditionally people dismissed the principle of human intellectual discovery except in minor matters (Lawrence 1964). Instead, myths were the sole and unquestionable source of all important truth. Myths told that all valuable parts of the culture were invented by the deities, who taught people both secular and ritual procedures for exploiting them, as Lawrence (1964, 33) explained:

> The body of knowledge was conceived to be as finite as the cosmic order from which it was contained. It came into the world ready made and ready to use, and could be augmented not by human intellectual experiment but only by further revelation by new or old deities. . . . There was no need – in fact, no room – for an independent human intellect.

Sacred elements were normally available only to select initiated males through formal education as adulthood approached and, later, in adult life. Ritualism, sacred rite and sorcery were important aspects. The knowledge was pragmatic and finite, revealed either by the gods or through instruction from those who already possessed it. The purpose of this secret knowledge was human survival and faithful transmittal of the culture, and it was controlled and regulated to these ends. From a pedagogical perspective, it was to be accepted not challenged. A learner gained new knowledge from initiation, dreams, purchase or ritual, which knowledge was neither self-generated nor critically assessed. Thus, knowledge was revelatory, and this usually applied to general technical knowledge as well as to sacred knowledge. The task of the learner was to look and to listen to people known to be trustworthy (Carrier 1980, 1984). Above all, learning was, and still is, 'a social construction based on relationships with teachers that are immediate, dialogical, and hierarchical' (Guy, Haihuie, and Pena 1997, 36).

6.2 Continuities in colonial formalism

Numerous elements of traditional pedagogy actually anticipated the formalistic schooling introduced in the colonial period (McLaughlin 1994; Guthrie 2003). Colonialism began in PNG from the 1870s in Papua (initially a British colony, from 1906 an Australian territory) and New Guinea (initially a German colony, from 1921 a League of Nations then United Nations mandated territory), which were jointly administered by Australia until self-government in 1973, followed by independence in 1975. Europeans brought a new variety of formal education institutionalised in schools (Weeks and Guthrie 1984). The little schooling that was imposed came mainly from Christian missions rather than the administration. The role of mission schools was to convert 'natives' for a limited role as Christian church members, clerks and labourers, with formal schooling mainly limited to basic literacy and numeracy (McNamara 1979; Smith and Guthrie 1980). Many indigenous people were reluctant to take up schooling, but over time it became accepted, indeed sought after, as a route to the advantages of the introduced way of life, which Carrier (1985) demonstrated in Manus Province.

Smith's (1985) research into the history of Catholic education by the Sacred Heart Order in Papua in the first half of the 20th century illustrated a system that was typical of both mission and administration colonial teaching. In 1916, the Order promulgated a formalistic curriculum and teaching methods in a pastoral letter that governed the mission's schooling until the 1960s. The letter aimed to regulate and improve schools by instituting a set programme of work and organising regular supervision similar to inspections. At the centre of the system were boarding schools where foreign religious staff taught. Feeder day schools in villages usually had paid Papuan teachers. A separate instruction for priests detailed supervision of these teachers and defined their three main roles as religious leaders, village schoolmasters, and family models for Christianity.

As schoolteachers, their main purpose was to facilitate evangelisation through instruction of children in the Christian doctrine and way of life. Teachers were required to prepare lessons well, be punctual, keep regular hours, ensure that discipline and order were kept, ring the bell early, keep the children silent and in good order, maintain rolls and be strict. Mission policy banned corporal punishment, but teachers commonly used it anyway. Teachers were to teach catechism using repetition and question and answer until material was learned by heart, with simple charts supplied as teaching aids. At the discretion of the supervising priests, the secular curriculum could include reading, writing, arithmetic, history, geography and other subjects. The Order's approach had considerable similarities with teaching and teacher education elsewhere in PNG, as shown by studies in Manus (Pomponio 1985), and elsewhere in Papua and the adjoining Torres Strait in Australia (Williamson 1985).

In the colonial period, education in schools was new, but formalistic colonial teaching was different from pre-colonial formalism in degree not kind (Guthrie 2003, 2011, 153–172). In traditional PNG, the learner's job was to find people who had knowledge and would teach it, which schools came to institutionalise. Leaving schooling in mission hands meant that the revelatory epistemological base of Christianity was compatible with the way knowledge was understood in traditional cultures. Pedagogy also had major commonalities, especially the underlying assumption that teachers know and transmit, and students do not know and receive. Both traditional and colonial formal education required students to play passive roles in receiving knowledge through memorisation of a curriculum of basic facts and principles. There is no indication that colonial educators deliberately sought to reinforce traditional teaching styles, so that the coincidence between traditional and modern was fortuitous. Nonetheless, the underlying similarities in epistemological and pedagogical principles do help explain why formalistic teaching in schools was (and still is) congruent with the pre-existing cultural paradigm.

6.3 Effects of tradition in modern times

Prior to World War II, the Australian administration took little part in schooling. After the war, it slowly took education more seriously. Initially, the emphasis was on schooling for rural life. Mass literacy and a gradualist approach to universal primary education became an objective in 1955, but still remains incomplete. With gradualism increasingly out of step with the international decolonisation agenda, the late 1950s and early 1960s saw expansion of primary schooling, establishment of more secondary schools, and increased teacher training. From 1960 to 1973, attempts were made to provide a curriculum that would allow Papua New Guineans to localise the expatriates who dominated the urban sector and plantation agriculture. When oversupply of primary school leavers started to become apparent in the late 1960s, the focus turned back on schooling relevant to village life (McNamara 1979; Weeks and Guthrie 1984). A major report (Weeden, Beeby, and Gris 1969) led to the creation of a

National Education System in 1970, including structural, teacher education and curricular reforms that tried to address the two inherently contradictory paths of schooling for the modern sector and schooling for the community.

Unsurprisingly, a great deal of continuity existed between colonial mission schooling and the national system's use of formalistic primary and secondary inspectorates. My own mixed methods research on the secondary inspectorate in the late 1970s found that the inspectorate was the keeper of school standards, a body of senior professionals trusted by its own seniors to evaluate teachers and schools, and allowed considerable authority to do so (Guthrie 1983a). The system was designed to ensure promotion by ability, as defined by professional acceptability to the Department of Education, rather than by seniority. The inspectorate's procedures made formal, written, professional judgements through a range of observation methods, standardised report requirements and strong peer review (Guthrie 2004). The approach to rating teachers was underpinned by an informal theory of formalism. This pragmatic theory placed the teacher firmly in control of whole-class processing of fixed syllabuses and textbooks, with the main emphasis on knowledge of basic facts and principles. Teachers were expected to have dominant roles and students generally to be passive, although limited overt teacher-student and student-student interaction was encouraged under conditions controlled by the teacher. Students were expected to have individual work and, on occasion, group work. Additionally, formalistic syllabuses, examinations and administration set the tone for schools and classrooms. The inspectorate had not expressed its formalistic construct in writing, but the underpinning could be inferred from the statutes, official notices, handbooks, inspectorial minutes, and procedures circulars detailing the inspectorial system, as well as from observation in schools and inspectorial meetings, and analysis of written reports on teachers and schools. Inspectorial formalism recognised that unsureness lay at the base of many new teachers' professional activities and attempted to generate confidence from understanding of educational routines with clear outcomes. The teacher, isolated in the classroom and often in a remote school, was linked to the system outside the school by the inspector and few other individuals with whom the teacher had direct contact. Undoubtedly, the inspection system restricted some teachers, for example by insistence on the keeping of full daybooks for three years after graduation. However, for most teachers, the inspectors were not restrictive of classroom behaviours because their orientation was to diversify and improve teachers' skills.

Discipline for teachers was largely external to the schools, and the inspectorate was the agent for this. Such discipline could be considered in two ways. First, there was discipline of the type that inspectors preferred: compliance with formal routines, which – even when not fully understood by teachers – provided a standard for assessing and improving performance. In their continual emphasis on lesson planning, daybook keeping, programme preparation, roll keeping, records maintenance and so on, the inspectors constantly tried to establish a disciplined approach to teaching. Teachers who followed the routines were likely to receive positive reinforcement in the form of promotion but, more importantly, their students were likely to benefit from a more thorough and systematic approach to schooling both in and out of the classroom. Teachers who did not follow the routines were likely to be the recipients of the second side of discipline: punishment for failure to follow requirements. Failure to be registered or promoted was a serious matter not taken lightly by the inspectors. Their inspections were designed to ensure that, within the available resources, teachers were assessed as systematically as possible, and that the assessment had built-in checks and balances.

Schooling has continued to change since the early 1980s, and the inspectorial system was modified along with the rest of the education system during the 1980s and early 1990s (Boorer 1993; Thompson 1993). However, its fundamental principles have continued to be entrenched as the means by which the Department of Education maintains operational stability and professional standards in schools (Mel 2007). The teaching style embedded in the inspectorate's formalism maintains continuity back through mission schooling to traditional formal education, a central aspect in all periods being the role of teachers in transmitting knowledge.

Other researchers throughout the post-colonial period have also noted the impact of local knowledge systems. Lindstrom (1990) observed that these systems are an important component of the deep cultural inclinations that both teachers and students bring to the classroom. Eyford (1993) noted that most children spend at least their first six years immersed in environments strongly influenced by cultural tradition rather than modern educational theories. Even after they enter school, a majority of learning time is spent in informal educational situations shaped more by cultural constructs than explicit pedagogy. Pickford (1998) found that inside the classroom, 'there are cultural meanings and sensibilities which mediate the activity structures of classroom practices, which also require acknowledgement if post-colonial teaching and learning are to be better understood' (6). Ope (2003), Kiruhia (2003), Kukari (2004, 2011) and Brownlee, Farrell, and Davis (2012) indicated that while such beliefs do alter, their essence still carries with the students through secondary school and teacher education. A formalistic construction of classroom behaviour helps link classroom pedagogy with the broader formalism of the education system as a whole, as well as with traditional culture. This formalist paradigm also affects the types of change teachers and students do and do not accept, and continues to affect strongly the type of pedagogy that teachers use and students accept intuitively.

Tradition has thus continued to be a real element in students' everyday lives and the learning styles they bring to school. The traditional paradigm based on revelatory epistemology is consistent with the underlying assumption in modern formalism that students attend school to obtain given knowledge from teachers. Both traditional and modern formalism require students to play passive roles in receiving revealed knowledge through remembering a curriculum of basic facts and principles. As Guy, Haihuie, and Pena (1997) put it, 'the problem is to find the right source or text, rather than engaging with the source or text in a creative fashion' (36). In distinct contrast, progressive knowledge is characterised by enquiry, reflectivity and creativity (McLaughlin 1994). Progressive Anglo-American education values questioning, creativity and problem-solving behaviours, but discussing, relating, sifting, appraising and hypothesising were not inherent in traditional education and might even be strongly discouraged. The lack of emphasis on enquiry, reflectivity and creativity in traditional epistemology is fundamentally incompatible with progressive reforms introduced in PNG in the late colonial period from the 1960s and in post-colonial society since.

6.4 Failure of progressive reforms

The inspectors' shared beliefs were held widely throughout the education system, reflecting a classroom culture that progressive curriculum and teacher education reformers have attempted – and failed – to break. Nationalistic and liberalising influences within the education system have attempted continuously to change schooling starting some ten years before independence in 1975. Progressive philosophies have appeared both to reject colonial gradualism and be relevant to ongoing needs. In the period before independence, C.E. Beeby was very influential, and a reformist director of education, K.R. McKinnon (1976), developed a similar progressive model of curriculum change, naming five curriculum 'stages' in PNG: Imitative, Derivative, Venturesome Local, Modern Local, and Integrated Modern Local (Guthrie 2011, 128–130). Since 1975, progressive influence has come through foreign aid, including for curriculum reform (Section 3.7) and for scholarships for study in Australia (Guthrie 2002). Extensive evidence shows that eight major progressive curriculum and teacher education reforms all failed in the sense that none had apparent sustained professional success at replacing classroom formalism (Guthrie 2003, 2011, 2012, 2014, 2015).

The evidence is summarised briefly here in overlapping chronological order.[2] The list is comprehensive in that it draws on the more solid empirical work, both qualitative and quantitative, particularly those where classroom outcomes have been studied, and on professional commentaries (the evidence is found in more detail in Guthrie 2011, 130–146). In contrast, long, deep and wide literature searches have not found examples of sustained progressive success. Professional documentation of other efforts tends to be free of data on classroom effects and is often buried in official and aid project files. The available evidence – most available publicly throughout this time – is that failure followed several paths.

Three earlier top-down change efforts, all in the 1970s, did not survive initial attempts at implementation and were allowed to fade away.

Primary mathematics

For a decade from the mid-1960s, TEMLAB (Territory Mathematics Laboratory) was an 'early modern local' attempt (in McKinnon's term) to reform primary mathematics teaching based on the work of the Canadian, Zoltan Dienes. TEMLAB introduced 'the new maths', which required teacher knowledge of this maths and progressive teaching skills using similar individual instruction methods to those entering Australia at the time. The progressive games approach failed, but was followed up with an even more ambitious attempt at a new maths curriculum called Mathematics for Community Schools (MaCS). It was introduced in 1978 and was considered relatively sophisticated compared even with Australian schools. Evaluations showed poor levels of student mastery, with the researchers concluding that the syllabus was not taught in the recommended spirit and placing much of the blame on the teachers rather than an inappropriate curriculum (Roberts 1978; Roberts and Kada 1979).

The community school

With independence in 1975, a major change attempted to transform primary schools into community schools in keeping with government policies encouraging community self-reliance. The reform adopted many elements of progressive education as part of an 'integrated modern local' approach. The curriculum was intended to be flexible and school-based, with only a framework provided for teaching so that instruction should be devised by the teacher to ensure that it was adapted to the community (Lancy 1979, 4). However, teachers lacked subject knowledge on which to build local curricula, including in science and mathematics. They could also lack both general knowledge and local knowledge about the community, and also its language, especially if posted outside their home area (Cheetham 1979). A Community Life Syllabus aimed to prepare pupils for returning to life in the rural community. Its progressive approach required teachers to be flexible and self-reliant, use improvised materials, and integrate the syllabus with other subjects as well as relate them to community activities. Many teachers preferred the previous more formalistic social studies programme, and the progressive syllabus was often unread and ignored (Watson 1979). Community schooling existed in name but not substance.

Generalist teaching (GT)

GT was another 'integrated modern local' approach in high school grades 7 and 8 from 1975 to 1979. In many ways, GT was a high school version of the progressive community school curriculum. It attempted to alter subject specialisation to subject integration using a primary teaching approach to class and subject organisation, as well as school-based curriculum development and changes to teaching styles. Field's (1981) comprehensive mixed methods evaluation found many contradictions between the policy and practice of GT. Teachers were given the freedom to experiment, to devise their own aims, objectives, teaching methods and content, but they were inadequately prepared and unable to cope. Schools usually met the Department of Education's timetabling requirements, but classroom approaches varied widely and only 30% of teachers attempted subject integration or thematic teaching. Teachers were formalistic, but GT required them to be willing and able to undertake curriculum development and teach progressively. Such responsibilities only showed young, generally inexperienced teachers more things they could not do and magnified feelings of insecurity, confusion and bewilderment. A Department of Education enquiry found GT adversely affected school standards (Roakeina 1977) and it was allowed to fade away.

A fourth curriculum reform was so heavily revised that it eventually bore little resemblance to the initial progressive precepts.

Secondary social science syllabus (SSSS)

From the 1960s to the 1990s, SSSS was a 'modern local' concept-based, spiral development effort at a student-centred, subject-integrated classroom after principles from Jerome Bruner and Hilda Taba. The approach was concept-based rather than fact-based with a spiral development of concepts from year to year. Pupils' community experiences were to be the basis of concept development involving as much as possible material from outside the classroom. Enquiry, experimentation and simulation were to be the key learning methods to develop concepts from pupil experience rather than teacher presentation. False assumptions in all this included an expectation that pupils working in a foreign language could derive abstract relationships and theoretical principles from social science concepts, the spiral development of concepts was therefore sound, teachers would have a solid grounding in academic subjects, and they could be facilitators of learning (Guthrie 1980). Classroom and student teachers had many difficulties with long and complex syllabus documentation and the department gradually adopted a textbook approach, albeit with a hope that it could involve some school-based curriculum development (Lornie 1982). Rewriting in the 1980s further downplayed the failed progressive approach, which evolved into a series of standalone student books with a mixture of geography, history and politics content far removed from the original integrated social science syllabus. Eventually the revised syllabus was replaced in 2006 with support from the Australian Curriculum Reform Implementation Project (CRIP). Despite the lessons involved in turning the original progressive syllabus into a more formalistic one, the new syllabus for grades 9 and 10 dubiously reverted to the progressive enquiry mantras at the centre of the original design 40 years previously (Guthrie 2011, 131–133).

A fifth reform using generalist teaching marked the beginning of unsustainable projectised reform using foreign aid.

Secondary School Community Extension Programme (SSCEP)

For some ten years from 1978, SSCEP was a high school pilot project with World Bank funding and international attention. This third 'integrated modern local' curriculum attempt took progressive elements from community and lower secondary a level higher to middle secondary grades 9 and 10. SSCEP introduced a 'relevant' curriculum that integrated classroom and practical work intended to lead students to value education for its contribution to improving village life (McNamara 1980). Like GT, SSCEP required major school-based change, including to teaching styles. The progressive approach stressed integrated curricula, activity methods, intensive school-based curriculum development and in-service teacher education (INSET), as well as practical work at boarding school outstations. Implementation of all these aspects was difficult, including a classic conflict between formalistic and progressive styles (Vulliamy 1983; Lipscomb 1985; Crossley and Vulliamy 1986). Evaluations by Crossley (1984) and Vulliamy (1985) found many positives in a well-funded pilot project under very favourable conditions, but many teachers found the development of integrated teaching-learning and assessment programmes excessively taxing. Many other factors also hampered implementation within schools. Staff and students were unwilling to move away from core subject study, unreasonable demands on teachers' time and skills involved an enormous level of INSET support, there were logistical problems providing enough practical work, and divisions between SSCEP and non-SSCEP staff occurred. With the end of the World Bank loan period in 1985, government funding could not be found and SSCEP faded away by the end of the decade.

From the 1990s, three further reforms derived from a 1986 Ministerial Committee into Education that recommended radical approaches to comprehensive classroom teaching and to greater equity and social justice influenced by integral human development themes.

The Education Reform

Progressive change derived from the Matane Report (1986) encompassed the whole elementary, primary and secondary school system, with recommendations for a far-reaching series of structural and curricular changes (Guthrie 2011, 138–146; Section 2.6). Structural change started with new village-based vernacular elementary schools for the first three years of schooling in grades K–2 (with a need to establish schools, provide a curriculum and teaching materials, and recruit and train vernacular teachers), removed grades 7 and 8 to primary schools (with an integrated generalist teaching approach and a requirement to retrain primary teachers for these grades), and added grades 11 and 12 to provincial high schools (with the necessity for changing curriculum and teaching methodology in secondary teacher education). Despite professional scepticism, the result was somewhat ad hoc reorganisation from 1993, which was completed by 2001 depending on provincial resources. The change was driven in considerable part by politicians in the belief that low-cost vernacular elementary schools would appear to meet election promises to increase enrolments. Little evidence emerged to suggest that planned school expansion targets or teacher education output requirements were met (Maha and Maha 2004; Webster 2006). The Education Department was able to resist some of the allied curricular pressures for a while, but Australian aid projects brought back progressive influences (McLaughlin 2011). At the beginning of this century, CRIP's attempts at progressive curriculum change derived from the Report targeted all elementary, primary and secondary school levels (Section 3.5). However, while the structural changes gave the appearance of reform, the curricular substance intended by the Matane Report did not actually require that the whole school system be restructured.

Despite some initial successes, two projectised 'integrated modern local' reforms did not outlast aid-funded trials.

Community Teachers' College Lecturers Professional Development Project (PDP)

In support of the Matane Report (of which it became, in effect, a subset), the 1989 McNamara Report argued against the formalistic approach dominating the theory and practice of teacher colleges, and recommended a qualitative shift to progressive teacher education programmes. PDP derived from this in the 1990s, funded by Australian aid and with implementation contracted from Australian universities. Project intentions called for a shift in teacher education away from the predominantly unreflective emphasis on basic skills towards 'critically reflective practice' and meaningful teaching. Formalism was viewed as an 'ideology' to be replaced, introducing a very value-laden term into a situation where the label 'cultural tradition' was rather more appropriate. Freirean adult education principles were also claimed to go 'beyond critical reflection/inquiry to transformative praxis.... based on critical reflection and transformative action.... Basically, lecturers were called upon to see themselves as political actors in a process of political (re-)socialisation' (Burke 1996, 41, 44, 47). Unsurprisingly in a well-funded and intensive programme, a mid-term review found professional development opportunities for college lecturers in Australia and PNG were having a positive effect on participants' competence and self-confidence (Toomey, Guthrie, and Penias 1992). The project was strong on rhetoric and might have had long-lasting effects on some lecturers, but there is no evidence that suggests radical reflection was sustained widely or had any flow-on in schools (Guy 1994).

Outcomes-based education (OBE)

The main curricular changes revolved around OBE, which was introduced from 2000 to 2006 by an Australian aid contractor through CRIP, which took up curriculum reforms derived from the Matane Report. The project included a central focus on measuring student outcomes, but was packaged with progressive theories about child-centred schooling such that implementation was associated with variously labelled integral human development, social constructivist and transformational themes (NDOE 2001; Norman 2006). As seen at length in Sections 3.5–3.7, CRIP displayed little if any awareness of the history of progressive failures, and produced little valid or reliable evidence that progressive curriculum reform impacted classroom formalism or student achievement. One outcome, reported in a major government planning framework, *Papua New Guinea Vision 2050*, echoed the reaction against OBE in South Africa, which PNG's experiences paralleled (NSPT 2010, 34):

> Extensive consultations throughout the country indicated that there is an overwhelming dissatisfaction with the newly introduced. . . . Outcome-Based Education (OBE) curriculum. Parents and teachers have revealed that the quality of learning and teaching has been greatly compromised by OBE. . . . It was also revealed that teachers are currently overworked because of the demands imposed on them by the teaching methodology prescribed by OBE. It is imperative that OBE is immediately replaced.

In 2014, the Minister for Education announced that OBE had been abolished and the Department of Education would replace it with a new Standards Based Curriculum (NDOE 2014, 2015).

6.5 Prevalence of formalism

Half a century of progressive curriculum reform efforts failed to generate paradigm shift from formalistic teaching styles in primary and secondary schools. The efforts were well meant, but their progressive assumptions usually received little critical scrutiny. Many of the reforms successfully delivered technical inputs, for example supplying materials to schools, but an absence of sound evidence of sustained classroom success contrasts with extensive agreement that none succeeded at shifting formalistic teaching towards progressive practice. The body of findings provides a damning case against progressive curriculum reform in PNG given the imbalance favours formalism 8–0 over progressivism.

With a long history of traditional formal education and colonial schooling, and half a century of progressive reform failure, it is no surprise that widespread and ongoing professional agreement exists in PNG that formalism has prevailed in schools for a century, and continues to do so:

- Formalism dominated in the colonial period (Pomponio 1985; Smith 1985; Williamson 1985);
- It pervaded the period surrounding self-government and independence in the 1960s and 1970s (Beevers 1968; Coyne 1973; Donohoe 1974; Larking 1974; Musgrave 1974; Guthrie 1983a, 1983b);
- It remained dominant in the post-colonial 1980s and 1990s (Matane 1986; McLaughlin 1990, 1995; Pearse, Sengi, and Kiruhia 1990; Ross 1991a; Avalos 1993; Burke 1993; Guy 1994);
- It has continued to prevail in schools in the 21st century (Monemone 2003; Wallangas 2003; Agigo 2010; Le Fanu 2011; Guthrie 2012); and

- It has been reinforced by formalistic
    - Teacher training (Guthrie 1983b, 1984; McNamara 1989; Avalos 1993; McLaughlin and O'Donoghue 1996; Guy, Haihuie, and Pena 1997; Kiruhia 2003),
    - Inspections (Guthrie 1983a; Weeks 1985; Boorer 1993; Thompson 1993; Guy 1994; Mel 2007), and
    - Examinations (Townsend, Guthrie, and O'Driscoll 1981; Ross 1991b; Mel 2007).

Widespread agreement has also existed, even among commentators who sought to replace it, that formalism is remarkably difficult to change, even at the tertiary level (Guy, Haihuie, and Pena 1997; Boorer 1999; Nongkas 2007).

Matters have not changed with time. Among the more recent reforms, no sound published evidence exists that the curriculum approach from the Matane Report was successful, that teaching styles changed consequently, or any of the goals of politicised rhetoric were met, despite large-scale professional, administrative and financial inputs through governmental and aid funding. The curriculum directions stemming from the Matane Report had major shortcomings. In claiming to present a PNG tradition of teaching, the report focussed on informal and non-formal education practices and overlooked the more relevant pre-colonial history of traditional formalism. The assumption of a more child-centred curriculum took little account of the cultural strength of the teacher-centred paradigm. In particular, the curricula ignored mistakes from the previous 30 years, particularly in re-introducing community schooling, generalist teaching and the progressive principles in the social science syllabus.

Many of the reforms also misjudged community attitudes in attempting to make schooling more relevant to village life. The populace generally saw schooling as an entry to modern life, not the village, and the reforms attempted to give children a type of education that parents did not seek (SSCEP being a prime example). Parents still widely view schooling as an investment targeting cash employment for their children and the ability for them to send home remittances, not an opportunity to learn skills for modernising village life. Even were community education now accepted as the primary purpose of schooling, orientation of formal schooling to village culture would not necessarily influence classroom teaching in the direction of progressivism. Community-focussed schools would be open to more influence from traditional formal pedagogy, not less.

A major difference between old and new is that traditional formalism in PNG is part of an oral culture, unlike the emphasis on literacy inside that institution of modern formalism, the school – and the content is also very different. Nonetheless, numerous elements of traditional education, especially formal education involving sacred knowledge, anticipated the formalistic classroom teaching that was introduced by colonial missions. A key assumption in traditional epistemology was that knowledge is revelatory. This is consistent with the underlying element in modern formalism that the teacher knows and transmits and the student does not know and receives. A second key element was that the learner's job was to find people who had knowledge and would teach it, which schools now institutionalise. Similar views of pedagogy in both traditional and modern times help explain the dominant role of teachers in traditional formal education and the acceptability of teachers as the source of knowledge in modern schools. Both traditional and modern formalism require students largely to play passive roles in receiving the ordained knowledge. Both share an emphasis on memorising a curriculum of basic facts and principles. The effect is that PNG has a formalistic paradigm that is inconsistent with the progressive Anglo-American alternatives that have been mediated through Australia.

6.6 Conclusion

Educational reformers in PNG cannot reject formalistic teaching merely as a colonial artefact. Formalism is grounded in epistemological constructs originally from pre-colonial times that are based on transmission of traditional knowledge – a cultural paradigm in existence long before British, German and the main Australian colonialism. Formalism was reinforced by the teaching style in colonial schools and has resisted reform since because it is far more consistent with cultural tradition than Australian versions of Anglo-American progressivism. The outcome has been a failure of paradigm shift from formalistic to progressive classroom methods despite continual reform efforts for some 50 years.

The wider relevance is that PNG is a long-term example of the worldwide failure of progressive reforms to compete outside their own Anglo-American cultural context with ancient revelatory epistemologies and formalistic paradigms. Progressivism is based primarily in a very different scientific epistemology involving intellectual enquiry and the generation of new knowledge, but the teaching paradigm derived from this has proven ineffective in developing countries. The progressive paradigm for curriculum development and teacher education in PNG has, like China and Africa, been a values-based policy imposed on teachers rather than a construct subject to field testing. In all the reforms in this chapter, progressive curriculums were imposed administratively, the teaching force (and usually the inspectorate) treated as an obstacle to change, and students as passive recipients. Despite half a century of effort, there is no evidence that progressivism has resulted in substantial modification of formalism.

The deep explanation for the lack of success in creating paradigm shift from formalistic classroom practices is that the progressive paradigm is alien to and inconsistent with traditional cultural epistemology and traditional pedagogy. Because of their pervasive influence, the formalist paradigm will remain embedded in PNG classrooms for the foreseeable future. Rather than adopting yet another round of confusing curriculum-driven progressive 'reform' intended fundamentally to change teaching styles, the clear implication is that teacher training and curriculum to replace OBE would do better to work at improving existing formalistic classroom practice. The way forward in PNG as elsewhere is methodology that elicits teaching and its improvement as culturally embedded acts, thus providing a constructive path for the development of a teaching style grounded in cultural epistemology (Part III). Formalism can provide a deep-rooted behaviour capable of modification to perform important educational functions in the foreseeable future. Curriculum development should derive from classroom practice and the use of progressive curriculum reform to foist inappropriate classroom change on teachers should be abandoned as a perennial failure.

Notes

1 Sections 6.1–6.3 derive in part from an article published in *Contemporary PNG Studies* (Guthrie 2015) with permission of the journal.
2 Section 6.4 summarises material in the *Papua New Guinea Journal of Education* (Guthrie 2014), published by the PNG National Research Institute, used with the permission of the Institute.

References

Agigo, J. 2010. *Curriculum and Learning in Papua New Guinea Schools: A Study on the Curriculum Reform Implementation Project 2000 to 2006.* Special Publication No.57. Port Moresby: National Research Institute.

Avalos, B. 1993. "Ideology, Policy and Educational Change." In *Participation and Educational Change: Implications for Educational Reform in Papua New Guinea*, edited by C. Thirlwall and B. Avalos, 99–124. Port Moresby: UPNG.

Beevers, R. 1968. *Curriculum Change in Developing Countries.* Unpublished Master of Education thesis, University of Leicester, Leicester.

Boorer, D. 1993. "School Inspectors as Agents of Change within the Papua New Guinea School System." In *Participation and Educational Change: Implications for Educational Reform in Papua New Guinea*, edited by C. Thirlwall and B. Avalos, 195–201. Port Moresby: UPNG.

Boorer, D. 1999. "Adopting the Andragogic Model in Papua New Guinea: Some Practical and Theoretical Considerations." *Papua New Guinea Journal of Education* 35 (2): 75–80.

Brownlee, J., Farrell, A., and Davis, J. 2012. "Understanding Learning and Teaching in Papua New Guinea: Elementary Teacher Trainers Engaged in Cultural Authorship in the Context of National Educational Reforms." *Australian Journal of Teacher Education* 37 (2): 25–40.

Burke, C. 1993. "From Basic Skills to Reflective Practice." In *Participation and Educational Change: Implications for Educational Reform in Papua New Guinea*, edited by C. Thirlwall and B. Avalos, 219–236. Port Moresby: UPNG.

Burke, C. 1996. "The Changing Agenda in Teacher Education in Papua New Guinea." *International Journal of Educational Development* 16 (1): 41–51.

Carrier, J. 1980. "Knowledge and Its Use: Constraints upon the Application of New Knowledge in Ponam Society." *Papua New Guinea Journal of Education* 16 (2): 102–126.

Carrier, J. 1984. *Education and Society in a Manus Village.* Report No.47. Port Moresby: Educational Research Unit, UPNG.

Carrier, J. 1985. "Education and the Transformation of Traditional Inequalities in Manus Province." In *Education and Social Stratification in Papua New Guinea*, edited by M. Bray and P. Smith, 86–97. Melbourne: Longman Cheshire.

Cheetham, B. 1979. "School and Community in the Huli Area of the Southern Highlands." *Papua New Guinea Journal of Education* [Special Issue on the Community School] 15: 78–96.

Coyne, G. 1973. "Education in Papua New Guinea Schools." *Papua New Guinea Journal of Education* 9 (1): 17–21.

Crossley, M. 1984. "Relevance Education, Strategies for Curriculum Change and Pilot Projects: A Cautionary Note." *International Journal of Educational Development* 4 (3): 245–250.

Crossley, M., and Vulliamy, G. 1986. *The Policy of SSCEP: Context and Development*. Research Report No.54. Port Moresby: Educational Research Unit, UPNG.

Donohoe, D. 1974. "Monitoring Educational Development in a Foreign Culture – Spotlight the Problem Areas." In *Educational Perspectives in Papua New Guinea*, 30–44. Melbourne: Australian College of Education.

Elkin, A. 1945. *Aboriginal Men of Higher Degree*. Brisbane: Queensland University.

Eyford, H. 1993. "Relevant Education: The Cultural Dimension." *Papua New Guinea Journal of Education* 29 (1): 9–20.

Field, S. 1981. *Generalist Teaching Policy and Practice*. Research Report No.36. Port Moresby: Educational Research Unit, UPNG.

Fitz-Patrick, D., and Kimbuna, J. 1983. *Bundi: The Culture of a Papua New Guinea People*. Nyrang: Ryebuck.

Guthrie, G. 1980. "Towards a New Social Science Syllabus for the 1980s." In *Introduction to the Revised Secondary Social Science Course*, edited by R. Lornie, 97–110. Occasional Paper No.3. Port Moresby: Teaching Methods & Materials Centre, UPNG.

Guthrie, G. 1983a. *The Secondary Inspectorate*. Report No.45. Port Moresby: Educational Research Unit, UPNG.

Guthrie, G. 1983b. *An Evaluation of the Secondary Teacher Training System*. Report No.44. Port Moresby: Educational Research Unit, UPNG.

Guthrie, G. 1984. "Secondary Teacher Training Effectiveness in Papua New Guinea." *Studies in Educational Evaluation* 10 (2): 205–208.

Guthrie, G. 2002. "Crumbs from the Table: The Impact of Globalization and Internationalization on the Poverty of Third World Universities." In *Internationalizing Education in the Asia-Pacific Region: Proceedings of the 2002 ANZCIES Conference*, edited by P. Ninnes and L. Tamatea, 325–338. Armidale: Australian and New Zealand Comparative & International Education Society.

Guthrie, G. 2003. "Cultural Continuities in Teaching Styles." *Papua New Guinea Journal of Education* [Special Issue on Formalism] 39 (2): 57–78.

Guthrie, G. 2004. "Typology of Educational Knowledge." *Papua New Guinea Journal of Education* 40 (1): 1–11.

Guthrie, G. 2011. *The Progressive Education Fallacy in Developing Countries: In Favour of Formalism*. New York: Springer.

Guthrie, G. 2012. "The Failure of Progressive Classroom Reform: Lessons from the Curriculum Reform Implementation Project in Papua New Guinea." *Australian Journal of Education* 56 (3): 241–256.

Guthrie, G. 2014. "The Failure of Progressive Paradigm Shift in Papua New Guinea." *Papua New Guinea Journal of Education* 41 (1): 1–28.

Guthrie, G. 2015. "The Formalistic Educational Paradigm in Papua New Guinea." *Contemporary PNG Studies* 22: 33–47.

Guy, R. 1994. "Reconstructing Teachers as Reflective Practitioners in Papua New Guinea." *Papua New Guinea Journal of Education* 30 (1): 45–59.

Guy, R., Haihuie, S., and Pena, P. 1997. "Research, Knowledge and the Management of Learning in Distance Education in Papua New Guinea." *Papua New Guinea Journal of Education* 33 (1): 33–41.

Kiruhia, J. 2003. "The Practicum as Experienced in the Student Teacher Role." In *Education for 21st Century in Papua New Guinea and the South Pacific*, edited by A. Maha and T. Flaherty, 109–116. Goroka: University of Goroka.

Kukari, A. 2004. "Cultural and Religious Experiences: Do They Define Teaching and Learning for Pre-service Teachers Prior to Teacher Education?" *Asia-Pacific Journal of Teacher Education* 32 (2): 95–110.

Kukari, A. 2011. "Cultural Construction of Indigenous Pre-Service Teachers' Identities Prior to Teacher Education." *Contemporary PNG Studies* 15: 134–145.

Lancy, D. 1979. "Introduction." *Papua New Guinea Journal of Education* [Special Issue on the Community School] 15: 1–6.

Lancy, D. 1983. *Cross-Cultural Studies in Cognition and Mathematics*. New York: Academic Press.

Larking, L. 1974. "Some Difficulties in Improving the Quality of Teachers in Papua New Guinea." In *Educational Perspectives in Papua New Guinea*, 130–137. Melbourne: Australian College of Education.

Lawrence, P. 1964. *Road Belong Cargo*. Melbourne: Oxford University Press.

Le Fanu, G. 2011. *The Transposition of Inclusion: An Analysis of the Relationship between Curriculum Prescription and Practice in Papua New Guinea*. Unpublished Doctoral dissertation, University of Bristol.

Lewis, M. (Ed.). 2016. *Ethnologue: Languages of the World* (19th ed.). Dallas: SIL International.

Lindstrom, L. 1990. "Local Knowledge Systems and the Pacific Classroom." *Papua New Guinea Journal of Education* 26 (1): 5–17.

Lipscomb, P. 1985. "Teacher Development through Curriculum Innovation." *Papua New Guinea Journal of Education* 21 (2): 219–228.

Lornie, R. 1982. "A Partial Evaluation of Grade 9 Social Science." *Papua New Guinea Journal of Education* 18 (1): 56–78.

Maha, A., and Maha, N. 2004. "Education Reform and Implementation in Papua New Guinea: The Missing Factor." *Papua New Guinea Journal of Education* 40 (1): 31–42.

Matane, P. (Chairman). 1986. *A Philosophy of Education for Papua New Guinea: Ministerial Committee Report*. Port Moresby: Department of Education.

McKinnon, K. 1976. "Curriculum Development in Primary Education: The Papua New Guinea Experience." In *Papua New Guinea Education*, edited by E. Barrington-Thomas, 49–56. Melbourne: Oxford University Press.

McLaughlin, D. 1990. "A Curriculum for Teacher Education: Some Preliminary Considerations." *Papua New Guinea Journal of Education* 26 (1): 29–35.

McLaughlin, D. 1994. "Through Whose Eyes Do Our Children See the World Now? Traditional Education in Papua New Guinea." *Papua New Guinea Journal of Education* 30 (2): 63–79.

McLaughlin, D. 1995. "Teaching for Understanding: The Melanesian Perspective." *Papua New Guinea Journal of Teacher Education* 2 (1): 7–15.

McLaughlin, D., and O'Donoghue, T. 1996. *Community Teacher Education in Papua New Guinea*. Port Moresby: UPNG Press.

McLaughlin, J. 2011. "Lost in Translation: Partnerships for Authentic Education in Papua New Guinea." *International Education Journal: Comparative Perspectives* 10 (2): 86–98.

McNamara, V. 1979. "Some Experiences of Papua New Guinea Primary Schools, 1953–1977." *Papua New Guinea Journal of Education* [Special Issue on the Community School] 15: 10–26.

McNamara, V. 1980. "School System Structure, Curriculum, SSCEP and Functional Motivation for Learning." *Papua New Guinea Journal of Education* 16 (1): 12–28.

McNamara, V. 1989. *Future Directions of Community School Teacher Education*. Port Moresby: Department of Education.

Mel, M. 2007. "Quality Assurance and Assessment in Education in Papua New Guinea." *Educational Research for Policy and Practice* 6 (3): 219–228.

Monemone, T. 2003. "Formalistic Teaching Is Not Imposed: It Is Indigenous to Papua New Guinea." *Papua New Guinea Journal of Education* [Special Issue on Formalism] 39 (2): 91–95.

Musgrave, P. 1974. "Primary Schools, Teacher Training and Change: Beeby Reconsidered – Some Data for the Pacific." *Papua New Guinea Journal of Education* 10 (1): 42–47.

NDOE (National Department of Education). 2001. *Annual Report*. Port Moresby: NDOE.

NDOE. 2014. "PNG Standards Based Curriculum Set for 2015." *Papua New Guinea Education News*. http://edu.pngfacts.com/standard-based-education/png-standard-based-education-set-for-2015

NDOE. 2015. "Awareness of Standards-Based Education (Statement by the Secretary for Education, M. Tapo)." http://edu.pngfacts.com/standard-based-education/png-standard-based-education-set-for-2015

Nongkas, C. 2007. *Leading Educational Change in Primary Teacher Education: A Papua New Guinea Study*. Unpublished PhD research thesis. Australian Catholic University.

Norman, P. 2006. "Outcomes-Based Education: A PNG Perspective." *Contemporary PNG Studies* 5: 45–57.

NSPT (National Strategic Plan Taskforce). 2010. *Papua New Guinea Vision 2050*. Port Moresby.

Ochs, E., and Schieffelin, B. 1984. "Language Acquisition and Socialisation: Three Development Stories and their Implications." In *Culture and Theory: Essays on Mind, Self and Emotion*, edited by R. Shwede and R. Levine, 276–320. New York: St. Martin's Press.

Ope, D. 2003. "The Implications of Educational Beliefs of Early Adolescents on their Learning Goals, Motivational Orientations and Achievements: A Case Study of Early Adolescents in Port Moresby North Schools." In *Education for 21st Century in Papua New Guinea and the South Pacific*, edited by A. Maha and T. Flaherty, 117–127. Goroka: University of Goroka.

Pearse, R., Sengi, S., and Kiruhia, J. 1990. "Community School Teaching in the Central Province: An Observational Study." *Papua New Guinea Journal of Education* 26 (1): 69–84.

Pickford, S. 1998. "Post-Colonial Learning: Classroom Rituals as Social and Cultural Practice." *Papua New Guinea Journal of Teacher Education* 5 (1): 6–14.

Pomponio, A. 1985. "The Teacher as Key Symbol." *Papua New Guinea Journal of Education* 21 (2): 237–252.

Roakeina, G. (Chairman). 1977. *Report of the Committee of Enquiry into Standards of High School Students Entering Colleges*. Port Moresby: Department of Education.

Roberts, R. 1978. "Primary Mathematics in Papua New Guinea." *Papua New Guinea Journal of Education* [Special Issue on the Indigenous Mathematics Project] 14: 205–220.

Roberts, R., and Kada, V. 1979. "The Primary Mathematics Classroom." *Papua New Guinea Journal of Education* [Special Issue on the Community School] 15: 174–201.

Ross, A. 1991a. "The Teacher Education Research Project." In *Teaching in Papua New Guinea: A Perspective for the Nineties*, edited by B. Avalos and L. Neuendorf, 73–91. Port Moresby: UPNG.

Ross, A. 1991b. "Examination Performance and Internal Assessment in School Certificate Science in Papua New Guinea: A Secondary Analysis of Published Examination Data." *Papua New Guinea Journal of Education* 27 (2): 1–7.

Smith, P. 1985. "'Labouring with Us in the Gospel': The Role of Papuan Teachers of the Sacred Heart Mission before the Pacific War." *Papua New Guinea Journal of Education* 21 (2): 151–161.

Smith, P., and Guthrie, G. 1980. "Children, Education and Society." In *The Education of the Papua New Guinea Child: Proceedings of the 1979 Extraordinary Meeting of the Faculty of Education*, edited by G. Guthrie and P. Smith, 5–21. Port Moresby: UPNG.

Thompson, P. 1993. "The Performance of the Secondary Inspector." *Papua New Guinea Journal of Education* 29 (2): 97–109.

Toomey, R., Guthrie, G., and Penias, W. 1992. *The Papua New Guinea Community Teachers' College Lecturers Professional Development Project: Report of the Mid-term Review Team*. Canberra: International Development Program.

Townsend, G., Guthrie, G., and O'Driscoll, M. 1981. *Criterion-Referenced Measurement: Towards a New School Assessment Policy*. Research Report No.37. Port Moresby: Educational Research Unit, UPNG.

Vulliamy, G. 1983. "Core Subject-Core Project Integration in SSCEP: Practice and Possibilities." *Papua New Guinea Journal of Education* 19 (2): 13–34.

Vulliamy, G. 1985. *A Comparative Analysis of SSCEP Outstations*. Report No.50. Port Moresby: Educational Research Unit, UPNG.

Wallangas, G. 2003. "Formalism Is Both Indigenous and Imposed." *Papua New Guinea Journal of Education* [Special Issue on Formalism] 39 (2): 96–100.

Watson, P. 1979. "The Introduction of New Curricula: Community Life." *Papua New Guinea Journal of Education* [Special Issue on the Community School] 15: 154–173.

Webster, T. 2006. "The Road to Universalising Primary Education in Papua New Guinea: Are We Really Serious About Getting There?" In *Sustainable Curriculum Development: The PNG Curriculum Reform Experience*, edited by P. Pena, 14–22. Port Moresby: Department of Education.

Weeden, W., Beeby, C. E., and Gris, G. 1969. *Report of the Advisory Committee on Education in Papua New Guinea*. Canberra: Department of External Territories.

Weeks, S. 1985. "The Teachers' Role: Research, Inspections and Standards." *Papua New Guinea Journal of Education* 21 (2): 197–204.

Weeks, S., and Guthrie, G. 1984. "Papua New Guinea." In *Schooling in the Pacific Islands: Colonies in Transition*, edited by R. Thomas and T. Postlethwaite, 29–64. Oxford: Pergamon.

Williamson, A. 1985. "Comparative Notes on the Role of the Indigenous Teacher in Papua, New Guinea and the Torres Strait Islands, 1871–1942." *Papua New Guinea Journal of Education* 21 (2): 163–172.

7 The failure of progressive paradigm reversal

Progressivism remains the dominant paradigm in the comparative education literature about schooling in 'developing' countries. It is a travelling policy among international, multilateral and bilateral aid organisations that often is supported by national governments and local innovators, for example as part of outcomes-based education in Papua New Guinea and South Africa. As Chapter 2 found, the evidence does not demonstrate that progressivism has made the transition to sustained classroom practice in primary and secondary schools, however it has continued to manifest as an axiom. The question that arises is whether it is appropriate any longer as the primary frame of reference for classroom change in developing countries. Jankowicz's (1999, 305) comment remains relevant:

> accounts of the measured development of ideas and practices within existing conceptual frameworks, well-accepted for their contemporary usefulness, should not exclude the periodic confrontation with the challenge of new thinking. . . . Whether as academics or practitioners, we need the stability of an agreed and enduring framework; but we need the challenge of alternatives, lest the paradigms which frame our thinking turn to cages which constrain it.

This interpretive chapter draws together previous material to analyse systematically the resistance of the progressive paradigm to deep-rooted alterations to its basic assumptions given its failure to compete beyond its own cultural domain. The commentary will follow Kuhn's lead in going past the reification of paradigms as abstract entities to the responsibility of believers for their worldviews. The approach will delve beneath the conventional academic surface to cognitive dissonance and other irrational side effects of goal-seeking behaviour to ask further, has progressivism become embedded in a cosmology of cumulative hallucination such that it has become an intellectual cage providing constructs that bound its proponents and restrict openness to alternatives?

7.1 Progressive paradigm shift in the classroom?

Kuhn's (1962) concept of paradigms was applied by Tabulawa (1997, 2011, 2013) to the social and educational constructs embedded in formalism and progressivism.[1] Tabulawa noted that one of the weaknesses of educational debate has been a failure to recognise the deep historical roots of teacher-centred and learner-centred classroom methods. Their assumptions about the social world, the nature of reality, and the learner are embedded historically in worldviews with antithetical epistemological assumptions and dialectically opposed value positions about the constitution of legitimate knowledge, how that knowledge should be transmitted, and how it is subsequently assessed. To propose that teachers and students undergo paradigm shift from a teacher-centred one to a learner-centred one is not just a technical issue or one requiring improved teacher training, but 'is necessarily a proposal that they fundamentally change their views of the nature of knowledge, of the learner and his/her role, and of classroom organisation in general' (1997, 192). Thus, the epistemologies underlying formalism and progressivism derive from opposed assumptions about the social world, the nature of reality, and the learner. Commonalities in cultures with revelatory epistemology – in which important knowledge comes from deities and the ancestors rather than from human inquiry – include a formalistic preference for teacher-centred methods to transmit given knowledge. In contrast, where scientific epistemologies prevail, the progressive view is that the student is the centre of the classroom rather than the teacher and knowledge is to be discovered, not transmitted (Guthrie 2011). In the face of such divergences, has paradigm shift from formalism to progressivism occurred in developing country classrooms?

Widespread evidence shows that progressive influences are inappropriate and/or reforms have had major difficulties, including in the 32 statistically representative developing countries cited in Section 2.8. Three detailed geographical examples in previous chapters included the study of Confucian culture in Chapter 4, which outlined Confucian epistemology that is documented for 26 centuries and links to a formalistic paradigm that continues to shape classroom teaching in China. Chapter 5 showed widespread examples of the failure of recent progressive reforms across 12 countries in Sub-Saharan Africa. In Chapter 6, Papua New Guinea (PNG) provided a longitudinal country study of the failure of eight major progressive reforms overlapping across some 50 years. There too, a traditional formalistic paradigm strongly influences the culture that teachers and students bring to the classroom. Any short-term progressive successes in pilot projects, particularly ones with high levels of aid funding, were not sustained.

The evidence about progressive reform failure manifests in the research and evaluation literature in several ways. The typology in Chapter 2 classified findings into six types from positive to negative.

1   The first type of evaluation was methodologically sound findings about progressive innovations in developing countries that have remained successful in the long term rather than just during pilot programmes. However, literature searches covering hundreds of studies of developing countries did not find sound evidence demonstrating long-term survival of progressive classroom reforms.

2   A second type of evaluation contained supportive findings derived from commercially contracted evaluations that can have vested interests in positive outcomes from progressive pilot projects. Such studies are prone to weak methodology and loose data interpretation (as illustrated in detail in the analysis of formative evaluations by the managing contractor of an Australian bilateral aid project in PNG in Section 3.5).
3   A third group of evaluations, seemingly the most common, found negative results about reforms, but perceived future success lying in further material and technical inputs, such as training. This was an issue particularly identified in Sub-Saharan Africa, where internationally influenced efforts at educational modernisation have essentially failed because technicist approaches focussed on inputs have considerably underestimated context (Chapter 5).
4   A not uncommon fourth type of evaluation questioned the effectiveness of progressive reforms on pragmatic grounds and looked to interim improvement in formalistic teaching methods. Such an approach in Beeby's educational 'stages' was a strong influence in the 1990s on writers associated with the World Bank who were focussed on educational reform in southern Africa (Section 5.3).
5   A small, fifth group of analyses recognised that technical inputs or time are insufficient and made more sophisticated recommendations for structural reforms to promote progressive change, especially where influenced by Bernstein's sociology of British pedagogy or, more radically, by the Marxist-influenced view that structural upheaval is necessary in society to remove tradition as an obstacle to modernisation (seen in PNG with 'The Education Reform' in Section 6.4).
6   A sixth group, often influenced by anthropology and cross-cultural psychology, variously rejected universal claims for progressivism. Such claims can be found in a positivist quest for universal laws that might give elegant predictions about the educational future (as underlying school effectiveness research), universalistic psychological assumptions about learning, and educational theories and practices from 'developed' countries.

Implicitly, all these groups recognise progressive failures – some more than others – with three types of theoretical response layered through the findings (Section 3.1). The first, most common and most surface layer is essentially managerialist. It interprets the lack of success of progressive reforms as due to poor resources, therefore necessitating further physical and professional inputs. Recommendations for these are commonly found in the econometric school effectiveness field and in educational analyses centred on classroom improvement. A second layer of findings, shaped variously by organisational sociology and post-colonial analyses, turns attention to political, economic and social systems as obstacles to change. The third, more fundamental layer sees underpinning cultural elements, either as organisational culture to be overcome as a barrier to change or to accept culture as an intergenerational grammar and a foundation for culturally embedded educational practice. Reactions to the evidence thus vary, but it is difficult to conclude anything other than that the shift to the progressive paradigm that occurred in the academic and official policy literature after the middle of the 20th century was not followed by paradigm shift inside formalistic developing country classrooms.

7.2 Gestalt-switch and paradigm reversal in the literature?

How has progressive paradigm theory responded to its failure to generate paradigm shift in classroom practice? As Patton (2008) put it, paradigms provide a 'worldview built on implicit assumptions, accepted definitions, comfortable habits, values defended as truths, and beliefs projected as reality' (267). The standard Kuhnian view is that science is conservative and that competition between incommensurable paradigms frequently involves values-based resistance to change among adherents to the 'normal science' paradigm that is under challenge (Bird 2013). This pro-change position implies that resolution of the tension between progressivism and formalism would require intellectually revolutionary change in constructs (a 'Gestalt-switch') among resistant formalists to generate paradigm shift to progressivism. To take analysis of paradigm shift further, the anomaly between progressive theory and sustained formalistic classroom practice opens up a different hypothesis to address failed scientific revolutions: a failure for paradigm shift to occur might require *paradigm reversal* involving revolutionary reversal of the challenger paradigm (this term has rarely been used in social science in considering paradigm shift between worldviews as far as I can ascertain, although narrower usages in neuropsychology relate to learning reversal). The anomaly between progressive theory and sustained formalistic classroom practice raises the possibility that a failure for progressivism to make the transition from theory to practice when exposed to competition outside its own cultural domain might require progressive paradigm reversal involving revolutionary reversal of the progressive worldview. Has Gestalt-switch and paradigm reversal occurred among adherents to resolve the anomaly and for theory to realign with reality, or has progressivism remained axiomatic?

Clearly, the middle four categories above sustain the axiom that formalistic methods need to be replaced by progressive ones. This literature often maintains simplistic assumptions despite the evidence.

- The Progressive Education Fallacy, that progressive teaching methods are necessary in primary and secondary schools in developing countries to develop enquiry skills, is rarely tested. On the contrary, there is no evidence that enquiry intellectual skills must be introduced in primary and secondary schools in revelatory cultures where knowledge is there to be revealed rather than created, nor that changing teaching styles is a necessary precondition.
- A false assumption is that all pedagogical options are possible and therefore likely. Rather, not all options are equally probable or desirable: progressivism may be possible in logic but improbable in practice.

- There is a widespread failure to recognise the considerable diversity within formalistic as well as progressive teaching styles, both of which are generic labels that encompass many teaching techniques. Diverse styles may be desirable in educational systems that encompass different types of epistemology, but the range of teaching styles that are appropriate options in many cultures are variations within formalism rather than between formalism and other styles.
- A false assumption can treat authoritarianism and formalism as synonymous. However, other cultures may not share Western perceptions of formalistic teaching as authoritarian, rather perceiving it as legitimate authority, especially when teachers are authoritative about their subjects.
- Ironically, in literature that purports to be child centred, enquiry into students' views about teaching and learning is very rare. There is a general lack of recognition that students can be complicit in co-constructing formalism with their teachers.
- There is also a lack of recognition of the extent to which students' individual needs may be addressed outside the classroom in some cultural contexts, including by formalistic teachers who can take into account students' learning needs during lesson planning. The effect is that formalistic teachers' objective behaviour may not be student-centred in the classroom, but their subjective thought may nonetheless consider learning needs in other ways.

In addition to these theoretical limitations, research and evaluations framed within the progressive paradigm have often been caged by a lack of methodological rigour. At one level, these are technical matters, as discussed in Section 3.3, but they interact with and compound the theoretical issues.

- Validity issues exist in specifying teaching style as dependent variable rather than student achievement, especially in classroom improvement research and evaluations of curriculum and teacher education reforms. School effectiveness research does use student achievement as dependent variable, but has commonly been caged by serious technical problems in measuring classroom factors, including use of data on class time from questionnaires that can provide only indirect and often inaccurate proxies for actual classroom behaviour. Too, recognition of context has usually been confined superficially to easily measured structural-functional variables rather than to culture. Allied to this, an absence of theory is common such that axiomatic assumptions are usually uncontested.
- Reliability issues exist in the statistical methods used in school effectiveness research, including the narrow range of variation in teaching practices in some developing countries that provides a lack of statistical discrimination and an underestimation of the impact of teaching styles.
- Relevance issues arise from the considerable effort trying to plant findings and methodology from developed to developing countries despite an absence of cross-cultural validation.

- Generalisability issues arise from operational constraints, which usually mean that the most common studies in developing country school systems are case studies of pilot projects (especially for classroom improvement studies) and questionnaire surveys (especially in school effectiveness research). With both approaches, basic sampling principles provide limitations that should (but often do not) restrict generalisation and prediction.

The literature often lacks recognition of such limitations or systematic rectification of methodological issues. Culturally biased and problematic assumptions about teaching styles in other cultures are often uncontested in curriculum and teacher education evaluations orientated to classroom improvement and in school effectiveness research. Manifestations were seen especially in contracted formative evaluations with vested interests. Overgeneralisation from pilot projects, case studies, and surveys was common, while more rigorous field experiments on the effects of teaching styles on student achievement are rare. With formative evaluations of pilot projects, the Hawthorne effect made prediction risky from any apparent early success to sustainability. Where reforms had implementation difficulties, the commonplace response was to recommend more resource inputs or time, with anomalies ignored, downplayed or mistreated as acceptable error. Ritual recommendations for more technical inputs or, more radically, calls for structural change embodied the ahistorical misinterpretation of anomalies in implementation as new challenges rather than chronic failure. It is hard to avoid the interpretation that most proponents treat progressivism as a value position to be implemented rather than a theory to be tested.

Insightful analysis of cultural effects does occur in some of the publications cited in this book as providing varying degrees of support for progressivism, but even these publications tend to skate on the cultural surface (below). Authors rarely question their faith in progressivism despite the lack of sound evidence of its success, so that an axiomatic faith in progressivism as a universal panacea is usually maintained even when its culturally biased and problematic assumptions about teaching styles in other cultures are contested. Rejection of universalistic claims means that the sixth evaluation group in Section 2.7 is the only one where thorough interrogations of the progressive paradigm are found. Otherwise, E.M. Rogers's (2003, 281) schema of five categories of adopters of innovation is relevant. He conceptualised innovators as the first 2.5% of a normal distribution to adopt a new idea; early adopters as the next 13.5%; an early majority of adopters as the next 34%; then the late majority as another 34%; and laggards as the last 16% of potential adopters. If rejection of the progressive paradigm is considered an 'adoption', then the appearance is that it has not proceeded much beyond Rogers's first group. Possibly, the increasing number of countries identified as having problems with progressive reforms and increasing discussion of cultural issues indicate that early adopters are starting to consider that progressivism is problematic in developing countries, but adherents to progressivism still usually maintain their axiomatic assumptions about the value of progressivism and appear unable to re-evaluate progressivism despite the evidence about its failures. Some exceptions serve to highlight a general absence of Gestalt-switch and a failure for paradigm reversal to occur.

Tan (2016) made a parallel interpretation in noting that a relatively under-explored topic in the current literature in comparative education is the problem of investigator bias in cross-cultural research. This type of bias can originate from theory-laden observation, so that everything a researcher perceives is influenced by and interpreted through the researcher's existing beliefs, values, assumptions and expectations. An explanation for lack of paradigm reversal lies in Tan's contrast of a 'weak approach' to theory-ladenness in the literature (where observations, although influenced by and interpreted through existing paradigms, are open to objective evaluation and revision) with a 'strong approach' (where worldviews are so strong they restrict openness to questioning because it is impossible for researchers to evaluate objectively the importance of their observations). The problem, Tan (2016, 85) considered, lies with the latter situation:

> Theory-ladenness is only detrimental to research if it results in investigator bias – where the researcher imposes one's existing beliefs, values, assumptions and expectations on the research subject, ignores the evidential impact of data (especially evidence that contradicts one's expectations), and draws conclusions that are aimed at reinforcing one's ideological preferences.

In Tan's terminology, the question that arises is, do progressives exhibit theory-laden bias to such a detrimental extent that they are caged by the strong approach to theory, or do they have an open-minded approach? Are adherents able to re-evaluate progressivism in view of the evidence, or are they unable to re-evaluate progressivism despite the evidence about its failures in developing countries? The answer is that the middle four groups, in particular, have generally exhibited strong theory-ladenness to such an extent that they are unable to re-evaluate progressivism despite the evidence about its failures. Progressivism has usually remained an intellectual cage that restricts rather than expands understanding of classroom change in developing countries.

7.3 Cultural issues and cognitive dissonance

Comparative education has a long history of interest in cultural context and a role for culture in schooling is virtually undisputed (e.g. Alexander 2000, 2008; Barrett 2007; Vavrus 2009); Schweisfurth 2013a). However, the actual role of culture is subject to different interpretations and is now the most crucial issue underlying theory and methodology in debate about formalistic and progressive paradigms.

One conceptualisation of culture focusses on behaviour change inside the classroom. Culture is treated as a background variable that can be observed but not readily altered – a critical precondition generating ecological validity for constructs about teaching, learning and the classroom (Guthrie 2011,

2015a; Section 9.2). Grounded mixed method research design starts with field experiments to identify the most effective teaching style for improving student achievement. Review of anthropological and sociological literature follows to analyse the style's cultural epistemology and pedagogic ontology and the extent to which they may be embedded in contextual educational paradigms as a background variable. Ethnographic and structured classroom observation then provide two different pathways to detail actual classroom behaviours and operational skills. Questionnaires, interviews and focus groups follow both pathways to elicit actors' perceptions, attitudes and constructs to explain their behaviours and their interpretations of the paradigms in which they are embedded. The intended outcome is identification of the most effective teaching style and of culturally appropriate choices for improvement of classroom practices, teacher education and curriculum design as independent variables and student achievement as dependent variable. This approach is based in philosophical pragmatism, working backwards from effective teaching styles to classroom interventions that are culturally grounded.

Another conceptualisation focusses on socio-politico environments and systemic issues outside the classroom that may generate greater understanding of educational systems and their potential for generating social change. Mindful of the many difficulties facing progressive reforms, culture is treated as a problematic 'implementation barrier' between progressive theories and their intended effects (Schweisfurth 2011, 2013a, 2013b). Along with complex expectations about reforms, resources, power, and agency, can be an emancipatory role for progressivism that is endorsed as rising above research evidence, Schweisfurth (2013b, 5) claimed:

> Human rights arguments rise above . . . questions of evidence; if LCE [learner-centred education] is the approach that respects learners' rights, as UNESCO and other agencies would have it, then the effort to implement it must go on. Context matters, but context isn't everything.

While the publications cited do not enter far into methodological issues, in effect culture is treated as an intervening variable between curriculum reform and teaching styles that can inhibit progressive change. A difficulty here is that even were systemic structural barriers involving governance and management resolved outside the classroom, culture is even less prone to interventions and would remain intuitive for teachers and students inside the classroom.

The two approaches have different conceptions of culture. The first follows Hall (1983) and Sternberg (2007) in treating it as an intergenerational grammar for understanding attitudes, values and beliefs that influence classroom behaviours. With *intergenerational culture* a critical precondition for ecological validity, progressivism becomes such an unlikely option in many developing countries that it is not a starting point at all – possible in logic but improbable in practice, although exceptions may occur in countries with distinctive cultural groups or at the higher cognitive levels in some schooling. As well, claims that developing country traditions may contain learner-centred elements (Thompson 2013; Smail 2014; Sarangapani 2015) have face validity, although they are open to interrogation and seem unlikely to overthrow findings that formalistic paradigms predominate.

The second approach to culture frequently follows Alexander's (2000) definition of pedagogy as both the act of teaching (the sense in which it is used in this book) and the discourse in which it is embedded. This approach collapses the meaning of cultural context and teaching style into one term concerned with *organisational culture*, which expands attention to structural elements, especially if influenced by Bernstein (2000), e.g. Barrett (2007) and Sriprakash (2012). Consistent with this, Schweisfurth (2015a, 2015b) interpreted school environments as 'a situated and resilient "pedagogical nexus" . . . in which culture, structures, and materials resonate across mutually-reinforcing dimensions of life in and out of school, including assessment, relationships, cohort formation, and parental and pupil aspiration' (2015a, 646). Such abstractions may have theoretical merit, but from a practical perspective the interweaving of so many elements is merely confusing in its failure to prioritise aspects that might lead to classroom interventions.

Further difficulties exist in migrating definitions of child- and learner-centred education associated with the second conceptualisation. Many studies retain progressivism as an axiomatic panacea even when they are insightful about cultural effects. O'Sullivan's (2004) mixed methods action research of learner-centred approaches among primary school teachers in Namibia found they would not only require new teaching skills, but would also have to change completely their cultural framework about teaching and learning. The solution was to redefine 'learner-centred' as 'learning-centred'. Mok (2006) reconstructed teacher-dominated lessons in China as an alternative form of 'student-centredness'; Vavrus (2009) offered 'contingent constructivism'; Ginsburg (2010) 'active-learning pedagogies'; and Sarangapani (2015) covered four bases with 'progressive/child-centred education/pedagogy'. In this semantic confusion, cognitive dissonance is apparent, while Gestalt-switch and paradigm reversal are not.

Confusion is also found in checklists for 'learner-centred education' that overlap considerably with formalism. The UNCF (2009, 151) report on UNICEF's Child-Friendly Schools programme used a Child-Centred Pedagogy observation schedule that contained 16 items. Inspection suggests that several could be as valid in teacher-centred classrooms as child-centred ones (e.g. the teacher presents lessons in a well-prepared and organised manner, moves around the classroom, communicates in a positive and friendly manner, and students pay attention and are respectful). Schweisfurth (2013a, 146) listed seven proposed minimum standards for learner-centred education. Each standard bore a qualification that interpretations of them might vary in different contexts, but five could well apply to good teacher-centred lessons (lessons are engaging to pupils and motivate them to learn, atmosphere and conduct reflect mutual respect between teachers and pupils, learning challenges build on learners' existing knowledge, curriculum is relevant to learners' lives, curriculum is based on skills and attitude outcomes as well as content). These five standards appear to fall into the trap (which Schweisfurth herself noted) that anyone can call anything learner-centred.

In the face of overwhelming evidence that progressivism has not replaced the formalistic paradigm in developing country classroom practice, and in the presence of extensively flawed research, even culturally aware reactions display cognitive dissonance in claims for progressivism that are migrated, nuanced or redefined confusingly so that progressive theory has not realigned with formalistic classroom reality. This cognitive dissonance is symptomatic of the progressive paradigm exhibiting classic symptoms of resistance to intellectual change, with few examples of Gestalt-switch and paradigm reversal. The effect is that progressivism is the 'normal science' paradigm that is now under challenge, with adherents exhibiting classic symptoms of values-based resistance to change.

7.4 A cosmology of cumulative progressive hallucination

The findings from the research and evaluation literature give rise to a fundamental question: why the stubborn and long-lasting faith in progressivism as an axiomatic panacea and the cognitive dissonance generated by findings about its failures such that paradigm reversal rarely occurs? In reading the literature on teaching styles, investigating the methodological issues, and in considering the absence of paradigm reversal that the data indicates is due, behavioural geography concepts about irrationality in human behaviour, published obscurely over 40 years ago, come to mind.[2]

Woolmington (1973) noted that rationality comes into play in information-based decisions taken in the light of clearly perceived goals. However, he posited irrationality limits the extent to which this occurs and is, he considered, the norm in human interaction with the social environment. Thus, he gave as a basic example the concern of some shoppers with the shopping environment rather than simply with price is financially irrational, which advertising exploits in its frequent focus on romantic imagery rather than the product. More widely, Woolmington considered that even in seemingly rational Western society much human behaviour shares characteristics with animistic cargo cults in PNG. The characteristics of cargo cults, the anthropological literature suggested, include that they occur when cargo (wealth) seeking fails and there is an absence of information about how to acquire it. These two characteristics generate regressive behaviour in the psychoanalytic sense because they represent failures to achieve something that is so little understood that seekers revert to ritual ceremony for explanation. As a modern example, Woolmington asserted that university examination systems are a coarse and faulty way of testing understanding. Their overt purpose is assessment, but too they are academically sacred ceremonial procedures, indeed covert ritual dances.

The effect of the continual representation of covert ritual behaviour as rational, Woolmington, Davey, and Walmsley (1972) further posited, is to generate a cosmology of cumulative hallucination. Human behaviour, they stated, is based on perceptual distortion, perception always being imperfect simply because of the physiological limitations of human sensory mechanisms. These limitations are compounded by the complexity of environmental texture and the intensity of emotional involvement with the perceived social environment. Thus, they hypothesised, human's view of interaction with their environment can be regarded in some cases as substantially hallucinatory dream worlds concocted through feedback processes that iterate continual and cumulative error. Negative feedback provides information to enable a system to correct its course, however positive feedback can actually be disequilibrating because false positives can lose the opportunity for corrective action, with compounding effect. The human environment becomes increasingly 'a clutter of man-made "stuff", which includes the fruits of... errors, the products of... hallucinatory behaviour, and the side-effects of goal-seeking actions' (2), so that humans are not rational actors as posited by classical economic theory but are delusional muddlers.

The claims of irrationality might be a stretch too far if they were taken to assert that research behaviour is necessarily bounded by perceptual distortion, delusion and hallucination. A more conventional expression is a statistical analogy. In inferential statistics, the process of falsification tests for the probability of 'true' negatives to assess the limits of universal claims to knowledge, but random false positives, misinterpretation of negative results as false, and explanations imposed upon the otherwise unknown residuals may all generate and iterate interpretive error indicative of cognitive dissonance. Otherwise, a succinct post-modern expression comes from the novelist Haruki Murakami (2002): 'understanding is but the sum of our misunderstandings' (146).

A vast anthropological and sociological literature demonstrates the cultural bases of mental constructs, however behavioural geography consideration of decision-making processes in spatial behaviour was derived from economics and psychology literature that is now common knowledge, but which had earlier challenged the dominant view in classical economics of 'man' as an economic maximiser: H. A. Simon's (1947) perspective that people are only intendedly rational decision makers who satisfice on the basis of imperfect knowledge bounded by a simplified model of the real world; G. A. Kelly's (1955) approach to perceptions as not just bounded by perceptual mechanisms but also derived from mental constructs that provide worldviews; Leon Festinger's (1957) insights about cognitive dissonance applying in situations where conflicting constructs create tension such that actors rationalise away the dissonant elements; Thomas Kuhn's (1962) concepts of paradigms and paradigm shift demonstrating the extent to which scientific constructs can consolidate into competitive schools of thought, as later introduced to debate over classroom change by Richard Tabulawa (1997); Anthony Ryle's (1975) rider that constructs can act as cages as well as frames, which is particularly relevant to failures of paradigm reversal; and Eric Woolmington's further rider that intendedly rational behaviour can be heavily distorted such that, consciously or unconsciously, it may become irrational and cumulatively so – to the extent, this book postulates, that rationally paradigm reversal should occur, but usually does not.

The emphasis in behavioural geography on the imperfections of perception arising from the physiological limitations of human sensory mechanisms had its foundations in a positivist ontology in cognitive psychology. Interestingly, Tan's (2016) discussion of theory-laden research recently reached its similar conclusion using epistemology derived from the philosopher Ludwig Wittgenstein. 'Comparativists', Tan (2016, 84) illustrated with Western research on China,

> are especially susceptible to investigator bias since they bring with them not only their subjective positionality but also their own cultural worldview and presuppositions that may differ from or even clash with those under study. Investigator bias is particularly relevant to research on policy borrowing.

The need, she commented, is to critically reflect on worldviews and the interaction between theory and data.

7.5 Progressive delusions

Counter-intuitive though the concept of cumulative hallucination in seemingly rational thought may be, it helps understand the ritual cage that progressive educational concepts can provide for policy reformers and academics to the extent that paradigm reversal is rare. As Alexander (2008, 1–2) sceptically wrote, a plethora of progressive claims about effective teaching and learning are rarely discussed, let alone evaluated against hard evidence, with the result that they rapidly acquire the status of unarguable pedagogical truth, become transmuted into policy and generate a self-reinforcing cycle. With progressivism in developing countries, the cycle has a basis in five regressive delusions that cage many reforms and their evaluations:

- Denial that the deeper cultural goal of reformers, consciously or unconsciously, is promotion of progressive 'enlightenment', in effect as part of cultural imperialism in the international culture wars (Chapter 1).
- Ritual recommendations that further progressive inputs will remedy problems that arise in pilot projects, when the body of evidence is that traditional paradigm behaviour usually overwhelms any progressive behaviours (Chapter 2).
- Cost-free recommendations for technical inputs that are financially unsustainable in poorer developing countries without aid support and its associated cultural imperialism (Section 2.4).
- Irrational confusion in setting reform goals as changes to teaching styles rather than to student achievement, based on the false premise (the Progressive Education Fallacy) that progressive classroom methods are necessary in the first place, such that there is a product-process confusion

between goal orientation to enquiry knowledge and enquiry learning as a teaching method (Sections 1.2, 2.9 and 3.3).
- Implicit failure to understand the cultural depths of resistance to progressive reforms, which is not rational in the presence of long-standing literature that makes common knowledge of the depths of cultural differences (Chapters 4–6).

Thus, the creation and maintenance of axiomatic claims for the progressive paradigm is based on weak cultural premises, suspect research methodology and the cumulative effects of interpretive error. Lack of recognition of, indeed resistance to, formalism and progressivism as a dialectic based in intellectually antagonistic worldviews means that debate on teacher- and student-centred styles is often superficial. Loose and culture-bound progressive goals have been prone to develop into data-free, value-ridden expressions of liberal ideals posing as theories rather than theoretical constructs subject to critical analysis and field testing. The bases of judgement that change is desirable are the educational norms of an individualistic, liberal Western academic subculture that have a hidden agenda of moral and philosophical values about desirable psychosociological traits for individuals and for society (Guthrie 1990, 222).

Progressive cognitive dissonance in consideration of the evidence is demonstrated when anomalies are incorrectly ignored, downplayed or mistreated as acceptable error. The effect is that random false positives are treated as indications of future possibilities and dissonant elements are ignored as false negatives, so that negative feedback ('the reform is less than successful') is mistreated as positive ('now we know what further inputs are required to generate success'). Ahistorical research, an absence of evaluation findings showing sustained progressive adoption, ritual recommendations for yet more technical inputs or, more radically, calls for structural change collectively embody the misinterpretation of anomalies in progressive implementation as new challenges rather than chronic failure.

The state of denial about the very strong evidence of progressive failure goes some considerable way to explain the lack of paradigm reversal that might otherwise occur from more rational understanding of reform goals, contrary evidence and the importance of cultural context. The outcome does not often appear to be new cognitions that generate fundamental changes to existing constructs. Despite all the failures of progressive reform, cognitive dissonance has proponents teetering away from the brink of Gestalt-switch, clutching at increasingly finely nuanced definitions of progressivism that are difficult to separate from formalism, and falling back on mantras such as human rights, even though intergenerational culture provides a more effective understanding of classroom change. Thus, the progressive paradigm, in claiming to produce more reliable and dependable knowledge than non-scientific paradigms, appears to be the opposite: a delusional intellectual straightjacket so heavily distorted by perceptual processes, the complexities of cultural environments, culture-bound constructs, research limitations and value judgements that it has led irrationally to a cumulative hallucination. Rather than a virtuous circle of increasingly informed decisions on improving the effectiveness of classroom teaching in developing countries, the outcome has often been a vicious circle of misinformation provided by recommendations for continuing the irrational pursuit of the unattainable.

7.6 Conclusion

A scarcity of deep reflection on findings is such that the progressive paradigm has often not been deconstructed. Widespread failure to generate paradigm shift has not led to paradigm reversal. Instead, it is now the progressive paradigm that is exhibiting classic symptoms of resistance to intellectual change. Regressive behaviour is apparent because the delusions are founded in lack of clearly set goals and in failures to achieve something that is so little understood that seekers revert to ritual publication ceremony for explanation. Iteration of progressive delusions in the literature can be understood as a cosmology of cumulative hallucination because the outcome is a self-reinforcing cycle of citations in evaluations and reviews such that continued repetition of the ritual dance camouflages the irrationality of the classroom reform goal that the publications purport to progress. Indeed, the ironic effect of child-centred progressive thought can be to position children in developing country schools as victims of the culture wars.

Perhaps the most fundamental flaw is a failure to understand the cultural depths of formalistic paradigms. As Morrison (2012) has similarly concluded from a very different perspective, 'there probably needs to be a paradigm reversal in development theory. It is indigenous culture which should be given normative status, with *modernity* given the status of that which needs to adapt and to develop' (185, emphasis in original). When cultural issues do receive attention, claims for progressivism are often migrated and nuanced. The resulting semantic confusion indicates cognitive dissonance when Gestalt-switch would be a more appropriate response to the evidence of progressive failure to generate paradigm shift among classroom formalists in developing countries. Until formalism replaces progressivism as the primary frame of reference for classroom change in contexts where it is appropriate, the continued effect is that the progressive paradigm will remain axiomatic as a travelling policy. Widespread failure to generate paradigm shift in classroom practice has not led to paradigm reversal. Instead, the progressive paradigm has become an intellectually caged, distorted and history-free educational ideology.

Irrational academic behaviour like this implies a contradiction within progressive thought that itself raises questions for research. Perhaps the research focus should turn from teachers and students in developing country schools to progressive reformers and evaluators from developed country universities, and to their failures to understand the depths of the formalistic paradigm and the lack of necessity to fundamentally change it. There is thus more to the commentary than an occasionally gleeful quickstep through a History of Cognitive Psychology. The purpose is to encourage a corrective to complacency, including the history-free cultural myopia that pervades aspects of classroom reform in developing countries. The extent to which comparative education can overlook the evidence before it partly comes from methodological blind spots, progressive intellectual cages, and culturally biased value positions that disguise the extent to which it can be a covert part of the soft power culture wars. Even more fundamentally, this all points to educational arrogance founded in notions of the superiority of Western civilisation that are quite delusional.

Notes

1 Sections 7.1–7.3 derive in part from an article published in *Compare* (Guthrie 2017, 63–64, 69–73), available online: www.tandfonline.com/doi/full/10.1080/03057925.2016.1138396.
2 Sections 7.4–7.5 are based closely on an article published in the *Southern African Review of Education* (Guthrie 2015b) with permission of the journal.

References

Alexander, R. 2000. *Culture and Pedagogy: International Comparisons in Primary Education*. Oxford: Blackwell.
Alexander, R. 2008. *Education for All, the Quality Imperative and the Problem of Pedagogy*. Create Pathways to Access Monograph No.20. London: Institute of Education, University of London.
Barrett, A. 2007. "Beyond the Polarization of Pedagogy: Models of Classroom Practice in Tanzanian Primary Schools." *Comparative Education* 43 (2): 273–294.
Bernstein, B. 2000. *Pedagogy, Symbolic Control and Identity: Theory, Research, Critique*. Lanham: Rowman & Littlefield.
Bird, A. 2013. "Thomas Kuhn." In *The Stanford Encyclopedia of Philosophy*, edited by E. Zalta. Stanford: Stanford University. plato.stanford.edu/entries/thomas-kuhn/
Festinger, L. 1957. *A Theory of Cognitive Dissonance*. Evanston: Row and Peterson.
Ginsburg, M. 2010. "Improving Educational Quality through Active-Learning Pedagogies: A Comparison of Five Case Studies." *Educational Research* 1 (3): 62–74.
Guthrie, G. 1990. "To the Defense of Traditional Teaching in Lesser Developed Countries." In *Teachers and Teaching in the Developing World*, edited by V. Rust and P. Dalin, 219–232. New York: Garland.
Guthrie, G. 2011. *The Progressive Education Fallacy in Developing Countries: In Favour of Formalism*. New York: Springer.
Guthrie, G. 2015a. "Culturally-grounded Pedagogy and Research Methodology." *Compare* 45 (1): 163–168.
Guthrie, G. 2015b. "The Cosmology of Cumulative Progressive Hallucination." *Southern African Review of Education* 22 (1): 7–18.
Guthrie, G. 2017. "The Failure of Progressive Paradigm Reversal." *Compare* 47 (1): 62–76.
Hall, E. 1983. *The Dance of Life*. New York: Doubleday.
Jankowicz, D. 1999. "Frames or Cages?" *Human Resource Development International* 2 (4): 305–307.
Kelly, G. 1955. *The Psychology of Personal Constructs*. New York: Norton.
Kuhn, T. 1962. *The Structure of Scientific Revolutions*. Chicago: University of Chicago Press.
Mok, I. 2006. "Shedding Light on the East Asian Learner Paradox: Reconstructing Student-Centredness in a Shanghai Classroom." *Asia-Pacific Journal of Teacher Education* 26 (2): 131–142.

Morrison, K. 2012. "The Promise of Orthodox Christianity for Sustainable Community Development." In *Radical Human Ecology: Intercultural and Indigenous Approaches*, edited by L. Williams, R. Roberts, and A. McIntosh, 179–204. Farnham: Ashgate.

Murakami, H. 2002. *Sputnik Sweetheart*. London: Vintage.

O'Sullivan, M. 2004. "The Reconceptualisation of Learner-Centred Approaches: A Namibia Case Study." *International Journal of Educational Development* 24 (6): 585–602.

Patton, M. 2008. *Utilization-Focused Evaluation*. Thousand Oaks: Sage.

Rogers, E. 2003. *Diffusion of Innovation* (5th ed.). New York: Free Press.

Ryle, A. 1975. *Frames and Cages: The Repertory Grid Approach to Human Understanding*. London: Chatto & Windus.

Sarangapani, P. 2015. "Viewing CCE Through an 'Indigenous' Lens." *Compare* 45 (4): 647–650.

Schweisfurth, M. 2011. "Learner-Centred Education in Developing Country Contexts: From Solution to Problem?" *International Journal of Educational Development* 31 (5): 425–432.

Schweisfurth, M. 2013a. *Learner-Centred Education in International Perspective: Whose Pedagogy for Whose Development?* London: Routledge.

Schweisfurth, M. 2013b. "Learner-Centred Education in International Perspective." *Journal of International and Comparative Education* 2 (1): 1–8.

Schweisfurth, M. 2015a. "Learner-Centred Pedagogy: Towards a Post-2015 Agenda for Teaching and Learning." *International Journal of Educational Development* 40: 259–266.

Schweisfurth, M. 2015b. "Make Learning, Not War." *Compare* 45 (4): 644–647.

Simon, H. 1947. *Administrative Behavior: A Study of Decision-making Processes in Administrative Organizations*. New York: Free Press.

Smail, A. 2014. "Rediscovering the Teacher within Indian Child-Centred Pedagogy: Implications for the Global Child-Centred Approach." *Compare* 44 (4): 613–633.

Sriprakash, A. 2012. *Pedagogies for Development: The Politics and Practice of Child-Centred Education in India*. New York: Springer.

Sternberg, R. 2007. "Culture, Instruction, and Assessment." *Comparative Education* 43 (1): 5–22.

Tabulawa, R. 1997. "Pedagogical Classroom Practice and the Social Context: The Case of Botswana." *International Journal of Educational Development* 17 (2): 189–194.

Tabulawa, R. 2011. "The Rise and Attenuation of the Basic Education Programme (BEP) in Botswana: A Global-Local Dialectic Approach." *International Journal of Educational Development* 31 (5): 443–442.

Tabulawa, R. 2013. *Teaching and Learning in Context: Why Pedagogical Reforms Fail in Sub-Saharan Africa*. Dakar: Codesria.

Tan, C. 2016. "Investigator Bias and Theory-Ladenness in Cross-cultural Research: Insights from Wittgenstein." *Current Issues in Comparative Education* 18 (1): 84–95.

Thompson, P. 2013. "Learner-Centred Education and 'Cultural Translation'." *International Journal of Educational Development* 33 (1): 48–58.

UNCF. 2009. *Child Friendly Schools Programming: Global Evaluation Report*. New York: UNCF Evaluation Office.

Vavrus, F. 2009. "The Cultural Politics of Constructivist Pedagogies: Teacher Education Reform in the United Republic of Tanzania." *International Journal of Educational Development* 29 (3): 303–311.

Woolmington, E. 1973. *Ritual Dancing*. Occasional Paper No.3. Canberra: Royal Military College.

Woolmington, E., Davey, C., and Walmsley, J. 1972. *A Cosmology of Cumulative Hallucination*. Occasional Paper No.1. Canberra: Royal Military College.

Part III
The formalistic frame

8 Theory of formalism

Despite long-standing evidence about the ineffectiveness of progressive reforms, the progressive paradigm remains the primary frame of reference for theory and policy about 'modernisation' of schooling in 'developing' countries. The international focus on progressive and formalistic styles has generated debate about the merits of child-centred versus teacher-centred teaching, so that the types of classroom teaching, teacher education and curriculum that are appropriate are becoming contested. However, instead of paradigm reversal at theoretical and policy levels given the failure of paradigm shift in the classroom, we witness the delusional maintenance of axiomatic claims for the progressive worldview. Cognitive dissonance is evident in consideration of the evidence and few examples of Gestalt-switch occur. Progressivism seems to have foundered in a cosmology of cumulative hallucination involving compounding errors of judgement. The dominant effect is that the paradigm has become a theoretical and policy cage rather than a frame.

The implication of the failure of paradigm shift to occur in the classroom is that formalism is likely to remain embedded in school systems for the foreseeable future. The issue that Part III of this book addresses is the role that formalism can have as the primary frame of reference for classroom change. The central proposition is that formalism is compatible with traditional and ongoing revelatory epistemology and can be treated as a deep-rooted cultural behaviour capable of modification to continue to perform important educational functions, including transmission of modern content. The progressive assumption that classroom formalism is an aberrant distortion of education systems overlooks its usual place as a subsystem that is part of and highly compatible with a symbiotic whole. As seen in Part II, formalistic teaching is consistent with the formalistic examinations, teacher training and inspections that provide coherence in many educational systems. As well, formalism is not necessarily as narrow as often supposed. Formalistic teachers do not necessarily rely just on lecturing and there can be variation among them. Teachers and students can share the same expectations about the value of formalism, which can be hierarchical without being authoritarian, and authoritative formalistic teaching can foster student engagement. Teaching, curriculum, and teacher education can build upon these positives to provide a constructive pathway forward rather than remain bounded by the cultural limitations of progressivism. The opportunity is to take culturally intuitive formalistic teaching styles and develop them further, instead of trying unproductively to push teachers and students to adopt progressive methods that are counter-intuitive to them.

Part III presents theory, methodology and some decision-making implications of formalism as a frame rather than a cage. This chapter provides theoretical perspective on formalism, for taking it seriously as a theory of teaching rather than an obstacle to change. The way forward requires methodology that elicits teaching and its improvement as culturally embedded acts (Chapter 9), providing a constructive path for the development of culturally effective teaching styles, for which the Teaching Styles Model in Chapter 10 provides some definitional clarity. Any proposed classroom changes also need to take into account teachers' perceptions, which Chapter 11 will discuss.

The focus here on classroom change is primarily about teaching styles inside the classroom. None of the analysis of classroom formalism is intended as an apology for dysfunctional elements in formalistic education systems. The compatibility of classroom formalism with formalistic systems means it is open to influences from outside the classroom and the school, such as the widely recognised problem of examination stress for children in Confucian education systems. Parental pressure for success is understandable for the opportunity it can provide for future careers, but can overload both teachers and students with demands for longer school hours and private tutoring. Societal demands like these have both negative and positive effects inside the classroom, but to a large degree they are independent of the case for upgrading classroom formalism. Put another way, improving classroom formalism can be beneficial regardless of the presence or absence of examination pressures.

8.1 Lessons learned from progressive failure

So far, this book has established that progressive education, derived mainly from Anglo-American culture, has been the primary frame of reference for classroom reform of developing country classrooms for some 50 years (Chapter 1). Progressivism is axiomatic in the comparative education literature, it is a central tenet of international and bilateral aid agency policies, which involve cultural imperialism, and it has strongly influenced local change agents' attempts at curriculum and teacher education reforms. Yet Part II did not find evidence that demonstrates sustained transition from formalism to progressivism in the classroom (Chapters 2, 4–6). The paradigm remains sustained by an extensive research and evaluation literature, even though that literature is subject to publication bias towards findings favouring progressivism and widespread validity, reliability, relevance and generalisability issues (Chapter 3). From the evidence in earlier chapters, the following lessons learned can be abstracted.

- Progressive curriculum reforms often naively promote classroom change in developing countries. The borrowing of fashionable progressive Anglo-American alternatives to formalism, such as outcomes-based education,

can display a gross lack of awareness of cultural contexts in non-Western, particularly non-English speaking countries. Revelatory cultures often include robust educational paradigms that are not fertile fields for progressive classroom reform.
- Little if any methodologically sound evidence in the research and evaluation literature demonstrates the long-term survival of progressive reforms in developing country classrooms. On the contrary, studies from 32 statistically representative countries show that progressive reforms were inappropriate and/or had major implementation difficulties. This evidence is not biased significantly by national per capita income, eligibility for foreign aid, levels of human development, or geographic distribution.
- Nevertheless, the progressive paradigm has rarely shown fundamental changes to its constructs. Paradigm reversal has not occurred and, ironically, the progressive paradigm is now the normal science position under attack and exhibiting classic resistance to intellectual change.
- The underlying cultural issues impact heavily on teaching styles and curriculum. A fundamental criticism of progressive curriculum reforms is that they often exemplify the Progressive Education Fallacy in confusing process with product. The universalistic assumption that teaching the enquiring mind requires enquiry teaching methods should not be accepted at face value, but should be tested through field experiments in each cultural context.
- Foreign aid projects are a recipe for failure if they ignore cultural context and override local curriculum expertise. This is particularly the case when they are coupled with weak evaluation processes that do not subject axiomatic progressive assumptions to independent classroom scrutiny. In the project design phase, cultural assumptions should be subject to careful literature review to seek guidance on traditional epistemology and pedagogy. In a trial phase, independent field experiments should evaluate whether proposed innovations improve student achievement.
- Additional problems with progressive reforms are the complexity of implementation and the financial costs of technical inputs and structural change. These may well be necessary, but they would be more efficiently and effectively directed to upgrading formalism rather than failing to change it to progressivism.
- Curriculum and teacher education reforms can give the appearance of educational change, but a litany of failure follows if they incorrectly assume that teacher-centred formalism is a culturally inappropriate colonial remnant and attempt to replace it with child-centred progressivism. Such efforts remain symptomatic of cultural imperialism.

Evidence from countries with formalistic classroom paradigms does not demonstrate that progressivism is superior to formalism at increasing student achievement. The thrust of the evidence is that the range of teaching styles that are appropriate options within many cultures are variations within formalism rather than between formalism and other styles. More usually, reforms would do better to implement subject syllabuses carefully and take steps to improve the quality of the formalistic style of teaching with which teachers and students usually feel comfortable. The sensible conclusion in those developing countries where it is appropriate is that formalism should replace progressivism as the primary frame of reference for classroom change.

8.2 Universal versus local

As previously (Guthrie 2011, 238–241), some terms need clarification. *Local* refers here to cultural contexts in nation states, whether uniquely indigenous traditions or modern accumulations of cultural influences. *Commonalities* are elements that case studies and surveys find in many settings, but whose extent cannot be defined accurately beyond those settings. *Generalisations* are findings from survey samples that might apply in whole or in specified part to the populations from which the samples were drawn. *Universality* is used here in the positivist sense as the objective of research to find universal laws, to which Popperian methodological principles of refutation apply. However, the quest for universal laws that might give theoretically elegant predictions about the educational future will not be found in this chapter. Nor will there be any universalistic psychological or cultural assumptions or ill-considered learning theories and practices from education in 'developed' countries. Any universality will come from an eclectic use of methodology to seek local solutions to local problems.

The possibility of a progressive universal pattern in theory implies the possibility of its absence in reality. The previous review in *The Progressive Education Fallacy* found a null pattern of evidence rather than a positive one, with any apparent progressive patterns quite possibly random ones (Guthrie 2011, 238–241). This was a trap, because random distributions always contain clusters that can give the illusion of possible systematic patterns and of potential generalisability. Thus, optimistic adherents could perceive progressive success. The accumulation of evidence seven years later in Section 2.8 now demonstrates a negative pattern. The state of the art has moved past progressive failures as an educational commonality to become a strong generalisation based on a considerable number of statistically representative developing countries, but not a universality.

However, even this generalisation is conditional methodologically. The generalisation will not be true of all developing countries, or of all cultures within them, or of all schools, or of all classrooms, teachers or students. Essentially, in the absence of much useful work on teaching styles in the school effectiveness field, the available classroom improvement research is an accumulation of ad hoc case studies and surveys where the original choices about research sites were often haphazard or purposive rather than random. At present, accurate mapping of formalism's extent is not possible, which bounds this book despite the 613 educational publications from which its findings derive. As well, hypothetically at least, progressive models sometimes may be effective with the higher cognitive levels where they exist in schools; they may be relevant in those parts of educational systems that aim for an 'international' education; and they may be appropriate in some cultural settings. Equally, some cultures not included in the area studies in previous chapters appear to have similar epistemological principles at play. For example studies in Islamic culture suggest, in accord with the Confucian culture seen in Sections 4.2–4.4, that Islamic traditions have formalistic classrooms underpinned by concern for the development of student understanding founded in deep textual knowledge (Dhofier 1999; Boyle 2006; Moosa 2015).

The effect is that the most fundamental issue in this book is not teacher versus student, as embedded in the contradiction between formalistic and progressive paradigms, highly important though the issue is. Rather, the most important issue is relevance to cultural context, not only of progressivism but also of different varieties of formalism. Pedagogies, be they student- or teacher-centred, from one cultural environment may be highly inappropriate in another. While the evidence is clear that in developing countries formalism prevails, there are no blanket formalistic solutions for them any more than there may be progressive ones because the countries and their cultures vary widely.

The context-oriented approach here bears similarities with Scheerens' (2015) multi-level model of educational effectiveness findings, which were conceptualised as an integration of top-down system-level, school-level, classroom-level, and student factors (to which levels cultural factors are an antecedent). Scheerens found that a range of different interpretations of the rationality paradigm (synoptic planning, contingency theory, market mechanisms and cybernetics) quite effectively explained both positive and negative outcomes from educational inputs. In particular, contingency theory has as its central thesis that the effectiveness of organisations depends on certain more basic contextual conditions. It holds that there is no universal best way to organise, and success depends on a good fit among internal organisational characteristics and between internal arrangements and contextual conditions (17–18). In Scheerens' systems analysis, influence runs hierarchically from higher levels to lower levels, with higher level processes contextualising and controlling lower levels; however, these relationships are loosely coupled so that the lower levels have considerable autonomy. Antecedents and societal factors influence higher level national policies in interaction with system ecology. National policies influence lower level school factors, where implementation is affected by school ecology and school leadership. In turn, school factors influence classroom and student factors, with student characteristics and abilities playing out in interaction with learning processes to provide learning outputs. The approach in this book amounts to a contingency approach to context that provides a middle level framework for analysis within particular cultural contexts (whether global clusters or individual countries) where progressive national policies are usually ineffective if they run counter to cultural antecedents and where teachers, usually unsupervised in the classroom, have considerable autonomy in practice to implement policies or not.

One need is for context-specific reviews of the literature that can identify local educational paradigms on which to build, and to help generate policy-oriented findings for decision makers operating within those cultural contexts. Theoretically inelegant though it may be, solutions need to be grounded in local realities. Academics searching for universalities may find the concern for context confusing or counter-intuitive, but administrators rarely need have any concern other than for their own situation, so context is not a practical administrative problem within educational systems unless different local educational paradigms collide. Methodological limitations in research are also of reduced concern in the real world of educational decision-making. Case studies can provide insights appropriate for use by context-based decision makers, which is highly relevant to the promotion of grounded educational change. The teaching styles that teachers adopt carry implicit information for educational authorities: the teaching medium is a cultural message.

8.3 Revelatory epistemology and the formalistic paradigm

Two sets of seemingly incommensurable epistemological assumptions and educational values underlie the international clash of educational cultures. A commonality in cultures with revelatory epistemology is that important knowledge comes from ancestors and deities rather than human inquiry. In Confucian epistemology, as a major example, the dominant concern is with social and ethical principles (Section 4.2). The customary transmission of a moral order originating in an idealised golden age is revealed through writings attributed to Confucius. Nature is a given, the emphasis being on social justice derived from ancient wisdoms about social relations. As Tabulawa pointed out in Botswana, traditional Tswana cosmology also runs deep (Section 5.2). The same is true of tribal Papua New Guinea (PNG), where Melanesian tradition has formal revelatory teaching (Section 6.1). That China should have a commonality with Africa or PNG is surprising, but the explanation lies in the level of abstraction of the concepts. The similarities in the principles underpinning their epistemologies (that knowledge is based on revealed truths from previous generations and the gods), should not be confused with any idea that the contents of their epistemologies (who revealed what, when, how, and to whom) or institutional manifestations (academies with written records or oral bush tradition) are similar. Equally, the reverse applies. The differences in the surface manifestations of these epistemologies should not blind us to their underlying commonalities. Revelatory epistemologies like these are consistent with the assumption in formalist pedagogy that teachers know and transmit, and students do not know and receive.

Deep-rooted revelatory epistemologies about the nature of their various truths provide the philosophical foundations for formalistic educational paradigms centrally concerned with the inter-generational transmission of knowledge. Paradigms are systems of intellectual thought which provide social constructs that constitute ways of viewing reality. In revelatory cultural systems, formalist pedagogy involves a body of teacher-centred educational knowledge valued highly by adherents for its congruence with traditional beliefs and its effectiveness in transmitting them. Confucian philosophy of knowledge has been embedded in Chinese civilisation for at least 3,000 years and still underpins the prevalence of didactic, teacher-centred classrooms. Similarly in Melanesia, 'the problem is to find the right source or text, rather than engaging with the source or text in a creative fashion', with the consequence that 'learning is, above all, a social construction based on relationships with teachers that are immediate, dialogical, and hierarchical' (Guy, Haihuie, and Pena 1997, 36). The formalist paradigm provides long-term patterns for teachers' and students' behaviour, notably a didactic approach to revelation of knowledge to learners. Both traditional and modern formalism require students to play passive roles in receiving revealed knowledge through memorisation of a curriculum of basic facts and principles, scientific and non-scientific.

In contrast, central concerns in Western philosophy are with the metaphysical, rational thought as a distinguishing characteristic of humans, and the scientific study of nature (Needham 1956; Popper 1979). Where scientific epistemologies prevail, formalistic transmissional views of pedagogy do exist, for example they are common to much of continental Europe. The progressive view of pedagogy, derived mainly from Anglo-American educational philosophy, values questioning, creativity and problem-solving to construct new knowledge. In the progressive view, the student is the centre of the classroom rather than the teacher, and knowledge is to be discovered rather than transmitted. The emphasis on enquiry, reflectivity and creativity in revelatory epistemology is incompatible with revelatory epistemologies that do not encourage these types of thought, for example in the fundamentalist varieties of many religions. The deep epistemological substance that underlies the surface classroom forms of Southern formalistic paradigms is the fundamental explanation for the failures to generate shift to the progressive paradigm outside its own Anglo-American cultural context.

Thus, the competition between formalism and progressivism, as the two main pedagogical paradigms in the international educational arena over the last 50 years, derives from opposed assumptions about the social world, the nature of reality and the learner. Both traditions have very distinct views about what constitutes legitimate knowledge, how that knowledge should be transmitted, and how it is subsequently assessed. The introduction of Anglo-American progressive cultural precepts into societies with different beliefs generates conflict with revelatory values. Regardless of any merits of progressive education reforms in the abstract, the evidence clearly indicates that formalistic paradigms continue to prevail in developing countries. The high likelihood of failure might be considered as the only necessary reason to reject progressive reforms. However, change agents often misdirect attention on the failures of progressivism to school conditions, teachers, teacher training, inspections and the educational bureaucracy, rather than to the key underlying reason, which is the compatibility of formalism with revelatory cultures. Cultural incompatibility is a key to the failure so freely of progressive reforms in the past and for the continuation of failure in the future.

Even where teachers are not particularly conscious of the underlying epistemology, formalism provides a model for the classroom with assumptions that students can and do share. Teachers' and students' intuitive, culturally derived assumptions about the nature of knowledge and the ways it ought to be transmitted, as well as their perceptions of their classroom roles and of the goals of schooling, influence their teaching and learning styles. Formalistic teaching is an organised processing of fixed syllabuses and textbooks, with emphasis on memorising basic facts and principles as a building block for future learning (Section 10.1). In formalistic classrooms, the teacher's basic role is to have knowledge and transmit it; the learner's basic role is to remember that knowledge, preferably develop an understanding of it, and later act on it in an appropriate fashion and teach others eligible to receive it. The formalistic teacher is hierarchical and didactic, but uses formalism as a path to knowledge rather than promoting obedience as such. Limited overt teacher-student and student-student interaction (such as question and answer routines and paired work) may be permitted under conditions controlled by the teacher, who will predominantly use closed questions to check student recall (whereas the progressive teacher will tend to ask open questions to check student understanding). Students generally play a passive role in whole-class teaching, but they can share formalistic values with teachers and be complicit in maintaining them in a dominant role. Good formalistic teachers are authoritative rather than authoritarian, and physical punishment is not necessarily used as negative reinforcement. The evidence is clear that formalism continues to be the predominant teaching style in primary and secondary schools in developing countries.

For educators, improving teaching is a legitimate act. None of the above is intended as an argument for accepting formalism in its totalities. Nor is it intended to legitimise lack of effort to improve the level of formalistic teaching. The thrust of the evidence is that incremental change within the formalistic teaching style may well succeed, but attempts to change to another style have not and will not. Successful attempts to improve the level of formalistic teaching, it can be hypothesised, might occur where they focus on elements considered marginal to the core of formalism, but not where they appear to contradict key cultural precepts, understood in terms of the culture in which they are embedded.

8.4 Lessons about formalism

Despite some insights, references to formalism in the educational literature are usually pejorative.[1] Examples across the decades include Beeby (1966), who viewed the ritualistic formalistic teacher as 'an unskilled and ignorant one who teaches mere symbols with only the vaguest reference to their meaning' (52); Kumar (1988), who criticised the official 'textbook culture' in India and its requirements for formalistic teachers to follow 'slavishly' official dictates; Ackers and Hardman (2001, 256), who wrote that formalistic classrooms can appear dull and repetitive, the teachers bored and uninterested, and the pupils quiet and passive; and Taylor (2014, 38), who described children in rural primary classes in South Africa as being socialised into passive and subservient recipients. Rather than a broad survey of such references, further examples of research give a fuller picture of formalism in practice and cast light on seven key issues about its nature: (1) formalistic teachers do not necessarily rely just on lecturing, (2) there can be variation among formalistic teachers, (3) students may share formalistic values with teachers, (4) formalism can be hierarchical without being authoritarian, (5) formalistic systems can be structured to upgrade teachers' skills, (6) teachers' constructs provide them with a basis for purposeful assessment of classroom change and (7) formalism derived from other cultural contexts can be just as inappropriate as progressive borrowings. These lessons are mostly based on case studies and there is no firm indication about how widely they apply, but they do indicate the merit of not making premature assumptions about formalism in any particular context. Some of these findings are long-standing and apparently not widely absorbed into the progressive literature, which is another indication of the classic symptoms of resistance to paradigm change seen in the previous chapter.

Lecturing

One long-standing finding is that formalistic teachers do not necessarily rely solely on chalk-and-talk. In a unique comparison, Pfau (1980) contrasted formalistic 5th grade science classes in Nepal with progressive ones (he used Beeby's Meaning label) in the United States, but without judgement about the teaching styles. Table 8.1 collapses the student-focussed data from the 11 categories of classroom behaviour used originally.

Pfau reported that the differences between the formalistic teachers in Nepal and the meaning style American ones were statistically significant, but the table shows that the differences were generally of degree not kind. In sum, the

Table 8.1 Contrasts between formalistic and progressive teachers in Nepal and the United States

Teaching Category	Nepal	United States
Lecturing	78%	40%
Teacher Demonstrations	0	5
Teacher Questioning	7	17
Student Speaking	7	19
Workbook Work, Laboratory Experiences, Group Projects, Student Demonstrations, Library Research, Field Trips	2	15
Silence or 'General Havoc'	6	4

Source: Author, based on Pfau (1980, 407).

formalistic Nepali teachers lectured about three-quarters of class time. Additionally, they asked questions that students answered (albeit they used few other student-focussed methods). While the American teachers lectured about half the time of the Nepali teachers, it was still their most frequent activity. They also had considerably more time in a variety of student-focussed activities. However, the difference between the types of teaching was not the presence or absence of teacher- or student-centred activities but their extent. Nepal had 78% of classroom time in lecturing and teacher demonstration, while 16% of activities had overt student involvement. The corresponding figures from the United States were 45% lecturing and teacher demonstration and 51% with overt student involvement. Nepalese classes were not restricted just to lecturing, and American ones were far from devoid of it.

Variation within formalism

Over the decades and in many countries, there is considerable evidence of some variety in formalism. Fuller and Snyder (1991) reported from a structured classroom observation study of three lessons each by 154 junior secondary and 127 primary teachers in Botswana. While teachers were predominantly formalistic, there were many variations in teacher practice. The teachers were vocal and dominant in most classrooms, but they did not always use chalk-and-talk and their pupils were not always passive and silent. Substantial variation was found in the extent to which teachers used textbooks, written exercises and materials, in part depending on the subject and the size of the class. A good deal of time was spent on question, answer and recitation, mainly involving closed-ended questions, but again with considerable variation and with many teachers attempting to generate pupil action. In China, Mok's (2006) case study of 15 videotaped lessons from a Shanghai mathematics classroom found 67% of lesson time was whole-class instruction, 22% was individual work, and 11% was small group or pair work. Whole-class instruction included frequent questions to the students, although very few student-initiated questions, but there was some variation within lessons. In Tanzania, Barrett (2007) also found considerable variation in the nature of pupil-teacher interactions. She studied primary schools in two regions of Tanzania in 2002–2003 using interviews with 32 teachers in 18 schools and observation in 28 lessons to compare what teachers said was good practice with their classroom behaviour. In classes averaging around 45 students, lessons were fairly standardised but there was variation that seemed influenced by school culture, exposure to in-service teacher education (INSET), plus teacher confidence, subject knowledge and pedagogical skill. In PNG, Le Fanu (2010) noted that primary teachers in his case study of three schools expertly used a variety of strategies to transmit skills and knowledge, including affective ones such as showing respect towards their students. In Kenya, Lattimer (2015, 13–15) also found variation among formalistic teachers (Section 10.1). More comprehensively, the literature survey by Nag *et al.* (2014) of 260 published research reports on foundation learning in a wide range of developing countries consistently found chorus, copy writing and drill the most visible aspects of instruction, but with some variety in these practices.

Student expectations

A notable finding is that teachers and students can share common expectations about the value of formalism. Tabulawa's (1997, 1998, 2004) unchallenged insights into the meanings attached to pedagogical practices by both teachers and students came from his grounded case study of geography classes in a rural secondary school in Botswana (Section 5.2). Tabulawa used qualitative methods, particularly unstructured ethnographic classroom observation of the school's three geography teachers over a two-month period, supplemented by semi-structured interviews with them, four other departmental teachers and 10 students.

To reiterate, Tabulawa (1998) found routine classrooms that provide a detailed example of formalism. Knowledge was a utilitarian commodity; the teachers' job being to impart it, the students' job to acquire it. The teachers usually started lessons with recapitulation of the previous lesson, followed by lecturing and writing of brief notes of the board. Few questions came from the students, who generally sat quietly. The lessons usually ended with recapitulation by the teachers or quizzing of the students. Teacher–student relationships were paternalistic and formal. Teachers expected traditional respect and deference and maintained a social distance. Limited verbal contact was initiated by the teachers in highly formalised question and answer sessions. Considerable emphasis was put on students demonstrating the 'right answers' to closed questions, part of a central concern about maintaining teacher control. Notably, the students had a very similar perspective to teachers (Tabulawa 2004). Students actually resisted variations in teaching practice, including group discussion. They viewed knowledge as external, a commodity possessed by the school and teachers, and found in textbooks. If they wanted to pass the examinations, they had to get it from these sources. Teacher dominance was not necessarily perceived just as a product of teachers' inherent desire for social control, but was a mutually constructed, negotiated product to which students contributed through their expectations of teacher behaviour. The teachers' apparent dominance was not so much imposed as a co-constructed, negotiated authority that was a product of teachers' and students' mutual expectations of schooling derived from a shared culture.

Authoritarianism

One of the main barriers to an acceptance of formalism as having desirable properties is its connotation to westerners of a domineering authoritarianism, indeed even as a contributor to the notion of schooling as violence (Harber 2002; 2017). Western perceptions of formalistic teaching as authoritarian may not be shared in other cultures. Rather, not atypical perhaps is a 'benevolent paternalism', as found in a classroom observation study in PNG. The study found teachers did nearly all the structuring, soliciting and reacting, while pupils did almost none of these but did all the responding. While critical of such an approach, Dunkin (1977) found it appropriate to comment that 'the teachers were warm and supportive in their dealings with the children and the atmosphere in all classes was one of enthusiasm and interest' (10). Another finding about the culture of teaching in Hong Kong and China was that authoritarian classroom practices did occur, but hierarchical classes were surrounded by active and more informal interactions outside the classroom (Cortazzi and Jin 2001; Ho 2001). Similarly, Rao, Chi, and Cheng (2009) found in large formalistic primary school classes in China that children were very engaged in the learning process, teachers did not have to manage disruptive behaviour, children were seldom criticised and the classroom atmosphere was very pleasant.

If such situations are common, the affective consequence of formalism may be rather less negative than is commonly assumed. Not all formalistic teachers use violence, nor is the definition tied to this. Some formalistic teachers do use physical punishment (which I regard as a sign of low-level formalism) and others do not (which can be considered a necessary but not sufficient condition to be a high-level formalist). Other types of weak teachers use corporal punishment too — it seems more an issue of personality than teaching style and, no doubt, these teachers need help to reduce the worst aspects of authoritarianism involved in physical and psychological abuse.

Student engagement and academic standards

The key element in formalism is that teacher talk predominates, even though there may be some variation in teacher behaviours. However, the sight of students sitting passively does not necessarily imply lack of intellectual engagement with the content of the lesson. Some of the evidence in this book about formalistic teaching happens to come from lesser developed countries not noted for high academic standards. However, the Paradox of the Chinese Learner is based on the apparent contradiction between large formalistic classes and high educational achievement by Confucian-heritage students in international studies of mathematics, science and language (Watkins and Biggs 1996, 2001; Chan and Rao 2009; Sellar and Lingard 2013; Kember 2016; Tan 2017). Rather than focussing on 'surface' remembering of facts, teaching encourages active, 'deep' understanding of underlying meaning. Students in China are not necessarily regarded by formalistic teachers just as passive receptors of information, but are expected to develop their ability through an active process of internal construction which can lead to higher level analysis (Tan 2015). Teachers often use formalistic methods in a highly sophisticated fashion that actually encourages student engagement in classroom material, which is the underlying explanation for the high academic performance. In formalistic classrooms, the obvious dominance of teachers does not necessarily imply an absence of mental engagement by the learners.

Upgrading teachers

A common assumption is that formalistic teachers often operate in hidebound systems where improvements to teaching are not encouraged. A sixth finding, also from China, is that formalistic systems can institutionalise incentives for teachers to systematically upgrade their performance. Cortazzi and Jin (2001) reported that the school system could provide incentives for teachers to learn from each other. Good teachers could be honoured with titles (such as 'special' or 'model' teacher) and salary incentives that were gained after public and competitive demonstration lessons in front of large groups of peers. Teachers recognised through this process would then act as mentors, including giving further demonstration lessons to younger teachers, with attendance required for promotion. Peer lessons had a modelling effect, spreading through a kind of 'cultural epidemiology' in a chain effect because teachers could see specific practices being managed effectively within their own context. Such findings are becoming more recognised in literature on communities of practice for teachers' professional development (e.g. Ali 2011; Anwaruddin 2015), although, as Hairon and Tan (2017) pointed out from differing Confucian cultures in Shanghai and Singapore, they need adaptation to local experience.

Adoption of change

Cultural perceptions help explain why progressive innovations rarely survive the trial period, especially when policymakers and evaluators do not adequately address the cultural environment in which innovations take place. Under trial conditions, it is possible to obtain considerable Hawthorne effects with commitments of time from those singled out for special attention through in-service. However, project extension phases are usually unsustainable if they require the same high levels of commitment, often without relief from normal duties and usually with less in-service support for teachers. Change issues will be discussed in the following chapters, including simplistic assumptions that the various difficulties facing progressive curriculum change are due primarily to teacher conservatism (Sections 11.1–11.3).

The perceptual view is that decision-making processes are based on learned mental constructs derived from social and cultural environments, and that such constructs provide teachers with a basis for purposeful assessment of classroom options. Constructs and the educational paradigms in which they are embedded are not just individual perceptions, but embody shared values that are culturally framed and shaped ultimately by cultural epistemology. Conversely, parents, teachers and children do not just passively and reflexively apply cultural tradition – their responses can represent purposeful, thoughtful, rational behaviour. Teachers, in particular, are often among the best educated people in their communities. In formalistic systems, changes that build on the existing classroom teaching style have greater relative advantage than progressive reforms. Modifications to extant teaching methods need not challenge fundamental personal values, while results can be understood by teachers and parents as likely to improve exam performance. Thus, change that does not require paradigm shift to progressivism but builds on existing formalistic behaviours is more likely to be adopted as long-term practice.

8.5 Formalistic borrowings?

A simple but superficial answer to lack of local research on upgrading teaching is borrowing solutions from other countries. However, the failures of international transfers, due in considerable part to their cultural limitations, are widespread. Indeed, formalism derived from other cultural contexts can be just as inappropriate as progressive borrowings. This point was illustrated in the *Southern African Review of Education* by a spirited theoretical debate, influenced by Beeby (1966) and Bernstein (2000), in which Hugo and Wedekind (2013a, 2013b), in an exchange with Zipin (2013), proposed 'zero pedagogy'. This was a concept derived from an analysis of the reproduction of social class in South Africa by Hoadley (2006), who asked whether pedagogy is present in a classroom encounter if there is no evidence of learning or intended or actual change in the learner.

Hugo and Wedekind (2013a) expanded the alleged absence of learning to teacher education, where they elucidated zero pedagogy as an absence of relevant pedagogical knowledge brought by tertiary students to their teacher education. Teachers might bring rich contextual knowledge with them, but this would not qualify them as teachers (2013b, 173). What would qualify them is specialisation into the logics and forms of curriculum, pedagogy and assessment. Only once teachers have learned specialised pedagogy might they have the technical skills to integrate everyday knowledge with the specialised knowledge held by properly inducted pedagogues. Hugo and Wedekind proposed that teachers in training should learn pedagogy as a transaction, a view that drew on formalistic pedagogy common to a wide swathe of continental Europe, notably as 'disciplinary induction' to provide access to established ways of enquiry (Alexander 2000). Unsurprisingly, Zipin (2013) labelled the privileging of their version of specialised knowledge as cultural imperialism. In agreement, I later wrote that any consideration of context by Hugo and Wedekind was heavily grounded in Bernstein's materialist sociology of education, which focussed attention outside schools on structural elements such as social class, and only superficially on culture (Guthrie 2015). Their version denied indigenous formal teaching styles unless filtered through induction into pedagogy as Eurocentric academic discipline. Knowledge about teaching held in 'other' cultures was treated as background noise unless re-interpreted through the prism of pedagogy as learned in formal education institutions. In sharp contrast, Chapter 5 showed long African traditions of formal education influence teacher and student behaviour in the classroom.

In partial agreement with Hugo and Wedekind, Hoadley (2016, 41–46) re-entered the discussion focussing on Bernstein's instructional discourse (in

Bernstein's cumbersome and opaque terminology, evaluative rules about the knowledge to be transacted in classrooms) and his regulative discourse (which distinguishes teaching styles). Her instructional discourse emphasis was on rules and measurement of curriculum knowledge, and she considered that Hugo and Wedekind over-generalised about regulative rules around teaching styles. Hoadley agreed with Zipin that heed should be taken of the socio-ethical purposes of teaching (i.e. of regulative discourse around teaching styles), but pointed out that it 'should not displace the need for children, especially children from disadvantaged backgrounds, to be given access to formal specialised school knowledge' (43) (i.e. to curriculum content instructional discourse). The central issue was the ordering principles (priority) accorded the discourses. She prioritised instructional discourse because both the authoritarian apartheid system in South Africa and post-apartheid progressivism generated educational impoverishment.

However, Hoadley misread Guthrie (2011, 2015) as privileging everyday knowledge in instructional discourse over codified subject knowledge derived from scientific epistemologies, about which I am agnostic. As was made clear in Guthrie (2013), an article published alongside those by Hugo, Wedekind and Zipin, the central focus in my analysis is teaching styles (regulative discourse). Within teaching styles, the analysis prioritises culturally relevant local pedagogical paradigms (as ontologies with revelatory epistemological roots) over any assumption that Northern classroom methods should prevail. However, the approach is agnostic about instructional discourse, then and now excluding curriculum content as a separate issue for national authorities (Section 9.3). If such knowledge is not indigenous, it does require structuring according to the methodologies in the various subject disciplines, where and whenever they may come from, given academic disciplines are subject to paradigm change. Thus, English language classes on grammatical structure may display one form of linguistic epistemology and Chinese language classes another, even though both are taught using similar teacher-centred methods; and a paradigm shift may occur from structural English to functional. It follows that Hoadley's (2016, 46) claim, that my approach runs the danger of marking developing country children as differently disposed to learning disciplinary knowledge than their Northern counterparts, was nonsense. The proposition is that the teaching styles through which students learn knowledge are affected by their cultural grammar, which is not a deficit view of their ability to learn content. In Bernstein terminology, the postulate is that regulative discourse is more likely to be effective within his teacher-centred performance mode than his learner-centred competence mode in many cultural contexts, including South Africa.

In her latest book, Hoadley (2017) omitted this element of her analysis but re-emphasised a requirement for instructional discourse to predominate over regulative discourse in the belief that a change in subject knowledge could allow teaching methods to become less authoritarian (210). Essentially, this seems to be a contextual issue for continued debate in South Africa. In the meantime, I remain in agreement with Zipin that Hugo and Wedekind's continental

European approach to teaching styles involved cultural imperialism. Formalistic cultural epistemology with roots in continental European paradigms, in which pedagogy as discipline is embedded, does have resonances with African formalism but, like progressivism, the contextual relevance is fraught. Pedagogy as academic discipline is in unlikely company with the child-centred progressive paradigm, but the parallel is with criticism of Anglo-American classroom progressivism as also embedded in notions of Northern economic, political and cultural superiority. Both approaches reveal lack of understanding of the deep epistemological substance that underlies the surface classroom forms of Southern formalistic paradigms.

Nor will South-South transfer of findings about formalism from one developing country necessarily be relevant to others (Guthrie 2011; Lam 2014). An example that suffices is the failure of The Education Reform in PNG in Section 6.4. The structural thinking behind the reform was derived from South America (Avalos 1992a, 1992b). While notionally emphasising 'participation', essentially the major school reorganisation recommended was based in a radical Marxist-influenced Latin American view that structural upheaval is necessary in society to remove tradition as an obstacle to modernisation. The relevance to an entirely different context on the far side of the Pacific was never established. No sound evidence exists that the curriculum approach was successful in PNG, or that teaching styles changed as a consequence, or that any of the politicised goals were attained despite large-scale aid funding. Thus, in recommending formalism as the primary frame of reference for classroom change in developing countries, we need to be clear that in any particular country formalism and its improvement should derive from local epistemology and local paradigms.

8.6 Cognition

Literature from cross-cultural psychology demonstrates further issues for schooling and student achievement testing that derive from opposed epistemological assumptions and educational values. A review of cross-cultural psychology research by Sternberg (2007) found that teachers from one culture teaching students of another culture may not understand how they think (e.g. linear Western teachers may not comprehend dialectical Asian students). Children may do poorly in school because they do not understand the instructions about what to do with material, rather than because they do not understand the material itself. As well, individuals in different cultures may think about concepts and problems in different ways and have different views about the meaning of intelligence (e.g. classifying hierarchically rather than functionally). Sternberg also found that when children are taught in culturally appropriate ways, their achievement increases (although this finding did relate to data on content teaching rather than teaching method). Indeed, the very act of assessing cognitive and educational performance affects performance differentially across cultures, and students do better on assessments with familiar and meaningful material. Additionally, children may have substantial practical skills that go unrecognised in academic tests and may develop contextually important skills at the expense of academic ones (perhaps having adaptive skills that matter in their own environment but that teachers do not view as part of 'intelligence').

Developmental understanding of when higher level cognitive skills manifest has been changed by an especially important and stable finding from neuroimaging in the 2000s about the nature of the brain and of its growth. Essentially, the brain's growth does not finish until well after earlier suppositions that it finished growing by the early teens (Guthrie 2011, 246–249). During adolescence the brain undergoes a thorough reconstruction (Badenoch 2008; Giedd 2008; Stiles and Jernigan 2010). Changes in connectivity, transmission speed and functional balance pave the way for a fully mature brain, with complex reasoning functions localised in the rostrolateral prefrontal cortex, which does not finish growing until the mid-20s (Burgess, Gilbert, and Dumontheil 2007). The prefrontal cortex is the home of the higher cognitive levels dedicated to the memory, planning or execution of actions in goal-directed behaviour, including higher level cognitive functions such as analysis, judgement, planning, problem-solving and fluid intelligence (Waltz et al. 1999; Fuster 2001; Goldberg 2001; Ellis 2006). Without physical maturation of the prefrontal cortex, school-age teens have less than consistent capacity for the integrated brain activity and mental coherence required by higher level cognitive functions that enquiry learning seeks to develop.

This is not a case of biological determinism. The social environment is particularly influential on the way in which the brain develops, especially during later periods of growth. The mind emerges in interaction between neurological and interpersonal processes and with other environmental features, developing as ongoing experience shapes the genetically programmed maturation of the nervous system (Siegel 2006). When neurons become activated, both experience and genes create the connections between them. In particular, the cortex is largely undifferentiated at birth, i.e. it has neural plasticity and is shaped heavily by experience and behaviour, including in schooling, and develops executive functions that can change during its lifetime.

This finding is consistent with Lancy's (1983) view that the nature of formal operations is culturally derived. His overriding explanation came from the development of Piagetian research into a new 'stage' theory of cognition from a socio-cultural perspective. Ethno-mathematical research among students in PNG found that the sequence of Piaget's developmental stages was similar but not identical to his European findings. Leaving aside objections to stages methodology as such, Lancy found that the first 'stage' was very similar to Piaget's sensorimotor and early concrete operational stages, the level at which genetic programming has its major influence. Socialisation is the key focus of communication and many children's activities are very similar across cultures. The second, concrete operational stage finds enculturation taking over from socialisation. With culture and environment more influential and genetics less, different cultures emphasise different knowledge and ideas. The third stage of meta-cognition has individuals acquiring theories of language and cognition.

Essentially, this level is based on cultural values. Different cultural groups emphasise different epistemologies that represent values lying behind language. Lancy considered that Piaget's formal operational stage was a cultural theory emphasised in Western culture, but neither in Melanesian nor Confucian cultures. One deduction from Lancy's case is the dubious nature of any assumption that teaching styles from one cultural context will accelerate similar cognitive results in another context.

Obviously enough, schooling is an important part of the social environment that helps shape neural activation. The case for bridging education and neuroscience has been put by Sigman *et al.* (2014). Usable research findings may come for schooling from studies of interactions among physical maturation and culture, the location in the lateral prefrontal cortex of complex reasoning, the type of teaching methods used in primary and secondary schools, and the timing of curricular activities. Some possibilities have been indicated by consideration of curriculum implications in a collection edited by Meltzer (2007), the use by Duijvenvoorde *et al.* (2008) of imaging to analyse the effects of different types of feedback on different age groups, Gilbert and Burgess's (2008) discussion of the implications of executive function and social cognition for education, Schmidt-Wilk's (2009) questions about the role of reflection in learning relative to recent advances in brain science, and Abadzi's (2014) discussion of the applicability of cognitive science to early grade basic skills.

The development and functioning of the brain are highly complex issues only briefly canvassed here. Especially, the findings about the growth of the brain have implications for the earlier assumption that the brain is fully developed by the early teens and that progressive teaching could help students apply brains that were already fully grown. Rather, the part of the brain where advanced capacities develop is not fully grown until a decade or so later. The implication is that progressive attempts to utilise such abilities in the mid- and late teens may be premature. If physical maturation is one fundamental, the underpinnings of the failure of progressive classroom reforms may in part be biological, and not only educational, cultural or social, and therefore apply as much to youth in developed as developing countries. If these conjectures help provoke further investigation, the results may raise the possibility that progressive education is as much a fallacy in developed countries as developing ones.

8.7 Conclusion

Incommensurable epistemological assumptions and educational values underlie the international clash of educational cultures. In revelatory cultures, epistemology holds that important knowledge comes from truths revealed by gods and previous generations, which provides the philosophical foundations for formalistic educational paradigms centrally concerned with the inter-generational transmission of cultural knowledge. In revelatory cultural systems, formalist pedagogy is a body of teacher-centred educational knowledge valued highly for its congruence with traditional beliefs and its effectiveness in transmitting them. The formalist paradigm provides long-term patterns for teachers' and students' behaviour, notably a didactic approach to revelation of knowledge to learners. Both traditional and modern formalism require students to play passive roles in receiving revealed knowledge through memorisation of a curriculum of basic facts and principles. Even where teachers are not particularly conscious of the underlying epistemology, formalism provides a model for the classroom with assumptions that students can and do share. Teachers' and students' intuitive, culturally derived assumptions about the nature of knowledge and the ways it ought to be transmitted, and their perceptions of their classroom roles and of the goals of schooling, influence their teaching and learning styles. In formalistic classrooms, the teacher's basic role is to have knowledge and transmit it; the learner's basic role is to remember that knowledge, preferably develop an understanding of it, later act on it in an appropriate fashion and teach others eligible to receive it. Knowledge is to be revealed and teachers are its agents. Students are to receive the light and pass it on.

In contrast, a central concern in scientific epistemology is the scientific study of nature and society. Progressive Anglo-American education founded in scientific epistemology values questioning, creativity and problem-solving to construct new knowledge. Where scientific epistemologies prevail, the progressive view of pedagogy is that the student is the centre of the classroom rather than the teacher, and knowledge is to be discovered rather than transmitted. The lack of emphasis on enquiry, reflectivity and creativity in revelatory epistemology is fundamentally incompatible with progressive reforms that encourage all these types of thought. The deep epistemological substance that underlies the surface classroom forms of Southern formalistic paradigms is the fundamental explanation for the failures to generate shift to the progressive paradigm in classrooms outside its own Anglo-American cultural context.

Rather than trying to generate systemic progressive change, strong theoretical and practical reasons exist for evolutionary modification of formalism from within. Formalism is a deep-rooted behaviour capable of adaptation and of performing important educational functions now and in the foreseeable future, including producing high academic outcomes. The productive approach is to develop further culturally intuitive formalistic teaching styles rather than trying unproductively to have teachers adopt counter-intuitive progressive methods. The future for school teaching in developing countries lies in operating within the constraints of formalistic systems and in working to improve classroom formalism in those cultures where it is appropriate.

Note

1 Section 8.4 derives from Guthrie (2011, 30–36, https://doi.org/10.1007/978-94-007-1851-7_2, © Springer Science+Business Media B.V. 2011) with permission of Springer Nature.

References

Abadzi, H. 2014. "How to Improve Schooling Outcomes in Low-Income Countries? The Challenges and Hopes of Cognitive Neuroscience." *Peabody Journal of Education* 89 (1): 58–69.

Ackers, J., and Hardman, F. 2001. "Classroom Interaction in Kenyan Primary Schools." *Compare* 31 (2): 245–261.

Alexander, R. 2000. *Culture and Pedagogy: International Comparisons in Primary Education*. Oxford: Blackwell.

Ali, S. 2011. "Communities of Practice and Teacher Development – Lessons Learnt from an Educational Innovation in Pakistan." *Journal of Research and Reflections in Education* 5 (2): 70–82.

Anwaruddin, S. 2015. "Teachers' Engagement with Educational research: Toward a Conceptual Framework for Locally-Based Interpretive Communities." *Education Policy Analysis Archives* 23 (40). https://doi.org/10.14507/epaa.v23.1776

Avalos, B. 1992a. "Education for the Poor: Quality or Relevance?" *British Journal of Sociology of Education* 13 (4): 419–436.

Avalos, B. 1992b. "The Need for Educational Reform and the Role of Teacher Training: The Case of Papua New Guinea." *International Journal of Educational Development* 12 (4): 309–318.

Badenoch, B. 2008. *Being a Brain-wise Therapist: A Practical Guide to Interpersonal Neurobiology*. New York: Norton.

Barrett, A. 2007. "Beyond the Polarization of Pedagogy: Models of Classroom Practice in Tanzanian Primary Schools." *Comparative Education* 43 (2): 273–294.

Beeby, C. 1966. *The Quality of Education in Developing Countries*. Cambridge: Harvard University Press.

Bernstein, B. 2000. *Pedagogy, Symbolic Control and Identity: Theory, Research, Critique*. Lanham: Rowman & Littlefield.

Boyle, H. 2006. "Memorization and Learning in Islamic Schools." *Comparative Education Review* 50 (3): 478–495.

Burgess, P., Gilbert, S., and Dumontheil, I. 2007. "Function and Localization within Rostral Prefrontal Cortex (Area 10)." *Philosophical Transactions of the Royal Society B, Biological Sciences* 362: 887–899.

Chan, C., and Rao, N. (Eds.). 2009. *Revisiting the Chinese Learner: Changing Contexts, Changing Education*. Hong Kong: Comparative Education Research Centre, University of Hong Kong.

Cortazzi, M., and Jin, L. 2001. "Large Classes in China: 'Good' Teachers and Interaction." In *Teaching the Chinese Learner: Psychological and Pedagogical Perspectives*, edited by D. Watkins and J. Biggs, 115–134. Hong Kong: Comparative Education Research Centre, University of Hong Kong.

Dhofier, Z. 1999. *The Pesantren Tradition: The Role of the Kyai in the Maintenance of Traditional Islam in Java*. Tempe: Monograph Series, Program for Southeast Asian Studies, Arizona State University.

Duijvenvoorde, A., Zanolie, K., Rombouts, S., Raijmakers, M., and Crone, E. 2008. "Evaluating the Negative or Valuing the Positive? Neural Mechanisms Supporting Feedback-Based Learning across Development." *Journal of Neuroscience* 28: 9495–9503.

Dunkin, M. 1977. "A Study of Classroom Interaction in Papua New Guinea." *Papua New Guinea Journal of Education*, 13 (2): 1–11.

Ellis, H. 2006. *Clinical Anatomy* (11th ed.). Malden: Blackwell.

Fuller, B., and Snyder, C. 1991. "Vocal Teachers, Silent Pupils? Life in Botswana Classrooms." *Comparative Education Review* 35 (2): 274–294.

Fuster, J. 2001. "The Prefrontal Cortex – an Update: Time is of the Essence." *Neuron* 30 (2): 319–333.

Giedd, J. 2008. "The Teen Brain: Insights from Neuroimaging." *Journal of Adolescent Health* 42 (4): 335–343.

Gilbert, S., and Burgess, P. 2008. "Social and Nonsocial Functions of Rostral Prefrontal Cortex: Implications for Education." *Mind, Brain, and Education* 2 (3): 148–156.

Goldberg, E. 2001. *The Executive Brain: Frontal Lobes and the Civilized Mind*. Oxford: Oxford University Press.

Guthrie, G. 2011. *The Progressive Education Fallacy in Developing Countries: In Favour of Formalism*. New York: Springer.

Guthrie, G. 2013. "Prevalence of the Formalistic Paradigm in African Schools." *Southern African Review of Education* 19 (1): 121–138.

Guthrie, G. 2015. "Culturally-Grounded Pedagogy and Research Methodology." *Compare* 45 (1): 163–168.

Guy, R., Haihuie, S., and Pena, P. 1997. "Research, Knowledge and the Management of Learning in Distance Education in Papua New Guinea." *Papua New Guinea Journal of Education* 33 (1): 33–41.

Hairon, S., and Tan, C. 2017. "Professional Learning Communities in Singapore and Shanghai: Implications for Teacher Collaboration." *International Journal of Educational Development* 47(1): 91–104.

Harber, C. 2002. "Schooling as Violence: An Exploratory Overview." *Educational Review* 54 (1): 7–16.

Harber, C. 2017. *Schooling in Sub-Saharan Africa: Policy, Practice and Patterns*. London: Palgrave Macmillan.

Ho, I. 2001. "Are Chinese Teachers Authoritarian?" In *Teaching the Chinese Learner: Psychological and Pedagogical Perspectives*, edited by D. Watkins and J. Biggs, 99–114. Hong Kong: Comparative Education Research Centre, University of Hong Kong.

Hoadley, U. 2006. "Analysing Pedagogy: The Problem of Framing." *Journal of Education* 40: 14–34.

Hoadley, U. 2016. *A Review of the Research Literature on Teaching and Learning in the Foundation Phase in South Africa*. Working Paper 05/16. Stellenbosch: Research on Socioeconomic Policy Group, University of Stellenbosch.

Hoadley, U. 2017. *Pedagogy in Poverty: Lessons from Twenty Years of Curriculum Reform in South Africa*. London: Routledge.

Hugo, W., and Wedekind, V. 2013a. "Six Failures of the Pedagogic Imagination: Bernstein, Beeby and the Search for an Optimal Pedagogy for the Poor." *Southern African Review of Education* 19 (1): 139–157.

Hugo, W., and Wedekind, V. 2013b. "The Ordering Principles and Operating Principles of Pedagogy: A Reply to Zipin." *Southern African Review of Education* 19 (1): 167–176.

Kember, D. 2016. "Why Do Chinese Students Out-Perform Those from the West? Do Approaches to Learning Contribute to the Explanation?" *Cogent Education* 3. https://doi.org/10.1080/2331186X.2016.1248187

Kumar, K. 1988. "Origins of India's 'Textbook Culture'." *Comparative Education Review* 32 (4): 452–464.

Lam, E. 2014. "'South-South' Borrowing: Lessons from the Caribbean and Implications for Post 2015 Agenda." *Canadian and International Education* 43 (2): Article 5. http://ir.lib.uwo.ca/cie-eci/vol43/iss2/5

Lancy, D. 1983. *Cross-Cultural Studies in Cognition and Mathematics*. New York: Academic Press.

Lattimer, H. 2015. "Translating Theory into Practice: Making Meaning of Learner Centered Education Frameworks for Classroom-Based Practitioners." *International Journal of Educational Development* 45 (1): 65–76.

Le Fanu, G. 2010. *Promoting Inclusive Education in Papua New Guinea*. EdQual Quality Brief No.7. Bristol: University of Bristol.

Meltzer, L. (Ed.) 2007. *Executive Function in Education: From Theory to Practice*. New York: Guilford.

Mok, I. 2006. "Shedding Light on the East Asian Learner Paradox: Reconstructing Student-Centredness in a Shanghai Classroom." *Asia-Pacific Journal of Teacher Education* 26 (2): 131–142.

Moosa, E. 2015. *What Is a Madrasa?* Chapel Hill: University of North Carolina Press.

Nag, S., Chiat, S., Torgerson, C., and Snowling, M. 2014. *Literacy, Foundation Learning and Assessment in Developing Countries: Final Report*. Education Rigorous Literature Review. London: Department for International Development.

Needham, J. 1956. *Science and Civilization in China, Volume 2: History of Thought*. Cambridge: Cambridge University Press.

Pfau, R. 1980. "The Comparative Study of Classroom Behaviours." *Comparative Education Review* 24 (3): 400–414.

Popper, K. 1979. *Objective Knowledge: An Evolutionary Approach* (2nd ed.). Oxford: Oxford University Press.

Rao, N., Chi, J., and Cheng, K. 2009. "Teaching Mathematics: Observations from Urban and Rural Schools in China." In *Revisiting the Chinese Learner: Changing Contexts, Changing Education*, edited by C. Chan and N. Rao, 211–231. Hong Kong: Comparative Education Research Centre, University of Hong Kong.

Scheerens, J. 2015. "Theories on Educational Effectiveness and Ineffectiveness." *School Effectiveness and School Improvement* 26 (1): 10–31.

Schmidt-Wilk, J. 2009. "Reflection: A Prerequisite for Developing the 'CEO' of the Brain." *Journal of Management Education* 33: 3–7.

Sellar, S., and Lingard, B. 2013. "Looking East: Shanghai, PISA 2009 and the Reconstitution of Reference Societies in the Global Education Policy Field." *Comparative Education* 49 (4): 464–485.

Siegel, D. 2006. "An Interpersonal Neurobiology Approach to Psychotherapy." *Psychiatric Annals* 36 (4): 248–256.

Sigman, M., Peña, M., Goldin, A., and Ribeiro, S. 2014. "Neuroscience and Education: Prime Time to Build the Bridge." *Nature Neuroscience* 17 (4): 497–502.

Sternberg, R. 2007. "Culture, Instruction, and Assessment." *Comparative Education* 43 (1): 5–22.

Stiles, J. and Jernigan, T. 2010. "The Basics of Brain Development." *Neuropsychology Review* 20 (4): 327–354.

Tabulawa, R. 1997. "Pedagogical Classroom Practice and the Social Context: The Case of Botswana." *International Journal of Educational Development* 17 (2): 189–194.

Tabulawa, R. 1998. "Teachers' Perspectives on Classroom Practice in Botswana: Implications for Pedagogical Change." *International Journal of Qualitative Studies in Education* 20: 249–268.

Tabulawa, R. 2004. "Geography Students as Constructors of Classroom Knowledge and Practice: A Case Study from Botswana." *Journal of Curriculum Studies* 36 (1): 53–73.

Tan, C. 2015. "Education Policy Borrowing and Cultural Scripts for Teaching in China." *Comparative Education* 51 (2): 196–211.

Tan, C. 2017. "PISA and Education Reform in Shanghai." *Critical Studies in Education*. https://doi.org/10.1080/17508487.2017.1285336

Taylor, N. 2014. *NEEDU National Report 2013: Teaching and Learning in Rural Primary Schools*. Pretoria: National Education Evaluation and Development Unit, Department of Basic Education.

Waltz, J., Knowlton, B., Holyoak, K., Boone, K., Mishkin, F., de Menezes Santos, M., Thomas, C., and Miller, B. 1999. "A System for Relational Reasoning in Human Prefrontal Cortex." *Psychological Science* 10 (2): 119–125.

Watkins, D., and Biggs, J. 2001. "The Paradox of the Chinese Learner and Beyond." In *Teaching the Chinese Learner: Psychological and Pedagogical Perspectives*, edited by D. Watkins and J. Biggs, 3–23. Hong Kong: Comparative Education Research Centre, University of Hong Kong.

Zipin, L. 2013. "Starting from Pedagogical Zero in Developing Contexts? Let's Re-imagine! A Response to Hugo and Wedekind." *Southern African Review of Education*, 19 (1): 158–166.

9 Culturally grounded methodology

Pedagogies, be they student- or teacher-centred, from one cultural environment may be highly inappropriate in another. In many ways, the methodology for identifying culturally appropriate teaching styles is more important than the theory because a grounded approach implies that it is not the nature of progressive or formalistic theory as such that is the primary issue, but the methodology for eliciting the nature of the contexts into which teaching styles must fit. From this perspective, the role of theories and methodologies is to be appropriate to the requirements of educational problem-solving in real world contexts. The approach is based in philosophical pragmatism, which views knowledge as useful in terms of its practical effect and the value of research methodologies as lying in their usefulness in engaging with practical issues (Guthrie 2010, 44–47). The requirement is to establish, first, what teaching styles are effective, then to derive classroom improvements that are culturally grounded, i.e. based on aspects of intergenerational culture that are effective in increasing learning. Otherwise, predetermining the methodology as, for example, positivist or post-positivist, restricts the choice of methods and techniques and their appropriateness for problem-solving.

McGinn and Schiefelbein (2010) have made the case for local research on the teaching practices that are most effective in 'developing' country classrooms, but without specifying methodology. The grounded pathway in this book is an eclectic approach to academic fields and methodology using mixed methods to triangulate both qualitative and quantitative techniques to optimise their strengths and weaknesses (Guthrie 2010, 86–98). The intended outcome from grounded exploration of traditional and current pedagogies practised in different cultural contexts is a base for authentic teaching styles as a constructive frame for upgrading classroom practices, teacher education, and curriculum design as independent variables and student achievement as dependent variable. In contrast, hypothetico-deductive research with universalistic assumptions from progressive theory or econometric models is vulnerable to the quite possibly culture-bound construct validity of researchers' hypotheses. However, nothing methodologically sophisticated is intended by the focus on grounded research, nor does it necessarily imply the use of Glaser and Strauss's (1967) post-positivist methodology. Field experiments, for example, can ground research in cultural and social settings. Accompanied by applied multidisciplinary research to identify classroom elements that are prone to improvement, the aim is to understand contextualised classroom experience and to generate recommendations that arise from it.

The discussion in this chapter particularly centres on analytical insights generated by research designs for field experiments on the effectiveness of teaching styles to identify which should be the object of classroom improvement research. Two intertwining themes run through the research methods discussed. One is the value of experimental design principles in evaluation of the effectiveness of educational interventions, including in aid projects. Field experiments should evaluate whether proposed changes improve student achievement (and aid evaluations need to be managed independently by competent professionals to avoid the conflicts of interest apparent in the mismanaged Curriculum Reform and Implementation Project (CRIP) evaluation in Sections 3.5–3.7). The other theme is the merit of mixed methods research in triangulating data and illuminating variables. A classroom improvement and a school effectiveness study from Indonesia demonstrate insights from experimental design variables to further illuminate evaluations based on case studies and surveys. These discussions cover familiar ground for researchers but are presented as clearly as possible to assist decision makers who are consumers of educational research, who may not be familiar with research design, or who could use some perspective on qualitative research where variables are often implied rather than stated. The discussion therefore leads to consideration of administrative decision-making about teaching styles.

9.1 Research strategy

The contrasting theoretical and methodological strengths and weaknesses in the school effectiveness and classroom improvement research fields have generated trade-offs among validity, reliability, relevance and generalisability (Section 3.3). Econometric school effectiveness studies rarely examine classroom processes or the cultural contexts that shape classroom behaviours. The surveys and case studies that dominate classroom improvement research as part of pilot studies and formative evaluations often have premature findings, especially if classroom findings come from questionnaires rather than observation. The naturalistic educational sociology within which most classroom studies fall rarely makes use of experimental design principles so that a widespread and persistent gap is experimental field research analysing under controlled conditions the impact of teaching styles on classroom learning in particular cultures.

A pragmatic first research step is field experiments to identify the most effective teaching style for improving student achievement in particular developing countries (Guthrie 2015, 166–167). While a contradiction may seem apparent between avoiding universalistic methodologies and encouraging experiments, the key is use of field experiments in natural settings. They can use the conceptual clarity provided by experimental design principles without generalising beyond the culture in which the research occurs. To measure which teaching methods are more effective, field experiments can treat different teaching methods (e.g. formalistic and progressive) as independent variables and student learning as dependent variable. Cultural context is treated as a background variable that is a critically important precondition for understanding the educational paradigms intuitively held students, their parents and teachers. Credibility among these stakeholders will increase if the dependent variable of student learning includes testing using papers from high-stakes public examinations.

With knowledge about which teaching style is most effective, the second research step is applied, mixed method research. Review of anthropological literature often can establish the cultural epistemology and pedagogic ontology embedded in traditional educational paradigms, and thus provide a cultural grammar for understanding actors' interpretations of schooling. Ethnographic and structured classroom observation then open two different pathways to detail actual classroom behaviours and operational skills. Questionnaires, interviews and focus groups follow both pathways to elicit actors' perceptions, attitudes and constructs to explain their behaviours and their interpretations of the paradigms in which they are embedded. The intended outcome is culturally grounded choices for improvement of the effectiveness of classroom practices, teacher education and curriculum design as independent variables and student achievement as dependent variable. This can come about through understanding of associated cultural constructs about teaching, learning and the classroom, with the intent of building inductively on them to increase the effectiveness of the most successful teaching style from the experimental phase. With formalistic teaching, for example, improvements to effectiveness can usefully explore change to elements marginal to the core of formalism, but not to elements that contradict key cultural precepts from the culture in which they are embedded (Guthrie 2013).

9.2 Design for field experiments on teaching styles

Formal designs for field experiments are intended to assess cause and effect, which requires careful analysis of the many different types of variables and of the relationships between them.[1] Experiments measure two key variables: the independent variable (which is the presumed cause) and the dependent variable (the presumed effect). However, other variables can also influence the results. Background variables are antecedents that affect the situation prior to the study, which we can observe but not usually change directly. Intervening variables are variables that we can anticipate will affect implementation and which we can 'control' through measurement. Extraneous variables are haphazard occurrences that can be observed and might affect the outcome during the study, but which cannot be controlled. Alternative independent variables suggest different causes from the presumed one.

A hypothetical example, but typical of the implied logic in much of the classroom improvement literature, is illustrated within the brackets in Figure 9.1.

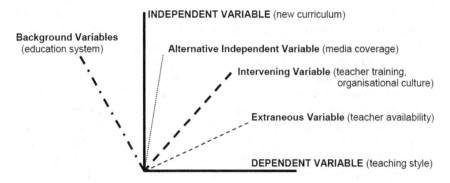

Figure 9.1 Invalid curriculum experiment
Source: Guthrie (2011, 219).

Here, a new student-centred curriculum is tested as an independent variable in an experimental school trial. The curriculum is hypothesised to generate change from formalistic to progressive teaching. In a true experimental design, some teachers use the new approach (the experimental group) and some the previous one (the control group), and the results are compared (although few curriculum reforms are tested this carefully). Typically, the dependent variable is teaching style. An intervening variable is conceptualised as the type of pre-service training previously undergone by teachers. If culture is considered, it is usually as organisational culture, an intervening variable taken as a barrier to change. A background variable is the education system and any formalistic requirements that it might impose through inspections. An extraneous variable might be changes in teachers during the trial (some might become sick, for example, requiring use of substitute teachers). Alternative independent variables are rarely considered but, hypothetically, one might be a high level of media attention to an issue related to the new syllabus, for example coverage of crime influencing outcomes from a new social science topic on the subject.

This particular experimental design is low on validity. The most important outcome should be improved student learning but the dependent variable is changes in teaching style, so that the design does not test the assumption that changes in teaching style will increase student achievement (i.e. it demonstrates the Progressive Education Fallacy). Often, this limitation in classroom improvement research is a practical one, especially where solo researchers have limited time and resources, for example to develop valid and reliable tests. However, failure to achieve the predicted change in teaching style most usually is not attributed to an inappropriate reform, but to inadequate technical inputs and conservative educational forces such as formalistic teacher training. They are treated as intervening variables that allegedly limit the ability of teachers to implement a progressive curriculum (many examples were seen in Chapter 5 on Africa). In effect, these variables are posited as alternative independent variables to explain negative results. Rarely do we see deep consideration given to cultural context as a key background variable that provides a subtle but powerful influence that can override the experimental trial. Research in the curriculum and school effectiveness fields that underestimates ecological validity or cultural context loses heavily in the trade-off with validity and relevance.

Measurement of learning gains from a new curriculum is uncommon in the classroom improvement field. The preferred scenario is Figure 9.2, where the critical dependent variable now is student learning, as properly found across the school effectiveness field. The independent variable is teaching style, with a control group of teachers using a formalistic style (as is conventional practice in most developing country contexts) and an experimental group using a progressive style. The research hypothesis – which is likely to be rejected – is that progressive teaching will result in greater student learning. An intervening variable is student cognitive level (given the indication that progressive teaching might operate more effectively at higher cognitive levels). Teacher availability remains an extraneous variable. The key background variable is intergenerational culture, which can be delineated separately through review of the anthropological, historical and sociological literature or, in large studies if necessary, through ethnographic research.

In this logic, there is no assumption that changes to teaching style will necessarily improve student learning: the point of the trial is to actually test this proposition as a hypothesis. Whether progressive teaching does result in increased student learning or whether formalistic teaching does, a key explanation lies in the epistemological and pedagogical patterns in teachers' and students' cultural frames. In particular, should the progressive hypothesis be rejected and formalism prevail, intergenerational culture now comes into consideration as an alternative independent variable, i.e. as one whose pervasive influence has overwhelmed the progressive experimental treatment such that culture is the underlying explanation for the success of formalism and the failure of progressivism.

Conventionally, as we saw in Chapter 2, failure to achieve positive results from progressive reforms is not attributed to an inappropriate reform but to

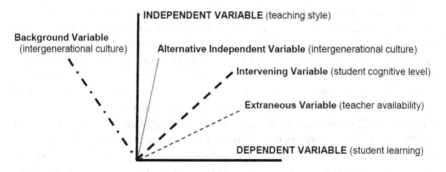

Figure 9.2 Valid teaching styles experiment
Source: Guthrie (2011, 221).

inadequate technical inputs and implicitly to conservative educational forces (such as formalistic inspections embedded in the education system, formalistic syllabuses or previous formalistic teacher training as intervening variables limiting the ability of teachers to implement the new curriculum). In the second design, these can be treated as intervening variables too, but studied for their effect on student achievement rather than teaching styles. Such a treatment need not assume that these variables will necessarily inhibit student achievement. Rather, it can be hypothesised that they will inhibit student achievement under progressive teaching and promote it under formalistic teaching, which are the independent variables being tested. The outcome of such a design approach is that whether progressive or formalistic teaching results in increased student learning, a key explanation lies in the epistemological and pedagogical patterns in teachers' and students' cultural frames.

Where, as is often the case, field experiments are not feasible, the variables in this design provide a checklist against which limitations can be delineated in case study and survey research. For example, the following shortcomings were common in the literature reviewed in Chapters 2 and 3: questionnaire surveys in school effectiveness studies that did not consider the impact of intergenerational culture as a background variable; measurement of student achievement as dependent variable that did not take into account performance in the examinations that parents often regard as essential to their children's life chances; and overgeneralised recommendations from case studies and surveys, including single case studies that did not provide statistically valid bases for recommendations to other cases and surveys that made recommendations for populations different from the one sampled. While operational research constraints can often prevent a researcher from investigating all the variables, there is no excuse for failure to recognise the design limitations when drawing conclusions and making recommendations from the research that was practicable. Likewise, the background variable of intergenerational culture means there is no excuse for unquestioned axioms in progressive reforms.

9.3 Relevant research methods

Briefly – because there is a huge literature on all of these matters – there are a number of pathways for mixed methods research to investigate each of the variables, whether in experimental designs, surveys or case studies. Despite being the most overlooked variable in conventional school effectiveness research, cultural background is usually the easiest to investigate because anthropological, historical and sociological material often exists on cultural epistemology and formal education paradigms. The starting point therefore is literature searches for such material, as seen in the earlier geographical chapters. In the unusual event that such evidence is not available, ethnographic studies commonly take a year of field work, in which case sole researchers face a difficult choice about whether to research this variable or others. Cultural variables can also be included within multivariate research as independent variables, as seen in

Section 5.4 with the Kenyan study by Daley *et al.* (2005), which provides an exception to the generalisation in this book about the lack of school effectiveness research into classroom culture and cultural context.

Examples of field experiments that have teaching styles as the independent variable remain rare. A still relevant example is Mulopo and Fowler's (1987) field experiment in Zambia, which researched the effectiveness of traditional and discovery approaches (as independent variables) for teaching scientific facts, understandings and attitudes (as dependent variables). The research found that the traditional, formalistic approach was efficient for teaching scientific facts and principles, while the progressive discovery approach tended to be more effective among formal reasoners in promoting scientific attitudes and understandings (Section 2.2). Another example was research in Singapore by Tan, Sharan, and Lee (2007) that did not support research hypotheses predicting the success of progressive cooperative learning (a constructivist approach based on small group investigation) over formalistic whole class instruction. A control group of 103 coeducational grade 8 students in two schools was taught two six-week geography units using the whole class method. The experimental group was 138 students taught the same units using group investigation. Analysis of covariance found both methods produced student achievement results at almost the same level. There were no significant differences in intrinsic motivation scores between the two types of class, although some differences between high and low achieving students occurred.

A vast array of international data derives from IEA testing of student achievement as dependent variable. More relevant to grounded research are public examination papers but, where they are not available or appropriate to grade level, tests constructed around Bloom's Revised Taxonomy of Educational Objectives remains a convenient tool. Figure 9.3 shows its cognitive domain, which has six levels from lower to higher order thinking. The typical actions indicate some of the expectations of learners at each level. The lower three levels of remembering (e.g. defining, listing, stating), understanding (e.g. describing, paraphrasing, summarising) and applying (e.g. calculating, illustrating, using) provide building blocks for later intellectual endeavour focussed on enquiry skills. They become foundations for the three higher levels of analysing (e.g. classifying, comparing, contrasting), evaluating (e.g. assessing, critiquing, justifying) and creating (e.g. designing, formulating, synthesising). In essence, formalistic methods are effective at the three lower levels, so are appropriate for students in primary schools and for the large majority in secondary schools whose intellectual abilities currently lie at those levels. Progressive enquiry methods aim to develop the three higher levels and generally seem more appropriate at tertiary level.

Research on the effectiveness of teaching styles does provide support for the hypothesis that formalistic styles are more effective with the lower cognitive levels found in primary and secondary schools and, conversely, some mixed support for the hypothesis that progressive teaching styles are more effective with higher cognitive levels and some affective aspects of learning. When transition

Cognitive Levels	Typical Actions
Creating: generating new ideas and patterns.	Construct Formulate Design Propose Devise Synthesise
Evaluating: making judgements.	Assess Judge Critique Justify Interpret Rate
Analysing: breaking material into parts to explore understandings and relationships.	Classify Distinguish Compare Illustrate Contrast Investigate
Applying: using information in another situation.	Calculate Practice Explain Show Illustrate Use
Understanding: explaining ideas or concepts.	Compare Outline Describe Paraphrase Explain Summarise
Remembering: recalling relevant knowledge.	Define Quote List State Present Tell

Higher cognitive levels ↑

Figure 9.3 Bloom's Revised Taxonomy of Educational Objectives
Source: Guthrie (2011, 223), based on Anderson and Krathwohl (2001).

from lower, concrete operational levels to higher, formal operational levels is appropriate is an issue that is in part context-based and in part biological. Piagetian evidence from second language students in the South Pacific has suggested that formal operations there generally started developing in the later teen years in upper secondary (especially with advanced students) and in tertiary education (Guthrie 2011, 165–167). Why they lie there seems a developmental consequence of human growth (Section 8.6). However, Lancy (1983) established a case that the nature of higher operations is actually culturally defined, i.e. they develop in interaction with the social environment, so it should not be assumed axiomatically that Piaget's Western intellectual styles will be followed in other cultures or be valued in them.

No universal answers indicate what educational objectives should be, other than they should focus on student learning as the key dependent variable in schooling. As Tabulawa (2013, 149–154) has discussed, the way in which objectives are set and are tied to the testing of content can have considerable impacts on teaching styles. Educational objectives too are context-specific and, that being the case, they should be chosen by appropriate authorities within each country, preferably conscious of influences from cultural imperialism. My personal view remains that primary and secondary curricula are often overloaded. Essentially, the core business of primary schools, especially where educational resources are scarce in the home, is to teach literacy, numeracy, and basic health and hygiene. Secondary schooling provides more scope for including physical, biological and social science content, as well as foreign languages, as appropriate. Bloom's standard division into cognitive, affective and skill domains provide targets for development and analysis of objectives so that textbook writers and teachers have a clear framework. However, it should not be assumed that the domains are entirely separate, merely requiring lists for each type of objective. As we have seen with the extensive discussion of epistemology and paradigms in this book, teaching skills not only convey particular knowledge, they also have affective elements buried deep within, particularly on the nature of intellectual and educational authority.

9.4 Classroom observation

Is a student who is wriggling paying attention, while another who is still and apparently attentive actually daydreaming or otherwise disengaged? Underlying this question are basic and long-standing technical issues in research about how self-meaning is attributed to classroom actors. The most valid data on teaching styles and classroom behaviour comes from observation, for which the two main methods in current use are videos coded with structured schedules (as commonly found in educational psychology) and ethnographic non-participant observation (usually influenced by anthropology and sociology). A vast literature exists on the underlying methodological issues, for which this basic discussion provides leads. For structured observation, technical analysis and the underlying measurement principles can be found in older positivist texts such as Kerlinger (1973) and Dunkin and Biddle (1974). Current textbooks tend to focus on classroom observation as a form of qualitative progressive action research in 'developed' countries (e.g. Wragg 2012; O'Leary 2014). Anthropological and sociological literature specialises in the ethnographic research necessary to gain deep understanding of cultural context and grounded research (e.g. Fife 2005; Corbin and Strauss 2015). Associated field issues in developing countries were discussed by Vulliamy, Lewin, and Stephens (1990), who wrote at length about the value of qualitative case studies and ethnographic research into the classroom. Bray, Adamson, and Mason's (2007) book on comparative education research contains several discussions of the study of cultures, while Milligan (2016) has written recently about participant observation issues.

Video provides externally observable, verifiable and therefore potentially reliable (i.e. replicable) data on classroom interaction, but cannot demonstrate actors' thought processes. Coding systems can either use high inference rating schedules (as also found with some types of available data, such as school inspection reports, that can be used as an alternative) or low inference category systems (such as structured observation schedules that usually attempt to remove judgements about mental processes and require researchers to make low inference categorisations of demonstrated teacher and student behaviours). Low inference categorisation was used by Pfau (1980) in a rare comparative analysis of teaching styles. The study used Caldwell's Activity Rating Instrument for coding 11 categories of behaviour every five seconds in 23 Nepalese schools in 1974. The results were then compared with prior data from 30 American teachers in 1966 (Table 8.1). The percentage of time found on each activity allowed reliable identification of aspects of behaviour that were specific to the two contexts, differences in the extent to which behaviours occurred within the two systems, and behaviours that were more universal in nature (407).

In contrast, ethnography provides narrative that can generate higher validity, particularly from long periods of field work, but can lack precision and be unreliable because it is difficult to standardise and relies heavily on high inference judgements by the observer (Guthrie 2010, 108–117). This is a limitation because such data cannot accurately quantify the extent to which patterns vary over time or allow reliable comparison within or between countries. However, highly structured low inference observation schedules and less structured high inference ethnographic observation have complementary uses. Quantitative data from structured observation can provide greater precision and allow systematic comparisons. Qualitative observation is more likely to provide insights into classroom behaviour and leads for enquiry into the actors' constructs about the behaviour. Without such constructs the percentages of classroom time allocated to various activities have little explanatory power. Only with such constructs can we begin to understand the significance of the time allocations. However, without quantification of those allocations we cannot have reliable measurement of similarities and differences.

Neither method of observation provides data directly on the mental processes at play among teachers and students. One approach to optimising methodological benefits is triangulation, the process of bringing multiple types of data to bear on the one problem. Triangulation of the meanings attributed to actors through ethnography, direct observation from structured schedules, and their many variations, is best conducted through questionnaires, interviews and focus groups. These methods are not valid for accurate reporting of classroom behaviour, for which they provide only second hand and often unreliable proxy data (Section 3.3). However, they are valid for investigating actors' perceptions, attitudes and cultural constructs of their behaviours. Grounded mixed methods research can thus help complement the strengths of the different observational approaches and overcome their limitations. An example is O'Sullivan's (2004) action study of three years of progressive in-service teacher education (INSET) for 145 unqualified teachers in 39 primary schools in Namibia. Her study increased validity by supplementing 450 hours of high inference semi-structured lesson observation with situational analysis using interviews, semi-structured and unstructured observations, assessment of learners, and documents. Teachers were familiar with reform policy and claimed to be using learner-centred methods. However, observation of the teaching skills of 75 of the teachers identified that they normally used formalistic methods, although they would adopt a few other skills, at least in the short term. Further interviewing indicated that adoption was heavily constrained by lack of cultural understandings about the constructivist view of knowledge, which was one of the underlying assumptions in the learner-centred reforms. For this action research as a formative project evaluation, high inference semi-structured observation was sufficient and had overriding value in leading to identification of progressive requirements that did not match cultural constructs.

9.5 Examples of variables in field research

Typically, experimental research is associated with laboratories and statistical measurement of the associations between quantitative variables. Field research involving qualitative case studies and quantitative surveys rarely expresses experimental design principles, but both can be understood using the variables from experimental design. Two studies from Indonesia demonstrate the point and further illustrate the limitations of the classroom improvement and school effectiveness fields that were summarised in Table 3.1. One study, a classroom improvement doctorate by Sopantini (2014), was an independent, grounded, mixed methods case study. It focussed on implementation of Indonesian national policy on progressive active learning, which was first introduced in the 1970s and subsequently rearticulated through four different national curricula that had support from numerous donor and government funded projects (29–42). Contrasting perspectives came from an extensive World Bank classroom effectiveness survey that did use experimental controls as part of an impact assessment of comprehensive 2005 laws that particularly focussed on upgrading the teaching profession (Chang et al. 2014, 1–37).

Sopantini (2014) observed a wide gap between curriculum policy and practice. Most schools and classrooms had changed little, with traditional chalk-and-talk teaching methods remaining prevalent. Her policy implementation research addressed two questions from the perspective of an insider: how do teachers translate active learning methodology in the classroom, and what factors impede the implementation of active learning? A theoretical framework used three broad perspectives: (1) the technical aspects dominant in the reforms, including teacher professional development and classroom practice involved in implementation, (2) the top-down political aspects, including global politics of international aid and policy transfer, national politics of policy development (including curriculum policy) and local school politics, and (3) cultural perspectives, including societal and intergenerational culture as well as organisational and educational culture (75, 273–291).

The multi-site case study used a purposive sample of three remote and economically disadvantaged districts in North Maluku, studying 10 schools and their teachers in eight urban and rural clusters in 2007 (135–176). Four main data gathering methods were triangulated: documentary analysis, a questionnaire survey ($N = 49$), 103 structured and unstructured interviews, and qualitative observation in 14 classrooms supplemented by informal discussions and field visits to schools. Constraints for an individual researcher included budget, time, accessibility and feasibility.

The research found a wide gap between central policy and local practices so that active learning policy had not been effectively implemented in the classroom. Sopantini (2014, 269) reported:

> In all classrooms observed, teaching was traditional, didactic and teacher-directed. In the two cases observed where efforts to implement active learning were attempted, the changes were mainly cosmetic, consisting of changing furniture arrangements to allow for group work, and occasionally taking children out of the classroom for activities such as observing plants in the playground. In these isolated cases, it was also clear that these approaches . . . were not yet integrated into daily practice and were implemented only on certain occasions and for specific lessons – for example when a visiting specialist was observing the class.

Effectively, a mixture of structural and cultural contextual elements were involved in the failure of the policy. Factors that impeded implementation were inadequate INSET and school supervision; lack of policy alignment from national to district, school and classroom levels; and community resistance. Implementation, Sopantini found, essentially had failed due to a combination of these interconnected technical, political and cultural factors, all of which were important. The cultural elements that contributed to this failure varied across a large number of ethnic groups in Indonesia, but one core value that Sopantini pointed to was social harmony. This emphasises a worldview with communal rather than individual values, with little emphasis on individual creativity. Instead, children are widely brought up to maintain harmonious social relationships, screen extreme emotions from others, and display obedience, especially to teachers who pass on received knowledge (48–57, 127–132).

Figure 9.4 reconceptualises the research design using the main experimental design variables. In effect, national technical, political and cultural factors provided three background contextual variables that were found to be essential preconditions for teaching style success. The active learning methodology constituted the independent variable, the success or otherwise of which was the focus of the study, assessed against classroom adoption as dependent variable. Local variations on the background variables acted as intervening variables impeding classroom implementation.

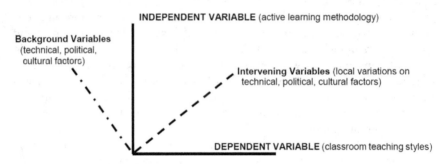

Figure 9.4 Evaluation of curriculum impact on classroom teaching

Source: Author, based on Sopantini (2014).

The large World Bank classroom effectiveness study by Chang *et al.* (2014) focussed on implementation of the teaching profession reforms introduced from 2005. The reforms had major structural elements, much of which centred on upgrading teacher qualifications and professional development, with increased pay as an incentive (56–96). One part of the evaluation focussed on whether increased teacher qualifications were impacting on student achievement using a sample of 1,714 teachers in 240 public primary schools and 120 public junior secondary schools. In 2009, all core subject teachers and all students in these schools were administered a multiple-choice subject matter test, all the teachers were interviewed, and 2009 Programme for International Student Assessment (PISA) data on 15-year-olds was used as dependent variable. The study included a repeat of the data collection in 2011. Extensive statistical testing used regression analysis.

Of direct interest is an experimental component of the study that evaluated the effects of salary increases and the associated certification process on teacher performance. Payment of the professional allowance did not significantly increase student learning (Chang *et al.* 2014, 113–121). Systematic statistical control of a range of measures found there was usually no significant difference in student achievement between certificated and non-certificated teacher classes. This could have been a consequence of different levels of teacher mathematical knowledge, but teachers without degrees did not actually have much lower levels of subject knowledge than teachers with degrees. Among degree holders, those with mathematics education degrees tended to outperform those with degrees just in mathematics, but correlations between teachers' degrees and student learning gains could not be explained solely by subject matter knowledge: teachers with degrees seem to be better teachers for reasons other than such knowledge. This conclusion was taken to imply quality issues in the certification programmes.

Figure 9.5 is a schema of the main variables in this part of the World Bank study. The background variable that gave shape to the research was the structural reforms to the education system that were introduced from 2005. While the study analysed the reforms more broadly than discussed here, the impact evaluation focussed on whether upgrading teacher pay and certification as independent variables improved student test performance as dependent variable. Finding that progressive training during the certification programme did not sustain in the classroom, the study, in effect, explained the outcome as being due to the quality of the certification programmes as an intervening variable. A search of the root 'cultur' found substantive use only 21 times in 192 pages of text, in contrast to Sopantini's 266 uses in 308 pages, indicating that culture was not given much consideration either as a background or intervening variable.

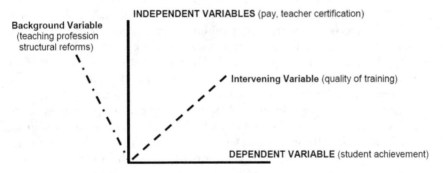

Figure 9.5 Evaluation of impact of certification on student achievement
Source: Author, based on Chang et al. (2014).

A further ex post facto experimental part of the evaluation correlated observed teacher behaviour in the classroom (labelled the 'black box') with student achievement. Grade 8 science and mathematics classrooms that participated in the 2007 Trends in International Mathematics and Science Study (TIMSS) study, were videoed, with a follow up in 2011 (Chang et al. 2014, 125–140). Against the reforms as background variable, here the independent variables were teacher classroom practices (time spent on exposition, discussion, problem-solving, practical work and investigation, as well as classroom interaction) (132–136; Section 3.3). Student achievement was the dependent variable. Intervening variables were a range of structural measures of student, home, classroom, school and community characteristics. This research identified teacher knowledge in both subject matter and pedagogy as having a large effect on student learning outcomes, but detailed quantitative and qualitative analysis of the teaching practices of 200 classroom teachers found 'some surprising results that tend to contradict some well-known teaching-learning theories' (126). Following upgraded certification with an emphasis on active learning, teachers actually tended to use much more exposition, while discussion, practical work and investigation all decreased: three-quarters of the teachers said this behaviour was influenced by the high-stakes national examination. There was only passing reference to formalistic teaching as a style, but the inferences are that teachers were predominantly formalistic (albeit some introduced limited flexibility into their teaching) and that the reform emphasis on active learning did not succeed in changing formalistic teaching styles.

The two studies serve to illustrate some of the relative strengths and weaknesses of classroom improvement and classroom effectiveness research, as discussed in Sections 3.2–3.3. Both found formalistic classroom teaching prevailed, reaching this conclusion from the contrasting theoretical and methodological limitations of the school effectiveness and classroom improvement fields with their trade-offs among validity, reliability, relevance and generalisability. Categorised according to Figure 3.1 on theoretical influences on types of research, the research by Chang and colleagues is an example of the second layer focus on teachers' working conditions, while Sopantini's study included a third layer focus on underpinning cultural elements. She paid considerable attention to intergenerational culture as one of the background factors that resurfaced locally as intervening variables. In this, the study is an exception to the many circular classroom improvement studies that have progressivism as a starting and an end point. However, the study, like most in this field, and constrained by doctoral requirements and resources, treated teaching styles as the dependent variable rather than student achievement. With extensive resources, the World Bank classroom effectiveness study listed nine authors and contributors compared to Sopantini's two short-term research assistants. The result was large samples and careful statistical cross-analysis of student achievement as dependent variable. Societal explanations were found in the reforms and their organisational consequences for teacher education, in particular, but there was a virtual absence of culture as a background variable or an explanation for the results. A lack of theory about culture and limited use of educational theory about teaching was reflected in the labelling of the classroom as a black box.

A major strength of the school effectiveness field is use of student achievement as dependent variable to give a valid output measure when test objectives match the taught curriculum. However, there can be complications, as indicated in an overview of the TIMSS test development process (Mullis *et al.* 2009). The TIMSS curriculum model has three elements: the intended curriculum based on national input, the implemented curriculum and the achieved curriculum. Thus, an official progressive intended curriculum that implies higher cognitive levels may be observed in the breach if teachers teach to national examinations that reflect a more formalistic approach and lower cognitive levels, as identified in the Bank research. Chang *et al.* (2014, 140) commented that

> This finding raises an important contradiction: . . . if teachers are 'teaching to the test' and these approaches tend to help students score better. . . . Could it, in fact, lead to better learning, albeit more through a mechanistic, rote-learning approach?

Clearly, where a teacher-implemented curriculum is based on high-stakes national examinations that do not match an intended progressive curriculum, there is a content validity issue for tests based on the intended curriculum.

One positive that arises is a direction for classroom improvement research where lack of use of student achievement as dependent variable reflects lack of testing resources. A culturally grounded methodology that puts teacher practice as the foundation for classroom improvement implies that the student achievement to be tested is that which their teachers actually implement. If public examinations provide the syllabus to which teachers teach, existing exam papers at matching grade levels could be a valid measure of the taught curriculum in classroom improvement studies.

9.6 Decision-making about classroom reforms

In establishing the relevance of this research methodology to real world decision-making, it is useful to acknowledge that major differences exist between the scientific emphasis on exactitude and nuance on the one hand, and administrative decision-making on the other.

- Researchers are used to thinking of high levels of probability – 95% or 99% in the social and psychological sciences – as being required before accepting a finding, let alone acting upon it in the real world where it might affect people's lives. Real world decision-making does not usually rely on scientific judgement, but as Popper (1979, 13–23) recognised, relies on use of the best tested of the available alternatives. The effect is that few decision makers can hope to achieve anything near the probabilities of success acceptable in the sciences, in the event that they consider probability at all.
- Where probabilities are known, the statistical significance of findings may not indicate their operational significance. Only variables within administrative control are of operational value even though they may be of lesser statistical significance compared to variables outside administrative control, whether known effects (such as student background) or residual effects (which by definition are unknown) (Husen, Saha, and Noonan 1978, 91).
- Effect sizes are more useful than probabilities, as discussed by Hattie (2009, 7–22). His influential analysis of teacher effectiveness research in 'developed' countries, took an effect size of 0.4 of a standard deviation as the

benchmark to judge whether effects on schooling are below or above average. No such norm has been established for research in developing countries as far as I am aware, but the implication is that findings from particular studies can be prioritised according to their effect magnitude and resources concentrated on those with greater benefits. Even although operational research results may be statistically significant, if their effect size is below average resources would be better applied to other significant effects that are above average, assuming similar costs.

- Even when statistical probabilities and effect levels are known, real world decision-making reduces to a choice between implementing a particular course of action (however complicated) or not implementing it. Thus, a logical decision maker can reduce all decisions to a binary choice (Act/Do Not Act), toss a coin, and make the 'right' decision 50% of the time with the superficial appearance of some success (Guthrie 2010, 196–203). For example, the Papua New Guinea (PNG) curriculum reforms seen in Section 6.4 resulted in eight failures and no long-term successes. Perhaps half of these failures could have been prevented had the education ministers making the final decisions merely tossed coins!
- Research can act to increase the likelihood of success: good judgement plus increased knowledge increases the probability of correct decisions. Equally, bad judgement can lower the probability of success, as with the poor progressive judgement behind recommendations to implement the various PNG reforms.

The binary effect in real world decision-making is to simplify matters considerably when the choice reduces to implementing a recommended course of action, such as a curriculum reform, or not implementing it. Additionally, when cultural commonalities basically occur in whole rather than in part, they effectively provide binary data because cultural context is not so much a correlate of educational success as a prior condition. Figure 9.6 is a simplified decision tree that is a consequence of the binary logic. The starting point is research reviewing the epistemological nature of cultural context as the background variable.

1. If literature review finds that revelatory cultural epistemology exists, the next question is whether traditional teaching styles are inherently formalistic. If they are, does field experiment show they are equally or more effective that progressivism? If so, a syllabus change is much more likely to be successful if attention is confined to improving formalism rather than trying to change it to progressive teaching.
2. (a) If the epistemology is not revelatory but scientific, then the next question is still whether teaching styles are inherently formalistic. If they are, does field experiment show they are equally or more effective that progressivism? If so, a syllabus change is more likely to be successful if it develops the formalistic teaching style.

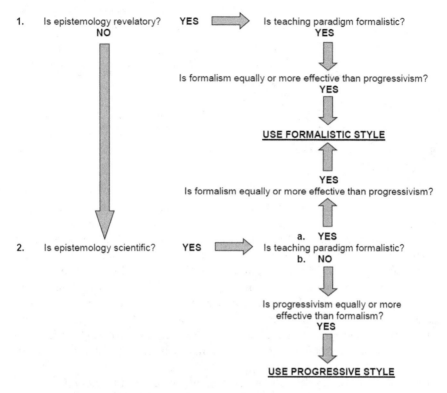

Figure 9.6 Simplified flow chart for decisions on teaching styles
Source: Adapted from Guthrie (2011, 226).

(b) If the culture is scientific and teaching styles are progressive, does field experiment show they are equally or more effective that formalism? If so, a progressive classroom style is appropriate.

The effectiveness and efficiency issues are shown in Figure 9.7. Situation A in Column 1 is the default no change, control situation in most experimental designs. Essentially, it accepts the existing style and makes no effort to change it. In fact, this is usually the real situation for teachers, who are often left to their own devices, and it may be that a valid experiment finds support for it. Leaving matters thus has a high probability of success in that change is not intended and little will occur except because of individual decisions by teachers within schools. Counter-intuitive to progressive sensibilities, this may nonetheless be rational behaviour if the decision is based on judgements that the present situation is indeed satisfactory (the religious message is being purveyed successfully, nobody is complaining about examination results or the field experiment has found it effective, for example). This is also rational behaviour if the present

Likelihood of Success	Amount of Classroom Change		
	1. No Change	2. Moderate Change	3. Major Change
High	A		
Medium		B	
Low			C

Figure 9.7 Relationships between amount and likelihood of change
Source: Guthrie (2011, 227).

situation is unsatisfactory, but resources are not available to initiate change or will not be available to sustain change after the withdrawal of any pilot funding.

The default no change Situation A is only likely to alter if there is a high level of external pressure and a high level of acceptance by teachers themselves that change is needed (e.g. the community demands and teachers believe in changes to their school, perhaps over vernacular teaching). In this case, there may be innovative change (e.g. attempts to introduce the vernacular, in which case Columns 2 and 3 come into play), or conservative change (e.g. rejection of the vernacular and reinforcement of an existing practice, such as keeping the existing national language of instruction, in which case Column 1 remains in play).

In Situation B, a moderate degree of change is sought (for example, a valid experiment showed that formalistic teaching is the most effective; now an INSET programme is aimed at encouraging improvements within the existing formalistic teaching style). Most teachers will accept such change because it does not threaten their basic professional identity. Although this approach encourages only a moderate level of change, it is the situation with the highest likelihood of actually achieving any change at all. In effect, the approach pragmatically accepts that evolutionary change is the most likely outcome of change efforts.

Situation C represents the seeking of major change, e.g. to a new teaching style (for example, in the many attempts at progressive reform of formalistic systems reported in this book). The evidence is that such reform efforts are highly unlikely to succeed beyond well-funded trials. These changes should not be attempted because in the long-term they are a waste of time, effort and resources, and are likely to be counterproductive for morale.

If there is no difference in effectiveness between teaching styles, the issue comes down to efficiency. In this case, there is no point in spending scarce financial and personnel resources on changing to a new style: the existing style (whatever it may be) is satisfactory and a new one will not improve student outcomes. Improving the existing style will be more cost-effective (which Section 10.4 will discuss further).

9.7 Conclusion

In many ways, the methodology for identifying culturally grounded teaching styles is more important than the theory because the grounded approach implies that it is not the nature of formalism (or of formalistic theory as such) that is the primary issue, but the methodology for eliciting the nature of the contexts into which appropriate teaching styles must fit. The Progressive Education Fallacy has led to the introduction of enquiry teaching styles in developing countries, using them, in effect, to test theories that confuse process and product. The critical issue is whether student learning actually benefits from changes to teaching styles, the extant hypothesis being that formalistic styles are more effective with the lower cognitive levels found in primary and secondary schools and, conversely, some mixed support for the hypothesis that progressive teaching styles are more effective with higher cognitive levels and some affective aspects of learning. However, where findings consistent with these hypotheses might apply is highly dependent on context and their geographic extent has not been fully mapped.

Progressive teaching styles have rarely been tested experimentally in developing countries to investigate whether they accelerate learning. The research designs discussed in this chapter indicate some grounded mixed method research possibilities and their implications for real-world decision-making. Traps for which researchers and administrators should be alert include premature optimism from pilot studies based on superficial questionnaire studies rather than direct observation in the classroom. Another area for alertness is lightweight research into curriculum change that focusses on teaching styles as dependent rather than independent variable and underestimates cultural effects. It is also well to be alert in hard-to-resist aid projects to project managers and evaluators who may have vested commercial interests. Their interests can lie in profiting from greater financial inputs to promote progressive change when the proper issue is the pervasive cultural context that makes incremental change to formalism the more constructive path.

Note

1 Section 9.2 derives from Guthrie (2011, 218–227, https://doi.org/10.1007/978-94-007-1851-7_9, © Springer Science+Business Media B.V. 2011) with permission of Springer Nature.

References

Anderson, L., and Krathwohl, D. (Eds.). 2001. *A Taxonomy for Learning, Teaching, and Assessing: A Revision of Bloom's Taxonomy of Educational Objectives.* New York: Longman.

Bray, M., Adamson, B., and Mason, M. 2007. *Comparative Education Research: Approaches and Methods.* Hong Kong: Comparative Education Research Centre, University of Hong Kong.

Chang, M., Shaeffer, S., Al-Samarrai, S., Ragatz, A., de Ree, J., and Stevenson, R. 2014. *Teacher Reform in Indonesia The Role of Politics and Evidence in Policy Making.* Washington, DC: World Bank.

Corbin, J., and Strauss, A. 2015. *Basics of Qualitative Research: Techniques and Procedures for Developing Grounded Theory* (4th ed.). Thousand Oaks: Sage.

Daley, T., Whaley, S., Sigman, M., Guthrie, D., Neumann, C., and Bwibo, N. 2005. "Background and Classroom Correlates of Child Achievement, Cognitive, and Behavioural Outcomes in Rural Kenyan Schoolchildren." *International Journal of Behavioral Development* 29 (5): 399–408.

Dunkin, M., and Biddle, B. 1974. *The Study of Teaching*. New York: Holt Rinehart & Winston.

Fife, W. 2005. *Doing Fieldwork: Ethnographic Methods for Research in Developing Countries and Beyond*. New York: Palgrave Macmillan.

Glaser, B., and Strauss, A. 1967. *Discovery of Grounded Theory: Strategies for Qualitative Research*. Mill Valley: Sociology Press.

Guthrie, G. 2010. *Basic Research Methods: An Entry to Social Science Research*. New Delhi: Sage.

Guthrie, G. 2011. *The Progressive Education Fallacy in Developing Countries: In Favour of Formalism*. New York: Springer.

Guthrie, G. 2013. "Prevalence of the Formalistic Paradigm in African Schools." *Southern African Review of Education* 19 (1): 121–138.

Guthrie, G. 2015. "Culturally-Grounded Pedagogy and Research Methodology." *Compare* 45 (1): 163–168.

Hattie, J. 2009. *Visible Learning: A Synthesis of Over 800 Meta-Analyses Relating to Achievement*. London: Routledge.

Husen, T., Saha, L., and Noonan, R. 1978. *Teacher Training and Student Achievement in Less Developed Countries*. Staff Working Paper No.310. Washington: World Bank.

Kerlinger, F. 1973. *Foundations of Behavioural Research* (2nd ed.). London: Holt Rinehart & Winston.

Lancy, D. 1983. *Cross-Cultural Studies in Cognition and Mathematics*. New York: Academic Press.

McGinn, N., and Schiefelbein, E. 2010. "Learning How Teachers Learn in Underdeveloped Countries." *Prospects* 40 (4): 431–445.

Milligan, L. 2016. "Insider-Outsider-Inbetweener? Researcher Positioning, Participative Methods and Cross-cultural Educational Research." *Compare* 46 (2): 235–250.

Mullis, I., Martin, M., Ruddock, G., O'Sullivan, C., and Preuschoff, C. 2009. *TIMSS 2011 Assessment Frameworks*. Boston: TIMSS & PIRLS International Study Center, Boston College.

Mulopo, M., and Fowler, H. 1987. "Effects of Traditional and Discovery Instructional Approaches on Learning Outcomes for Learners of Different Intellectual Developments: A Study of Chemistry Students in Zambia." *Journal of Research in Science Teaching* 24 (3): 217–227.

O'Leary, P. 2014. *Classroom Observation: A Guide to the Effective Observation of Teaching and Learning*. London: Routledge.

O'Sullivan, M. 2004. "The Reconceptualisation of Learner-Centred Approaches: A Namibia Case Study." *International Journal of Educational Development* 24 (6): 585–602.

Pfau, R. 1980. "The Comparative Study of Classroom Behaviours." *Comparative Education Review* 24 (3): 400–414.

Popper, K. 1979. *Objective Knowledge: An Evolutionary Approach* (2nd ed.). Oxford: Oxford University Press.

Sopantini. 2014. *Reforming Teaching Practice in Indonesia: A Case Study of the Implementation of Active Learning in Primary Schools in North Maluku*. Unpublished Doctor of Education thesis, University of Tasmania.

Tabulawa, R. 2013. *Teaching and Learning in Context: Why Pedagogical Reforms Fail in Sub-Saharan Africa*. Dakar: Codesria.

Tan, I., Sharan, S., and Lee, C. 2007. "Group Investigation Effects on Achievement, Motivation, and Perceptions of Students in Singapore." *Journal of Educational Research* 100 (3): 142–154.

Vulliamy, G., Lewin, K., and Stephens, D. 1990. *Doing Educational Research in Developing Countries: Qualitative Strategies*. London: Falmer.

Wragg, E. 2012. *An Introduction to Classroom Observation*. London: Routledge.

10 Teaching Styles Model

Within the general field of comparative education, the orientation of this book is to development education, with the theory oriented to problem-solving in applied and policy research in 'developing' countries. So far, the focus has been on the two predominant classroom styles, which essentially are teacher- and learner-centred. In part, this framing is because debate has been couched in these terms for several decades, but mainly it is because the dichotomy reflects the underlying epistemological issues. However, by the time these paradigms filter down and transmute into classroom practice, considerable variety in classroom behaviour may ensue. For more detailed study of classroom practice, as Alexander (2001) and Barrett (2007) stated, the dichotomy is oversimplified. Discussion now needs to be more specific about teaching styles for research and decision-making directly affecting the classroom. Detailed analysis of classroom behaviour can contribute to decisions about teaching styles by helping separate the *empirical issues* (the scientific study of what is, as embodied in formalistic practice) from the *ethical issues* (the rational analysis of what should be, as with claims for progressive theory).

The Teaching Styles Model in this chapter provides a framework for classifying research data arising from application of the methodological principles in the previous chapter. The model's first and main use is for basic, systematic, grounded within-country classroom research focussed on teaching styles and learning results, whether through qualitative case studies, sample surveys or designs for field experiments. The model can generate more focus through taxonomic clarity in identifying classroom styles and for analysis of different types of classroom practice. Classroom research can also provide a focus for identifying elements that keep styles static, upgrade them or move them towards other styles. As well, they can be useful for analysis of impact on student achievement, particularly in the school achievement field when focus on disaggregated classroom variables loses the bigger picture about teaching styles. The model is also compatible with Alexander's (2001) call for comparative international pedagogy by allowing between-country comparisons of like data.

These types of research can be helpful in clarifying some of the conflicts about different types of teaching that are implicit in pre-service training, inspections, in-service training, curriculum design, and syllabus and textbook production in different countries. Firm policies on teaching styles and consistent efforts to implement them would do much to improve teaching in many places. Choices over reforms to classroom conditions in developing countries are also heavily constrained by practical barriers, especially costs, and rectification of such realities can benefit formalism without being tied to progressive reforms. The many systemic and financial barriers to change will also be discussed in this chapter, while cultural factors that are key to the willingness of teachers and students to adopt change will be explored in the final chapter. The aim is to make policies appropriate to what actually occurs in the classroom.

10.1 The model

As an ideal-type, the Teaching Styles Model has no pretensions to sophistication, but aims to provide a technically correct foundation for basic research – in the sense of establishing sound empirical baseline data – classifying teaching styles. The model uses the same design principles as the typology of findings about progressive educational reforms in Figure 2.1 and removes the extensive methodological failings of Beeby's (1966) 'stages' model (analysed at length in Guthrie 2011, 43–60), from which some of the terminology derives. The styles are intended to apply to formal schooling at primary, secondary and tertiary levels, although in the descriptions that follow some flexibility is required at each level in interpreting terms such as classroom, teacher, student and reinforcement.

The model in Table 10.1 posits five classroom teaching styles in a continuum from more to less teacher-centred, using commonsense labels: Authoritarian, Formalistic, Flexible, Liberal and Democratic.[1] In light of the theory underlying the model, the Authoritarian, Formalistic and Flexible styles are all subsets of revelatory epistemology, and are encompassed by previous generic use of the term formalism in this book. The Liberal and Democratic styles have foundations in scientific epistemology and have been encompassed by the term progressivism. A grey area in the literature is that the Flexible style is often identified as sufficiently learner-centred to constitute a progressive style (e.g. Barrett 2007) because it implies more attention to variety of methods suited to different students or types of knowledge. Here it is seen as related to formalist pedagogy because the underlying element is still transmission rather than construction of knowledge.

In part, the model helps address the inadequacy of multivariate regression techniques in accounting for the presence or absence of teaching styles by providing a basis for ordinal classification, albeit one where statistical variance will remain narrow as a consequence of a limited range of teaching styles in most developing countries. There, the evidence suggests that when the previous more generic use of formalism in this book in separated out into the three styles, most teachers will be classified as Formalistic, many as Flexible and some as Authoritarian, thus providing limited but distinguishable variance for school effectiveness research.

The model does not incorporate Anglo-American progressive education as the basis for predicting direction of change. The styles are represented ordinally

Table 10.1 Teaching Styles Model

Variables	Authoritarian	Formalistic	Flexible	Liberal	Democratic
Teacher Role (authoritarian to democratic)	Formal, domineering. Imposes rigid norms and sanctions.	Formal with well-established routines and strict hierarchical control. Uses closed questions.	Uses variety in methods and some relaxation of controls, but still dominant. May use open questions.	Actively promotes student-centred classroom. Encourages pupil participation in decisions.	Leader of democratically based group. Coordinator of activities.
Student Role (passive to active)	Passive recipient of teacher-defined roles in behaviour and learning. Little overt interaction.	Often complicit in passive learning role, although some overt interaction.	More active role within constraints defined by teacher.	Works within fairly wide boundaries, especially in learning decisions.	Actively participates in decisions. Increasingly responsible for own actions.
Content Approach (teaching to learning)	Teaching of rigid syllabus with closely defined content for rote learning.	Organised processing of syllabus with emphasis on memorisation.	Some flexibility in use of syllabus and textbooks, with attention to learning problems.	Wide degree of curricular choice. Emphasis on learning processes rather than content.	Strong emphasis on student learning at individual pace. Teacher a resource.
Reinforcement (negative to positive)	Strict teacher control with strong negative sanctions (e.g. corporal punishment) enforcing obedience.	Teacher-based negative sanctions, especially focussed on learning.	Greater attempts to use positive reinforcement backed by strong negative sanctions.	Increased emphasis on positive reinforcement.	Positive response to internal motivation, although with latent teacher authority.

More to less teacher-centred

Source: Guthrie (2011, 205).

as being more or less teacher-centred, but the model is intended to be taken at a purely nominal level as far as evaluation of the desirability or undesirability of teaching styles and their components is concerned, i.e. no one style is defined as 'better' than another, such evaluative judgements being deliberately excluded as a matter external to the model. My personal view is that the best teachers can use any or all of these styles, separately or in combination, as the situation warrants.

The typology is based on the four variables of Teacher Role (from authoritarian to democratic), Student Role (passive-active), Content Approach (teaching-learning) and Reinforcement (negative-positive). The basis of the model is the teacher role, which deliberately implies that the teacher is more important than the other variables in creating a classroom style. The teacher has the most important organisational role whether the classroom is authoritarian and teacher-centred, with students not allowed to speak, or whether the classroom is democratic and student-centred, with active pupil participation in decision-making. Even where student-teacher relationships in democratic classrooms are based on a form of ethical egalitarianism, or where students have countervailing power in formalistic classrooms, the teacher wields considerably more direct and indirect authority as controller of time, knowledge resource, organiser of materials, arbiter in disputes and, especially, as the person usually responsible for allocating student grades. Furthermore, educational bureaucracies and school organisation place the teacher in a key hierarchical role as implementer of policy, whether progressive or conservative (Section 11.4).

The model has deliberately not been made more complex, as is the practice in econometric school effectiveness research (which, where it does quantify teaching process variables, does not identify teaching style patterns) and educational psychology literature (which commonly encapsulates variables in an abundance of detailed flow charts on teaching and learning – see examples on the Chinese learner in Chan and Rao 2009). Both school effectiveness and educational psychology fields represent researchers' complex attempts to provide holistic descriptions rather than the more bounded and action-orientated perspectives of practitioners. Nonetheless, the model takes into account in three ways Barrett's (2007) point that more nuance is needed in considering classroom practice. One way is the style labelled Flexible. Another is that improvements to Formalism or any other style may increase variation in classroom techniques, which proposition encompasses a third point, that Formalism is not defined as narrowly as Barrett assumed. Any assumption that formalistic teachers never use variety in their methods and never involve students is misplaced. Formalism does allow for some overt teacher-student and student-student interaction.

The five teaching styles in the model follow.

Authoritarian

The authoritarian teacher is very formal and domineering; indeed, the prime role of the authoritarian teacher is to require obedience to organisational norms.

This may be true, for example, of total institutions such as armies and some religious orders, where use of the style is a deliberate attempt to socialise recruits into following orders in strongly hierarchical authority systems. The authoritarian teacher typically teaches a rigid syllabus and operates through rote learning of facts and principles, whether the three Rs, recitation of religious tracts or the operation of a rifle. The teacher defines the norms of behaviour and of learning. The students' overt role is to be obedient and to respond to directions, but they may elect to be subject to this induction and be complicit in understanding of their role as receivers of given knowledge. In schools, a variety of reasons suggest themselves for teachers to organise classrooms in such a way. The predominant one is compatibility with the teachers' and students' culture (or at least the subculture into which students are being inducted). Additionally, teachers may have authoritarian personality traits, or be insecure and use authoritarianism as a mask or, simply, large groups may necessitate rigid organisation. Reinforcement is essentially negative and frequently involves physical sanctions such as corporal punishment both for breaches of behaviour codes and failure to learn.

Formalistic

The formalistic teacher is also hierarchical, formal and dominant, but promotes formalism as a route to knowledge rather than to obedience as such. Teaching is an organised processing of fixed syllabuses and textbooks, with emphasis on memorising basic facts and principles at lower cognitive levels. Student learning needs are likely to be taken into account in lesson preparation rather than overtly in the classroom, where students may be complicit in playing a passive role in whole-class teaching. Limited overt teacher-student and student-student interaction may occur under conditions controlled by the teacher, such as question and answer routines (where the formalist will typically use closed questions to check student recall) and paired work. Formalistic teachers are authoritative rather than authoritarian, and there is no necessary use of physical punishment as a negative reinforcement. Formalistic teaching is especially common in the many developing countries with revelatory cultures.[2]

Flexible

The flexible teacher uses a variety of methods to transmit given knowledge; however, the different methods are often limited in scope and frequency of use and are teacher-dominated. The variety may serve as positive reinforcement of other forms of teaching, to increase interest and motivation, and to adapt to individual differences. Formal controls may be relaxed and more attempt made to explain norms to help students internalise them and use them informally. Nonetheless, the teacher retains and uses the hierarchical role, and strong negative reinforcement is a backstop. However, syllabuses and textbooks are used with some flexibility, open questions may sometimes be used to check student understanding, and students are encouraged to think problems through and to apply knowledge to their own circumstances. Many teachers who are predominantly formalistic may use some flexibility in their methods; for example, the social studies teacher organising a debate on current affairs or the science teacher supervising student experiments in the laboratory are often doing so in the context of limited variation in methods of teaching. Many of the examples in this book of some variation among formalistic teachers and within formalistic lessons (e.g. in Section 8.4) amount to them having a degree of flexibility, albeit within a revelatory framework and with the teacher clearly in charge.

Liberal

The liberal teacher is essentially student-centred and works to base classroom activities around student needs. The teacher structures the knowledge, but students work within fairly wide boundaries established by the teacher and take an active role in decision-making about learning. Open questions are used to promote student understanding and discovery. Teachers have a wide range of choice in adapting the curriculum to class needs and students have options between and within subjects. Syllabuses are based around learning processes rather than cognitive content and encourage problem-solving. Learning resources are wide-ranging. Many primary classrooms, especially in the Anglo-American world, operate in this fashion, and secondary and tertiary classes often have similar emphases.

Democratic

The democratic teacher's role is to coordinate activities that promote students' self-concepts and construction of knowledge, especially through their own decision-making, encouragement of taking responsibility for their own actions, and in focussing on student discovery and construction of knowledge. Classes may occur in open spaces, include a range of student ages, and involve team teaching. Students actively participate in democratic decision-making at all levels, although teachers, backed by the school, have considerable latent powers. A major focus is on having students decide what they want to learn, when and at what individual pace, which may involve individual learning contracts. Internal motivation is promoted and teacher reinforcement is generally a positive response to success. A wide range of study options is available and there is access to a wide variety of resources and materials. Thus there may be no official curriculum at all. The free school movement in the 1970s had primary schools operating in this fashion, and postgraduate university seminar courses have many similarities, but secondary level democratic classrooms are more uncommon if for no other reason than the higher levels of secondary systems generally become driven by the selection function of external examinations.

Classroom research that used the Teaching Styles Model without any judgements about their relative merits or direction of change was undertaken by

Lattimer (2015) in Kenya. She researched secondary mathematics lessons in two similar schools in Nairobi to identify instructional practices. During a two-year period, more than 60 detailed classroom observations and video recordings were made. Despite many similarities between the classrooms, variations in instructional practice occurred across and within the schools. Subtle classroom differences resulted in distinct differences in placement on the model compared to Schweisfurth's (2013) seven minimum standards for learner-centred education (LCE), which were used as two approaches responsive to the context specific demands of students and communities. Detailed analysis of the lessons found that teacher behaviour around three elements – teacher questioning, student participation, and assessment practices – contributed to quite different learning environments. While a majority of teachers used formalistic methods, a number engaged students with elements of learner-centred practices. Two lessons were used to describe this finding in detail. A form 1 lesson fitted squarely in the Formalistic style in the model and met only one of Schweisfurth's seven learner-centred standards. A form 2 mathematics lesson demonstrated the characteristics of the Flexible style in the model and met all seven of Schweisfurth's standards. Both teachers were firmly in control of their classes at all times but subtle differences in their behaviour occurred, e.g. seeking chorus responses to closed questions or individual student responses to open questions. No data was available on student achievement, so no conclusions could be drawn about which approach was more effective. It can be added that Schweisfurth's minimum standards for LCE matched the Flexible style in the Teaching Styles Model and thus did not meet the progressive criteria in the Liberal and Democratic styles, but Lattimer (2015, 74) properly cautioned that,

> the analysis should not be seen as an endorsement for privileging one approach, for example a 'flexible' teaching model versus a 'formalistic' teaching model, as inherently superior to another. The goal is not to be prescriptive but rather descriptive, providing an example of how researchers, policy makers, and practitioners might analyze and describe instructional practices in-depth so that teachers and site-based administrators can be intentional about choosing the specific practices that are most responsive to their instructional goals and local context for purposes of strengthening teaching and learning.

Research like this can contribute to informed ethical judgements about what teachers should be doing in any particular context in light of systematic knowledge about what they are doing. Which approaches create greater student learning in particular cultures? Which approaches develop more skilled workers? Which approaches develop individuals who are constructive citizens? These questions can involve empirical research, preferably with experimental designs if cause and effect is to be established clearly in the field. The distinction between empirical and ethical analysis is also important in making judgements about the likelihood of success of change strategies. Attempts to promote teaching styles too far removed from empirical reality will usually fail. Thus, directions for change should not stem from the type of self-fulfilling prophecy of axiomatic progressive studies, but should be based on independent criteria relevant to each country. 'Progress' is thus not necessarily a case of moving to the right of the continuum (e.g. to the Democratic style), but can well be a case of improving within a style (e.g. improving the level of Formalism) (Guthrie 1981, 166, 1990, 228, 2011, 208–211). Progress may also occur through reversing attempts to change formalistic styles to progressive.

10.2 Changing styles

When might alterations within formalism actually be classified as a change of style? This issue was raised by the research of O'Sullivan (2004) and Barrett (2007) in Section 5.3. In both cases, teacher change was observed in the direction of the Flexible style. Barrett asserted that the variation she found in primary classrooms in Tanzania challenged assumptions in stereotypes of teaching in Sub-Saharan Africa. She considered that the belief by some teachers in the importance of understanding pupils' conceptualisation of subject matter meant that they had some values consistent with Bernstein's (2000) learner-centred 'competence mode', but they operated predominantly within his teacher-centred 'performance mode'; a similar view to Gao and Watkins's (2001, 37–38) distinction between teachers' 'ideal' constructs of teaching and competing 'practical' constructs that dominate in the classroom. Barrett (2007) equated the teacher-centred performance mode with poor quality, authoritarian, inequitable and teacher-dominated classrooms. However, her view that 'It is possible to recognise and build on learners' prior knowledge; to recognise and cater for different learning styles; to value individuals' contributions and celebrate individuals' achievements within whole-class "teacher-centred" practice' (290) is not necessarily inconsistent with the definition of Formalism used here. One alternative explanation is that formalistic teachers do not necessarily ignore student learning, but can try to understand students' conceptualisation of subject matter in order to shape their own preparation and presentation of material, even though in class they apparently demonstrate little attention to student understanding in asking few if any open questions when delivering the material. Another possibility is that Barrett was describing Flexible teaching rather than progressive transformation. In either case, as Tabulawa (2013, 49) pointed out, Barrett's case for pedagogical flexibility does not grapple with the deeper epistemological issues, both explanations being founded in revelatory epistemology rather than scientific.

O'Sullivan's (2004) research in Namibia did find that some basic classroom techniques for checking on student understanding had success in introducing variety into lessons and considerable improvement in student reading skills. On the basis of this finding, she reconceptualised the official student-centred policy approach to indicate the effectiveness of an adaptive strategy examining the realities within which teachers work. The strategy would use whichever approaches, methods and skills that best brought about *learning*-centred teaching rather than a *learner*-centred approach. The learning-centred approach, she claimed, challenged my views on the appropriateness of formalism (Guthrie 1990). However, four caveats need to be entered into her finding that teachers did change their approach: the new techniques introduced were very limited in range (e.g. they involved teachers asking student opinions, checking students' understanding by asking questions, and using time efficiently); the changes were achieved under non-experimental conditions without tight controls; aid funding provided outside support for three years; and there was no indication that the changes outlasted the in-service teacher education (INSET) programme. Whether the new techniques thus represented a sufficient change so that the new label of learning-centred had substance, or whether the label was merely a semantic device for appearing to meet the requirements of a non-functional progressive policy, seems a moot point. The likelihood is that formalism was being upgraded with a very limited range of skills.

The effect of this discussion is to illustrate four matters. One is that the Formalistic style should not be confused with the Authoritarian one. The second is that Formalism is not as narrow as sometimes assumed. The third is that much of the teaching described in the literature as having more variation that Formalism amounts to the Flexible style rather than paradigm shift to progressivism. The fourth is that none of the styles is intended to be discrete, i.e. the model does not require that teachers' behaviour be forced entirely into one category. A teacher might have a teacher role with well-established routines and strict control, a content approach emphasising memorisation shaped by some understanding of students' own conceptualisations, and use negative sanctions such as low marks, but on occasion broaden the student role to become more active (such as choice of assignment topics). In this example, three of the four categories are formalistic, with the student role on occasion but not always flexible. Overall, the teacher might be rated in an observation study as a Formalist, perhaps with the addition of a high inference judgement that the teaching is good quality because corporal punishment is not used, the teacher is conscious of learning outcomes, and students are sometimes allowed to exercise learning choices.

10.3 Systemic barriers to change

Even if progressive methods are culturally appropriate and teachers support change, educational systems have many practical barriers change over which teachers have little or no control.[3] Systems-based issues discussed in the literature as part of barriers to change have long recognised that unwillingness to adopt change may have a foundation in realism as a rational response to objective systemic problems (e.g. MacDonald and Ruddock 1971; Crossley 1984; Guthrie 1990). Project extension phases, in particular, face several systemic barriers to sustainability beyond any pilot phase. Five main practical problems are evident: (1) classroom facilities may be inappropriate for some teaching styles,

(2) class sizes may be too large for progressive teaching styles, (3) teachers may not have sufficient time to innovate, (4) examinations may emphasise learning inconsistent with innovations and (5) educational administrators may not be able to provide support. An important qualification is that rectification of such realities can benefit formalism without being tied to progressive reforms.

Classroom conditions

Attempts to upgrade teaching through changes in teaching style may find classroom conditions overwhelm the desired behaviours. In practice, working conditions, especially in 'lesser developed' countries, usually do not favour innovation. Where teachers have to cope with large classes, changes in teaching styles that require small group work, experiential enquiry or laboratory work may not be practicable because of fixed classroom furniture, lack of space, absence of equipment and lack of classroom insulation, making even moderate noise a disturbance in other classrooms.

Extensive quantitative research into the poverty of school conditions was reported by Postlethwaite (1998) based on a comprehensive 1995 UNESCO and UNICEF sample survey of 857 primary schools in 14 'least developed' countries in Africa and Asia. The survey found that many school buildings were in need of repair, toilets were often unusable and many classes took place in temporary facilities, including in the open. Only three countries were relatively well off for basics such as chalkboards and wall charts, while very few classrooms had wall maps, cupboards, bookshelves or a library corner, and only about half the classrooms had a teacher's table or chair. In many countries, children had to sit on dirt floors that turned to mud when rain entered. Class sizes of 40–70 were common. Only in one country did all students have a seat at a bench or desk: the writing place was often the shoulder of the next student. Except in two countries, virtually none of the students had supplementary reading books. The dismal conclusion was that conditions in many, if not most, of the schools surveyed were not conducive to teaching or to learning.

Any assumptions that conditions have improved, at least in poorer developing countries, can be quite unfounded. In the UNESCO study, head teachers reported more decreases than increases in school facilities in the preceding five years, despite increases in school enrolments being the norm. Uduku (2015) recently pointed out in relation to low-income countries that schools designed for the poorest remain inadequate for basic requirements, with classrooms designed for 40 regularly accommodating more than 60, and with poor access to infrastructure, electricity, drinking water, sanitation, and computing and library spaces. Thus, progressive innovations can be naïve if they rely implicitly on uncrowded classroom conditions, for example to permit students to move around readily, or furniture to allow group work. A study by Victorini and Wambiya (2016) in Tanzania demonstrated many such resource limitations. The study used questionnaires with 580 secondary students and 115 teachers, interviews with six secondary principals and a school inspector and observation. Some 85% of teachers and students considered that classroom supplies were inadequate, while school facilities were even worse for implementation of the government's learner-centred pedagogy (which the researchers took as a given). The observation schedule indicated that many schools lacked progressive requirements such as computers, internet facilities, libraries, recreation facilities and adequate teaching aids, and had too few teachers.

Class size

Notably, school effectiveness research has long questioned the progressive assumption that scarce financial resources should be used to reduce class size (Lockheed and Verspoor 1991; Gannicott and Throsby 1992). More recently, the school achievement meta-analysis of quality econometric studies by Glewwe et al. (2011, 23–24) found 101 separate estimates from 29 studies in developing countries from 1990 to 2010 that included class size effects on student learning. A majority of estimates (56, or 55%) reported no statistically significant impacts from increased size on learning outcomes (generously interpreted at $p > .10$). Among those with significant effects, another 15 (15%) actually found positive effects, i.e. learning was greater in larger classes. Only 31% (30) found increased class size impacted negatively and significantly on achievement.

A review of the international evidence about the impact of large classes on teaching and learning by O'Sullivan (2006) noted that a general absence of research on class size in developing countries, with most of the evidence from 'developed' countries, where studies had not demonstrated that teachers with small classes actually bring about improved performance. The main evidence was that classes smaller than 20 in the early years of primary school led to improved performance, but class sizes above 20 were not associated with improved student performance. Using these figures, 20 is beyond the resources of some developed countries and is not a realistic number in developing countries. My own commonsense interpretation is that teachers, whether in developed or developing countries, cannot realistically provide meaningful individual attention in a typical 40-minute lesson unless class size is below 20 (and even then only two minutes per student, assuming no other activity occurs). Above that size, it does not much matter whether 30 students or 50 receive teacher talk because few, if any, can receive separate attention. Once classes average 20, cost-effectiveness implies they may as well increase in size, although how large they can become is dependent on contextual factors and no rules exist. While lack of space, fixed classroom furniture and absence of equipment are not desirable in any school, they are easier to cope with in large classes and whole-class teaching than with small group work or individual attention. The effect is that large class size is a barrier to progressive teaching but not necessarily to formalistic. O'Sullivan sensibly considered that the critical issue was not reducing class size but making teaching in large classes more effective, which has implications for teacher training and for government and school policies.

The issue of class size also goes to cultural perceptions. Cortazzi and Jin (2001) reported that class sizes in China in the 1990s commonly ranged from 30 to 70 or more. While school resources were often available to reduce class sizes, frequently this did not happen. The reasons given by teachers included that large classes permitted fewer lessons per week for each teacher and therefore more time for preparation, supervision of study, and the expected individual attention to students outside the class. Thus, the progressive mantra that class sizes should be smaller is caged by the view that teachers' responsibilities are mainly limited to inside the classroom. Where teachers have outside responsibilities to pupils, less classroom time can be a rational trade-off for more time in which to carry out these responsibilities. Paradoxically, large class sizes can permit more teacher attention to students.

Time

The basics of daily life, especially in rural areas with poor infrastructure, can be very time-consuming. Teachers just may not have enough spare hours to innovate long term. This remains particularly the case for teachers in communities lacking modern facilities, where fetching water and firewood can occupy rather more time than for the innovators comfortably located at headquarters. Thaman (1987) tellingly illustrated this point with the story of a Tongan primary teacher with multiple roles as teacher, income source for her extended family, secretary of the village women's group, informal educator of her own children into traditional customs and church member. Each role absorbed considerable time and carried traditional cultural values that generated particular expectations of behaviour. Additionally, a professional expectation was that she would prepare her class 6 for success in the high school selection exam.

The outcome is that the normal work of preparation, teaching, marking and supervising, as well as time for spouse, children, relatives and community groups, means that teachers like this simply might not have the time to invest in complex curriculum reforms. Because modification to existing classroom practice is generally less time-consuming and requires less value change than progressive reform, teachers are more likely to have the time and willingness to adopt and sustain change. Were their time freed up, it could be beneficially applied to formalistic routines, such as preparation and written feedback to students when marking assignments.

Examination pressures

Where syllabus reforms promote progressive teaching to develop enquiry skills and attitudinal change, but examinations emphasise lower level recall of cognitive knowledge, teachers have a dilemma. Usually, their path will follow their own and their students' formalistic expectations of exam-oriented teaching, as shown over the decades by Morris (1985) in Hong Kong, Tabulawa (1997) in Botswana, and Chang *et al.* (2014) in Indonesia. Long-standing academic criticism of the 'diploma disease' (Dore 1976; Little 1997) does not appear to have influenced such attitudes. The implication is that a necessary but not sufficient condition for attempts to change classroom practice is that they should be congruent with teachers' and pupils' perceptions of the requirements of any public examination system (Crossley and Guthrie 1987).

If curricular innovations are unlikely to succeed because they are incompatible with the requirements of the examination system, one solution within the power of educational authorities is to change the exams, as has long been pointed out (e.g. Heyneman 1987; Kellaghan and Greaney 2001). The main function of public exams is selection for higher levels of education and for employment. Traditional practice was usually norm-referenced when the function was selection based on students' relative performance. The alternative of criterion- or domain-referenced testing, which concentrates on assessing student achievement against defined educational objectives, has become common (as found in the more traditional versions of outcomes-based education identified by Norman 2006), albeit sometimes taken to incorporate progressive approaches, as with the more radical versions of outcomes-based education (OBE) that failed in Papua New Guinea and South Africa. In part, criterion-referenced testing can rank students and also meet the selection function. Indeed, under criticism from proponents of criterion-referenced testing, norm-referenced examinations are now likely to be tied to explicit learning objectives, so that the objectives can promote the desired types of learning. This is simple in principle, but is time-consuming, very technical, expensive of time, skills and money (not least for computer operations), requires systematic rewrite of syllabuses in performance terms, and should not be undertaken lightly (Guthrie 1990, 230). Even this assessment was optimistic, at least in the case of Hong Kong, where criterion-referenced examination reforms in the 2000s met further difficulties because teachers simply could not see what the problem was with the existing norm-referenced system and the changes were prescribed in a top-down approach that made little attempt to take into account parents' or teachers' perceptions (Watkins and Biggs 2001, 16). Where formalistic syllabus changes are compatible with existing examinations, teachers, parents and students are more likely to accept them as meeting their own goals as well as system goals.

Administrative support

Insufficient support from departmental administrations may be embedded in the formal bureaucracies that surround formalistic teaching. Stephens (1991) typified very clearly the hierarchical system impinging upon a primary classroom in Nepal, but which could apply in many places elsewhere. The student at the bottom of the hierarchy received knowledge passively and with little control over what he learned and when. The teacher passed on the knowledge she learned in her day and was more a transmitter than a decider, constrained by her limited knowledge of choices and lack of resources. The head teacher, even with a degree in education, decided little that was new or innovatory. He managed rules and procedures that left little time or energy for INSET, curriculum development or school-community relations. His immediate superior, the inspector of schools, was unsure of her exact duties because she had recently been promoted from head teacher and had not received induction. She concentrated on administration, leaving curriculum development and materials writing to specialists in the capital city. At the top of the hierarchy was the government department, heavily constrained by aid conditionality imposed by donors (albeit benevolently and in the interests of efficiency and relevance in mind). This description showed formalistic teachers at work in a formalistic system. The system was designed to keep routine operations on track, but quite possibly had a long cultural history of preference for revelatory rather than scientific knowledge, and therefore with more meaning for the participants than Stephens admitted.

Administrative systems like this can inhibit a desired change. They are more likely to have the capability to support incremental formalistic change (especially if funded routinely from recurrent budgets) rather than substantial progressive change (especially if funded from aid funds with extra accountability procedures). Progressive reforms can generate considerable overhead costs for administrative support, as well logistical problems, because they usually require procurement and delivery of greater quantities and varieties of books and other supporting equipment and materials, as well as delivery of professional inputs such as INSET in progressive methods. Lack of funding can severely compromise sustainability by limiting continued provision of support materials and replacement equipment, such as computers. A typical outcome can be seen from Victorini and Wambiya's (2016) observation schedule, which indicated that many schools in Tanzania lacked progressive requirements such as computers, internet facilities, libraries, recreation facilities and adequate teaching aids – all of which overlap with the more fundamental cultural issues associated with retraining of teachers.

10.4 Financial implications

In Western countries, education often is seen as a form of consumption, a human right that society should provide to meet popular demand. Although it is not always possible to provide what is wanted, and although this view is long lost for tertiary education, it is still the ideal around which much educational provision revolves at the lower levels of schooling. However, progressive demands for more individualised attention to pupils and smaller classes require increased numbers of teachers and greater funding for teacher training and teacher salaries. In other words, almost invariably progressive reforms add to costs. In developing countries, economics require planners to approach education as an investment in human resources for national development. Maintenance of existing formalistic systems with routine supply of professional and technical inputs are more financially sustainable.

Even if progressive reforms are appropriate, economics is a barrier. The example of Papua New Guinea (PNG) is again illustrative. PNG is asset rich but income poor. Total revenue in the 2017 government budget was forecast as AUD 5.45 billion, including an estimated AUD 0.44 billion in grant aid (8.1% of revenue) (GOPNG 2016; PNG 1.00 = AUD 0.42). In comparison, the small Australian state of Tasmania had a similar estimated annual revenue of AUD 5.58 billion in 2016–2017, including AUD 1.21 billion in grants from the Australian Commonwealth Government (21.7% of revenue) (GOT 2016). However, Tasmania, with 102% of PNG's estimated revenue, was only 15% of its area, had 7% of its population, and had to provide a lesser range of services that did not include foreign relations and defence. Gas and mineral projects have increased PNG's income considerably during the 2010s, but the government's service delivery remains hampered by endemic financial management issues, including planning and budgetary processes, cash flow management, service delivery capability and accountability, as well as now endemic corruption. Even were these inefficiencies resolved, revenue would be insufficient for a modern state with a fast growing population. Other developing countries often have similar stories.

During trial or pilot phases, additional funding from aid projects may temporarily overcome such barriers, although the example of SSCEP in PNG (outlined in Section 6.4) demonstrated that aid trials are highly vulnerable to sustainability problems. With the end of World Bank loan funding, the project was to be disseminated from 10 trial schools to all provincial high schools, however government funding could not be found in a difficult economic period, and SSCEP faded away within five years. Progressive reforms require not just extra start-up costs, but they can be unrealistic in assuming restricted educational budgets can sustain higher running costs in the long term.

In contrast, one of formalism's strengths is its functionality and affordability within poorly resourced classroom settings. Teachers in developing countries often face large classes in rooms with very basic furniture and materials, and may not have even that. The functionality of formalism in such conditions is a considerable asset, nonetheless formalism should not be considered merely as a coping mechanism for lack of resources. None of the analysis in this book about the cultural roots of classroom teaching is intended to deny any of the needs for resource inputs and structural changes identified in the literature classified earlier in Figure 3.1. The evidence about the failures of progressive reforms implies that technical and professional inputs, when and if available, would be applied more efficiently and effectively to upgrading formalism rather than attempting to change it to progressivism. Superficially attractive, additional aid funding outside the normal governmental budgetary processes can upgrade conditions as part of progressive reforms; however, aid funding has long lead times. Incremental improvements funded through existing recurrent budgets are less glamorous but nonetheless realistic. Section 11.5 will outline eight cost-effective, evidence-based incremental paths that are available to educational planners, curriculum designers and teacher trainers.

10.5 Conclusion

A great deal of research needs to be carried out if theoretical propositions are to be useful in improving education systems. The Teaching Styles Model focusses solely on teaching styles inside the classroom. As an ideal-type, the model is not sophisticated methodologically, but aims to provide a technically correct foundation for basic classification. Collection of data on teaching styles using the model can help identify conditions and processes affecting changes within and between styles, as teased out through Lattimer's (2015) research in Kenya. The range of possible data collection techniques is wide: their corresponding strengths and weaknesses indicate the merit of triangulation through mixed methods research. Grounded research can provide information relevant to the basic policy question for many countries: formalistic or progressive teaching? The model is ordinal in the sense of spreading teaching styles along a continuum from more to less teacher-centred, but is purely nominal as far as evaluation of the desirability or undesirability of teaching styles and their components is concerned. The absence of an evaluative dimension in the model carries the implication that conscious, independent choices should be made about the appropriateness of a teaching style or styles, and these choices should be based on country-specific evidence.

Firm policies on teaching styles and consistent efforts to implement them would do much to improve teaching in many places. Clear strategies can help resolve some of the conflicts about different types of teaching that are implicit in pre-service training, inspections, in-service training, curriculum design, and syllabus and textbook production. Choices over reforms to classroom conditions in developing countries are also heavily constrained by practical barriers, especially costs. Insufficient financial and administrative capacity makes innovation vulnerable even if appropriate. Equally, extra financial and administrative capacity when available can be applied for the benefit of formalistic schools, classrooms and teachers. The aim is to make change appropriate to what actually occurs in the classroom rather than to attempt to force social change on teachers derived from exogamous theories, thus avoiding the cultural imperialism inherent in many progressive reforms.

Notes

1 Sections 10.1–10.2 derive from Guthrie (2011, 203–210, https://doi.org/10.1007/978-94-007-1851-7_10, © Springer Science+Business Media B.V. 2011) with permission of Springer Nature.
2 This definition has been modified slightly from Guthrie (2011, 206–207) to reflect Tabulawa's (2004) analysis of student complicity in formalism and to make closed questioning more evident.

3 Section 10.3 derives from Guthrie (2011, 67–72, https://doi.org/10.1007/978-94-007-1851-7_4, © Springer Science+Business Media B.V. 2011) with permission of Springer Nature.

References

Alexander, R. 2001. "Border Crossings: Towards a Comparative Pedagogy." *Comparative Education* 37 (4): 507–523.

Barrett, A. 2007. "Beyond the Polarization of Pedagogy: Models of Classroom Practice in Tanzanian Primary Schools." *Comparative Education* 43 (2): 273–294.

Beeby, C. 1966. *The Quality of Education in Developing Countries.* Cambridge: Harvard University Press.

Bernstein, B. 2000. *Pedagogy, Symbolic Control and Identity: Theory, Research, Critique.* Lanham: Rowman & Littlefield.

Chan, C., and Rao, N. (Eds.). 2009. *Revisiting the Chinese Learner: Changing Contexts, Changing Education.* Hong Kong: Comparative Education Research Centre, University of Hong Kong.

Chang, M., Shaeffer, S., Al-Samarrai, S.; Ragatz, A., de Ree, J., and Stevenson, R. 2014. *Teacher Reform in Indonesia The Role of Politics and Evidence in Policy Making.* Washington, DC: World Bank.

Cortazzi, M., and Jin, L. 2001. "Large Classes in China: 'Good' Teachers and Interaction." In *Teaching the Chinese Learner: Psychological and Pedagogical Perspectives*, edited by D. Watkins and J. Biggs, 115–134. Hong Kong: Comparative Education Research Centre, University of Hong Kong.

Crossley, M. 1984. "Strategies for Curriculum Change and the Question of International Transfer." *Journal of Curriculum Studies* 16 (1): 75–88.

Crossley, M., and Guthrie, G. 1987. "Current Research in Developing Countries: INSET and the Impact of Examinations on Classroom Practice." *Teaching and Teacher Education* 3 (1): 65–76.

Dore, R. 1976. *The Diploma Disease.* London: Allen and Unwin.

Gannicott, K., and Throsby, D. 1992. "Educational Quality in Economic Development: Ten Propositions and an Application in the South Pacific." *International Review of Education* 38 (3): 223–239.

Gao, L., and Watkins, D. 2001. "Towards a Model of Teaching Conceptions of Chinese Secondary School Teachers of Physics." In *Teaching the Chinese Learner: Psychological and Pedagogical Perspectives*, edited by D. Watkins and J. Biggs, 27–45. Hong Kong: Comparative Education Research Centre, University of Hong Kong.

Glewwe, P., Hanushek, E., Humpage, S., and Ravin, R. 2011. *School Resources and Educational Outcomes in Developing Countries: A Review of the Literature from 1990 to 2010.* Working Paper 17554. Cambridge: National Bureau of Economic Research.

GOPNG (Government of Papua New Guinea). 2016. *2017 National Budget Speech*, 1 November. www.treasury.gov.pg/html/national_budget/files/2017/2017%20Treasurer's%20Budget%20Speech.pdf

GOT (Government of Tasmania). 2016. *Budget Paper No. 1*: www.treasury.tas.gov.au/Documents/2016-17-Budget-Paper-No-1.pdf

Guthrie, G. 1981. "Teaching Styles." In *Teachers and Teaching: Proceedings of the 1980 Extraordinary Meeting of the Faculty of Education*, edited by P. Smith and S. Weeks, 154–168. Port Moresby: UPNG.

Guthrie, G. 1990. "To the Defense of Traditional Teaching in Lesser Developed Countries." In *Teachers and Teaching in the Developing World*, edited by V. Rust and P. Dalin, 219–232. New York: Garland.

Guthrie, G. 2011. *The Progressive Education Fallacy in Developing Countries: In Favour of Formalism*. New York: Springer.

Heyneman, S. 1987. "Uses of Examinations in Developing Countries: Selection, Research, and Education Sector Management." *International Journal of Educational Development* 7 (4): 251–263.

Kellaghan, T., and Greaney, V. 2001. *Using Assessment to Improve the Quality of Education*. Paris: UNESCO International Institute for Educational Planning.

Lattimer, H. 2015. "Translating Theory into Practice: Making Meaning of Learner Centered Education Frameworks for Classroom-Based Practitioners." *International Journal of Educational Development* 45 (1): 65–76.

Little, A. 1997. "The Diploma Disease Twenty Years On: An Introduction." *Assessment in Education* 4 (1): 5–22.

Lockheed, M., and Verspoor, A. 1991. *Improving Primary Education in Developing Countries*. Oxford: Oxford University Press.

MacDonald, B., and Ruddock, J. 1971. "Curriculum Research and Development Projects: Barriers to Success." *British Journal of Educational Psychology* 41 (2): 148–154.

Morris, P. 1985. "Teachers' Perceptions of the Barriers to the Implementation of a Pedagogic Innovation: A South East Asian Case Study." *International Review of Education* 31 (1): 3–18.

Norman, P. 2006. "Outcomes-Based Education: A PNG Perspective." *Contemporary PNG Studies* 5: 45–57.

O'Sullivan, M. 2004. "The Reconceptualisation of Learner-Centred Approaches: A Namibia Case Study." *International Journal of Educational Development* 24 (6): 585–602.

O'Sullivan, M. 2006. "Teaching Large Classes: The International Evidence and a Discussion of Some Good Practice in Ugandan Primary Schools." *International Journal of Educational Development* 26 (1): 24–37.

Postlethwaite, N. 1998. "The Conditions of Primary School Classrooms in Least-Developed Countries." *International Review of Education* 44 (4): 289–317.

Schweisfurth, M. 2013. *Learner-Centred Education in International Perspective: Whose Pedagogy for Whose Development?* London: Routledge.

Stephens, D. 1991. "The Quality of Primary Education in Developing Countries: Who Defines and Who Decides?" *Comparative Education* 27 (2): 223–233.

Tabulawa, R. 1997. "Pedagogical Classroom Practice and the Social Context: The Case of Botswana." *International Journal of Educational Development* 17 (2): 189–194.

Tabulawa, R. 2004. "Geography Students as Constructors of Classroom Knowledge and Practice: A Case Study from Botswana." *Journal of Curriculum Studies* 36 (1): 53–73.

Tabulawa, R. 2013. *Teaching and Learning in Context: Why Pedagogical Reforms Fail in Sub-Saharan Africa*. Dakar: Codesria.

Thaman, K. 1987. "A Teacher's Story." *International Review of Education* 33: 276–282.

Uduku, O. 2015. "Designing Schools for Quality: An International, Case Study-Based Review." *International Journal of Educational Development* 44: 56–64.

Victorini, S., and Wambiya, P. 2016. "Assessment of the Adequacy of Resources and Facilities to Enhance Learner Centred Pedagogy in Secondary Schools in Kilimanjaro Region, Tanzania." *European Journal of Education Studies* 2 (2): 142–161.

Watkins, D., and Biggs, J. 2001. "The Paradox of the Chinese Learner and Beyond." In *Teaching the Chinese Learner: Psychological and Pedagogical Perspectives*, edited by D. Watkins and J. Biggs, 3–23. Hong Kong: Comparative Education Research Centre, University of Hong Kong.

11 Teacher constructs and classroom change

A long-standing issue has resurfaced in recent years at the centre of current international managerial reforms in education. As Bonal (2013) observed, 'teachers are back as protagonists, but what has not changed is the *blaming the victim* strategy used by many educational policy makers' (iv, emphasis in original). An earlier expression of the same approach was Beeby's (1966) unsympathetic view of the ritualistic formalistic teacher as 'an unskilled and ignorant one who teaches mere symbols with only the vaguest reference to their meaning' (52). In his influential view, professional conservatism was affected by five factors: lack of clear goals in the system affecting teachers' thinking, lack of understanding and acceptance by teachers of reforms, teachers as products of a system not being prone to innovate, isolation of teachers in their classroom slowing down diffusion of innovations, and a wide range of ability of teachers making diffusion rates uneven. The pejorative implication was that the inability of formalistic teachers was the key obstacle to progressive 'development'. One widespread inference from this approach was a need for curriculum reform to accelerate teacher development through the 'stages'. Another inference attributed curriculum failures to teachers rather than to the innovators who failed to understand the formalist paradigm and the school situation adequately.

Three types of response to the research evidence about the ineffectiveness of progressive reforms were layered through the typology of findings in Chapter 2. The surface layer identified the lack of success of reforms as due to school and classroom conditions (Figure 3.1). Consequent recommendations for more technical inputs naively assumed that extra resources and training would overcome the barriers. The second layer identified structural conditions, such as teacher status or more deeply in the education system itself, as being at fault. The third layer identified the more fundamental cultural elements underlying both these layers, either organisational culture as a barrier to change or intergenerational grammar as a foundation for culturally embedded educational practice.

Researchers who focussed on the first layer were often informed by econometric models about school effectiveness or by classroom subject specialisations and education theory about curriculum and teacher education. The second layer tended to be informed by sociological, political economy and critical theories that turn attention to political, economic and social systems as structural obstacles to change. The third layer tended to be informed by cross-cultural psychology and cultural anthropology, which turned attention to paradigms and epistemology. This book is firmly in the last group. The final chapter refocuses on the teachers who, all the evidence and analysis suggests, are the most important element in classroom change. Rather than treating formalistic teachers as obstructive, this chapter considers teachers' and students' perceptual constructs, teachers' various attitudes to adoption of change, and some possible improvements to teaching that are consistent with the formalist paradigm.

11.1 Teachers' constructs

When the modern curriculum movement began in the United States in the 1950s, it initially used a top-down, centre-periphery model (Crossley 1984a, 1984b; Guthrie 1986).[1] Innovations were successfully disseminated as far as the classroom, but lack of behavioural change by teachers inside the classroom soon became apparent. By the end of the 1960s, attention turned to problems of diffusion and to persuasion of resistant teachers, followed in the 1970s with school-based curriculum strategies that tried to expand the change process to include teachers. Curriculum reform in 'developing' countries often followed these patterns soon after they occurred in 'developed' counties, partly under the influence of contracted expatriate curriculum specialists. Increasingly through time, local change agents returned from study in developed countries with borrowed progressive theories. However, despite the seeming congruity of top-down models with formalistic school systems, implementation of directives by teachers was often tokenistic and not sustained in the long term. The sustainability of school-based curriculum development was also low in large part because of its extra demands on teachers' time and skills.

A more realistic stepwise change model later combined the strengths of the centre-periphery and school-based models. It has been common since the 1980s, especially in well-funded and well-staffed pilot projects funded by aid programmes. Project design and management principles structure change management, for example using the logical framework favoured in the World Bank and the Australian Agency for International Development (AusAID). Under systematic trial conditions, teachers singled out for special attention through in-service can make considerable commitments of time. These Hawthorne effects are often interpreted as a sign of success. However, project extension phases that require ongoing levels of time and commitment, often without relief from normal school duties and usually with less in-service teacher education (INSET) support, are usually unsustainable professionally. Another major limitation is financial sustainability, especially when external funding ceases.

Two simplistic assumptions are that teacher conservatism and resource limitations between them explain the difficulties faced by the three curriculum change models. Additional and deeper understanding lies in perceptual and cultural issues associated with paradigm shift. Perceptual analysis focusses on decision-making processes based on learned mental constructs that derive from social and cultural environments, and which provide teachers with a basis for purposeful assessment of classroom options. A conceptual starting point for this type of analysis came from H.A. Simon (1947) in economics. He viewed people not as economic maximisers, but as intendedly rational satisficers who make decisions based on imperfect knowledge. Bounded by simplified models of the real world, individuals evaluate their environments in terms of subjectively based aspiration levels that adjust on the basis of experience. Construct theory derived from psychology further postulates that individuals' perceptions derive from their constructs, which are ways of making sense of past experiences to give meaning to present and future ones (Kelly 1955). Too, constructs provide a worldview that itself can change through experience. Some agreement with Beeby's pessimism about teachers lies in the view that constructs can act not only as frames, but also as cages (Ryle 1975).

Once adopted in education, the perceptual approach contributed to a number of different research themes, including teachers' practical knowledge, classroom ecology, knowledge-in-action, images and frames (Tabulawa 1998, 251–253) (the student-centred 'constructivist' view of knowledge creation has perceptual roots too, but is very different from the concern here with teachers' formalism as a construct). The themes identified by Tabulawa have remained infrequent in research in developing countries, however, as can be inferred from extensive literature reviews on teacher professional development (Villegas-Reimers 2003, 145–195), quality in education (Barrett *et al.* 2006, 18–21), school effectiveness (Yu 2007, 58–61) and foundation learning (Nag *et al.* 2014). Rather, sociological research with other theoretical bases has emphasised constructs not just as individual perceptions, but as culturally framed and derived from the social environment (e.g. Clarke 2003 in India), to which Tabulawa (1997) applied the concept of paradigms. In turn, the perceptual approach to decision-making implies that formalistic teachers do not necessarily apply cultural tradition in a passive and reflexive fashion – they are usually among the most educated members of their communities – but instead their behaviour can be rational, purposeful and thoughtful. Another implication of constructs is that different people can ascribe different meanings to the same phenomenon. A curriculum innovator's progressive enlightenment can be a classroom teacher's professional nightmare.

An example of research based in constructs is Morris's (1985) Hong Kong study of the effects of examinations on progressive curriculum reform in a school system that long had placed great importance on public exams and formalistic teaching that promoted rote learning (Choi 1999). In the early 1980s, curriculum planners attempted a counter with innovations involving progressive approaches to teaching and learning. These required pupil participation and a heuristic teaching style but, Morris found, classroom observation demonstrated that the approaches were actually not implemented despite teachers expressing favourable attitudes to progressive approaches. The study attempted to assess why economics teachers did not implement the new techniques in forms 4 and 5. Semi-structured interviews were conducted with 45 teachers, each from a different secondary school. After observation of a lesson, teachers were asked what factors had influenced their approach to the lesson, later followed by supplementary interviews. The results demonstrated the formalistic context: 29% of teachers gave as the sole influence for a lesson pattern the need to cover the syllabus in the available time, 16% gave pupils' expectations. A majority cited the examinations as the main influence on their teaching. Teachers repeatedly viewed knowledge as information, requiring them to lecture rather than to adopt the heuristic learning process in the new syllabus.

Morris did not view these teachers as resistors of change, but as rational decision makers concerned with factors that could limit successful implementation. They weighed the innovations according to practicality in the classroom, congruence with prevailing conditions, and professional costs. Their decisions not to use the progressive innovations were rational choices between alternatives. Teachers said they used traditional didacticism because it was more efficient than progressivism for transmitting information specified by the examination syllabus. Examinations and their selection functions were regarded as normal. They gave purpose and a framework for teaching in a social and economic context of very unequal distribution of income. Examination success was crucial to pupils' life chances, and teachers perceived the progressive approach as inefficient for achieving such important ends. Undesirable consequences could occur if the syllabus was not covered, and teachers were blamed for student failure. Teachers also considered progressivism was not congruent with existing teaching and learning styles and not consistent with how colleagues and principals assessed teachers' work. The teachers' perception was that any intrinsic merit of the progressive approach did not outweigh its lack of extrinsic worth for exam results. Change would not occur unless they perceived it as necessary for pupils to pass the exams. However, this was not a simple case of an errant examination system or caged teachers. Teachers' constructs derived from classical Chinese culture with deep rooted epistemology about the nature of knowledge and its purposes, and associated views on the merits of pedagogy and memorisation of knowledge, as Chapter 4 showed.

11.2 Perceptions of change

The Hong Kong study demonstrated that teachers bring their existing knowledge and prior experiences to school, which interact with their current perceptions to shape classroom behaviour. Teachers' mental constructs classify their reality under the influence of the cultural, social and educational environments in which they operate. These constructs can provide stability in educational systems marked by change, so that perceptions influence heavily attempts to change teaching styles, and can undercut administrators and change agents who assume falsely teachers will passively implement change directives. The need is to understand how teachers perceive innovation and the extent to which curriculum reforms are consistent with their beliefs about education. Rogers's (2003) sociological perspective is relevant, especially his delineation of five distinct attributes of innovations that are weighed up by individuals in an organisation (15–16):

i   *Relative advantage* (the degree to which innovations offer advantages over other innovations or over present circumstance).
ii *Compatibility* (the extent to which innovations align with prevalent values, previous experiences or ideas, and the needs of clients in the social system).
iii *Complexity* (the extent to which innovations are considered difficult to learn and apply).
iv *Trialability* (the degree to which innovations can be tried on a small scale).
v   *Observability* (the degree to which outcomes from use of a new idea are visible to clients).

Innovations perceived as having greater relative advantage, compatibility, simplicity, trialability and observability are adopted more rapidly than innovations that do not have these attributes.

Where pilot projects and trials provide inducements and support for reforms, Hawthorne effects may provide initial appearances of success. The longer term perspective on pilot projects is that traditional paradigm behaviour usually overwhelms progressive behaviours, so that initial appearances of paradigm shift do not sustain. The reluctance of formalistic teachers to maintain progressive reforms as routine practice can be understood as reasoned responses to complex changes that offer no relative advantage in the classroom, are not compatible with existing methods, are complex to implement, and offer no observable outcomes for clients such as parents concerned with examination results. On the other hand, formalistic developments compatible with extant teaching methods can have a relatively easy path to adoption because modification of existing methods is simpler than attempting fundamental change in teaching styles, and results can be accepted by teachers and parents if they improve examination performance. Change that does not require paradigm shift to progressivism, but builds on existing formalistic behaviours, is more likely to be tried out and, if successful, adopted as long-term practice.

11.3 Adopters of innovation

Teachers are not equally open to or equally resistant to change. Perceptual and systemic issues show teachers in general can weigh reforms rationally, but not all potential adopters or rejecters are alike. Columns 1 and 2 of Table 11.1 show Rogers's (2003, 281) equally relevant schema of five categories of adopters of innovation, which can be adapted to help understand how change is affected by the structural position of various professional groups within school systems.

The application in column 3 of the table distributes educators hypothetically along a continuum based on their different integration as professional

Table 11.1 Adopters of innovation

Adopters	Rogers's Schema	Education System Application
Innovators	Venturesome risk takers greatly interested in innovations. Seek information actively. Can understand complex technical knowledge and cope with high levels of uncertainty associated with innovation. Critical role in adoption and diffusion of innovations as the first members to introduce new ideas to their social system.	Designers of a new curriculum, usually located in headquarters and closely tied to official policy concerns.
Early Adopters	More integrated into the social system. Tend to be cautious about decisions on innovation to maintain respect of other members. Other potential adopters seek information and advice from them as role models and opinion leaders. Peers perceive their adoption as a stamp of approval.	Head teachers, deputies and subject heads operating under field conditions often inadequately accounted for in official policy. Required officially to support change, which duty may be responsible for their promotion of a new curriculum rather than personal conviction.
Early Majority	Rarely perceived as opinion leaders, but interact frequently with peers and willing to be adopters. Will deliberate for some time before committing fully to an innovation.	Younger teachers with something to gain from adoption of an innovation, especially during a trial phase, perhaps because this may benefit their professional opportunities.
Late Majority	Sceptical and cautious in approach. To reduce uncertainty will wait until most colleagues have adopted an innovation. Growing peer pressure and, in some cases, economic gain drive their adoption.	Experienced older teachers who have reached their ceiling and for whom professional life is incidental to personal life external to the school.
Laggards	Interact primarily with others perceived as adhering to traditional ways. Show virtually no leadership in opinion making. Tend to be suspicious of innovations and change agents. Their decisions influenced by the past.	Teachers overlooked for promotion, alienated from the system, feeling undervalued and unwilling to invest time and effort in change.

Source: Columns 1 and 2 based on Rogers (2003); column 3, author.

groups into an education system's structure. The implication of the professional groups in column 3 is that they will approach adoption of classroom change quite differently. Innovators, usually located in headquarters and closely tied to official policy concerns, might be the designers of a new curriculum, for which school staff in leadership positions are co-opted as early adopters required to implement official policy. Younger teachers for whom uptake can earn recognition may make up an early majority; however, older teachers at their professional ceiling may be a less enthusiastic late majority, and laggards alienated from the system may remain resistant. Many progressive curriculum projects will often receive only lip service and will not diffuse far into the third group, the early majority, let alone the late majority who comprise the fourth group. Any changes are unlikely to be sustained if they offer no relative advantage once pilot support and official attention ceases. Perhaps with the laggards, Beeby's attitude to teachers as caged resistors of change had a target. However, there is no reason to assume that formalistic teachers are the only type who act as laggards or that people stay fixed in one category over time.

Whether a new syllabus, teaching style or wider curriculum change does become accepted by both early and late majorities is a complex issue. Adoption is dependent on teachers' personal and professional constructs and structural inducements, a school's professional climate, and countervailing work and social pressures, as well as the systemic issues discussed in the previous chapter. Even if many of these factors are positive, the influence of cultural context on teachers' formalistic professional constructs may well outweigh – quite rationally from their perspective – the alleged benefits of any progressive reform.

11.4 Students' constructs

Teachers are not the only people in the classroom putting constructs into behavioural effect. Students too can be rational decision makers weighing the practicality of innovations, their congruence with prevailing conditions, and personal costs – especially possible effects on the examination results that might provide a rare opportunity for upward mobility and escape from poverty. Thus, particularly in formalistic systems, students' and teachers' constructs may have common ground.

This point is established by Tabulawa's (2004) highly insightful investigations into the meanings attached in common to pedagogical practices by both teachers and students in Botswana, as detailed in Section 5.2. His research found little variation in routine, formalistic classroom practice. Knowledge was a utilitarian commodity; the teachers' job being to impart it, the students' job to acquire it. Teacher-student relationships were paternalistic, formal and deferential. However, students actually resisted changes to these roles. Students viewed knowledge as an external commodity possessed by the school and teachers, and found in textbooks. If they wanted to pass the exams, they had to obtain knowledge from these sources. Teacher dominance was not necessarily perceived just as a product of teachers' inherent desire for social control. In many instances, teachers were 'forced' into a dominant position by the students themselves, so that teacher dominance was a mutually constructed, negotiated product. Students contributed to teacher-centredness through their expectations of teacher behaviour and through considerable informal power over teachers' reputations. The teachers' apparent dominance was not so much imposed as co-constructed, a negotiated legitimate authority that was a product of the expectations of schooling that teachers and students derived from their shared cultural context.

However, while teachers share the classroom space, their structural position of authority in schools does outweigh any countervailing power held by students. Teachers, subject department heads and principals all have more important organisational influences on both teacher- and student-centred classrooms. School staff have considerable direct and indirect authority as controllers of time and resources, as arbiters in disputes and, particularly, in streaming students and allocating student grades. Further, the school system places teachers in a key hierarchical role as implementer of policy, whether progressive or conservative. A recent attempt to change this situation in Ethiopia involved neo-liberal democratic efforts to broaden local stakeholder (including student) participation in school leadership (Mitchell 2017). While management did become more transparent, its agendas dominated consultative and decision-making forums and the fundamental authority system remained in place.

The effect is that students' responses to change can represent purposeful behaviour. They may not be able to control whether reforms occur, but they can have considerable impact on their success. Tabulawa (2004, 70) provided a telling classroom challenge for progressive change agents:

> Conceptualizing classroom reality as a co-construction has important implications for the [progressive Botswanan] pedagogical reforms. . . . In such reform endeavours, no cognizance is taken of the students. This is in line with the tacit assumption that students do not make any significant contribution to classroom practice. For this reason, whenever change is proposed, in-service and pre-service programmes are mounted for teachers, never for students. It is often assumed that students' classroom behaviour will change as and when that of the teacher changes. However, this position becomes a fallacy once it is acknowledged that classroom reality (such as 'teacher-centredness') is as much a student construction as it is a teacher construction.

11.5 Improving formalistic teaching

The formalistic teachers prevalent in many developing country classrooms need not be seen as problematic obstructions to modernisation.[2] Rather than trying to generate systemic progressive change, strong theoretical and practical reasons exist for gradual modification from within. In this approach, formalism is accepted as a deep-rooted cultural behaviour capable of adaptation and of performing important educational functions now and in the foreseeable future. Despite concerns about lack of testing of curriculum innovations, the absence of experimental research is not a reason to ignore upgrading existing classroom practices; although it does provide reason not to attempt to change teachers to other styles. The productive approach is to take culturally intuitive formalistic teaching styles and develop them further, rather than trying unproductively to have teachers adopt methods that are counter-intuitive to them. In those cultures where it is appropriate, formalism can be both a legitimate means and a legitimate end point. Formalistic teaching is often embedded in formalistic teacher training, examination, inspection and administrative systems that are parts of a symbiotic, mutually reinforcing whole. Progressive or radical attempts to replace them are unlikely to succeed but, like teaching within the classroom, they are open to evolutionary improvement.

Regardless of the presence or absence of evidence from field experiments, improving teaching is a professional responsibility and an end in itself that need not be embedded in curriculum change. In the absence of large-scale reforms, teachers can use ongoing professional support through pre-service and in-service teacher training to upgrade their performance, whether or not new syllabuses are pending. Plenty of scope exists for upgrading formalistic teachers' skills within the classroom and its school setting. Many textbooks for teachers provide tips on techniques: for example, one written for Melanesia abounded with constructive ideas that were neither overburdened with angst about the formalism of schools nor unapologetically accepting of it (Kubul 2001).

Long-standing evidence, in part outlined in Section 10.3, indicates several cost-effective alternatives to progressive reform efforts that are compatible with the predominant formalism in the classrooms of developing countries: (1) increase time on task, (2) improve facilities, (3) increase class size, (4) provide textbooks, (5) provide supplementary language readers, (6) increase attention on subject knowledge in teacher training, (7) use distance education for subject in-service and (8) teacher practice of moderate versions of reflection. The eight approaches illustrate some pathways that are available to educational planners, curriculum designers and teacher trainers. However, none of the approaches is prescriptive given that teaching and teacher education are specific to context. Another caveat is that, while more straightforward and more cost-effective than complex progressive reforms, there can nonetheless be implementation difficulties. An abundant literature exists on all of these approaches, including many warnings that implementation can be difficult and that they require persistence, which is another reason for administrators to focus on long-term recurrent funding rather than search continually for short-term project funding.

Increase time on task

Increased time on task has long been observed to correlate with increased student achievement. Montero-Sieburth (1989) examined literature in developing nations on classroom use of instructional materials and teacher-managed time to promote learning. For learning to occur, the indications included that stable teacher and student attendance patterns must exist; the teacher as classroom manager has the greatest influence on learning; and the use of classroom time and instructional materials depends on the teacher's ability to organise, pace, monitor and provide feedback to students. Similarly, Abadzi (2009) found that since the 1970s, studies in developing country schools on use of instructional time and its impact on student achievement have consistently shown that the amount of time spent in learning tasks is related to student performance. Significant amounts of time are often wasted due to informal school closures, teacher absenteeism, delays, early departures and poor use of classroom time. Pfau's (1980) study in Nepal found 6% of classroom time was taken up by silence or the evocatively labelled 'general havoc' (Table 8.1), while Frost and Little (2014), in a large scale survey in Ethiopia, found that 15% of student time in lessons was 'off-task'. These and other studies suggest that improved classroom management, including use of appropriate materials such as textbooks and workbooks, can allow students to stay on task even when the teacher is otherwise occupied. Teacher time on task can be increased by reducing absenteeism and time on non-academic activities, and increasing time on the formal curriculum. Essentially, these improvements can be brought about by improved school and classroom management without requiring complex changes to teaching styles or the curriculum.

Improve facilities

Among the many variables in the search of the school effectiveness literature by Glewwe *et al.* (2011), only three main ones had significant effects on student learning, one of which was availability of desks. Their evidence suggested that 'adequate amounts of desks, tables and chairs raise student test scores' (19). Of 28 estimates from eight studies, 54% were positive. Provision of blackboards and other visual aids, school libraries and better quality buildings were also supportive of student learning results, however provision of computers was not: 'Given that computers can be relatively expensive, this suggests caution when deciding whether scarce funds for education should be used to purchase computers and related products' (20). The effect is that basic, low technology interventions can be cost-effective in formalistic classrooms because they are consistent with the classroom skills and computer literacy of teachers and will require less funding for ongoing repair and replacement.

Increase class size

Contrary to conventional progressive wisdom, smaller classes do not necessarily increase student learning, at least above a class size of about 20 (Section 10.3). A commonsense explanation is that below 20, teachers do have a chance of providing individual attention within a typical 40-minute lesson, but much over 20 and they do not. The indication is that increasing student-teacher ratios will not necessarily have a negative effect on student achievement. Educational efficiency would, however, be improved, especially if funds were liberated from relatively well staffed educational sub-sectors, such as tertiary education, for upgrading teachers' work in other sub-sectors. Increasing class size in all sub-sectors was recommended for Papua New Guinea (PNG) by a high-level sector-wide planning committee in the mid-1980s (Guthrie 1985a). While this was educational policy during the late 1980s, it was never implemented, in part because of the resistance of entrenched university interests and partly because an economic downturn in the late 1980s meant that any savings were deployed outside the education sector. The relevance is that even reform proposals that are simple in principle may be difficult to implement because of educational politics.

Provide textbooks

The provision of textbooks is cost-effective, especially in large-scale systems. In the late 1970s, studies generally revealed positive associations between textbook provision and student achievement (Heyneman, Farrell, and Sepulveda-Stuardo 1978). In light of this, the World Bank was notable for funding a considerable number of textbook projects. Once written, large-scale production rapidly reduces unit costs, although design, logistical and quality problems have long been considerable and persistent (Crossley and Murby 1994; Askerud 1997; Milligan et al. 2017). Long-term benefits were confirmed by Glewwe et al.'s (2011) meta-analysis. The evidence, from 60 separate estimates from 21 studies in developing countries that included the effect of textbooks and workbooks on student learning, 'strongly suggests that textbooks and similar materials (workbooks, exercise books) increase student learning' (19).

The relevance of textbooks to formalistic classrooms was shown by Kumar (1988), who described two approaches to textbook use in India. The first approach had textbooks recommended by the authorities and gave the teacher the freedom to decide what materials to use. The other approach required the teacher to follow textbooks prescriptively, about which she was hostile; however, in both situations, textbooks can be appropriate for teachers to set practice tasks, class reading and homework. School texts will be more effective if carefully written in relation to integrated performance objectives, but it is possible to do so without rewriting the original syllabuses or renovating examination systems. Glewwe, Kremer, and Moulin (2009) did find in Kenya that textbook provision benefitted students with a strong initial academic background, but the bottom line is that a motivated student with reading skills but a teacher ill-trained in a particular subject can at least continue to learn independently from a textbook. Where teachers have the freedom, the ability, and supplementary materials to adapt to the classroom, the result may turn out to be a higher level of formalism; where they do not, the result may be low-level formalism.

Provide supplementary language readers

One simple innovation to do with book supply has been tested with considerable success in a number of countries. Elley (2000) reported that it is possible to double the rate of reading acquisition in primary schools with a 'book flood' of about 100 high-interest books per class and short teacher training sessions. Studies of teaching English as a second language in Niue (1979), Fiji

(1980–1981), Singapore (1985–1989), Sri Lanka (1995), the Solomon Islands (1995–1998) and South Africa (1997) found that the benefits for reading skill and enthusiasm were consistent across diverse cultures, languages and age levels, and appeared to generate corresponding improvements in writing, listening comprehension and related language skills.

An interesting aspect of an early experimental study in Fiji was that INSET was not necessary to improve student achievement. In grades 4 and 5 of 12 rural primary schools, classes taught by teachers who had INSET on a shared book method did not perform significantly better than those where teachers were not provided with assistance other than instruction to provide 20–30 minutes a day for silent reading. Both groups had much higher proportions of students passing the grade 6 examinations than a control group, with the benefit of the programme accruing to all examined subjects (Elley and Mangubhai 1981a, 1981b). Classes where teachers did little other than provide silent reading time for students to read books of their own choice had twice the expected gains in reading comprehension and grammatical structures. They also had smaller but considerable gains on tests of writing, word recognition and oral language. Uninterrupted reading time is a simple method for improving student achievement involving low costs, little support, and easy for even the most lacklustre teacher to implement.

Increase attention to subject knowledge in teacher training

A pragmatic implication of the role of revelatory knowledge has to do with the amount of subject knowledge in teacher education courses. Glewwe *et al.* (2011, 22, 31) found moderate support for the impact of teacher knowledge (measured by teacher test scores) on student learning. Of the 33 findings, 88% had positive effects and 55% were statistically significant. The analysis did not distinguish between teaching styles, but the relevance of the finding to formalistic environments, in particular, is that where the teachers' job is to know and transmit, their classroom credibility depends in considerable part on authoritative display of that knowledge.

Analysis of the implications is helped by a formalistic 'integrative model' of teacher cognition presented by Gess-Newsome (1999, 10–14), in contrast to a progressive 'transformative model'. The integrative model distinguishes between the overlapping domains of subject knowledge, pedagogical knowledge and contextual knowledge. Formalistic paradigms have implications for the mixture of these domains in both pre-service and in-service training. The main implication for the subject knowledge domain is consideration whether teacher training should spend more time on this domain, and less on the pedagogical and contextual knowledge domains, so that trainees can become more authoritative about their teaching subjects. It would also be logical, when faced with the choice, to train in fewer teaching subjects, especially for secondary teachers. As well, classroom teachers can be encouraged in pre-service training and upgrade courses, including at post-graduate level, to study their teaching subjects rather than professional courses. An implication for training formalistic teachers in the pedagogical knowledge domain is to discard courses on universalistic curriculum and psychology theories relevant to the progressive paradigm. For the contextual knowledge domain, the implication is that courses should include the history, sociology and anthropology of the local formalist paradigm. In all these matters, teacher trainers can continue to exercise their professional judgement, but informed by any local research with implications for the effectiveness of teachers in the three domains rather than by progressive theories fashionable internationally.

Use distance education for in-service

Another finding by Glewwe et al. (2011, 22) is that overall teacher in-service has a moderate positive impact on student learning. Distance education in subject content does bear consideration because it can be a cost-effective alternative to other types of INSET, and need not be complicated or credentialed. For example, in a simple experimental study in Zaire, Bimakunu (1982) found improved student performance in French reading was associated with a correspondence in-service course for teachers untrained in teaching the language. The in-service course consisted of instruction in types of reading, purposes of reading, the identification of general ideas and specific information, practical application and critical evaluation. No other assistance was given to the teachers.

The long-established economics are such that distance education is better reserved for courses with large-scale enrolments (Guthrie 1985b; Rumble 2004). The costs of physical and administrative establishment can be high, and course development costs are high regardless of the number of students. However, unit costs decrease rapidly as enrolments increase, which is a major potential economic advantage over school-based or teacher college-based in-service. In some situations, a major area of potential cost savings lies in opportunity costs because savings can accrue both to teachers who do not have to face loss of income during full-time study and to education departments not required to fund replacement teachers. Costs are heavily dependent on the type of media used, and considerable material now exists on using e-learning and associated technologies (e.g. Sife, Lwoga, and Sanga 2007). The establishment and recurrent costs and practical constraints on information and communication technologies in the field indicate caution is needed (Kundi and Nawaz 2014). The enthusiasm of information and communications technology specialists may not translate to field conditions.

Practise reflective formalism

In its more progressive forms as a particular teaching style, reflection is open to the criticism that it represents a naïve transfer of fashionable ideas. In its more moderate forms, as a process of self-reflection, it has potential as an active tool for improvement by formalists of their own teaching without necessarily threatening their cultural identity. The role for this form of reflection is that teachers can be encouraged in pre-service and in-service education to cogitate on their own teaching, perhaps as part of communities of professional learners (Anwaruddin 2015; Hairon and Tan 2017). This approach can be consistent with undergraduate and postgraduate teacher education courses, as the following course description from Papua New Guinea (University of Goroka 2003, 26) illustrates:

> The emphasis of this course is on the improvement of the processes of conceptualisation, planning, and practice of teaching and learning through critical reflection. The course will equip the students with the essential knowledge, skills, and attitudes to systematically plan, implement, and evaluate their own performances.

Nonetheless, even moderate reflective practice can be incompatible with cultural values in some settings, as Minnis (1999) found in Brunei Darussalam.

11.6 Conclusion

A propensity for change agents to blame teachers and their training for the failure of inappropriate progressive reforms has a very limited view of teachers' roles, their cultural contexts and their decision-making processes. Failure of teachers to innovate may be rational responses to complex progressive reforms that offer no relative advantage in the classroom, are not compatible with existing methods and offer no observable outcomes for students and parents concerned with examination results. Nor are teachers equally open to or resistant to change. Blanket categorisation of teachers as obstructionist does not go far, and may indeed reveal as much about the prejudices of the critics as the attitudes of the teachers. Much deeper understanding is required for effective educational reform. Whether or not a new syllabus, teaching style or wider curriculum change diffuses through classrooms depends especially on teachers' personal and professional constructs. As well, systemic barriers impede change, including school resources, countervailing work and social pressures, schools' professional climates and lack of structural inducements. Even if many of these factors are positive, the influence of context-specific cultural paradigms on teachers' formalistic professional constructs may well outweigh – quite rationally from the perspective of them and their students – the alleged benefits of any progressive reform.

Theory-laden progressive change agents serious about classroom reform as such can retain a stubborn and long-lasting faith in progressivism as an axiomatic panacea and demonstrate intellectual confusion over findings about its failures. Cultural imperialists with a conscious ideological mission hidden behind progressive educational language as part of soft power projection are even less likely to be persuaded by such conclusions. However, those targeted for change can know that the comprehensive evidence reported here does not support the progressive case, and they should be wary of the cultural imperialism underlying claims for progressive education.

There is little if any evidence to support sustained progressive success in developing country classrooms. Yet progressive theory has not aligned with classroom reality. Progressive resistance to change manifests in many ways in the research and evaluation literature. One manifestation is retention of an axiomatic faith in progressivism as a universal panacea even though its culturally biased and problematic assumptions about teaching styles in other cultures are not often contested. Theoretically superficial and methodologically flawed studies commonly lead to weak research findings, notably in vested commercialised evaluations subject to financial conflicts of interest. An absence of methodological rigour exists in overgeneralisation from pilot projects, case studies and surveys. The Hawthorne effect is apparent in formative evaluations of pilot projects, which often appear to have the beginnings of success, especially when wishful evaluations assume that positive responses in questionnaires and interviews with teachers are a valid reflection of their classroom practice. Where implementation difficulties are found, the commonplace response has been to recommend more resource inputs or time. Cognitive dissonance in consideration of the evidence is demonstrated when anomalies incorrectly are ignored, downplayed or mistreated as acceptable error. In effect, random false positives are treated as indications of future possibilities and dissonant elements are ignored as false negatives, so that negative feedback ('the reform is less than successful') is mistreated as positive ('now we know what further inputs are required to generate success'). Ahistorical research, an absence of evaluation findings showing sustained progressive adoption, ritual recommendations for yet more technical inputs or, more radically, calls for structural change collectively embody the misinterpretation of anomalies in progressive implementation as new challenges rather than chronic failure.

A scarcity of deep reflection on findings is such that the progressive paradigm has often not been deconstructed. Widespread failure to generate paradigm shift has not led to paradigm reversal. Instead, it is now the progressive paradigm that is exhibiting classic symptoms of resistance to intellectual change. The effect in the literature is that this paradigm remains axiomatic as a travelling policy whose most fundamental flaw is a failure to understand the cultural depths of competing formalistic paradigms. When cultural issues do receive attention, claims for progressivism are often migrated and nuanced. The resulting semantic confusion indicates cognitive dissonance when Gestalt-switch and paradigm reversal would be more appropriate responses to the evidence of progressive failure to generate paradigm shift among classroom formalists in developing countries. Indeed, the progressive paradigm has become an intellectually caged, distorted and history-free educational ideology; a delusional intellectual straightjacket that has led to a vicious circle of misinformation for continuing the irrational pursuit of the unattainable.

Much of the literature, especially on Africa, blamed the failure of progressive innovations on systemic issues and recommended further inputs to overcome the shortcomings. These are legitimate issues, but they are as applicable to improving formalistic systems as to attempting to change them to progressive ones. Even were such conditions rectified, progressive success remains unlikely because financial support for technicist inputs does not provide a solution that overrides the cultural issues associated with the prevalence of formalism. Amid many practical barriers to change, deeply held, culturally based perceptions of the role of schooling provide a rational basis for rejecting progressive innovations that offer little comparative advantage over formalistic styles for teachers targeted for change. Using funds to upgrade school conditions for formalistic teaching would be much more cost-effective.

Formalism need not be taken as a problematic obstruction to modernisation. The assumption that classroom formalism is an aberrant distortion of education systems overlooks its usual place as a subsystem that is part of and highly compatible with a symbiotic whole. Rather than trying to generate systemic progressive change, strong theoretical and practical reasons exist for evolutionary modification of formalism from within. Formalism should be treated as a deep-rooted cultural behaviour capable of adaptation and of performing important educational functions now and in the foreseeable future, including producing high academic outcomes. The productive approach is to seize the opportunity to develop further culturally intuitive formalistic teaching styles, rather than trying unproductively to have teachers adopt methods that are counter-intuitive to them. In those cultures where it is appropriate, the future for improving teaching lies in operating within the constraints of formalistic systems and in working to improve classroom formalism. Clearly, the sensible conclusion in those developing countries where it is appropriate is that formalism should replace progressivism as the primary frame of reference for classroom change.

Notes

1 Sections 11.1–11.2 derive from Guthrie (2011, 62–65, https://doi.org/10.1007/978-94-007-1851-7_4, © Springer Science+Business Media B.V. 2011) with permission of Springer Nature.
2 Section 11.5 derives from Guthrie (2011, 228–232, https://doi.org/10.1007/978-94-007-1851-7_11, © Springer Science+Business Media B.V. 2011) with permission of Springer Nature.

References

Abadzi, K. 2009. "Instructional Time Loss in Developing Countries: Concepts, Measurement, and Implications." *World Bank Research Observer* 24 (2): 267–290.
Abadzi, H. 2014. "How to Improve Schooling Outcomes in Low-Income Countries? The Challenges and Hopes of Cognitive Neuroscience." *Peabody Journal of Education* 89 (1): 58–69.
Anwaruddin, S. 2015. "Teachers' Engagement with Educational research: Toward a Conceptual Framework for Locally-Based Interpretive Communities." *Education Policy Analysis Archives* 23 (40). https://doi.org/10.14507/epaa.v23.1776
Askerud, P. 1997. *A Guide to Sustainable Textbook Provision*. Paris: UNECSO.

Barrett, A., Chawla-Duggan, R., Lowe, J., Nikel, J., and Ukpo, E. 2006. *The Concept of Quality in Education: Review of the 'International' Literature on the Concept of Quality in Education.* EdQual Working Paper No.2. Bristol: University of Bristol.

Beeby, C. 1966. *The Quality of Education in Developing Countries.* Cambridge: Harvard University Press.

Biniakunu, D. 1982. "In-Service Teacher Training Improves Eighth Graders' Reading Ability in Zaire." *Journal of Reading* 25: 662–665.

Bonal, X. 2013. "Foreword." In *Global Managerial Education Reforms and Teachers: Emerging Policies, Controversies and Issues in Developing Contexts*, edited by A. Verger, H. Altinyelken, and M. de Koning, iv–v. Brussels: Education International.

Choi, C. 1999. "Public Examinations in Hong Kong." *Assessment in Education* 6 (3): 405–417.

Clarke, P. 2003. "Culture and Classroom Reform: The Case of the District Primary Education Project, India." *Comparative Education* 39 (1): 27–44.

Crossley, M. 1984a. "Relevance Education, Strategies for Curriculum Change and Pilot Projects: A Cautionary Note." *International Journal of Educational Development* 4 (3): 245–250.

Crossley, M. 1984b. "Strategies for Curriculum Change and the Question of International Transfer." *Journal of Curriculum Studies* 16 (1): 75–88.

Crossley, M., and Murby, M. 1994. "Textbook Provision and the Quality of the School Curriculum in Developing Countries: Issues and Policy Options." *Comparative Education* 30 (2): 99–104.

Elley, W. 2000. "The Potential of Book Floods for Raising Literacy Levels." *International Review of Education* 46 (3–4): 233–255.

Elley, W., and Mangubhai, F. 1981a. *The Impact of a Book Flood in Fiji Primary Schools.* Wellington: New Zealand Council for Education Research.

Elley, W., and Mangubhai, F. 1981b. "The Long-Term Effects of a Book Flood on Children's Language Growth." *Directions* 7: 15–21.

Frost, M., and Little, A. 2014. "Children's Learning Practices in Ethiopia: Observations from Primary School Classes." *Oxford Review of Education* 40 (1): 91–111.

Gess-Newsome, J. 1999. "Pedagogical Content Knowledge: An Orientation and Introduction." In *Examining Pedagogical Content Knowledge: The Construct and Its Implications for Science Education*, edited by J. Gess-Newsome and N. Lederman, 3–20. Dordrecht: Klewer.

Glewwe, P., Hanushek, E., Humpage, S., and Ravin, R. 2011. *School Resources and Educational Outcomes in Developing Countries: A Review of the Literature from 1990 to 2010.* Working Paper 17554. Cambridge: National Bureau of Economic Research.

Glewwe, P., Kremer, M., and Moulin, S. 2009. "Many Children Left Behind? Textbooks and Test Scores in Kenya." *Applied Economics* 1 (1): 112–135.

Guthrie, G. 1985a. "The Role of Teachers in National Development." *Papua New Guinea Journal of Education* 21 (2): 265–281.

Guthrie, G. 1985b. "Current Research in Developing Countries: Teacher Credentialing and Distance Education." *Teaching and Teacher Education* 1 (1): 81–90.

Guthrie, G. 1986. "Current Research in Developing Countries: The Impact of Curriculum Reform on Teaching." *Teaching and Teacher Education* 2 (1): 81–89.

Guthrie, G. 2011. *The Progressive Education Fallacy in Developing Countries: In Favour of Formalism.* New York: Springer.

Hairon, S., and Tan, C. 2017. "Professional Learning Communities in Singapore and Shanghai: Implications for Teacher Collaboration." *International Journal of Educational Development* 47(1): 91–104.

Heyneman, S., Farrell, J., and Sepulveda-Stuardo, M. 1978. *Textbooks and Achievement: What We Know.* Staff Working Paper No.298. Washington: World Bank.

Kelly, G. 1955. *The Psychology of Personal Constructs*. New York: Norton.
Kubul, G. 2001. *Practical Tips for Teachers in Melanesia: A Survival Guide for Student Teachers and Beginner Teachers*. Sydney: Longman.
Kumar, K. 1988. "Origins of India's 'Textbook Culture'." *Comparative Education Review* 32 (4): 452–464.
Kundi, G., and Nawaz, A. 2014. "From e-Learning 1.0 to e-Learning 2.0: Threats & Opportunities for Higher Education Institutions in the Developing Countries." *European Journal of Sustainable Development* 3 (1): 145–160.
Milligan, L., Tikly, L., Williams, T., Vianney, J-M., and Uworwabayeho, A. 2017. "Textbook Availability and Use in Rwandan Basic Education: A Mixed Methods Study." *International Journal of Educational Development* 54: 1–7.
Minnis, P. 1999. "Is Reflective Practice Compatible with Malay-Islamic Values? Some Thoughts on Teacher Education in Brunei Darussalam." *Australian Journal of Education* 43 (2): 172–185.
Mitchell, R. 2017. "Democracy or Control? The Participation of Management, Teachers, Students and Parents in School Leadership in Tigray, Ethiopia." *International Journal of Educational Development* 55: 49–55.
Montero-Sieburth, M. 1989. *Classroom Management, Instructional Strategies and the Allocation of Learning Resources*. BRIDGES Research Report Series No.4. Cambridge: Institute for International Development, Harvard University.
Morris, P. 1985. "Teachers' Perceptions of the Barriers to the Implementation of a Pedagogic Innovation: A South East Asian Case Study." *International Review of Education* 31 (1): 3–18.
Nag, S., Chiat, S., Torgerson, C., and Snowling, M. 2014. *Literacy, Foundation Learning and Assessment in Developing Countries: Final Report*. Education Rigorous Literature Review. London: Department for International Development.
Pfau, R. 1980. "The Comparative Study of Classroom Behaviours." *Comparative Education Review* 24 (3): 400–414.
Rogers, E. 2003. *Diffusion of Innovation* (5th ed.). New York: Free Press.
Rumble, G. 2004. *The Costs and Economics of Open and Distance Learning*. London: Routledge Falmer.
Ryle, A. 1975. *Frames and Cages: The Repertory Grid Approach to Human Understanding*. London: Chatto & Windus.
Sife, A., Lwoga, E., and Sanga, C. 2007. "New Technologies for Teaching and Learning: Challenges for Higher Learning Institutions in Developing Countries." *International Journal of Education and Development Using ICT* 3 (2). http://ijedict.dec.uwi.edu/viewarticle.php?id=246/&layout=html
Simon, H. 1947. *Administrative Behavior: A Study of Decision-Making Processes in Administrative Organizations*. New York: Free Press.
Tabulawa, R. 1997. "Pedagogical Classroom Practice and the Social Context: The Case of Botswana." *International Journal of Educational Development* 17 (2): 189–194.
Tabulawa, R. 1998. "Teachers' Perspectives on Classroom Practice in Botswana: Implications for Pedagogical Change." *International Journal of Qualitative Studies in Education* 20: 249–68.
Tabulawa, R. 2004. "Geography Students as Constructors of Classroom Knowledge and Practice: A Case Study from Botswana." *Journal of Curriculum Studies* 36 (1): 53–73.
University of Goroka. 2003. *Handbook of Postgraduate Studies in Education, 2003–2004*. Goroka: UOG.
Villegas-Reimers, E. 2003. *Teacher Professional Development: An International Review of the Literature*. Paris: UNESCO International Institute of Educational Planning.
Yu, G. 2007. *Research Evidence of School Effectiveness in Sub-Saharan Africa*. EdQual Working Paper No.12. Bristol: University of Bristol.

Index

academic standards 82, 94, 109, 172–173
Africa 9–11, 15, 44–46, 166, 215; classroom formalism 104–107, 116–117; pedagogical traditions 102–104, 107, 117–118; research on progressive reforms 107–113; Sub-Saharan 36, 39–40, 63–64, 67, 102–122, 144–145, 213
aid programmes 1, 37, 225; bilateral 69–77; multilateral 9–13
Alexander, R. 13, 14, 17, 102, 151, 154, 174, 206
Altinyelken, H. 11, 12, 43, 65, 112–113
Anglo-American progressivism xv–xvi, 4, 14–16, 37, 82–83, 102, 137, 176, 207, 225
Asia 14–15, 34, 44–46, 215
AusAID 70–77, 132–135
Australia 9, 15, 75, 126, 137, 220
authoritarianism 11, 22, 109, 171–172
Authoritarian teaching style 207–210, 214
axioms 6, 33, 35, 46–50, 61, 152–157, 237–238
Azerbaijan 43, 46

Barrett, A. 10–11, 48, 111, 170, 206, 209, 213
barriers to change 59–60, 187, 214–219, 239
Beeby, C. E. 10–11, 40–41, 46, 108, 127, 130, 168, 174, 207, 224
Bernstein, B. 17, 111, 151, 174–175, 213
Biggs, J. 42, 82, 91, 92
Bloom's Revised Taxonomy 190–192
Botswana 18–19, 43, 66, 103–107, 115, 117, 166, 170, 171, 230–231
Buddhism 13–14, 45, 84, 86
bureaucracy 9, 59, 218–219

Cambodia 17, 39, 43, 45, 47, 65
case studies 44, 61, 67–68, 104, 148, 164–166, 185, 193–194, 238
child-friendly schools 37–38, 151

child soldiers xvi, 49–50, 156
China 19, 36, 42–43, 82–101, 154, 166, 217; recent educational reforms 92–97; *see also* Confucianism
Chinese Learner Paradox *see* Paradox of the Chinese Learner
Christianity 46, 83, 91, 103, 126–127
classroom conditions, facilities 22, 39, 59, 211, 215–217, 219, 233
classroom improvement field 4–5, 58–68, 77–78, 113, 147–148, 164, 185–189, 194, 198–199; methodological influences, limitations 61, 64–68; theoretical influences, limitations 59–64
classroom observation 61, 64–65, 95, 150; ethnographic, structured 186, 192–194
class size 93, 215–217, 233–234
cognition 176–178; cognitive levels 37, 88, 116, 188, 190–192, 198–199, 210; prefrontal cortex 177–178
cognitive dissonance xv–xviii, 6, 50–51, 149–157
collectivism 14, 94, 102
colonialism, post-colonial issues 9, 11, 60, 75, 103, 107, 126–130, 135–137
commonalities 66, 102–104, 144, 164–166, 200
communalism 14, 102–104, 195–196
communities of professional learning 95–97, 237
comparative education 3–6, 16–17, 21, 58–59, 143, 149, 157; *see also* classroom improvement field; school effectiveness field
Confucianism 14–15, 82–101; epistemology 85–86, 166–167, 178; history 83–84; modern influence 15, 42, 82–83, 89–92, 95–98, 162, 172–173; Neo-Confucianism 84, 87–92; paradigm, pedagogy 86–89; vernacular 92

constructivist learning 8, 13, 48, 75, 82, 97, 102, 109–110, 190, 194
constructs 18–20, 123–124, 129, 146–153, 173, 186, 193–194; students' 105–106, 171, 230–231; teachers' 105–106, 171, 213, 224–241; *see also* perceptions
context 4–5, 12–13, 16–21, 33, 47–50, 67, 102, 149–151, 155; cultural, structural elements 17, 61–64, 106–107, 163–166, 174–178, 184–193, 200, 235–236; local 12, 164, 212
contingency theory 21, 165
cosmology of cumulative hallucination xvi, 152–157
costs 39, 219–221, 232–236; cost effectiveness, efficiency 200–202
CRIP (PNG Curriculum Reform Implementation Project) 69–77, 132, 134
Crossley, M. 4, 8, 33, 133, 218, 225
cultural clusters 15, 19, 22, 45, 64, 82, 102, 123
cultural imperialism xv–xviii, 3–29, 75–77, 174–176, 192
cultural relativism 16–17
culture 4, 12–16, 22, 42, 63, 143–149, 153–157, 161–166, 174–178, 184–205, 226, 231, 237–239; Africa 102–107, 110, 113–118; China 82–87, 91–92, 96–98; intergenerational, organisational 14, 17–18, 49, 59–60, 92, 149–152; Papua New Guinea 123–130, 136–138; revelatory 8, 166–168
culture wars xv, 3–29, 50–51, 156–157
curriculum 4, 19–20, 59, 77, 86–89, 125–129, 148, 161–163, 174–176, 179, 200–201, 227–230; evaluation 64, 67–78, 150, 186–189, 195–196; intended, taught, achieved 64, 198–199; reforms 9, 33, 36, 40, 82, 92–95, 102, 107–113, 130–138, 224–227

DAC (OECD Development Assistance Committee) 3, 44–45
decision-making 153–154, 173–174, 199–203, 226, 231, 237–239
Democratic teaching style 8, 207–213
democratisation 5, 10–12, 38, 41, 47, 107–108, 231
'developing' country categories 43–45
DfID (UK Department for International Development) 12, 68–69
direct instruction 8, 114
distance education 236

Education for All (EFA) 9, 12, 13, 68
Egypt 20, 39, 43, 47

empirical, ethical issues 9, 16, 85, 91, 175, 206, 212–213
English language 3–4, 13–15, 62, 102, 117
epistemology 7, 15–16, 46, 59, 110, 113, 125–130, 144, 154, 178–179, 189, 207; Confucian 85–86; revelatory, scientific 18–20, 117–118, 166–168, 200–201
Ethiopia 34, 39, 43, 231, 233
evaluation 6, 33–41, 64–74, 77, 113, 144–149, 154, 162–164, 185; independence 37–38, 47, 50–51, 70, 76
examinations 22, 104–105, 116–117, 186, 198–199, 217–218, 228; China 82–90, 93–94, 162; Hong Kong 218, 226–227
experimental design, field experiments 36–37, 184–190, 194–199, 200–202

false negatives, positives 40, 51, 63, 72, 153, 155
Fataar, A. 9, 108
Festinger, L. 6, 153
Fiji 234–235
flexible teaching, variety in teaching 10, 34, 70, 75, 106, 111–114, 170–171, 206, 213–214
Flexible teaching style 207–214
focus groups 39, 64–65, 150, 194
formal education 18, 103–104, 124–129, 136–137, 174, 189; *see also* informal education; non-formal education
formalism xv–xviii, 4, 6–23, 33–42, 44–51, 61, 82–98, 123–130, 135–138, 146–147, 203, 220, 237–239; borrowings 7–8, 174–176; definition 8, 210; frame 6–7, 21–22, 156, 161–183; improving 75, 231–237; lecturing 169–170; paradigm 18–20, 102–122, 143–146, 166–168; variation 170–171, 214
Formalistic teaching style 207–214

generalisability, generalisation issues 4, 41, 61–62, 67–68, 148, 164, 185–186, 238
Gestalt-switch 20, 146–149, 155–156
Ghana 12, 34, 43, 49, 107, 113
Ginsburg, M. 39–40, 47, 151
Glewwe, P. 36, 62, 63, 216, 233–236
globalisation 11–12, 16, 47, 75
GLOBE project 15, 45, 82
Guthrie, G. 8, 11, 14, 17, 20, 23, 33–41, 49–50, 65–68, 93, 104, 123, 126–128, 132, 174–175, 184–186, 193, 225, 233

Hall, E. 17, 150
Hinduism 14, 46
Hoadley, U. 109, 174–176
Hong Kong 82, 92, 96, 172, 217–218, 226–227
Human Development Index (HDI) 44–45

Index

India 34, 40, 43, 49–50, 168–169, 234
individualism 12, 14, 102, 155
Indonesia 43, 66, 194–199
informal education 103–104, 123–124, 129, 136
innovation 35–39, 173, 225; adopters 148–149, 228–230; attributes 227–228
INSET 60, 68, 74, 83, 95–96, 108, 114, 133, 173, 195, 214, 219, 235–236
inspections 22, 128–130, 167, 189, 193
interviews 39, 64–65, 150, 194, 238
Iraq 37, 67
Islam 14, 18, 46, 103

Jamaica 43, 63

Kazakhstan 11
Kelly, G. 153, 226
Kenya 34, 43, 64, 66, 113–117, 212, 234
Korea 11, 82
Kuhn, T. 20–21, 143, 146, 153
Kyrgyzstan 39, 43, 47

Lancy, D. 15, 42, 131, 177–178, 192
language readers 234–235
Lattimer, H. 117, 211–212
Lesotho 43, 112–113
lessons learned 154–155, 162–164
Liberal teaching style 8, 207–212
Libya 43

Macau 42, 82
Malawi 39, 43, 47, 49, 112–113
maturation 177–178
measurement scales 34–35, 66, 200, 207–209, 221
Melanesia 19, 76, 167, 178, 232
meta-analyses xv, 33, 62, 67, 216, 234
Mexico 34, 43
'modernisation' 9, 13, 23, 39–41, 91, 97–98, 104, 107, 161, 176, 231
Morocco 43
Morris, P. 5, 58, 62, 66–67, 226–227
Mozambique 43
Myanmar 13, 43

Namibia 11, 43, 108, 110, 114, 151, 194, 213–214
neo-liberalism, 'New Paradigm' 5, 10–12, 41, 60, 231
Nepal 169–170, 218–219, 233
Nigeria 43, 64, 113–114, 116–117
non-formal education 18, 88, 103–104, 124, 136

OECD 3, 9, 44–45
O'Sullivan, M. 8, 110, 114, 151, 194, 213–214, 216
outcomes-based education (OBE) 70, 218; Papua New Guinea 69–77, 134–135, 138; South Africa 108–109

Pakistan 34, 43
Papua New Guinea 36, 41, 43, 69–77, 123–142, 166, 172–173, 176–177, 218, 220, 233–234, 237; colonial education 126–127; formalism 135–137; progressive educational reforms 130–135; traditional education 123–130
paradigms xv–xviii, 5–7, 18–23, 46, 48, 50–51, 59–60, 143–144, 161–168, 173–179, 235–239; Africa 102–122; China 42, 86–87; definition 18–21; 'normal science' 6, 20–21, 62, 152; Papua New Guinea 123–129, 135–138; paradigm reversal 21–22, 146–157; paradigm shift 6–7, 20–21, 43–45, 50–51, 68, 143–146, 214, 228; see also formalism; progressivism
Paradox of the Chinese Learner 42, 82, 91, 172
pedagogy 4, 7, 11–21, 38, 47–48, 174–176, 206–213; definition 17, 151; see also Africa; China; formalism; Papua New Guinea; paradigms; progressivism; Teaching Styles Model
perceptions 46, 65, 103–104, 152–154, 173, 225–228
Peru 34, 43
Pfau, R. 169–170, 193, 233
Piagetian research 116, 177–178, 192
pilot projects 35–39, 61, 67–68, 132–133, 144–148, 238
policy borrowing, transfer 4–10, 17, 33, 58, 67, 82, 96, 107–108, 154, 174–176, 195, 225
Popper, K. xvi, 19, 40–41, 123, 164, 167, 199
process and product 8–9, 58–64, 66, 91
Progressive Education Fallacy xvi, 8–9, 47, 186–189, 203; examples 47, 64, 71, 113
progressivism xv–xviii, 3–29, 143–149, 237–239; axiom 46–51; cultural imperialism 9–13; definition 8, 207; delusions 154–156; geographic failure 42–46; lessons learned 162–164; limitations in research 58–81; paradigm 9, 18–20; reform findings 33–57; see also Africa; Anglo-American progressivism; China; Papua New Guinea; paradigms

questionnaires 61, 64–65, 147–148, 186, 194, 203

reflection 134, 236–237
relevance issues 8, 21, 61, 66–67, 165, 175–176
reliability issues 61–62, 65–66, 70–73
religion 18–19, 45–46, 50, 83–85, 91, 103, 126–127
research design 22, 44, 77–78, 113–116, 150, 184–189, 194–199; limitations 61, 64–68, 147–148; methods 189–194; *see also* classroom improvement field; evaluation; experimental design; measurement scales; school effectiveness field; variables
Rogers, E. 39, 148, 228–230
Ryle, A. 6, 153, 226

Scheerens, J. 21, 62–67, 165
school effectiveness field 4–5, 10, 36, 58–68, 77–78, 115–116, 147–148, 185–189, 194, 207–209; methodological influences, limitations 61–68; theoretical influences, limitations 59–64
Schweisfurth, M. 4, 14, 17–18, 36, 42, 47–48, 50, 149–152, 212
Senegal 43, 49
Simon, H.A. 153, 226
Singapore 82, 173, 190, 235
soft power 3–29, 50, 90, 157, 237
Sopantini 194–198
South Africa 9–11, 43, 66, 103–104, 108–109, 113, 115, 135, 169, 174–175, 235
South America 14, 41, 44–45, 176
South-South borrowings 7–8, 176
Sri Lanka 235
'stages' of educational development xvii, 10–12, 33, 40–41, 47, 108, 123, 130, 207, 224
Sternberg, R. 17, 42, 150, 176–177
student achievement 5, 17, 58, 61–64, 147–150, 176, 184–190, 197–199, 218, 232–235; *see also* constructs, students'; examinations; variables, dependent
subject knowledge 36, 106, 175, 192, 235–236
surveys 44, 61, 64–67, 148, 164, 185, 189, 194, 238
syllabuses 22, 164, 168, 188–189, 199, 200–201, 206–211, 218

Tabulawa, R. 8, 11–12, 18, 39, 41, 47–48, 50, 103–107, 113–114, 143–144, 153, 171, 192, 226, 230–231
Tan, C. 46, 49, 82, 88, 92, 94, 96–98, 149, 154, 172–173

Tanzania 43, 48–49, 111–115, 170, 213
Taoism 84–91
teacher education, training 4, 9, 22, 33, 40, 49, 58–67, 112–113, 130, 134, 147–148, 161–163, 174, 184, 234–237; *see also* INSET
teaching styles *see* pedagogy
Teaching Styles Model 206–213, 221
teleology 12, 40, 46–47, 85–86
textbooks 22, 59–60, 105–106, 168–169, 206–211, 234
time on task 232–233
Timor-Leste 43, 65
Tonga 217
traditional education 7, 18–20, 22–23, 86–91, 102–104, 123–130, 137–138, 166–168, 186
travelling policies 4–12, 156
Trinidad and Tobago 113
Turkey 11, 43
typology of progressive reform findings 33–42, 46, 50–51, 59

Uganda 43, 49, 65, 112–114
UNCF 37–38, 151
UNDP 44–45
UNESCO 9–10, 12–13, 150, 215
UNICEF 9, 37–38, 151, 215
United Kingdom 3, 12, 15; *see also* Anglo-American progressivism; DfID
United States 9, 15, 169–170, 225; *see also* Anglo-American progressivism
universal claims, universalities 6, 14–17, 21, 40–42, 46, 60–67, 123, 164–166, 184–185, 236
USAID 39, 47

validity issues 6, 16, 39, 61–66, 147–151, 187–188, 193, 199
values 3–23, 46, 49, 75–76, 91–92, 102–107, 130, 137, 144–152, 166–169, 173, 178, 213, 228
variables 17, 34–35, 61–66, 115–116, 184–199; alternative independent 186–188; background 49, 149–150, 186–189, 196–200; dependent 150, 184–190, 196–199; extraneous 186–188; independent 150, 184–190, 196–199; intervening 150, 186–190, 196–198
variation in teaching *see* flexible teaching
Vavrus, F. 48, 111–112, 115, 151
Vietnam 43, 82

Western, westernisation 3–5, 9–14, 19–20, 49, 82–91, 96–98, 103–104, 116, 154–157, 167, 171, 178, 192, 219
Woolmington, E. 152–154
World Bank 3–5, 9–12, 40, 44–45, 62–63, 108, 132–133, 198, 234

Yu, G. 36, 63, 67

Zaire 236
Zambia 36–37, 43, 116, 190
zero pedagogy 174–176
Zimbabwe 103